CALIFORNIA STUDIES IN THE HISTORY OF ART

Walter Horn, General Editor

LEONARDO DA VINCI ON PAINTING

A LOST BOOK (*LIBRO A*)

Leonardo da Vinci. Lady pointing into distance.
Black chalk; *ca.* 1513–1515. Windsor, Royal Library, 12,581.

LEONARDO DA VINCI ON PAINTING
A LOST BOOK (*LIBRO A*)

REASSEMBLED

FROM THE CODEX VATICANUS URBINAS 1270

AND FROM THE CODEX LEICESTER

BY CARLO PEDRETTI

With a Chronology of Leonardo's "Treatise on Painting"

FOREWORD

BY SIR KENNETH CLARK

University of California Press, Berkeley and Los Angeles, 1964

UNIVERSITY OF CALIFORNIA PRESS
BERKELEY AND LOS ANGELES, CALIFORNIA

LIBRARY OF CONGRESS CATALOG CARD NUMBER: 64-17171

DESIGNED BY JANE HART

PRINTED IN THE UNITED STATES OF AMERICA

Look over all these cases tomorrow and copy them and leave them in Florence so that, if you should lose the notebooks you carry with you, the invention will not be lost. CODEX ATLANTICUS 214 r-d, *ca.* 1508

FOREWORD

By Sir Kenneth Clark

IT WOULD NOT BE EXTRAVAGANT to claim that Leonardo da Vinci's Treatise on Painting is the most precious document in the whole history of art. To find out even a little more about this extraordinary work would be a valuable contribution to knowledge. Carlo Pedretti, in the work which follows, has found out a great deal.

As is well known, the greater part of the Treatise has not come down to us in Leonardo's own hand, but in a compilation, evidently made in the first half of the sixteenth century, now known as the Codex Urbinas 1270. This raises a number of questions. How far is the compilation accurate? How far does it represent Leonardo's final intentions? At which date in Leonardo's career was the greater part written? And, finally, who was the compiler? To all these questions Mr. Pedretti produces convincing answers. He does so in the course of reconstructing one of the lost original manuscripts from which the Treatise was compiled, the one listed by the compiler as Libro A. By a close analysis of the text he establishes the exact size of this manuscript, even the length of the lines, and proves that it must have been the companion to Libro B, which has in fact survived in the Bibliothèque de l'Institut under the title Manuscript E. He then goes on to prove that the Libro A (like MS. E) was written by Leonardo quite late in his career, probably 1508–1515, and was to some extent a fair copy which Leonardo may have intended to use directly in the final edition of his Treatise on Painting. In fact the compiler split it up between five of the eight sections of his book, although the greater part is in section three. Mr. Pedretti has found it possible to rearrange all the extracts in their original order, so that in reading his reconstruction of Libro A we are able to follow the movements of Leonardo's mind almost exactly as if we were reading the original manuscript. Furthermore, he has found that the last pages of this manuscript, which were not concerned with art, but with hydraulics, and so are not included in the Treatise, exist in Leonardo's writing in the Codex Leicester. In this compilation on the movement of water Leonardo included twenty-five notes copied from Libro A, and for each note he gave the reference to the page of the lost manuscript. This system was used again in the compilation of the Treatise on Painting for the chapters copied from Libro A and Libro B.

Mr. Pedretti then asks who was the compiler and copyist of the Treatise, and concludes that it was none other than Francesco Melzi, Leonardo's closest friend during the last twelve years of his life, and the inheritor of his manuscripts. I confess that the evidence of hand-writing does little to support this conclusion, but taken in conjunction with other arguments, it seems to me convincing, and is of great importance, as we can be sure that Melzi's copy would be scrupulously accurate (occasionally, like everyone else, he had difficulty in reading a word) and close to Leonardo's intentions. Mr. Pedretti gives many instances of the patient and systematic manner in which Melzi sought material for his compilation in all Leonardo's manuscripts, and the very fact that he copied into a book of which the leaves were already bound means that he often preserved Leonardo's order. In fact the Treatise is shown to be considerably closer to what Leonardo himself might have produced than has hitherto been believed.

This conclusion is linked with Mr. Pedretti's discovery that the greater part of the Treatise was written by Leonardo late in his life. Because one of the few parts to have survived in the original is the so-called Manuscript A in the Bibliothèque de l'Institut (and its missing section in the Ashburnham Codex), a manuscript of the 1490's, it has been generally supposed that the whole Treatise dated from the Sforza period. It is now clear that both Libro A and Libro B were written after 1510 and in fact only a small portion of the Treatise can date from the 1490's. It is revealing to find how often Leonardo goes back to subjects which had interested him twenty years earlier, for example the so-called *Paragone*, and incorporated earlier points of view with later observations. In this, too, we have the feeling that he is consciously preparing the ground for a final attempt at putting his Treatise into a definite order.

In addition to establishing the text and sequence of Libro A, Mr. Pedretti annotates each chapter with a fullness of knowledge which has seldom been equalled in Leonardo studies. Not only can he bring to bear on every passage references to Leonardo's other writings, but he makes most interesting comparisons with other early theorists. In particular he confirms Leonardo's debt to Leon Battista Alberti's *della Pittura*. Again and again an observation in Libro A can be related to a passage in the earlier writer, and one is left with the feeling that Alberti's book was not merely an influence on Leonardo, but the crucial experience which led him to produce his own Treatise.

Finally Mr. Pedretti includes a number of appendices on subjects connected with the Treatise, each of which is a fresh contribution to our knowledge of Leonardo. He combines a miscroscopic eye, a relentless logic and an almost incredible memory in a way which must command the admiration of all those who have attempted work of this kind. Leonardo studies have recently passed through a slack time, and scholars have supposed that there was little further to be discovered. Mr. Pedretti's writings, however, have shown that by the careful relation of neglected details, whole new aspects of Leonardo's life and work can be revealed. Would that he could be entrusted with a new edition of the *Codice Atlantico*—even though the resulting volumes might fill a library.

I suppose it is over thirty years since I last read Leonardo's thoughts on painting. Reading them again in this form which, by restoring their order, gives them back much of their original freshness, I find them far more impressive than I did then. During that time accepted theories about the nature of art have changed several times, and one is less inclined to judge Leonardo by current aesthetic fashions. When his approach seems strange or his instructions unduly oppressive, one may reflect that on the subject of painting he is really more likely to be right than most people. Of course his conception of art as a form of creative knowledge is at the opposite pole from abandonment to pure sensation, abstract expressionism, or any of the other aesthetic theories which hold good today. But the greatest thinkers who have ever applied themselves to the subject, men as different from one another as Poussin, Goethe, Lessing and Ruskin, would certainly have agreed with Leonardo rather than with present-day theorists; and the general reader may find the Libro A a bracing antidote to the metaphysics and hyperbole of modern criticism.

CARAE CONIVGI

PREFACE

THE INITIAL INSPIRATION for this work resulted from A. Philip Mc-
Mahon's facsimile edition of Leonardo's *Trattato della Pittura*, the present Codex
Urbinas 1270 (*Treatise on Painting by Leonardo da Vinci* [Princeton, N.J.: Princeton University Press, 1956]). My primary purpose in reassembling Leonardo's notes
on painting identified as having been copied from the lost *Libro* A was to ascertain
the character and date of the lost manuscript. The works of Gerolamo Calvi and
Sir Kenneth Clark on the chronology of Leonardo's manuscripts and drawings made
it possible for me to undertake such a project.

The present new translation of the notes from *Libro* A has been made by Florence B. Longman directly from the Italian text of the Codex Urbinas after checking
every previous translation of the *Trattato della Pittura*, not only in English, but also
in French, German, and Spanish (the Elmer Belt Library of Vinciana, Los Angeles,
has a complete collection of the editions of the *Trattato*). The notes on hydraulics
from the Codex Leicester are presented here in English translation for the first
time. It is well known that the best way to comment upon the writings of an author
is to translate them. Mrs. Longman's translation of *Libro* A serves this purpose,
while my commentary is mainly concerned with the chronology of Leonardo's lost
notebook and with new interpretations of the Italian text. Mrs. Longman and I have
found an indispensable tool in the McMahon edition of the *Treatise on Painting*.
Princeton University Press kindly permitted me to use the McMahon translation of
the Codex Urbinas both as a basis for a new translation of the notes from *Libro* A
and for quotations of passages related to problems of the chronology of Leonardo's
Trattato.

Seventy-one of the 107 notes (or "chapters") on painting in *Libro* A are found in
the abridged Du Fresne edition of the *Trattato della Pittura* (Paris, 1651), which
was translated into English as early as 1721. The English translation by J. F. Rigaud
(London, 1877; a revised, enlarged version based on the first edition of 1835), which
Sir Kenneth Clark judged to be the only good English edition available, is particularly useful because it was made by a painter who had a deep understanding of the
art and technique of the Italian Renaissance. In my reconstruction of *Libro* A the
passages that are found in the abbreviated edition of the *Trattato* bear references to
the chapter-number of the Rigaud translation. These are the chapters that contain
the famous Leonardo "precetti," which were adopted by painters and theorists for

three centuries—from Pietro Accolti in his *Discorso sul Disegno* (Florence, 1625) and Francisco Pacheco in his *Arte de la Pintura* (Spain, 1649), through De Piles's and Sir Joshua Reynolds' teachings in France and England in the eighteenth century, to Goethe in his *Farbenlehre* (Germany, 1810).

The Leonardo drawings from the Royal Library at Windsor Castle are reproduced by the gracious permission of Her Majesty Queen Elizabeth II. The text and figures from the Codex Vaticanus Urbinas 1270 are reproduced by permission of the Prefetto of the Vatican Library. The late Lord Leicester permitted me to use some of the notes and figures from the Codex Leicester. The photographs of the covers of the Leonardo manuscripts in the Institut de France, which are reproduced here for the first time, have been made available through the courtesy of M. Tremblot de la Croix, Conservateur en Chef, Bibliothèque de l'Institut de France.

My thanks are due to several libraries and institutions in Italy, including the Raccolta Vinciana, Castello Sforzesco, Milan; the Ambrosian Library; the Bibliotheca Hertziana, Rome; the Biblioteca Vaticana; and the Biblioteca dell'Istituto di Archeologia e Storia dell' Arte, Rome.

Professor Anna Maria Brizio, Mrs. Marilyn Aronberg Lavin, and Mrs. Kate T. Steinitz read my manuscript and gave me invaluable advice. I should also like to thank Professor André Chastel for information concerning the physical structure of the Leonardo manuscripts in the Bibliothèque de l'Institut de France, Paris.

A first study of the chronology of the Codex Urbinas which I published in the Italian journal *L'Arte* in 1959–1960 was somewhat imperfect; nonetheless it was favorably accepted by scholars, and has been used by Maria Rzepinska as a basis for her doctoral dissertation at the University of Warsaw. Dr. Rzepinska's publication of parts of her study has in turn given me the great opportunity to improve my work.

Professor Lester D. Longman, former chairman of the Art department, University of California, Los Angeles, who has contributed most effectively to the creation of a center of Leonardo studies on the Los Angeles campus of the University, offered me the opportunity of presenting my unpublished material in a seminar on Leonardo and assisted me in the preparation of the present book. Professor Frederick S. Wight, the present chairman of the Art department, has also been most helpful in supporting my studies. My thanks are also due to the University Library at Los Angeles, whose resources in Renaissance material have been increased considerably in the last few years, thanks to the librarian Mr. Robert Vosper and his enthusiastic staff.

I have been particularly indebted throughout this and my other studies to Elmer Belt, M.D., the founder of the Elmer Belt Library of Vinciana, Los Angeles, whose merits as a scholar equal his liberality. The donation of his Library to the University of California, Los Angeles, will in time be recognized as one of the most important contributions to Leonardo studies, comparable to the foundation of the Raccolta Vinciana in Milan in 1905.

My gratitude to R. Y. Zachary and Geoffrey Ashton of the University of California Press, Los Angeles, is not easily expressed in words. Not only were they able to produce a book that is in keeping with the splendid tradition of the Leonardo editions but they made it possible to have a foreword written by Sir Kenneth Clark, an honor that only the Leonardo section of the book deserves.

The first outline of this book goes back to my work on the catalogue of Leonardo's fragments at Windsor Castle in 1957. Seven years of work may well appear to be too long a period for such research. Most of this time, however, I have spent profitably according to Leonardo's advice:

As the body with great slowness produced by the length of its contrary movement turns in greater space and thereby gives a stouter blow, whereas movements which are continuous and short have little strength—so study upon the same subject made at long intervals of time causes the judgment to become more perfect and the better to recognise its own mistakes. And the same is true of the eye of the painter as it draws farther away from his picture.

C. P.

University of California
Los Angeles

CONTENTS

LEONARDO DA VINCI ON PAINTING
A LOST BOOK (*LIBRO A*)

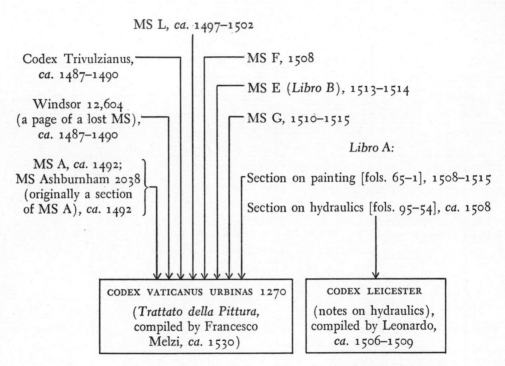

MS L, *ca.* 1497–1502

Codex Trivulzianus,
 ca. 1487–1490

Windsor 12,604
(a page of a lost MS),
 ca. 1487–1490

MS A, *ca.* 1492;
MS Ashburnham 2038
(originally a section
of MS A), *ca.* 1492

MS F, 1508

MS E (*Libro B*), 1513–1514

MS G, 1510–1515

Libro A:

Section on painting [fols. 65–1], 1508–1515

Section on hydraulics [fols. 95–54], *ca.* 1508

CODEX VATICANUS URBINAS 1270

(*Trattato della Pittura,*
compiled by Francesco
Melzi, *ca.* 1530)

CODEX LEICESTER

(notes on hydraulics),
compiled by Leonardo,
 ca. 1506–1509

The known sources of the Codex Urbinas and the Codex Leicester

Brief History of Leonardo's Trattato della Pittura

1487–1519

At the end of his compilation of the *Trattato della Pittura* ("Treatise on Painting") from Leonardo's notes on painting, Francesco Melzi listed eighteen manuscript sources (*see* Appendix I), of which only six and a fragment are extant (see diagram on facing page): from Leonardo's early period *ca.* 1487–1497 we have the MSS Trivulzianus (*ca.* 1487–1490), Windsor 12,604 (a page of a lost manuscript; *ca.* 1487–1490), and A & Ashburnham 2038 (*ca.* 1492); from his intermediate period *ca.* 1497–1505 we have MS L (*ca.* 1497–1502); and from his late period, after 1505, we have MSS F (1508), E (*Libro B*; 1513–1514), and G (1510–1515), plus the lost *Libro* A. (Extant manuscripts containing notes on painting which were not used in the compilation of the *Trattato della Pittura* are also listed in the table on page 8. See also Appendix V: General History of the Leonardo Manuscripts; especially the chart.)

1498

February 9. In the dedicatory letter of his *Divina Proportione* (Venice, 1509) Luca Pacioli remarks that Leonardo had completed a treatise on painting and human motion.

1519

Francesco Melzi inherits all Leonardo's manuscripts and drawings. In the following years he compiles the *Trattato della Pittura* ("Treatise on Painting"), the present Codex Vaticanus Urbinas 1270, from eighteen of the manuscripts (but *see* Appendix I for details of MS C, which, although listed by Melzi, was not used in his compilation).

1542

Benvenuto Cellini acquires from an impoverished nobleman at the court of Francis I a book on sculpture, painting, architecture, and perspective copied from a manuscript of Leonardo. He lends it to Sebastiano Serlio.

1568

Giorgio Vasari, *Le vite de più eccellenti pittori* . . . (Florence, 1568), parte iii, pp. 7–8, mentions the manuscripts of Leonardo belonging to Francesco Melzi, and affirms that an anonymous Milanese painter owned another Leonardo manuscript on painting and methods of drawing and coloring: "This person, not long since, came to Florence to see me, wishing to print this work; and he took it to Rome, in order to give it effect, but I do not know what may afterwards have become of it."

ca. 1570

At the death of Francesco Melzi, Orazio Melzi, Doctor of Law, inherits Leonardo's manuscripts.

1582–1590

The dispersion of Leonardo's manuscripts begins with Pompeo Leoni and others, as one learns from Ambrogio Mazenta's *Memorie su Leonardo da Vinci*. (In 1631 Mazenta recalled having possessed 13 Leonardo manuscripts about fifty years earlier.)

1584

Giovan Paolo Lomazzo, *Trattato dell'arte de la pittura* (Milan, 1584), p. 158, mentions an autograph manuscript on the comparison between painting and sculpture written by Leonardo at the request of Lodovico Sforza.

ca. 1600

Mazenta gives MS C, a treatise on light and shade, as a present to Cardinal Federico Borromeo. He also gives a manuscript to the Duke of Savoy and another to the painter Ambrogio Figino.

1609

Cardinal Borromeo founds the Ambrosian Library in Milan, depositing there MS C. A copy of the abridged version of the *Trattato della Pittura* is acquired by the Ambrosian Library as part of the library of G. V. Pinelli (1535–1601).

ca. 1620

The painter Matteo Zaccolini (1590–1630) composes a great treatise on optics and perspective, written in mirror script in imitation of Leonardo's and making use of original manuscripts of Leonardo's. Zaccolini's work is lost.

1625

Pietro Accolti publishes in Florence a treatise on perspective and painting, making use of a manuscript copy of Leonardo's *Trattato della Pittura.*

1630–1640

Cassiano dal Pozzo (1588–1657), secretary to Cardinal Barberini in Rome, sponsors the great project of transcribing Leonardo's manuscripts, and prepares an abridged copy of the *Trattato della Pittura* with illustrations by Poussin. (See Appendix IV.)

1631

Francesco Maria della Rovere (1548–1631), the last duke of Urbino, dies. His library is transferred in twelve crates from Castel Durante to Urbino.

1636

Galeazzo Arconati gives a manuscript copy of Luca Pacoli's *Divina Proportione* (which may contain drawings by Leonardo), ten Leonardo manuscripts, and the Codex Atlanticus to the Biblioteca Ambrosiana. Previously he had given permission for many notes on optics and perspective to be copied from these manuscripts at the request of Cassiano dal Pozzo. Cassiano also arranged for some chapters of his abridged version of the *Trattato della Pittura* to be checked against the original manuscripts.

1640

Leonardo's *Trattato* is discovered at Urbino in one of the crates of manuscripts, prints, and drawings belonging to Duke Francesco Maria della Rovere which were formerly preserved in the Ducal Library at Castel Durante.

1651

The first edition of the *Trattato della Pittura* is issued in Paris, based on the abridged copy provided by Cassiano dal Pozzo.

1657

The Library of Urbino is moved to the Vatican Library in Rome. The *Trattato* is mentioned, with a reference to the old and new crates in which it was kept.

1796

Napoleon enters Milan with his victorious army and declares that "all men of genius . . . are French, whatever be the country which has given them birth." Accordingly, Leonardo's manuscripts in the Ambrosiana are judged to be French and are sent to France. The Codex Atlanticus goes to the Bibliothèque Nationale and the others, to the Institut de France.

ca. 1797

The *Trattato* is catalogued in the Vatican Library as Codex Vaticanus Urbinas 1270.

ca. 1809

The librarian of the Vatican Library, Abate Gaetano Luigi Marini, has the entire Codex Urbinas transcribed at the request of Giuseppe Bossi.

1810

Giuseppe Bossi, *Del Cenacolo di Leonardo da Vinci. Libri Quattro* (Milan, 1810), p. 52, states that he is preparing an edition of the Codex Urbinas. (Bossi's death in 1815 halted this project.)

1817

The full text of the Codex Urbinas is published for the first time by Guglielmo Manzi, in Rome. (The first critical edition was prepared by Heinrich Ludwig [Vienna, 1882] and the first facsimile edition with English translation by A. Philip McMahon [Princeton University Press, 1956].)

INTRODUCTION

EXTANT LEONARDO MANUSCRIPTS CONTAINING NOTES ON PAINTING
(*see also* APPENDIX I)

Manuscripts used in the compilation of the Codex Urbinas [with Melzi's mark in brackets]	*Manuscripts not used in the compilation of the Codex Urbinas*
EARLY PERIOD, *ca.* 1487–1497	
Codex Trivulzianus, *ca.* 1487–1490 [F]	MS C, *ca.* 1490
Windsor 12,604 (a page of a lost manuscript), *ca.* 1487–1490	MSS H₁, H₂, H₃, *ca.* 1493–1495
MS A,* *ca.* 1492	Codices Forster I, II, III, *ca.* 1493–1497
MS Ashburnham 2038 (originally a section of MS A), *ca.* 1492	MS I, *ca.* 1495–1497
	Codex Atlanticus (1478–1518), *passim*
	Codex Arundel (1478–1518), *passim*
INTERMEDIATE PERIOD, *ca.* 1497–1505	
MS L, *ca.* 1497–1502 [Y]	MS M, *ca.* 1500–1502
	MS K: I–II, *ca.* 1504–1505; III, *ca.* 1506–1507
	Codex Atlanticus, *passim*
	Codex Arundel, *passim*
LATE PERIOD, *ca.* 1505–1515	
MS F, 1508 [⊠]	MS D, *ca.* 1508
MS E (*Libro B*), 1513–1514 [B]	Codex Leicester, *ca.* 1506–1509 (one note on human movement [Richter, I, 386]; some of the notes on hydraulics were copied from *Libro A*)
Libro A, *ca.* 1508–1515 [A]	Folio Resta, *ca.* 1508–1510
MS G, 1510–1515 [Φ]	Codex Atlanticus, *passim*
	Codex Arundel, *passim*

* Melzi's mark has been erased from the cover. See Appendix I.

Introduction

Libro A* AND Libro B

LEONARDO DA VINCI made notes for a "Treatise on Painting" throughout his career, but the project was not completed during his lifetime. Moreover, much of the source material is lost. The extant manuscript in the Bibliothèque de l'Institut de France, Paris, known as MS A is only a draft for a book on painting, and can be dated *ca.* 1492. Luca Pacioli informs us that in 1498 Leonardo had completed a treatise on painting and human motion.[1] In 1584 Giovan Paolo Lomazzo states that Leonardo wrote such a treatise at the request of his patron Lodovico Sforza.[2] This request helps to explain why Leonardo began to write on painting after he was about forty years old. During his first Florentine period and in the first decade of his sojourn in the service of the Sforza, that is, before 1490, there is no evidence of his having been concerned with the writing of such a treatise. His notes on painting before the date of MS A are simply recipes for the preparation of colors and they reflect the practice of Florentine studios.[3]

At the fall of the Sforza dynasty in 1499 Leonardo is again in Florence; this is the beginning of the later period of his activity. In 1502, when he is in the service of Cesare Borgia as a military engineer, he is fifty years old. The year after, he is

---

* NOTE: Throughout this study the references to *Libro* A denote the "chapter" (or "note") number if the number is set in italic; otherwise, the number denotes the carta (e.g., *Libro* A *12* refers to "chapter" 12 and *Libro* A 12 refers to carta 12).

1. Pacioli (1509*a*), Introduction, fol. 1: ". . . hauendo già con tutta diligentia al degno libro de pictura e mouimenti humani posto fine . . ." (Leonardo with all diligence has finished his praiseworthy Book on Painting and Human Motion).

2. Lomazzo (1584), p. 158: "Nel qual modo va discorrendo & argomentando Leonardo Vinci in vn suo libro letto dà me questi anni passati ch'egli scrisse di mano stanca à prieghi di Lodouico Sforza, Duca di Milano, in determinatione di questa questione se è piu nobile la pittura, ò la scultura . . ." (In this way Leonardo da Vinci continues to discuss and reason in his book, which I read in recent years, and which he wrote with his left hand, on request of Lodovico Sforza, Duke of Milan, in order to decide the question whether painting or sculpture is more noble . . .).

3. *See* Brizio (1952), pp. 49–50.

Recent research indicates an additional reason for Leonardo's decision to write a treatise on painting: the reading of Leon Battista Alberti's *della Pittura. See* Clark (1944), pp. 16–17. Although Leonardo never mentions Alberti's book, he certainly was acquainted with it, for his early writings show its influence even in the sequence of subjects. See below, pp. 21, 59–60, and 117.

back in Florence engaged in the painting of the "Battle of Anghiari," having the young Michelangelo as a rival. Then in 1506 another Milanese period begins for Leonardo; this time as an architect in the service of the French governor of Milan and concurrently as a painter for the King of France. In 1513 he moves to the Vatican, where he remains until 1516, making excursions around Rome and on occasions going to north Italy and to Florence. The last three years of his life he spends in France, in Amboise as a painter and architect for Francis I.

During the nineteen years after 1500, notwithstanding the difficulties of a wandering life, Leonardo increases his activity as a writer. He uses pocket notebooks in order not to miss any opportunity of recording an observation while traveling, and he maintains unbound files in which he starts copying and organizing his notes according to subject matter. He envisages treatises on mechanics, on hydraulics, on anatomy, and of course on painting. His early project of a book on painting has to be amplified, to include notes on plants and landscape, and new observations on light, shade, and color. This new phase of his work is preserved in notebooks dating from 1508 to 1515, but we have no evidence that the project went any further.

At Leonardo's death in 1519 his manuscripts went to his pupil Francesco Melzi, who had been his assistant since about 1508.[4] From Leonardo's notes on painting Melzi compiled the *Trattato della Pittura*, now known as Codex Urbinas 1270 in the Vatican Library. At the end of the Codex Urbinas the eighteen original manuscripts used in the compilation are listed according to their original code marks (plates 2 and 3). Some of the extant manuscripts still have these marks, usually on the cover. By comparing Melzi's list with extant manuscripts, one can see which manuscripts remain and which are lost. Of the eighteen manuscripts listed, only six and a fragment have unquestionably survived (see Appendix I).

When the *Trattato della Pittura* had been compiled a scholar was called in as an adviser. He made several suggestions concerning modifications in the headings and in the sequence of certain chapters. Familiar as he was with the manuscripts of Leonardo, he must have envisaged the opportunity of identifying each passage of the Codex Urbinas with the reference to its source. He actually started this patient concordance by identifying all the chapters that were copied from two notebooks, *Libro* A and *Libro* B. *Libro* B still exists; it is the MS E in the Bibliothèque de l'Institut de France, Paris—a notebook originally composed of 96 folios, written in 1513–1514.[5] *Libro* A is lost. We may assume that Pompeo Leoni did not dis-

---

4. Calvi (1925), pp. 254–260.

5. *Libro B* was given the mark "E" in 1796, when G. B. Venturi listed the Leonardo MSS in the Bibliothèque de l'Institut with letters from A to N. The original mark "B" is still visible on the cover (see plate 31). Sixteen folios, that is, the last signature, of *Libro B* disappeared around 1840. Some notes of the missing folios are known from copies by G. B. Venturi. *See* G. B. De Toni (1924), p. 78. *Libro B* measures 15.4 × 9.6 cm. It was used by Leonardo in 1513 and 1514, both in Milan and in Rome. The date on the first folio refers to Leonardo's journey to Rome: "I departed from Milan for Rome on the 24th day of September, 1513, with Giovan Francesco de' Melzi, Salai, Lorenzo, and il Fanfoia." The date 25 September 1514 on folio 8or refers to Leonardo as being in Parma, probably as a military architect in the service of Lorenzo di Piero de' Medici.

member it in order to form the Codex Atlanticus or other miscellaneous collections of Leonardo's folios, because no fragment of *Libro* A can be identified in these collections.

The present book concerns the reconstruction of this lost manuscript of Leonardo. One hundred and seven passages in the body of the Codex Urbinas are marked as being derived from *Libro* A, and the folio number in *Libro* A is given (but the references do not specify whether recto or verso). The first step in the reconstruction of *Libro* A was to arrange all these passages in their original order. It turned out that they came from folios 1 to 65 of *Libro* A. By textual analysis and comparison with extant manuscripts we were able to establish the date of the notes as being *ca.* 1508–1515. An error in transcription made it possible to determine the length of the lines in the original notebook, which proved to be the same as the length of the lines in three other late notebooks of Leonardo's, MSS E, F, and G. From these observations we drew the conclusion that *Libro* A was probably identical in dimensions and number of folios. But so far we had reconstructed only 65 folios, whereas MSS E, F, and G had 96 folios. Where, then, were the notes originally on folios 66 to 96? We found them in the Codex Leicester, which is a compilation of notes on hydraulics made by Leonardo himself in the period *ca.* 1506–1509. In this codex references to an original source in the notebook that Leonardo called *Libro* A are frequently noted in connection with various passages. Again, the folio number is given each time (for his citations Leonardo uses an A and a number; only once, on folio 21r [plate 4], does he give a full quotation: "89 in libro A"). (Melzi's method of gathering and transcribing passages from various notebooks to make the Codex Urbinas was thus evidently based on Leonardo's own practices.) In the Codex Leicester, as Gerolamo Calvi had already pointed out,[6] the folios of *Libro* A from which passages are quoted run from 54 to 95.

Another date in *Libro* B was in a note transcribed by Venturi from the missing folio 96, next to a drawing of waterfalls and rocks: "Sulla riva di Po vicino a Santo Angiolo nel 1514, adi 27 di 7mbre" (On the bank of the Po river, near Sant'Angelo, 1514, the 27th of September). Doubts as to the late date of MS E, that is, *Libro* B, have been raised by R. Marcolongo (1937), pp. 161–164. Marcolongo states that several of the problems on statics in the first 30 folios of the Codex Arundel are found in draft in MS E, and MS E should therefore be dated before March, 1508, the date of Leonardo's compilation of the first 30 folios of the Codex Arundel. But this is not the case. The notes in MS E are not the drafts of those in the Codex Arundel; they are compiled from drafts in Codex Atlanticus 271 r-f and 113 r-b. These two folios, together with folio 12 r-b, v-b, originally formed a single sheet containing archaeological studies of the harbor of Civitavecchia, *ca.* 1514. (Cf. Pedretti [1962c], pp. 84 ff., and figs. 47–48.) The drafts of notes on mechanics were added later in the space left free around these architectural drawings, thus providing evidence that the compilation of the notes on mechanics in MS E dates *ca.* 1514.

6. Calvi (1925), pp. 223–224. Calvi suggests that another trace of *Libro* A could be recognized in Codex Atlanticus 267 r-a (*ca.* 1495), in a figure and note on mechanics on which Leonardo had written the words "copied in A." The note and figure, however, were copied by Leonardo in Codex Forster II 97r, so it is unlikely that the cross-reference refers to our *Libro* A. It is possible, of course, that Codex Forster II, one of the earliest notebooks of Leonardo, was originally marked "A," even though no trace of this mark

The lost notebook, therefore, had probably no more than 96 folios, that is, six signatures of 16 folios each, as in MSS E, F, and G. Since no record is left of folio 96, we can assume that this was a blank folio or a folio filled with notes not pertaining to painting or hydraulics. Obviously, the lost notebook, in common with any other Leonardo manuscript dealing with painting, also contained notes and drawings on other subjects, such as geometry and mechanics. In fact, between folios 1 and 95 in our reconstruction there are several folios of which no record is left: folios 2–11, 45, 46, 52, 53, 55–60, 62, 63, 66–73, 76–84, 90, 91, 93, 94. However, in spite of these gaps, the present reconstruction of *Libro* A gives us a fairly good idea of the contents and date of the lost manuscript: the first part concerned painting and the second part hydraulics, although, since Leonardo started at the back and worked forward in filling his notebooks, the notes on hydraulics are *earlier* in date.[7]

Two questions immediately arise: How long before the compilation of the Codex Leicester was the section on water in *Libro* A written? And, since the compilation of the Codex Leicester, which is not dated by Leonardo himself, is usually referred to the period 1506–1509, were the notes on water in *Libro* A written before 1506 or nearer to 1509? An answer to these questions can be provided by an analysis of the notes in the second part of *Libro* A. One of these notes (*Libro* A 110) is illustrated with a topographical sketch of the confluence of the Mugnone brook and the Arno river. A date before 1503 can thus be excluded, for this was the year of Leonardo's studies on the straightening of the Arno above Florence in connection with the project of a Prato–Pistoia canal—and Sir Kenneth Clark points out that the paper of the maps of the Arno and the Mugnone in Windsor 12,677 and 12,678 has the same watermark as that of the drawings for the "Battle of Anghiari," 1503–1504. Moreover, the diagram of the movement of wind in *Libro* A 130 can be related to Leonardo's studies on aerodynamics and the flight of birds around 1505. Further, a note on the flight of birds was written on carta 51 of *Libro* A [8] at the beginning of the section on painting, representing a logical transition from

---

remains on its vellum cover. Since this codex is written without *pentimenti*, it must have been compiled from notes drafted in other manuscripts. One such note, in fact, is found on folio 101r, being the copy of one in Codex Atlanticus 318 r-a, a folio dated on its verso 2 January 1496; *see* Pedretti (1957a), pl. 20. Thus Codex Forster II can be dated after January, 1496. Calvi (1925), p. 149, interpreted the date "venerdì 4 di settembre" on folio 159 of the Codex Forster II as referring to 1495. On folio 64v there is the well-known record of the burial of Caterina, perhaps Leonardo's mother.

7. The Codex Forster I is another two-part manuscript of Leonardo's, with an even greater difference in time and content (stereometry and hydraulics); *see* Calvi (1925), pp. 79–80.

8. *Libro* A 105. It is not surprising that the lost notebook, in common with the similar MSS E, F, and G, included notes on the flight of birds, but it is curious that one of the notes was copied in the *Trattato della Pittura*. The note was included in the *Trattato* as part of a discussion on the center of gravity—other notes on the same subject having been copied from the same carta 51 of *Libro* A. Comparisons with notes in the *Codex on the Flight of Birds* and elsewhere indicate the year 1505 as a *terminus a quo* for dating *Libro* A.

the problems on dynamics in the section on hydraulics to those on statics (center of gravity) in the section on painting. Finally, the section on water in *Libro A* can be dated around 1505–1507 because it carries out a program of discussion outlined in MS K 65r (*ca.* 1506): "Describe in how many ways water hollows out the bottom, and in how many ways it deposits earth upon the bottom. And the same of the banks: where it raises them and where it forms them, and in how many ways it hollows out the soil of the banks."

An indirect relationship between the section on painting in *Libro* A and the Codex Leicester can be recognized in notes on the blue of the sky, which are found both on folio 4r of the Codex Leicester (which is one of the latest sheets of that codex, as Calvi demonstrated) and on carta 1 of *Libro* A. If Calvi's assumption that the Codex Leicester was written nearer to 1509 than to 1506 is correct, no great interval of time would have elapsed between the compilation of the two parts of *Libro* A. In that event, the whole of *Libro* A would have a chronological and contextual unity.

Windsor 12,579r (plate 1) was folded in half when Leonardo drew on the left an old man in profile seated on the bank of a river. On the right side of this folio are four drawings of the motion of water which are similar to those in MSS F and G and the Codex Leicester. The note pertaining to these drawings appears to be of about the same date as the notes on painting in *Libro* A. It reads: "Observe the motion of the surface of the water, which resembles that of hair, which has two motions, of which one depends on the weight of the hair, the other on the direction of the curls; thus the water forms eddying whirlpools, one part of which is due to the impetus of the principal current and the other to the incidental motion and return flow." [9] These drawings may thus be considered to be a synthesis of the material in the lost notebook of Leonardo: The pictorial image of the undulation of hair, suggested by his observation of the motion of water, seems to unite in a single symbol the material on hydraulics in the second part of *Libro* A and the notes on painting in the first part.

FORMAT OF THE LOST NOTEBOOK

Through textual analysis of the reconstructed *Libro* A we can estimate the size of the lost notebook and the approximate date of the entries.

As we have seen, Melzi used *Libro* A from folios 1 to 65 in the compilation of the *Trattato della Pittura*; Leonardo used it from folios 54 to 95 in his Codex Leicester notes. We know that at least three of Leonardo's late notebooks, MSS E, F, and G, all have 96 folios, their format being about 15 × 10 cm. *Libro* A, which had at least 95 folios, was probably the same type of notebook as MSS E, F, and G, for its contents are also akin to those of these manuscripts. Further evidence of such relationship is that *Libro* A and its companion *Libro* B, that is, MS E, had lines of writing of similar length.

---

9. J. P. Richter (1883), I, 389.

It may appear impossible to detect the length of a line of writing in a manuscript no longer extant. However, almost everyone has experienced a mistake quite easy to make when transcribing a note onto a fresh sheet, that is, to start to omit a line that happens to begin or end with the same word as the one beginning or ending the preceding line. Melzi made such an error in copying one of the notes from *Libro* A. He corrected himself by crossing out the words he had started to copy from the wrong line. Thus one can easily determine which line he started to omit. In Melzi's copy on folio 156v of the Codex Urbinas we find the text of *Libro A 38* reading as follows:

> . . . *tu le fai che quella parte*[*cipa*
> *d'esso lume*] *del corpo che' più remota dal lume manco*
> *partecipa d'esso lume.* . . .

The words crossed out by Melzi are shown within brackets. Thus the passage can be reconstructed as it was in Leonardo's original manuscript:

> . . . *tu le fai che quella parte*
> *del corpo che' più remota dal lume manco parte*[-]
> *cipa d'esso lume.* . . .

Here the line is composed of 37 letters plus 8 spaces between the words, which is approximately the type of line that can be found in MSS E, F, and G.

An indication of the width of the original manuscript is given by the diagrams of the classification of the profiles of the nose in *Libro* A 30. As all the illustrations in the Codex Urbinas are reproduced in their original size, we can safely assume that these diagrams occupied almost the entire width of a page of the lost manuscript. They measure 9.6 cm. In MS E, that is, *Libro B*, there are diagrams of similar length,[10] varying from 8.5 cm. to 10 cm. One of them, on folio 40v, measures 9.6 cm., the precise width of those in chapter 30 of *Libro* A. The width of these diagrams does not correspond to the width of the lines of the notes, of course, but to the width of the manuscript page. If we write the above reconstructed line of *Libro A 38* using letters of the size of those of the notes in *Libro B*, we obtain a line width of 7 cm., the same as that of the notes on folio 40v of *Libro B* and of the notes on most of the other folios of the same manuscript.

Libro B 40v

Libro A 38

This length of line in *Libro B* means that a margin of about 2.5 cm. is always left on the right side of the page to provide space for figures, diagrams, or supplementary annotations. Several of the small figures and diagrams of the lost *Libro* A are of the same size as the marginal figures and diagrams in *Libro B*. *Libro* A, therefore,

10. Cf. MS E: fols. 6r (8.5 cm.), 29v (8.5 cm), 40r (10 cm.), 40v (9.6 cm.), 43v (9.7 cm.); also MS G 19v (9.4 cm.), copied in Codex Urbinas 230v.

must have been similar to *Libro B* in this characteristic page layout, a characteristic that does not appear in Leonardo's manuscripts before 1500.

As can be checked in the present reconstruction of *Libro* A, the pages with the greatest amount of writing never exceed the capacity of the pages of MSS E, F, and G.[11] This is an indirect confirmation of the assumption that *Libro A* was similar in format to these notebooks.

Another such indirect confirmation is provided by the list of Leonardo's original manuscripts at the end of the Codex Urbinas (plates 2–3). In this list the Leonardo manuscripts seem to have been arranged in order of page size, from the largest at the beginning ("Libro intero segnato .i.") to the smallest at the end ("librettini"). *Libro* A appears twice: in the ninth and fourteenth positions. This repetition can be explained, however. The ninth book was previously listed as *Libro F*, then the F was crossed out and an A substituted. Since a *Libro F* was actually used in the compilation of the Codex Urbinas (it is the present Codex Trivulzianus), the "Libro segnato .A." in the fourteenth position should presumably have been changed to *F*. One might surmise that the person who corrected the mark of the ninth book without correcting the fourteenth entry had probably intended to list *Libro* A among notebooks of similar format, such as the present MS F and the *Libro B* (the present MS E). However, even in the fourteenth position *Libro* A was already associated with a notebook similar in format, the present MS G,[12] so there was no need to change its position, other than for the purpose of giving it a more prominent place in the list. However, the only reasonable conclusion we may draw from such conjectures is that someone was certainly attaching special importance to *Libro* A.

CHRONOLOGY OF *Libro* A

The 107 notes copied by Melzi from *Libro* A are distributed in five of the eight parts of the *Trattato della Pittura:* the first part contains 4 notes from *Libro* A; the second, 26; the third, 58; the fifth, 18; and the sixth, 1. Parts iv, vii, and viii contain no notes from *Libro* A. We see that most of the notes taken from *Libro* A were gathered in the third part of the Codex Urbinas.

Because of the four notes copied in the first part, one might assume that *Libro* A dates from an early period of Leonardo's activity. In fact, it is usually believed that the subject of the first part of the Codex Urbinas—the comparison of the

---

11. However, as the references to *Libro A* do not specify the recto and verso of the folios of the original notebook, some of the longest passages may have occupied both faces of a single folio.

12. Ravaisson-Mollien (1881), pp. 18 ff., describes the covers of Leonardo's manuscripts in the Bibliothèque de l'Institut de France, but gives the original code marks only for MSS C, E, and F. Thus MS C is the fourth of the list in the Codex Urbinas, recorded as *Libro d'Ombra e lume segnato* .G.; MS F is the eighth, marked with a square with diagonals; and MS E is the eleventh, marked *Libro B*. MS G is now identified as the thirteenth of Melzi's list. The problems related to the code marks of Leonardo's manuscripts are discussed in Appendix I.

arts—concerned Leonardo only during his Sforza period,[13] *ca.* 1492. But a note
in Windsor 19,010 proves that Leonardo was still interested in this subject about
1510. The Windsor note, which can be compared to chapter 31 of the McMahon
edition of the *Treatise on Painting,* is one of the clues to the fact that Leonardo returned to the subject of the "Paragone" in his late period. From his new studies
on light and shade, on perspective, and on atmosphere he gained new assurance
in proclaiming the superiority of painting over the other arts, especially sculpture.
This new approach is recognizable in *Libro* A 48: "[Sculpture] cannot represent
luminous and transparent bodies, such as veiled figures which show the nude
flesh beneath the veils covering them, and it cannot show small pebbles of various
colors beneath the surface of transparent waters."

Codex Atlanticus 277 v-a, a folio of blue-gray paper of *ca.* 1510, contains a discussion of the comparison between painting and sculpture in one of the notes
that was intended as an introduction to the Book on Light and Shade:

How the eye cannot discern the shapes of bodies within their boundaries except by
means of shadows and lights; and there are many sciences which would be nothing
without the science of these shadows and lights: as painting, sculpture, astronomy,
a great part of perspective and the like. As may be shown, the sculptor cannot
work without the help of shadows and lights, since without these the material
carved would remain all of one colour; and by the ninth of this [book] it is shown
that a level surface illumined by uniform light does not vary in any part the clear-
ness or obscurity of its natural colour, and this uniformity of colour goes to prove
the uniformity of the smoothness of its surface. It would follow therefore that if
the material carved were not clothed by shadows and lights, which are necessitated
by the prominences of certain muscles and the hollows interposed between them,
the sculptor would not be able uninterruptedly to see the progress of his own work,
and this the work that he is carving requires, and so what he fashioned during the
day would be almost as though it had been made in the darkness of the night. Paint-
ing, however, by means of these shadows and lights comes to represent upon level
surfaces scenes with hollows and raised portions, separated from each other by dif-
ferent degrees of distance and in different aspects.[14]

Even more significant is a passage in Codex Atlanticus 305 v-a: "One of the chief
proofs of skill of the painter is that his picture should seem in relief, and this is
not the case with the sculptor, for in this respect he is aided by nature." [15] This
note in red chalk can be considered to be a draft for chapter 18 of *Libro* A. This
folio of the Codex Atlanticus can be dated about 1506–1508 because of the topographical relief associated with Leonardo's activities in the service of Charles
d'Amboise, governor of Milan.[16]

The notes on the "Paragone" from *Libro* A provide one of the several indications
that Leonardo in his late period resumed discussions on problems related to

13. Cf. Brizio (1956), pp. 309–320; *see* also below, pp. 121 ff.
14. MacCurdy:II.397–398.   15. *Ibid.:*II.230.
16. *See* Pedretti (1960*a*), fig. 4.

theories of the Quattrocento.[17] Other passages, if isolated from the context of the reconstructed notebook, may appear early in date; for example, the precept that admonishes one to avoid the "common defect of Italian painters," [18] namely, their tendency to imitate themselves and to imitate the work of other painters, instead of following nature as the true and only master. This advice goes back to Cennini and Alberti, as does his criticism of the perspective employed by certain contemporary painters, which is actually a criticism of Trecento painting, in *Libro A* 55.

Chapter 90 of *Libro A*, "To Make a Figure Which Appears to Be Forty Braccia High in a Space of Twenty Braccia," in the Codex Urbinas precedes an analogous chapter copied from MS A 38v, *ca.* 1492. Again, it would be perfectly justifiable to suggest an early date for the chapter coming from the lost notebook, but in Leonardo's original manuscripts there is evidence of elaboration in 1514 of notes on perspective written as early as 1492.[19] Moreover, a note in Codex Arundel 62r, *ca.* 1508, deals with a problem of anamorphosis analogous to that treated in these two chapters.

In his Introduction to his edition of *The Codex Huygens* Professor Panofsky states that only two chapters of the "Treatise on Painting" are concerned with the principles of division and variation *in infinitum* of human motion, although this subject is extensively developed in the Codex Huygens.[20] These two chapters come from *Libro A*.

The Codex Huygens, a late sixteenth-century compilation, was based primarily on notes from Leonardo's late period. Its treatment of the theory of human movement and perspective reflects a very late phase of Leonardo's theory of art, because it can be related to a note in *Libro B*, that is, MS E 17r: "Observe how the shoulder changes with all the movements of the arm, moving up and down, inwards and outwards, backwards and forwards, and so also with turning movements or any other movements. And do the same with the neck, the hands and feet and the chest above the hips." [21]

That part of *Libro A* which has not been preserved through Melzi's copies might have been the source for the compiler of the Codex Huygens. The above-mentioned note on the manner of making a figure "Which Appears to Be Forty Braccia High in a Space of Twenty Braccia" would be appropriate in the context of the notes on perspective in the Codex Huygens.[22]

---

17. *See* below, pp. 54–55, 121 ff.   18. *Libro A* 72.
19. *See* below, pp. 169–171.   20. Panofsky (1940), pp. 122–125.
21. MacCurdy:I.194. See also the passage in Windsor 19,005v (*Fogli A dell'Anatomia* 6v), quoted in note 46 (*Libro A* 39).
22. Because of these similarities, the Codex Urbinas and the Codex Huygens can be considered to have a closely related, if not identical, origin. Numerous notes in the Windsor folios transcribed by the compiler of the Codex Huygens are marked with the characteristic dashed circle with which Melzi designated Leonardo's notes on painting that were to be copied in the Codex Urbinas. Moreover, the handwriting of the Codex Huygens resembles that of certain marginal notes of the Codex Urbinas. *See* below, pp. 104–105, and *Post Scriptum*, pp. 263–264.

Leonardo wrote *Libro* A during a period in which he was, for the second time, greatly interested in anatomy. The lost notebook contained many notes on muscles and bones, as well as notes on the balance and movement of the human figure.

The Windsor anatomical folio 19,010, *ca.* 1510, contains a list of topics that Leonardo intended to discuss:

After the demonstration of all the parts of the limbs of man and of the other animals you will represent the proper method of action of these limbs, that is in rising after lying down, in moving, running and jumping in various attitudes, in lifting and carrying heavy weights, in throwing things to a distance and in swimming, and in every act you will show which limbs and which muscles are the causes of the said actions, and especially in the play of the arms.[23]

The human movements mentioned here, and the movements involved in lifting oneself from a seated position, which are described in *Libro* A 36, are illustrated in many chapters of the third part of the "Treatise on Painting." Some of them come from MSS G and E, but many others come from lost manuscripts of Leonardo, which may all be dated in the same period as *Libro* A.

Original manuscripts that contain such notes include not only MSS G and E but also folios of similar date at Windsor, as, for example, nos. 19,149–19,152 and 19,141–19,142.[24] Folio 19,149 contains a note on human movement and some notes on light and shade.[25] In other folios at Windsor—usually concerned with anatomy—dating in his late period, Leonardo often records observations on the mechanics of the human body and on optics, with specific reference to his plans for a book on painting. Such notes, which are still in draft form, precede the compilation of *Libro* A; for example, those in Windsor 19,121r (plate 26), all of which are crossed out, evidently because they were copied or better developed elsewhere. They constitute the outline for a discussion on how to represent *istorie*, how to depict drapery, and how one should avoid the defect of certain painters who repeat the same poses. They also include a draft of a discussion on the practice and ethic of painting.[26] All these subjects are considered in *Libro* A.

The Windsor anatomical folios that contain notes on human movement related to those in *Libro* A also contain notes on light and shade. Similarly MSS E and G, containing notes on light and shade and on hydraulics, also have notes on anatomy and human movements. Evidently between 1508 and 1515 Leonardo intensified his study of these subjects as well as his observations on color and landscape.

---

23. MacCurdy:I.108.   24. *See* Clark (1935), pp. 188–191.
25. *See* MacCurdy:II.287; Steinitz (1958), p. 20.
26. *See* below, pp. 144–145. Similar crossed-out notes are also found on folios of the Codex Atlanticus, e.g., folio 345 v-b [plate 25 of the present book], which can be dated 1508–1510 because of the sketches on the canalization of the Adda river. Cf. Calvi (1925), pp. 295 ff. In order to date the lost notebook accurately it would be necessary to trace preparatory notes in extant manuscripts. But this possibility is limited because *Libro* A was a notebook, not a codex like the Leicester in which Leonardo had copied and organized his own writings.

In a manuscript of the early period, MS C, *ca.* 1490, Leonardo had already started to gather notes for a Book on Light and Shade, probably as part of a book on painting, but only after 1506 did he develop this project as an individual book, as happened also with his book on perspective.[27] In a note in Windsor 19,076, *ca.* 1513, Leonardo reminds himself to reserve for the last part of his Book on Light and Shade a discussion of "the figures which appeared in the studio [*scriptoio*] of Gherardo Miniatore in San Marco at Florence." A *scriptoio* in San Marco is obviously one of the cells decorated by Fra Angelico (1387–1455); unfortunately, we have no evidence as to which of them Leonardo referred to as Gherardo's. This note, however, proves that in 1513 Leonardo, then on his way to Rome, was planning to devote space in his book to a discussion of certain paintings of his Florentine predecessor. He was probably interested in commenting on the effects of reflected color and of colored shadows displayed in Fra Angelico's frescoes.

Libro A contained a great many notes on color. None of Leonardo's extant manuscripts has so many notes on this subject, which seems to have occupied him increasingly after 1505. In Codex Atlanticus 181 r-a, *ca.* 1508, Leonardo writes:

The surface of each body takes part of the colour of whatever is set against it. The colours of the objects in light are reproduced on each other's surface at different spots according to the varieties in the positions of these objects . . . and the rest will be set forth in the Book on Painting. In that book it will be demonstrated, by transmitting the images of the bodies and colours of the things illuminated by the sun through a small round hole in a dark place on to a smooth surface which in itself is white. But everything will be upside down.[28]

Such a program of analyzing the nature of colors by means of the *camera obscura* is developed in *Libro A 19.*

Commenting on the notes on painting in MS G, 1510–1515, Sir Kenneth Clark points out that "in these writings Leonardo anticipates the impressionistic doctrine that everything is more or less reflected in everything else, and that there are no such things as black shadows." [29] In the notes on color gathered from *Libro A* we find a similar anticipation of impressionistic doctrine:

I have often seen a white object with red lights and bluish shadows. This happens on snow-clad mountains at sunset, when the horizon appears on fire.[30]
. . . often happens when the face is high in color or white, and its shadows make it yellowish. This occurs because wet streets are more yellowish than are dry ones, and the parts of the face nearest those streets are tinted by the yellow tones and shadows of the streets which reflect on them.[31]

---

27. *See* below, pp. 146 ff.   28. MacCurdy:II.277.
29. Clark (1952), p. 148.   30. *Libro A* 24.
31. *Libro A* 96. Alberti was perfectly aware of this effect: "You may have noticed that anyone who walks through a meadow in the sun appears greenish in the face" (Spencer: 51).

In *Libro* A 44 Leonardo specifically states that shadow must be regarded as an element of chromatic value: "And remember that the shadows should never be so dark that you must lose color in the area where they are found. . . ." And it is also in *Libro A*, chapter 83, that Leonardo writes the famous definition: "Painting is a composition of light and shade, combined with all the various kinds of simple and compound colors."

Leonardo certainly knew the treatise on color attributed to Aristotle, from which he may have taken his first idea about the blue of the sky. In 1508 Leonardo was reading Aristotle's *De Physica*, since notes in MS F and in other manuscripts of that time specifically refer to it.[32] Thus it may not be a coincidence that MS F and the Codex Leicester as well as *Libro* A contained discussions of the origin of the blue of the sky. Leonardo's research developed in a direction that Alberti had already intuited, that is, toward a study of the gradations of intensity in colors due to varied densities of atmosphere.

Observations on landscape are frequent in the notes on painting written by Leonardo around 1510. Likewise, *Libro* A contained notes on atmosphere, on mountains and valleys, on vegetation, and on water.

On the whole, almost every note from *Libro* A has formal and stylistic similarities to notes preserved in Leonardo's manuscripts dated from 1508 to 1515. Particularly significant is the similarity of chapter 108 of *Libro* A to Windsor 19,001 (on bone structure), which dates from about 1510. Similar relationships will be pointed out in our commentary.

---

32. MS F 84v and cover; *see* also MS D 10v.
A study of the sources of Leonardo's studies on color and vision would provide precious information about the influence of Aristotelian theories on Renaissance writers and painters. Before Solmi's pioneering work on the subject of the sources of Leonardo's manuscripts (1908), an almost forgotten contribution to the knowledge of Leonardo's indebtedness to Aristotle was given by Charles Lock Eastlake in his edition of Goethe's *Theory on Colours* as early as 1840 (pp. 379–389). Eastlake's juxtaposition of Leonardo's chapters from the *Trattato* and passages from the *Treatise on Colors* attributed to Aristotle (published in 1497) is an example of a greater work of comparison that could be profitably extended to the writings of other Renaissance theorists. The subject of Aristotle's *De Coloribus* was discussed by Simon Portius in a series of lectures in Florence early in the sixteenth century. The years 1505–1508 represent a crucial point in the development of Leonardo as a theorist of art. During this period he must have carried out a vast program of reading, including the works of classical as well as medieval authors. Many of what we may irreverently call the "obsessions" of Leonardo originated from these readings; for example, the principles of "continuous quantity" and their application to the geometrical game of the *lunulae*, the definitions of point and line as the basic principles for his treatises on painting and on water, and finally the problem of Alhazen in his studies on optics. Manuscript D, which is a treatise on the eye and on the theory of vision, was written *ca.* 1508 under the influence of the *Opus Majus* of Roger Bacon. (Cf. Codex Arundel 71v: "Rugieri Bacon fatto in istampa." Leonardo may have had access to a manuscript of Roger Bacon's *Opus Majus* as Ghiberti did, or he might have used the translation of Bacon's *Optical Science* in Ghiberti's Third Commentary.) Leonardo's studies on light and shade and color carried out after 1505 teach a pitch that is almost beyond human understanding. In *Libro B* (MS E) 31v a note written in microscopic script above a diagram of light and shade reads: "Non si debbe desiderare lo impossibile" (One ought not to desire the impossible).

The classification of the profiles of the nose in chapters 29 and 30 of *Libro* A continues a subject Leonardo had already considered during his early discussions on painting. Many notes from the lost notebook are concerned with the study of expression. Some of them have been considered basic in Leonardo's early formulation of his theory of art.[33] Thus, to be able to date them would help to clarify the development of Leonardo's theory of art.

If the MS A in the Institut de France is the main source for the study of Leonardo's theory of art during his Sforza period, the reconstruction of *Libro* A provides us with an equivalent source for the study of Leonardo's theory in his late period. It is significant that these two manuscripts (the early one still extant and the later one lost) have in common a basic characteristic: both treat painting at length and both have a section on hydraulics. This is evidence of Leonardo's habit of developing his early studies in his late period—a habit that helps to account for the repetition in *Libro* A of ideas already expressed in the manuscript of the Sforza period.[34] Something similar happened to Leonardo's anatomical studies. In *Fogli B dell'Anatomia* at Windsor one can see how often Leonardo elaborated after 1500 upon notes he had written in 1489–1490 (see plates 22 and 23). Such reconsiderations of his ideas on the theory of art demonstrate his continuing allegiance to the Florentine tradition of the Quattrocento. In this respect the reconstruction of the sequence of passages in *Libro* A is revealing: chapters 55 to 58 actually repeat the sequence of passages on *Decorum* in Alberti's *della Pittura*, providing evidence that Leonardo used Alberti's book not only in the Sforza period, as usually believed, but also after 1500.

A date after 1505 for *Libro* A is suggested by the style of its drawings. Some of the chapters are illustrated with sketches of human figures which reflect the style of the lost originals. Such small "standing figures" as those of chapter 81 are comparable in style to many fragments at Windsor.[35] The drawing illustrating chapter 67, "On the Figure Which Moves against the Wind," deserves particular attention. In this drawing the copyist even reproduces the left-handed direction of hatching. The Windsor fragment 12,708, which Pompeo Leoni took from Codex Atlanticus 289 r-c, contains a similar figure of a woman.[36] Since the Windsor fragment can be safely dated about 1505, the similar drawing in *Libro* A should not be dated before that time.

---

33. Cf. Blunt (1959), pp. 23–38.

34. MS C (1490) and MS E (1513–1514) are also similar in contents, although of different size. Both treat light and shade and hydraulics. Some of the notes in the later manuscript were even copied from the earlier. *See* below, p. 147.

35. *See* Windsor 12,707 (Pedretti [1957a], pl. 25).

36. *See* Pedretti (1957a), pl. 18. Beneath the space produced by the extraction of the Windsor fragment, this folio of the Codex Atlanticus has another *lacuna*, which may have contained a short note on painting. But the contents of the folio (notes on geometry) do not have the characteristics of the notes usually found in pages of notebooks. Moreover, in the cut-off sketch a man is running after the woman, and other figures are in the foreground. Thus the Windsor fragment cannot be identified as the original drawing from *Libro* A.

HISTORY OF *Libro A*

Little is known of the history of *Libro* A other than its mention in the Codex Urbinas. Obviously Melzi inherited *Libro* A together with the other Leonardo manuscripts. We know that around 1585 Ambrogio Mazenta obtained thirteen manuscripts of Leonardo's from the heirs of Francesco Melzi.[37] In his *Memorie* Mazenta states that some of the manuscripts were *in folio* and others *in quarto*. At the request of the Melzi family Mazenta returned seven of these thirteen manuscripts; and he also gave away three of the six remaining manuscripts as presents: one, the present MS C in the Institut de France, to Cardinal Borromeo; a second to the painter Ambrogio Figino; and a third to the Duke of Savoy. The Figino

---

37. For the early story of Leonardo's manuscripts see Appendix V, this volume.

The hypothesis that *Libro* A was known at the end of the sixteenth and the beginning of the seventeenth century is suggested by a paraphrase of the chapter on the center of gravity of birds (*Libro* A 105) in Jean Baptiste Villalpand's *Apparatus Urbis ac Templi Hierosolymitani* (Rome, 1604) (see P. Duhem [1903–1913], I, 80–82): "When a bird flies, the vertical line that passes through the middle of the surface of the wings passes also through the center of gravity of the body of the bird. When the bird wishes to raise the fore part of its body and lower the rear part, it puts the wings (that is, its supporting base) forward. And when it wishes to descend it does the contrary, placing its wings backward. In so doing the bird changes the position of the center of gravity of its body."

Villalpand's other passages on the center of gravity quoted by Duhem echo similar chapters in *Libro* A, including chapter 36, "On a Man's Rising-Up from Sitting on Level Ground," which is actually a derivation from Aristotle's *Mechanical Questions*, XXX (see R. Marcolongo [1937], p. 183, n. 60). Similarly, Bernardino Baldi develops these problems of the center of gravity in his *Sylloge Commentariorum et exercitationum in questiones mechanicas Aristotelis* of 1582 (Venetiis, 1623), omitting, however, the passage on the flight of birds, but including an explanation of the vortex effects of water. Duhem's suggestion (Vol. I, pp. 53 ff.) that both Villalpand and Baldi had access to a lost manuscript of Leonardo makes us wonder whether such a manuscript was our *Libro* A. Villalpand's teacher was P. Jérôme Prado, who was commissioned by Philip II of Spain to write a commentary on the vision of Ezekiel. In carrying out the work left unfinished at Prado's death in 1595, Villalpand undertook a systematic archaeological study of the temple of Jerusalem, including problems of statics and, consequently, of the center of gravity. Philip II, the sponsor of so monumental a project, was the patron of Pompeo Leoni, the sculptor who brought the Leonardo manuscripts to Spain. It is possible that Jesuits in the service of the king of Spain could have seen those manuscripts, but the evidence given by the works of these writers is not enough to support such an attractive hypothesis. Villalpand and Baldi could have used one of the several abridged versions of the *Trattato della Pittura* which were made available as early as the second half of the sixteenth century. (The abridged version of the *Trattato* contains all the passages paraphrased by these writers, with the exception of *Libro* A 36, which derives from Aristotle.) Baldi could even have seen the Codex Urbinas, since he had access to the library of the Duke of Urbino. On the other hand, we have always to bear in mind that such similarities of contents between the manuscripts of Leonardo and the works of later writers can be explained by the fact that both Leonardo and his successors might have used the same sources. A study of the works of the alleged plagiarists of Leonardo (Cardano, Baldi, Villalpand, Kircher, Niceron, and so forth) may help us to define better the classical and medieval sources of Leonardo's writings.

and Duke of Savoy manuscripts are lost. It is thus possible that *Libro* A was one of them. Certainly it was not one of the three manuscripts left to Mazenta, because these came to Pompeo Leoni, who took them apart in order to have more Leonardo material to be gathered into the huge scrapbook known today as the Codex Atlanticus.

We do not know whether Leoni obtained *Libro* A directly from the Melzi family, but it is certain that he did not dismember it to mount its folios on the pages of the Codex Atlanticus. Obviously he considered *Libro* A as a manuscript complete in itself, to be preserved as an individual book, as he preserved the other manuscripts now in the Bibliothèque de l'Institut de France.

After Leoni's death, *ca.* 1610, the Leonardo manuscripts passed on to Galeazzo Arconati. Among them was *Libro B*, the notebook known today as MS E. *Libro* A was already lost.

Arconati had recovered a large part of the Leonardo manuscripts from the Leoni collection brought back from Spain, among them the Codex Atlanticus and the small notebooks described in the deeds of his donation to the Ambrosian Library, in 1637.[38] At that time, or shortly before, certain copies requested by the secretary of Cardinal Barberini, Cassiano dal Pozzo, were made from the Leonardo manuscripts owned by Arconati.[39] Cassiano was the one who gave Raphael du Fresne the manuscript copy of the abbreviated version of the *Trattato della Pittura* which was used for the first edition in 1651. In order to have the text of his copy corrected, Cassiano dal Pozzo sent Galeazzo Arconati a list of chapters to be checked against the originals: "Chapters in which are found difficulties in understanding the work of Leonardo da Vinci on painting, the title of which are the following, according to the copy that we have here in Rome, from which a copy has been made and sent to Padre Gallo in order to have it checked by him" [*per avere il favor del riscontro*].[40] Padre Gallo, a priest of the Ambrosian Library, marked the list with small crosses to indicate the chapters he had checked against the originals, specifying at the end of the list that "the chapters marked are checked; the others were not found in these books" (plate 5). Two of the checked chapters, 34 and 298 in Cassiano's list, come from carta 38 of *Libro* A, that is, chapters 75 and 79 in the present reconstruction. Padre Gallo failed to find the originals of fifteen chapters listed by Cassiano. Actually four of these chapters are to be found in MS Ashburnham 2038 and three in *Libro* A. These omissions can be explained by the difficulty in reading Leonardo's handwriting; however, they would not affect the validity of Padre Gallo's checking, for even if he had checked only some of the chapters written in *Libro* A, this would be enough to prove that he had seen this notebook. But this is not the case. We are able to prove that Padre Gallo could not have seen *Libro* A. When he checked the chapters of Cassiano's list, in 1639, the Leonardo manuscripts were already in the Ambrosian Library: no *Libro* A is

38. Uzielli (1884), pp. 235–254.
39. Steinitz (1958), pp. 94–116; Pedretti (1957*b*), pp. 257–263.
40. Steinitz (1958), p. 96.

described in the deeds of the Arconati donation in 1637. Moreover, in the first edition of 1651, as well as in all the copies of the abridged version of the *Trattato*, chapter 34 of Cassiano's list, that is, *Libro A 75*, has the last paragraph omitted.[41] If Padre Gallo had seen the original he would most likely have sent the missing paragraph of that chapter to Cassiano. Finally, if *Libro A* had been among the Arconati manuscripts, the compilers of the Codices H 227 inf. and 229 inf. in the Ambrosian Library and the treatise on *Del Moto e Misura dell'Acqua* in the Barberini Library would have excerpted its section on hydraulics.[42] We have reason to believe that Padre Gallo did not check the chapters of Cassiano's list against the originals but against an early copy of the abridged version of the *Trattato* which entered the Ambrosiana with the Pinelli library.[43]

As a last hypothesis, we may assume that *Libro A* had been separated from its companion *Libro B* even before Melzi's death. Vasari mentions a manuscript that Leonardo had written in mirror-writing on "painting and on the method of drawing and colouring." [44] This indication of the contents of the manuscript also describes a large part of the contents of *Libro A*. Vasari does not specify the name of the Milanese painter who owned this manuscript. The anonymous owner could not be Melzi because Vasari had just described the Leonardo manuscripts in the Melzi collection when he came to speak about a manuscript owned by another person: "Not long ago this person came to Florence to see me, wishing to print this work; and he took it to Rome in order to do so, but I do not know what became of it afterwards." [45]

We have no way to prove that the anonymous Milanese painter was acquainted with Melzi. It is therefore doubtful that the Leonardo manuscript he took to Rome for reproduction was one of those excerpted by Melzi for the compilation of the *Trattato della Pittura*.

RECONSTRUCTION OF *Libro* A

The reconstruction of the section on painting in *Libro A* is based on transcriptions executed directly from the Codex Urbinas. Although the rearrangement of Leonardo's notes according to their original sequence is simpler than the solution of

41. Du Fresne (1651), p. 7.
42. Steinitz (1958), pp. 188–190, 204–205; *see* also Pedretti (1962a), pp. 61–70.
43. Codex Pinellianus D 467 in the Ambrosian Library, Milan; *see* Steinitz (1958), p. 53. A table of contents of MS D 467 is found in MS H 267 in the Bibliothèque de la Faculté de Médecine, Montpellier; *see* Steinitz (1958), p. 109. At the beginning of this table is a note by Cassiano dal Pozzo proving that the Codex Pinellianus was mistaken for an original manuscript of Leonardo: "Capitoli o Indice de' Capitoli del libro originale di Leonardo da Vinci M.S. che si troua à Milano nella libreria Ambrosiana o Borromea che si dica, delle Regole della Pittura, che fu donato a quella libreria dal Conte Arconato. Mandato questo Indice dal Canonico Giovanni Alfieri."
44. Vasari (1568), III, pp. 7–8.
45. *Ibid*. "This person," often thought to have been Aurelio Luini, may in fact have been G. P. Lomazzo. See Appendix V, note 13.

the "jigsaw puzzle" of the Windsor fragments, a determination of the correct reading of the notes requires some care. Owing to the difficulty in reading Leonardo's handwriting, Melzi incorrectly transcribed certain words, making some sentences obscure. However, although Leonardo's original manuscript is lost, we are able to restore the correct reading of such words by tracing in reverse the process of their misinterpretation. For example, in one place Melzi gives us a word, *neri,* which does not make sense in Leonardo's sentence. If we write this word using Leonardo's handwriting of his late period, we can see that it can be read as *non,* giving clarity of meaning to the obscure sentence.[46]

The chapters on each folio of the reconstructed *Libro* A are arranged in order of their appearance in the Codex Urbinas. This sequence seems reasonable because we know that Melzi transcribed from the original manuscripts. He selected from them the notes on painting and placed these notes in the eight parts of the Codex Urbinas in accordance with eight basic classifications of the material. Within each classification Leonardo's notes were usually copied in the sequence they followed in the original notebooks. Melzi must have used one notebook at a time, with the result that the whole Codex Urbinas still closely reflects the structure of Leonardo's original material. Melzi probably attempted some rearrangement of the material, occasionally modifying the original sequence of the passages, but his system of copying prevented much alteration in compiling the *Trattato della Pittura.* Had he first copied each passage on individual sheets, he could have improved the arrangement of the material in the final copy. But since the Codex Urbinas in which he was writing was probably a volume of blank sheets, he could not rearrange the material after it was written down. That is why, fortunately for us, the Codex Urbinas preserves the structure of Leonardo's original manuscripts to a considerable extent.

Thus the present reconstruction of *Libro* A is correct in the sequence of folios and largely correct in the sequence of chapters in each folio. Exceptions would occur only when Melzi may have changed the order. Nevertheless, only twice did the system we adopted prove to be unsatisfactory: our chapter 39 should come before 38, because it is found on folio 104 of the Codex Urbinas whereas chapter 38 is on folio 156v. We reversed the sequence because chapter 40 appears to be a continuation of chapter 39. Also, chapter 23 could have been placed before chapter 22, because the first chapter on carta 20 (chapter 24) was transcribed following the first chapter on carta 19 (chapter 22).

Sometimes the mark "L⁰ .A." in the Codex Urbinas refers only to one paragraph of a chapter that is otherwise taken from other manuscripts. These identifications of the passages from *Libro* A are certainly complete and correct, as are those of the passages from *Libro* B. Thus, it was possible to reconstruct the notes that were broken up and incorporated with others; as, for example, chapter 48, "Comparison of Painting and Sculpture," which was originally placed at the end of chapter

---

46. Codex Urbinas 137–137v: ". . . in modo ch' el termine de lumi *neri* sia congionto col termine della finestra." Cf. *Libro* A 79.

52 of the McMahon edition of the Codex Urbinas, whereas it should be kept together with McMahon's chapter 46, that is, *Libro A 49*.

Because of such peculiarities, we have taken from the Codex Urbinas only the notes that are marked "L⁰ .A." and have excluded paragraphs placed before or after them. The same criterion has been followed in the transcriptions from the Codex Leicester.

The reconstruction of *Libro A* unfortunately lacks two of the most important elements characterizing every original manuscript of Leonardo: drawings and autobiographical notes. The loss of these elements is the more lamentable since the lost manuscript belonged to one of the most interesting as well as the least documented periods of Leonardo's career—the years of his sojourn in Milan after the unsuccessful painting of the "Battle of Anghiari," when he worked as an architect for Charles d'Amboise and as a painter for the King of France. At the same time, he was still at work on such masterpieces as the "Mona Lisa," the "Leda," the "St. Anne," and the project for the Trivulzio monument.

The text of the reconstructed *Libro A* can be used as a tool for many new probes and reëvaluations of the *Trattato della Pittura* as a whole. The extant Leonardo manuscripts contain only one-fourth of the material gathered by Melzi in the *Trattato*. Thus, three-fourths of that material could not be dated with certainty. However, the 107 notes that were copied from *Libro A* represent almost one-fifth of the whole *Trattato della Pittura*. Although this material is missing, we know its approximate date, 1508–1515. Thus, almost half (one-fourth plus one-fifth) of the whole *Trattato* can now be dated with reasonable accuracy. Many other chapters can be dated on the basis of comparisons with dated notes; hence for only a few chapters of the whole *Trattato* is the chronology still uncertain.

The problems of the chronology of the *Trattato* are discussed at length in the second part of the present book. The contents of the *Trattato* will be analyzed according to their sequence, which is, to a certain extent, chronological. At the beginning of his compilation Melzi used early manuscripts of Leonardo, whereas toward the end he used exclusively manuscripts of the late period.

The second part begins with an analysis of the handwriting of the Codex Urbinas. As a result of this analysis, Francesco Melzi is now recognized as the person who transcribed in the Codex Urbinas all the notes on painting he could find in Leonardo's manuscripts. Up to now, Melzi's hand has been tentatively identified either as that which made some spelling corrections (Manus 2) or as the other which suggested modifications in the titles and in the sequence of certain passages. This latter hand (Manus 3) is of the greatest importance, because it is that of an unknown person who had so deep a knowledge of Leonardo's manuscripts as to be able to recollect several characteristics of the originals. It was this person, in short, who identified in the Codex Urbinas all the passages copied from *Libro A* and *Libro B*.

Our analysis of the *Trattato* is followed in Part Three by a list of all the titles of the chapters in the Codex Urbinas with our dating of each. An up-to-date concordance will also be included. The benefits of such a list are many. Above all, we may expect that it will prove to be of value for the study of the long evolution of Leonardo's theory of art.

PART ONE

LIBRO A

EDITORIAL NOTES

Each chapter of the reconstructed *Libro* A bears a reference to the source, which is the Codex Vaticanus Urbinas 1270 for chapters 1–105, 108, and 109, and the Codex Leicester for the chapters on hydraulics 106, 107, and 110–131.

The source of the notes on painting from the Codex Urbinas is indicated as follows: *CU* refers to the folios of the Codex Urbinas; *Lu,* to the chapter-numbers in Ludwig's edition of the *Trattato* (1882); *McM,* to the chapter-numbers in McMahon's English translation (1956); and *Rig,* to the chapter-numbers of Rigaud's English translation of the abridged edition of the *Trattato della Pittura* (1877). (A concordance Rigaud–Du Fresne is given by Rigaud's "General Index.")

The transcriptions have been made directly from the facsimiles of the Codex Urbinas and Codex Leicester according to the standard method known as "trascrizione critica." The text has been changed only in that it gives the modern equivalent of certain archaic forms (such as *t* for *z* and *u* for *v*) and punctuation has been introduced. Textual alterations have been made only within brackets or with explanatory footnotes.

A literal translation of Leonardo's term "corpo ombroso" could be misleading. Rigaud and McMahon often translate it as "shadowy body" or "shaded body," whereas it it actually means a "body that casts a shadow," as opposed to a "transparent body." Richter always translates it as "opaque body" or "opaque object." In the following English translation the word "opaque" as a qualification of "body" or "object" is placed between fences (⟨ ⟩) because it is not strictly necessary for our comprehension.

Fences in the Italian text are used to indicate passages or words that have been omitted from the chapters of *Libro* A included in the first edition (1651) of the *Trattato.*

Chapters 17, 21, 25, 31, 32, 47, 49, and 109 do not have titles in the corresponding chapters of the Codex Urbinas, being notes incorporated in other chapters. (However, the titles of the chapters of the *Trattato della Pittura* are rarely by Leonardo himself, and the transcriber often changed them.) The notes on hydraulics from the Codex Leicester are reproduced without titles, according to the original manuscript. Calvi's edition of the Codex Leicester (Milan, 1909) has been used as a basis for transcription and translation.

References to Alberti are to his *della Pittura* (edited by Luigi Mallè; Florence: Sansoni, 1950) unless specified otherwise, with the English renderings from John R. Spencer's *Leon Battista Alberti, On Painting* (New Haven, Conn.: Yale University Press, 1956).

Libro A

CARTA 1

CU 154v, LU 490, MCM 519; RIG 303]

1. De pittura

L'azzurro dell'aria è di color composto di luce e di tenebre. La luce dirò per causa dell'aria alluminata nelle particule dell'umidità infra essa aria infusa. Per tenebre dirò l'aria pura la qual non è divisa in attimi,[1] cioè particule d'umidità nella qual s'abbi a percotere li razzi solari; e di questo si vede l'esempio nell'aria che s'interpone infra l'occhio e le montagne ombrose per l'ombra della gran copia delli alberi che sopra di essa si trovano, ovvero ombrosa in quella parte che non è percossa dalli razzi solari; la qual aria si fa azzurra e non si fa azzurra nella parte sua luminosa, e peggio nella parte coperta di neve.

1. On Painting

The blue of the sky is a color composed of light and darkness; I say of light, because of the moist particles floating in the air, which reflect the light. By darkness, I mean the pure air which has none of these extraneous particles [1] to stop and reflect the rays. Of this we can see an example in the air interposed between the eye and some dark mountains, rendered so by the shadow of a great quantity of trees; or else shaded on one side by the natural privation of the rays of the sun: this air becomes blue, but not so on the side of the mountain which is light, and less on the parts covered by snow.

CARTA 12 *

CU 192v–193, LU 652, MCM 763]

2. Delle qualità d'ombre e di lumi

Molto maggiore fia la differenza de' lumi dalle loro ombre nelli corpi posti alli potenti lumi, che in quelli che sono posti ne' luoghi oscuri.

2. On the Quality of Lights and Shadows

The difference between light and shadow is much greater on bodies in a strong light than on those placed in the shade.

---

1. Codex: "attimi." Ludwig: "attomi." In a note on Codex Leicester 4 which also deals with the blue of the sky, Leonardo uses the word "attimj." Cf. Brizio (1952), p. 588, and MacCurdy: I.418–421. See also Lu 226. Small particles of water are only one of the causes producing blue scattering centers. Rayleigh's law of scattering for particles smaller than 0.1 of the wavelength of light is illustrated by Minnaert (1954), pp. 238–239. Maria Rzepinska, in her dissertation on Leonardo's theory of art (chap. iv), comments on this and similar passages as follows: "He explains why

the sky is blue more or less in the same way as it is interpreted by modern science, i.e., that the blue is a result of the diffusion of light; but the conclusion he draws, namely that azure is not a primary color, is evidently wrong, because as we know, azure belongs to the colors of the solar spectrum. Leonardo takes advantage of this phenomenon to back up his own technique of painting, namely that of obtaining a tint that acts as substitute for azure, by mixing adequate black and white components." Cf. Codex Leicester 4r and Libro A 86.

* There are several folios of Libro A of which no record is left. The first gap in the present reconstruction occurs between carte 1 and 12. For the other gaps see the Introduction, p. 12, ll. 6–8.

CARTA 13

CU 39V, LU 81, MCM 77; RIG 354]
3. De l'imitare li pittori[2]

Dico alli pittori che mai nessuno debbe imitare la maniera dell'altro perchè sarà detto nipote e non figliolo della Natura, in quanto all'arte. Perchè, essendo le cose naturali di tanta larga abbondanza, più tosto si vuole e si debbe ricorrere a quella, che alli maestri che da quella hanno imparato. ⟨E questo dico non per quelli che desiderano mediante quella pervenire a ricchezze, ma per quelli che di tal arte desiderano fama ed onore.⟩[3]

CU 108, LU 287, MCM 414]
4. Qualità d'arie de' visi

Fa che i visi non siano d'una medema aria, come nei più si vede operare, ma fa diverse arie secondo l'ettadi, e complessioni, e nature triste e buone.

CU 127–127V, LU 386, MCM 390; RIG 108]
5. De' posati d'infanti

Nell'infanti e vecchi non debbe essere atti pronti fatti mediante le loro gambe.

---

2. Manus 3 has added: "Sarà meglio dire Come il Pittore non debbe imitare la maniera d'alcun altro Pittore" (It would be better to say: How the painter ought not to imitate the manner of any other painter). Blunt (1959), p. 33, states: "The danger of copying the style of another painter is that it leads to mannerism, and that, in Leonardo's eyes, is one of the worst sins, since mannerism excludes naturalism." See Leonardo's passage dealing with the evolution of painting in Codex Atlanticus 141 r-b, ca. 1491 (Richter [1883], I, 660); Pedretti (1957a), pl. 8. Cennini, chap. xxvii, suggests choosing only one master, so that "you will find, if nature has granted you any imagination at all, that you will eventually acquire a style individual to yourself." Alberti represents a further step toward nature: "Quando si volesse copiare l'opere altrui meglio varrebbe prendere una mediocre scultura che una buona pittura, chè, almeno, s'imparerebbe a rinvenirvi e a riprodurre le luci giuste" (Alberti, ii, 109; Spencer:94). Cf. Panofsky (1952), p. 35 and note 14. Leonardo, however, is not against the method of copying the

3. On Imitating Other Painters[2]

I say to painters that nobody should ever imitate another's manner, because as far as art is concerned, he will be called a grandson rather than a son of Nature. Since things exist in such great abundance in nature, we wish—and indeed ought—to have recourse to her rather than to masters who have learned from her. I say this not for those who wish to become wealthy through the art, but for those who desire fame and honor from it.[3]

4. Quality of Expressions of Faces

See that your faces do not all have the same expression, as one sees with most painters, but give them different expressions, according to age, complexion, and bad or good character.

5. On Poses of Infants

Infants and old people should not be represented with lively movements of their legs.

works of other painters as a means of acquiring practice, providing that these works are by excellent masters, but he concludes that on account of the scarcity of good masters in his day it is safer to go direct to the works of nature, "for he who has access to the fountain does not go to the waterpot" (Codex Atlanticus 199 v-a, ca. 1506–1507; reproduced in this volume, plate 24). In a Latin dialogue written before 1524, Paolo Giovio speaks of Leonardo as follows: "He would forbid youths under the age of twenty to touch brushes and colors, and he would have them practice only with the lead stylus, choosing as models the best examples left of the ancients, in order to become able to render the force of nature by means of essential lines . . ." (Beltrami [1919], n. 256).

3. Cf. MS G 33; Brizio (1952), p. 444; Richter, I, 402: ". . . it will be well that you should represent everything from nature, and not despise such study as those do who work (only) for money." See also Alberti, iii, 103: "La fine della pittura, rendere gratia et benivolentia et lode allo artefice molto più che richezze" (Spencer:89).

CU 127V, LU 387, MCM 392; Rig 107]

6. *De' posati di femmine e giovanette* 4

Nelle femmine e giovanette non debbe essere atti di gambe sbarlate 5 o troppo aperte perchè dimostrano audacia e al tutto privazione di vergogna, e le strette dimostrano timore di vergogna.

6. *On Poses of Women and Girls* 4

In women and young girls there should be no awkward or too open movement of the legs,5 because these show boldness and complete lack of shame, while legs pressed together show timidity and modesty.

CARTA 14

CU 113, LU 314, MCM 304; Rig 58]

7. *De' piegamenti*

Tanto quanto l'uno de' lati de' membri piegabili si farà più lungo, tanto la sua parte opposita sarà diminuita. La linea centrale estrinseca de' lati che non si piegano, de' membri piegabili, mai diminuiscano o crescano di loro grandezza.

7. *On Bending*

Flexible parts of the body will lengthen exactly as much on one side as they shorten on the other. The sides of flexible members that do not bend never increase or diminish in magnitude.

CU 113–113V, LU 315, MCM 340; Rig 81]

8. *D'equiparanza* 6

Sempre la figura che sostiene peso fuor di sè e dalla linea centrale della sua quantità, debbe gittar tanto peso naturale od accidentale dall'opposita parte, che faccia equiparanza di pesi intorno alla linea centrale che si parte dal centro della parte del piè che si posa e passa per tutta la somma del peso sopra essa parte de' piedi in terra posata.

Vedesi naturalmente uno che piglia un peso da l'un de' bracci, gittare fuori di sè il braccio opposito, e se quello non basta a fare l'equiparanza vi porge tanto di peso di sè medesimo, piegandosi, che si fa sufficiente a resistere all'appicato peso.7

8. *On Equilibrium* 6

The figure which carries a weight outside itself or the central line of its mass, must always throw enough natural or accidental weight to the opposite side, to create a balance on either side of its axis. This line begins at the center of that part of the foot resting on the ground and passes through the whole weight above that part of the foot.

We see that a man who lifts a weight with one arm, naturally thrusts out the opposite arm, and if that is not enough to keep his balance, he adds as much of his own weight as necessary by bending

---

4. In the codex the word "giovanetti" is changed to "giovanette." Cf. Alberti, ii, 97 (Spencer:80).

5. "Gambe sbarlate" is translated by McMahon as "legs raised." "Sbarlato," or "imberlato," is synonymous with "storto," so that it could be translated "crooked." This word, however, does not quite render the meaning of Leonardo's sentence. "Sbarlato" is rather a reference to the clumsy attitude of a standing woman, as one can see, for example, in the "Vanitas" of the School of Memlinc; cf. Clark (1959), fig. 258.

6. The number 13 after the mark *L⁰* A in the

Codex Urbinas has been corrected and changed to 14. Favaro (1926–1927), pp. 249–250, considered this passage in order to refute the interpretation given by Duhem (1909–1913), I, 77.

7. Cf. Alberti, ii, 96: "Posi mente come l'huomo, in ogni suo posare, sotto statuisca tutto il corpo a sostenere il capo, membro fra li altri gravissimo; et posandosi in uno piè, sempre ferma perpendicolare sotto il capo, quasi come base d'una colonna; et quasi sempre di chi stia diritto il viso si porge dove si dirizzi il piè. I movimenti del capo veggo quasi sempre essere tale che sotto a sè anno qualche parte del corpo a sostenerlo, tanto è

Si vede ancora in un che sia per cadere riverscio l'un de' suoi lati laterali che sempre gitta infuori il braccio dall'opposita parte.

enough to counterbalance the added weight.[7] Also in the case of one about to fall backward to one side, one sees that he always thrusts out the arm on the opposite side.

CU 116v, LU 333 & a, MCM 321; Rig 45]

9. De' muscoli [8]

Li membri non debbono avere nella gioventù pronunciazione di muscoli perchè è segno di fortezza attempata, e ne' giovanetti non è tempo nè matura fortezza.

Sieno li sentimenti delle membra pronunciati più o meno evidenti, secondo che più o meno saranno affaticati.[9]

Sempre i muscoli di quelle membra saranno più evidenti i quali in maggior fatica saranno esercitati.

Quelli muscoli saranno ne' lor membri manco sculpiti li quali fieno da minor fatica esercitati.

Sempre li muscoli che sono affaticati sono più alti e più grossi che quelli che stanno in riposo.

Mai le linee centrali intrinseche de' membri che si piegano stanno nella lor naturale lunghezza.

9. On Muscles [8]

Youthful limbs should not have pronounced musculature because that is a sign of strength which develops with age, and in the young there is neither age nor mature strength.

Strength of limbs should be more or less pronounced in accordance with greater or less exertion.[9]

Muscles will always be most evident in those members which are involved in the greatest exertion.

Those muscles will be least sculptured in those members which are involved in the least exertion.

Muscles that are being exerted are always higher and larger than those in repose.

The central inside lines [axes?] of limbs that are bent never retain their natural length.

CU 121v–122, LU 353, MCM 316; Rig 53]

10. Delle pieghe della carne [10]

Sempre la carne è piegata e grinza dall'opposita parte da che l'è tirata.

10. On Creases in the Flesh [10]

The flesh is always creased and wrinkled on the side opposite to that which is stretched.

---

sì grande peso quello del capo; overo certo in contraria parte, quasi come stile d'una bilancia, distende uno membro quale corrisponda al peso del capo; et vegiamo che chi sul braccio disteso sostiene uno peso, fermando il piè quasi come ago di bilancia, tutta l'altra parte del corpo si contra ponga a contra pesare il peso" (Spencer:79). See also Accolti, p. 147: "Et vedesi naturalmente, che chi piglia, o porta un peso con l'uno de bracci, gettare incontinente, et protender fuori di sè l'altro, et se quello non basti a librar il peso, porgervi tanta parte di sua persona (piegandosi col fianco nella contraria parte) che si renda sufficiente a resistergli, senza esserne tirato a terra."

8. The mark *L⁰ A* is repeated at each paragraph. The title "De' muscoli" (On Muscles) is repeated after the second mark. The last paragraph is copied from carta 20 (see n. 24). Cf. MS E 20 (Lu 126, McM 127): "Describe which muscles and tendons, through various movements of each limb, become exaggerated, or hidden, or do neither

one nor the other. Remember that such a study is most important and necessary for painters and sculptors who would become masters." See also Windsor 19,141–19,142 (C VI 22r) (MacCurdy: I.190–191), not dated by Clark but *ca.* 1506–1508, which contains a list of topics for discussions on muscles to be carried out in books "Concerning the Human Form" and "On Painting."

9. Accolti, p. 146: "Et per ciò secondo, che più, o meno ciascuna parte affatica, così più, o meno devono detti lor muscoli pronunciarsi."

10. The mark *L⁰ A* is placed at the beginning of folio 122.

These notes on muscles are chronologically related to the note in Codex Arundel 44, *ca.* 1508–1510 (MacCurdy:II.286), in which Leonardo explains the necessity for study on this subject: "In the last folds of the joints of any limb everything which was in relief becomes a hollow, and similarly every hollow in the last of the said folds is changed into a protuberance when the end of the

CARTA 15

CU 157, LU 499, MCM 437]

11. *Come le figure spesso somigliano alli loro maestri*

11. *How Figures Often Resemble Their Masters*

Questo accade chè il giudizio nostro è quello che move la mano alle creazioni de' lineamenti d'esse figure per diversi aspetti, in sino a tanto ch'esso si satisfaccia. E perchè esso giudizio è una delle potenze dell'anima nostra,[11] con la quale essa compose la forma del corpo dov'essa abita, secondo il suo volere, onde, avendo co' le mani a rifare un corpo umano, volentieri rifà quel corpo di che essa fu prima inventrice. E di qui nasce che chi s'innamora volentieri s'innamorano di cose a loro simiglianti.

This happens because our judgment is that which moves the hand to create lineaments of figures through varying aspects until it is satisfied. Because judgment is one of the powers of the soul,[11] by which it shapes, according to its will, the form of the body wherein it resides, thus, having to reproduce with the hands a human body, it naturally reproduces the one which it first invented. From this it follows that he who falls in love, naturally loves things similar to himself.

---

limb is straightened. He who has not knowledge of this, often makes very great mistakes through relying too much upon his own skill, and not having recourse to the imitation of nature. And such variation is found more in the middle of the sides than in front and more behind than at the sides." Favaro (1918–1919), pp. 147–148, had already pointed out a relationship between this passage and Lu 353. See also *Libro A* chapters 40 and 108, and note 112.

11. "Anima," i.e., unconscious. Cf. Alberti, *De re aedificatoria*, ix, 5: "animis innata quaedam ratio." According to Gombrich (1954), p. 211, this note must be, to some extent, autobiographical. Only introspection could have led Leonardo to discover what we would call the "unconscious." See also *Libro A* 45 and 46. These passages in *Libro A* are related to Lu 108 (McM 86). According to Chastel (1961), p. 225, the latter is clearly inspired by the type of Platonic thought standard in the intellectual atmosphere of Florence in which Leonardo was educated. "But as usual with Leonardo, this tradition is here accompanied by observation and consequently enriched and modified: This passage describes in a positive manner, is supported by an incontrovertible fact, and summarily analyzes the intervention of the unconscious in the painter's activity." Leonardo's indebtness to neo-Platonism is echoed in Vellutello's commentary to Petrarch (1545), 45b, in a passage explaining the sonnet

> *In qual parte del ciel, in qual idea*
> *Era l'esempio; onde natura tolse*
> *Quel bel viso leggiadro. . . .*

"*Et in qual idea*, rispetto a l'opinione di Platone, la qual fu, che l'imagini delle cose fossero tutte a principio nella mente divina create, perchè Idea è quella imagine de la cosa che nella nostra mente si forma prima che la facciamo, come per figura, Leonardo Vinci vuol far l'imagine di Maria Vergine, ma prima che metta mano a l'opera, ha stabilito ne la mente sua di che grandezza in che atto & habito e di che lineamenti vuol ch'ella sia." (*Et in qual idea*, is referred to Plato's opinion that all things were conceived as images in the mind of God before being created, because *Idea* is that image we first form in our mind of the things we are about to make, as in the case of a figure: Leonardo da Vinci wants to make the image of the Virgin Mary, but before he starts painting he has already in his mind the size, posture, dress, and countenance he wants to give to his Madonna.) As Vellutello had been at the court of Leo X, he may refer to the painting of a Madonna that the Pope commissioned of Leonardo. This early reference to Leonardo, as far as I know, has not appeared before in Vincian literature.

Finally, it must be noted that the present passage from *Libro A* is the only one in the whole *Trattato* in which Leonardo uses the term "creazione" instead of "generazione." Cf. Panofsky (1960), p. 188, n. 3: "Leonardo da Vinci, though justly proud of the fact that the painter is 'lord and god' of the world which he can arrange according to his own pleasure, studiously avoids the terms *creare* and *creazione* in favor of *generare* and *generazione*, a fact unfortunately neglected in all available translations and paraphrases."

CU 157, LU 500, MCM 549; Rig 335]

12. *Del figurare le parti del mondo*

Sarai avvertito, che ne' luoghi marittimi o vicini a quelli volti alle parte meridionali, non farai il verno figurato nelli alberi e prati, come nelle parti remote da essi mari e settentrionali faresti, eccetto che nelli alberi li quali ogni anno gittano le foglie.

CU 157–157v, LU 501, MCM 548; Rig 334]

13. *Del figurare le quattro cose de' tempi dell'anno o partecipanti di quelli*

Nell'autunno farai le cose secondo l'età di quel tempo; cioè, nel principio li alberi cominciare a impallidire le foglie ne' più vecchi rami, più o meno secondo che la pianta è figurata in loco sterile o fertile,[12] ed ancora più pallide e rosseggianti a quelle specie d'alberi li quali furono primi a fare i loro frutti. E non fare come molti fanno a tutte le sorte degli alberi, ancora che da te siano equalmente distanti, d'una medesima qualità di verde.[13] Così, dicendo de' prati come delle piante ed altre qualità di terrami e sassi e pedali delle predette piante, varia sempre, perchè la Natura è variabile in infinito; ⟨non che nelle spezie ma nelle medesime piante trovera' vari colori, cioè, nelle vimine son più belle e maggiori

12. On Portraying the Parts of the World

You should also be advised that, in places on or near the sea toward south, you should not represent winter by means of trees and fields, as you would in places remote from the sea and in the north, except for trees that shed their leaves every year.

13. On Depicting the Four Seasons of the Year or Things Connected with Them

In autumn you should depict things in accord with the progress of the season. That is, at the beginning the leaves on the oldest branches of trees commence to turn more or less pale, depending on whether the tree is represented as growing on sterile or fertile soil.[12] Even more pale and reddish are the leaves of those trees which were first to produce fruit. Do not, as many do, paint all kinds of trees, even when equally distant, the same shade of green.[13] In the same way, fields, as well as plants and other characteristics of the terrain, and stones and roots of trees, are always varied because Nature is infinitely variable, not only as regards species. On the same plant you will find different colors, for instance, on the wil-

---

12. This passage is chronologically related to Lu 806 (McM 839), a long chapter on portraying the characteristics and component parts of mountainous landscapes: "The grass and trees will be paler in color, in the degree that the soil that nourishes them is meager and lacking in humidity. . . ." Both this chapter and the note from *Libro* A can be compared to one of the notes in Windsor 12,412 transcribed for the first time and translated by Gould (1947), pp. 239–242: "L'erba bassa che si fa campo della ghiara ha diversi colori secondo la diversa grassezza o magrezza del suo terreno e per questo è alcuna volta morella, alcuna gialla, alcuna di tanè verdeggiante, altre verde gialle, altre verde azzurre e così son tutte variate" (The short grass which grows by the gravel is of different colours according to the differing fertility or barrenness of its soil, and for this reason sometimes appears blackish, sometimes yellow, sometimes greenish brown, at others greenish yellow and again greenish blue, and thus it is all dif-

ferent). This Windsor folio dates from 1511 as Windsor 12,416 (plate 12 of this volume), one of a series of landscape drawings in red chalk on brick-red prepared paper.

13. Cf Codex Arundel 114v, *ca.* 1508–1510, MacCurdy:II.318: "The trees in landscapes are of various different shades of green. . . ." Leonardo must have kept in mind, once again, Botticelli's indifference to realistic landscapes. (Cf. Lu 60 [McM 93]: "This painter [Botticelli] of whom I have spoken makes very dull landscapes.") In his advice to avoid tapestry Leonardo displays a great concern for color. His description of plants evokes the landscape of Giorgione's "Tempesta," which is not just a background but the real subject of the painting. Battisti (1960), p. 159, considers such paintings of landscape and of still-life as a product of Aristotelianism opposed to the monumentality of Florentine Classicism. Giorgione depicted plants according to their seasonal state and to the condition of ground, as Leonardo suggested.

le foglie [nei rami maggiori] [14] che negli altri rami; ed è tanto dilettevole Natura e copiosa nel variare, che infra li alberi della medesima natura non si troverebbe una pianta ch'appresso somigliassi all'altra, e non che le piante, ma li rami o foglie, o frutti di quelle non si troverà uno che precisamente somiglia ad un altro. Sicchè abbi tu avvertenza e varia quanto più puoi.⟩

low the larger and more beautiful leaves are found on the upper branches.[14] Nature is so delightful and abundant in its variety that among plants of the same kind there will not be found one which closely resembles another, and this is so, not only of the plant as a whole, but of the branches, leaves, and fruit, for not one will be found precisely like another. Therefore, observe this and vary them as much as you can.

CARTA 16

CU 153v–154, LU 486, MCM 506; RIG 264]

14. De' termini

I termini delle cose seconde non saranno mai cogniti come li primi.

Adunque tu, pittore, non terminare immediate le cose quarte colle quinte, come le prime colle seconde, perchè 'l termine d'una cosa in un'altra è di natura di linea matematica, ma non linea.[15] Perchè il termine di un colore è principio di un altro colore e non ha da essere però detta linea, perchè nissuna cosa s'intramette infra il termine di un colore che sia antiposto a un altro colore, se non è il termine il quale è cosa insensibile d'appresso. Adunque tu, pittore, non lo pronunciare nelle cose distanti.

14. On Outlines

The outlines of second-plane objects will never be as clear as those of foreground objects.

Therefore, painter, do not outline as sharply fourth-plane objects against those of the fifth plane, as you do the first against the second, because the contour of one object against another, while of the nature of a mathematical line, is not a line.[15] Since the end of one color is the beginning of another, it must not be called a line, for nothing intervenes between one color placed in front of another except its end, which is imperceptible even when viewed from near at hand. Therefore, painter, do not accentuate it in distant objects.

14. It is obvious that Melzi omitted to copy some words which specified in what part of the willow the leaves are most beautiful and larger. He probably omitted the words "nei rami maggiori" because of the proximity of two similar words: "*maggiori* le foglie," and "nei rami *maggiori*." Cf. Lu 921 (McM 903): "The thickest tips of branches of trees send out the largest leaves, or leaves in larger quantity than does any other end of a branch." See also Lu 919a (McM 947): "The upper branches of trees are more heavily covered with leaves than the lower ones."

15. A similar definition of "termini" is found in Leonardo's discussion on "l'essere del nulla" in Codex Arundel 132r, *ca.* 1508, namely, in his draft of an introduction to his "first book on water": "The limiting surface of one thing is the beginning of another. . . . That which has no limitations has no form. . . . The limitations of two conterminous bodies are interchangeably the surface of each" (Richter [1883], I, 46). Cf.

Windsor 19,151, *ca.* 1508 (Richter [1883], I, 47): "The line has in itself neither matter nor substance and may rather be called an imaginary idea than a real object. . . ." The quality of boundaries is fully discussed in MS G 37r (MacCurdy: II.285): "The boundaries of bodies are the least of all things. The truth of this proposition is proved by the fact that the boundary of the substance is a surface, which is neither a part of the body enclosed by this surface nor a part of the atmosphere which surrounds this body, but is the medium interposed between the atmosphere and the body, as is proved in its place. But the lateral boundaries of these bodies are the boundary line of the surface, which line is of invisible thickness. Therefore, O painter, do not surround your bodies with lines, and especially when making objects less than their natural size, for these not only cannot show their lateral boundaries, but their parts will be invisible, from distance." *See also* MS D 10v (note to the first figure).

CU 164, LU 527, MCM 527; RIG 286]
15. Delle diminuzioni de' colori e corpi
Sia osservata la diminuzione delle qualità de' colori insieme con la diminuzione de' corpi ove s'applicano.[16]

CU 164, LU 528, MCM 517; RIG 208]
16. Delle interposizioni de' corpi trasparenti infra l'occhio e l'obbietto
Quanto maggiore fia la interposizione trasparente infra l'occhio e l'obbietto, tanto più si trasmuta il colore dell'obbietto nel colore del trasparente interposto.

CU 164, LU 528a, MCM 449; RIG 208]
17. Dell'obbietto infra l'occhio e il lume
Quando l'obbietto s'interpone infra l'occhio e 'l lume per la linea centrale che s'astende infra 'l centro del lume e l'occhio, allora tal obbietto fia totalmente privato di lume.

15. On Diminution of Colors and Bodies
Observe the diminution in intensity of colors with the diminution of the bodies to which they are applied.[16]

16. On Interposing Transparent Bodies between the Eye and the Object
The greater the transparent body placed between the eye and the object, the more the color of the object will be changed toward the color of the transparent object in between.

17. On the Object between the Eye and the Light
When the object is interposed between the eye and the light along a line which extends from the center of the light to the eye, then the object will be completely deprived of light.

CARTA 17

CU 27–27v, LU 45, MCM 54]
18. Differenza che è dalla pittura alla scultura
La prima meraviglia che apparisce nella pittura è il parer spiccato dal muro od altro piano, ed ingannare li sottili giudizii con quella cosa che non è divisa dalla superfice della parete. Qui, in questo caso, lo scultore fa l'opere sue che tanto paiono quanto elle sono; e qui è la causa che 'l pittore bisogna che faccia l'offizio della notizia nelle ombre che sieno compagne de' lumi. Allo scultore non bisogna tale scienza perchè la Natura aiuta le sue opere, com'essa fa ancora a tutte l'altre cose corporee, dalle quali tolto la luce sono d'un medesimo colore e rendutole la luce sono di vari

18. The Difference between Painting and Sculpture
The first marvel of painting is that it appears detached from the wall or other flat surface, deceiving people of subtle judgment with this object that is not separated from the wall's surface. In comparison with this, the sculptor makes his works so as to appear exactly as they are. And this is why the painter must make it his concern to study shadows which are the companions of lights. The sculptor does not need this knowledge, because Nature aids his works, as it does all other objects. If the light is taken away from them, they are all of the same tone; when the light is re-

16. The concept is further developed in Windsor 12,639 (C VI 18), *ca.* 1504–1508 (MacCurdy:II.380): "Make the perspective of the colours so that it is not at variance with the size of any object, that is that the colours lose part of their nature in proportion as the bodies at different distances suffer loss of their natural quan-

tity." This Windsor fragment gives an idea of the type of notes and drawings of the lost *Libro A*; it contains a note on hydraulics ("Of the waters which impinge against each other the less potent is always repelled") and notes on human movements. Cf. Clark (1935), *sub numero*. See also Richter (1883), I, 379 and plate xxiii–4.

colori, cioè chiaro e scuro. La seconda cosa [17] è che 'l pittore con gran discorso bisogna che con sottile investigazione ponga le vere qualità e quantità dell'ombre e lumi. Qui la Natura per sè le mette nelle opere dello scultore.[18] Terza è la prospettiva, investigazione ed invenzione sottilissima delli studi matematici, la quale per forza di linee fa parere remoto quello ch'è vicino e grande quello che è piccolo. Qui la scultura è aiutata dalla Natura, in questo caso, e fa senza invenzione dello scultore.[19]

turned, they are of different tones of light and shade. The second thing [17] is that the painter must, through serious reasoning and subtle investigation, fix the true quantity and quality of light and shade. Nature herself takes care of this in the works of the sculptor.[18] The third thing is perspective, which is a most subtle discovery in mathematical studies, for by means of lines, it causes to appear distant that which is near, and large that which is small. Sculpture is aided by Nature in this case, which accomplishes its end without any artifice of the sculptor.[19]

CARTA 18

CU 74–74v, LU 248, MCM 196; RIG 245]
19. *De' colori*

Il lume del fuoco tinge ogni cosa in giallo. Ma questo non apparirà esser vero se non v'è al paragone le cose alluminate dall'aria; e questo paragone si potrà vedere vicino alla fine della giornata, o sì veramente dopo l'aurora, ed ancora dove in una stanza oscura [20] dia sopra l'obbietto uno spiraculo d'aria, ed ancora uno spiraculo di lume di candela, e in tal loco certamente fia vedute chiare e spedite le lor differenze. Ma senza tal paragone mai sarà conosciuta la lor differenza, salvo che i colori che han più similitudine, ma fien conosciuti, come bianco da giallo chiaro, verde dall'azzurro; perchè, gialleggiando il lume che allumina l'azzurro, è come mischiare insieme azzurro e giallo, i quali compongono un bel verde; e se misti poi giallo col verde esso si fa più bello.

19. *On Colors*

The light of fire tinges everything with yellow, but this will not appear to be true except through comparison with things illuminated by the air of daylight. This comparison can be made near the end of the day, or just after the dawn, and also where through an opening in the wall of a dark room [20] there falls upon the object a thin beam of light from the air and through another opening a thin beam of light from a candle. In such a situation, the difference can certainly be seen clearly and quickly. But without such a comparison the difference will never be seen, except between colors which are very similar but still distinguishable, such as white from light yellow, green from blue. The light which illuminates the blue, having a yellow tinge, produces the same effect as mixing together blue and yellow, which compose a beautiful green. If afterward you mix yellow with the green, it becomes even more beautiful.

---

17. Codex: ". . . la seconda cosa ch'el pittore con gran discorso bisogna che. . . ." Ludwig proposes: ". . . bisogna, è che. . . ."

18. Codex: ". . . nelle opere dello scultore, la prospettiua inuestigatione. . . ." Ludwig's correction is accepted.

19. See the draft for this chapter in Codex Atlanticus 305 r-a, 1506–1508, quoted on page 16 above. Infra-red photographs of this folio are reproduced in Pedretti (1960a), p. 92. Cf. *Libro A* 48–50. Leonardo's discussions on the comparison

between painting and sculpture are echoed by Galileo in a letter to Lodovico Cigoli, June 26, 1612: ". . . Sculpture receives light and shade from Nature herself whereas painting receives it from Art." For Panofsky's comment on Galileo's letter see note 58 below.

20. Cf. Codex Atlanticus 181 r-a, quoted on page 19 above. This folio can be dated from 1506–1508 because of notes on the problem of Alhazen which occupied Leonardo at the time of his MS F (1508).

CU 164, LU 526, MCM 447; RIG 310]

20. *Delli obbietti*

Quella parte dell'obbietto sarà più alluminata che fia più propinqua al luminoso che l'allumina.

CU 164, LU 526a, MCM 513; RIG 310]

21. *Della similitudine*

La similitudine è sustanzia delle cose: in ogni grado di distanza perde gradi di potenza.

Cioè quanto la cosa sarà più remota dall'occhio, sarà tanto men penetrabile infra l'aria co' la sua similitudine.

20. *On Objects*

That part of the object will be most illuminated which is closest to the light source.

21. *On Likeness*

Likeness is the substance of things: for every degree of distance it loses degrees of clarity.

That is, the more remote from the eye an object is, the less its appearance will be able to penetrate through the air.

CARTA 19

CU 74v–75, LU 249, MCM 159; RIG 278]

22. *De' colori de' lumi incidenti e reflessi*

Quando due lumi mettono in mezzo a sè il corpo ombroso, essi non posson variarsi se non in due modi, cioè o essi saran d'equal potenza o essi saranno inequali, cioè parlando de' lumi infra loro; e se saranno equali essi posson variare in due altri modi il loro splendore sopra l'obbietto, cioè con equale splendore o con disequale. Equale sarà quando saranno in equale distanza. Disequale, nelle disequali distanze. ⟨In equale distanza si varieranno in due altri modi, cioè meno sarà l'obbietto alluminato dalli equali lumi in splendore ed in distanza, [quanto] i lumi equali in potenza ed equali in distanza [saranno lontani] dall'obbietto opposito.⟩ [21]

L'obbietto situato con equale distanza infra due lumi equali in colore ed in isplendore, può essere alluminato da essi lumi in due modi, cioè o equalmente d'ogni parte o disequalmente. Equalmente

22. *On the Color of Incidental and Reflected Lights*

When two lights have an object between them, they may differ in only two ways; they will be of equal or unequal intensity—that is, speaking of the lights themselves. Being equal in power, they may vary in two other ways their brilliance on the object—that is, they may shine on it with equal or unequal brilliance. This will be equal when they are at equal distance; unequal if the distances are unequal. The distances being equal, there will be two other possible variations—that is, the object will be less illuminated by lights of equal brilliance and at equal distance, as these lights, equal in power and distance, are placed farther from the object.[21]

The object placed half-way between two lights equal in color and in brilliance may be illuminated in two ways, namely either equally on each side or unequally. It will be equally illuminated when

---

21. Codex: ". . . et in distantia, i lumi equali in potentia et equali in distantia dall'obbietto opposito." Ludwig proposes: ". . . et in distantia remota dall'obbietto opposito, che da i lumi equali in potentia et equali in distantia uicina dall'obbietto opposito." McMahon translates: "At equal distance they differ in two other ways, that is, the object will be less illuminated by equal lights in respect to brilliance and distance." In the first edition of the *Trattato* (Paris, 1651) this chapter (157) is abbreviated and some sen-

tences modified in an evident attempt to make some sense out of the obscure text. But the result is even more misleading because the printer made the mistake of repeating a line of the text he was using. See Appendix IV, p. 243. Actually, only the first part of the passage between the fences is understandable; but the meaning of the entire passage can be restored easily. The mark *L° A* is repeated before the second paragraph. For Leonardo's theory of colored shadows see note 23 below.

sarà da essi lumi alluminato quando 'l spazio che resta intorno alli due lumi sarà d'equal colore e oscurità o chiarezza. Disequale sarà quando essi spazi intorno ai due lumi sarà vario in iscurità.

CU 193, LU 653, MCM 599]
23. *De l'ombre e lumi e colori*

Quella parte del corpo ombroso si mostrerà più luminosa che da più potente lume sarà alluminata.

Tanto sarà maggiore in sè la quantità de l'ombre ne' corpi ombrosi che la sua quantità alluminata, quanto è maggiore la quantità de l'oscurità da lui veduta che quella de lo splendore che l'allumina.

the spaces around the two lights are of the same color and darkness or brightness. It will be unequally illuminated when these spaces differ in darkness.

23. *On Shadows and Lights and Colors*

That side of an ⟨opaque⟩ figure will appear most luminous which is illuminated by the strongest light.

On ⟨opaque⟩ figures, the quantity of shadow will exceed the quantity of illumination by as much as the quantity of darkness to which it is exposed exceeds that of the brightness which illuminates it.

CARTA 20

CU 75, LU 250, MCM 203; RIG 261]
24. *De' colori d'ombre*

Spesse volte accade l'ombre ne' corpi ombrosi non essere compagni ne' colori de' lumi, o saran verdeggianti l'ombre e lumi rosseggianti, ancora che 'l corpo sia di colore equale.

Questo accade, chè 'l lume verrà da oriente sopra l'obbietto e alluminerà l'obbietto del colore del suo splendore, e da occidente sarà un altro obbietto del medesimo lume alluminato il quale sarà d'altro colore che 'l primo obbietto, onde con suoi razzi reflessi risalta in ver' levante e percote con suoi razzi nella parte del primo obbietto a lui volta, e lì si tagliano i suoi razzi e rimangono fermi insieme co' loro colori e splendore.[22]

Io ho spesse volte veduto a uno obbietto bianco i lumi rossi e l'ombre azzurreggianti. E questo accade nelle montagne di neve quando il Sole tramonta e l'orizzonte si mostra infuocato.[23]

24. *On the Colors of Shadows*

Many times, a shadow is not consistent with the color of the light. The shadows may be greenish and the lights reddish, even though the object is all of the same color.

This happens when light coming from the east falls on the object and illuminates it with the color of its glow. To the west another object is illuminated by the same light, but the object is of a different color from the first. Rays reflected eastward from the second object meet the nearest side of the first object, on which their color and brilliance is thus visible.[22]

I have often seen a white object with red lights and bluish shadows. This happens on snow clad mountains at sunset, when the horizon appears on fire.[23]

---

22. The diagram must have had an explanation that Melzi omitted. Such an explanation can be restored by following in part Lu 554 (McM 711): "Let O be the body casting the shadow, and N be the light which causes the primary shadow (M) and throws the derivative M B C. I say that if the body casting the shadow is white and the light N is red the illuminated part O

will be red, and the dark part M will be bluish, being illuminated by the reflection of the blue object A B C D." The letter M in the diagram is invisible because it is covered by hatching.

23. Leonardo had the intuition that the phenomenon of colored shadows on snow is not only physical as a result of reflection of color but also psychological in the way demonstrated by The-

CU 116v, LU 333a, MCM 321]

25. *De' muscoli* [24]

Li muscoli grossi e lati sieno fatti alli potenti con le membra concorrenti a tal disposizione.

25. *On Muscles* [24]

Thick, broad muscles should be represented for the strong, with limbs that are consistent with such character.

CU 123, LU 361, MCM 412; RIG 160]

26. *De attitudini* [25]

Negli atti affezionati [26] dimostrativi di cose propinque per tempo o per sito, s'hanno a dimostrare

26. *On Gestures* [25]

Affective gestures [26] pointing to things near either in time or space should be made with the hand

---

odor Fechner; cf. Solmi (1905), pp. 202–203. In fact, in *Libro A 19* Leonardo considers the phenomenon of an object illuminated by two lights of different colors: "The light of fire tinges everything with yellow, but this will not appear to be true except through comparison with things illuminated by the air of daylight. This comparison can be made near the end of the day. . . ." On this passage Goethe based his experiment of a pencil illuminated on one side by candlelight and on the other side by moonlight; cf. Minnaert (1954), p. 134. The phenomenon of changes of color in "after-images" was also known to Ghiberti, who took it from Roger Bacon's *Opus Majus*, II, 449; see *I Commentari*, III, 2: "Look at a meadow of thick grass illuminated by the sun, and after you have dwelt sometime at observing it, turn your eyes to a dark place. There you will still see the shape of the meadow, that is the green light of its grass. And if the place is not too dark, the light that is in it will blend with the green light of the grass. Similarly, you can observe an object of any other color, such as blue, yellow, reddish, or green, and always experience the same effect." See also Codex Atlanticus 204 r-a, *ca.* 1492 (MacCurdy:II.326).

24. This is the last paragraph of chapter McM 321. The preceding paragraphs were copied from carta 14 (see *Libro A 9*).

25. Manus 3 (see pp. 104 ff.) has added: "De gl'atti dimostrativi" (Of demonstrative gestures). The last sentence of Leonardo's note was misunderstood by the first editor of the Codex Urbinas. Manzi (1817), p. 187, transcribes: "e la faccia del viso volta a ciò che si dimostra." Also Ludwig's transcription suggests the idea that the figure should be looking at the object being pointed to: "e la faccia del viso volta a che si dimostra." Curiously enough, the early transcriptions in the abridged version of the "Treatise on Painting" were correct, according to the text of the Codex Urbinas: "e la faccia del viso volta

a chi si dimostra." In the French translation by R. Freart Sieur de Chambrai (Paris, 1651), p. 80, we find: ". . . que le visage de celui qui monstre foit tourné vers celuy auqueil il le parle"; and in the first English translation of the "Treatise on Painting" (London, 1721), p. 127: ". . . the Face of him that Points, being at the same time turned, toward him for whose sake that Action is intended." See also Rigaud (1877), no. 160: ". . . and the faces of the figures pointing must be turned towards those to whom he is pointing it out."

Leonardo's drawing of a pointing lady in Windsor 12,581 (frontispiece) may serve as an illustration to this precept. Leonardo frequently emphasizes the foreground figure turned to the spectator and pointing to the subject of the picture. The advice goes back to Alberti, ii, 94: "Et piacemi sia nella storia chi admonisca et insegni ad noi quello che ivi si facci: o chiami con la mano a vedere . . ." (Spencer:78). Domenico Veneziano's altarpiece of St. Lucia had already introduced such a device, which was to become one of the rhetorical gestures in manneristic painting. The figure on the right of Leonardo's "Adoration of the Magi," usually considered a self-portrait, and the angel in the Louvre "Madonna of the Rocks" are examples of such intermediary figures. These figures point to "things near either in time or in space," and thus the hand is not too far from the body. The woman in the Windsor drawing is pointing to something far away—one might well say "far in time," suggesting an abstract concept to Leonardo's idea. Her arm is fully extended in foreshortening, the face turned to the spectator. Raphael applied Leonardo's precept in depicting some pointing figures in the "Stanza della Segnatura," and in the Madonna of Foligno, in which the figure of St. John recalls Leonardo's St. John in the Louvre.

26. "Atti affezionati" is translated by McMahon as "Friendly gestures." "Expressive ges-

con la mano non troppo remota da essi dimo-
stratori; e se le predette cose [27] saranno remote,
remota debbe essere ancora la mano del dimostra-
tore e la faccia del viso volta a chi si dimostra.

not too far from the body of the person pointing;
and if the objects [27] are remote, the hand of the
pointer should be the more extended and the face
turned toward the person to whom he is pointing
them out.

CU 193v, LU 655, MCM 794]

27. *De ombre e lumi nelli obbietti* [28]

La superfice d'ogni corpo ombroso partecipa del
colore del suo obbietto.

Gran rispetto bisogna al pittore nel situare le
cose sue infra obbietti di varie potenze di lumi e
di vari colori alluminati, conciosiachè ogni corpo
da quelli circondato non si mostra mai integralmente del suo vero colore.

27. *On Lights and Shadows on Objects* [28]

The surface of every ⟨opaque⟩ object partakes of
the color of the adjacent object.

The painter must take great care in placing
things among other objects of different intensities
of light and illuminated by different colors, keeping in mind that no subject so surrounded is ever
seen entirely in its true color.

CARTA 21

CU 193–193v, LU 654, MCM 793]

28. *De' lumi e ombre e colori di quelli*

Nessun corpo non si dimostrerà mai integralmente
del suo vero colore.

Quel che si propone può accadere per due
diverse cause, delle quali la prima accade per interposizione del mezzo che s'include infra l'obbietto
e l'occhio. Seconda è quando le cose che alluminan
'l predetto corpo ritengano in sè qualità d'alcun
colore.[29]

Quella parte del corpo si dimostrerebbe del suo
natural colore il quale fusse alluminato da luminoso senza colore e che in tale alluminamento non
vegga altro obbietto che 'l predetto lume. Questo
non accade mai potersi vedere, se non nel colore
turchino [30] posto per piano in verso il cielo sopra
un altissimo monte, acciò che in tal loco non
possa vedere altro obbietto e che il Sole non sia
occupato, nel suro morire, da bassi nuvoli, e che 'l

28. *On Lights and Shadows and Their Colors*

No object is ever seen entirely in its natural
color.

What is proposed above may happen from two
different causes, of which the first occurs through
interposition of the existing medium between the
object and the eye. The second happens when
things that illuminate the above-mentioned object
have some color of their own.[29]

That part of the object would appear in its true
color if it were illuminated by a colorless light,
provided that in this illumination no other object
were visible than the aforesaid light. It so happens
that this can never be seen except in the case of a
blue surface [30] face-up to the sky, on top of a very
high mountain so that no other object is visible,
the setting sun is covered with low clouds, and the

---

tures," or simply "gestures," would be closer to
the meaning of Leonardo's sentence. Cf. Alberti,
ii, 95: "Sono alcuni movimenti d'animo detti
affezione: come era dolore, gaudio et timore,
desiderio et simili altri" (Spencer:78).

27. Codex: ". . . da essi e s'elle predette cose.
. . ." Ludwig's interpretation is accepted.

28. The mark *Lº A* is repeated before the second paragraph. Cf. Alberti, ii, 98: "Resta a dire
del ricevere de lumi. Ne i dirozzamenti di sopra
assai dimostrammo quanto i lumi abbino forza

a variare i colori chè insegnammo come istando
uno medesimo colore, secondo il lume et l'ombra
che riceve altera sua veduta" (Spencer: 81–82).

29. Codex: ". . . le cose che allumina el predetto corpo, e ritegnalo in se qualita d'alcun
colore." Ludwig's correction is accepted. The
mark *Lº A* is repeated before the second paragraph.

30. Baldinucci (1681), p. 172: "Turchino,
Color simile al ciel sereno; & è di più e diuerse
sorte, cen'è del più pieno e del più chiaro."

piano [31] sia del colore de l'aria. Ma in questo caso i' mi ridico: perchè il rossato anch'egli cresce di bellezza quando il Sole che l'allumina nell'occidente rosseggia, e insieme con li nuvoli che se gli interpongono; benchè in questo caso si potrebbe ancore accettare per vero, perchè, se 'l rossato alluminato dal lume rosseggiante mostra più che altrove bellezza, gli è segno che i lumi d'altri colori che rossi gli toglieranno la sua bellezza naturale.

flat surface [31] is the color of the air. But here I retract because even rose grows more beautiful when the sun in a reddish sunset illuminates it together with the intervening clouds; although in this case it might still be accepted as true. Because if rose, illuminated by a reddish light, is more beautiful than otherwise, that is a sign that lights of colors other than red take away some of its natural beauty.

CARTA 22

CU 108–108v, LU 288, McM 417; Rig 22]

29. De' membri e descrizioni d'effigi [32]

Le parti che mettono in mezzo il gobbo del naso si variano in otto modi, cioè o elle sono equalmente diritte o equalmente concave o equalmente convesse, prima; o sia veramente elle sono disequalmente rette concave e convesse, seconda; ovvero elle sono nelle parti superiori rette e di sotto convesse, terza; ovvero di sopra rette e di sotto convesse, quarta; ovvero di sopra concavo e di sotto retto, quinta; o di sopra concavo e di sotto convesso, sesta; [33] ovvero di sopra convesso e di sotto retto, settima; o di sopra convesso e di sotto concavo, ottava.

L'appicatura del naso col ciglio è di due ragioni, cioè o che l'è concava o che l'è diritta. La fronte

29. On Features and Description of the Face [32]

The parts into which the projection of the nose is divided vary in eight ways— that is, first, they are equally straight, equally concave, or equally convex; second, they are irregularly straight, concave, or convex; third, they are straight on the upper and concave on the lower part; fourth, straight above and convex below; fifth, concave above and straight below; sixth, [33] concave above and convex below; seventh, convex above and straight below; eighth, convex above and concave below.

The juncture of the nose and the brow is of two types: that is, either concave or straight. The fore-

---

31. Codex: "panno." Leonardo does not specify that the flat surface of color placed face-up to the sky was meant to be an object, namely a cloth. Perhaps in the original manuscript the word "panno" was actually "piano": *ᴜᴨᴧ૧*,

piano; *ᴜᴨᴧ૧*, panno. Furthermore, Leonardo speaks of a large colored surface, which can hardly be thought of as that of a sheet placed on the top of a high mountain! He must rather refer to the color of rocks or to that of snow or trees, as in Windsor 12,414 (Gould [1947], p. 241): "The rocks of this mountain take on naturally a colour tending to blue and the intervening air makes them appear bluer still, particularly in the shadows. They also show certain dark marks which are caused by the minute trees which grow among them. . . ." See also *Libro A 24*.

32. Cf. Lu 290 (McM 415) from MS Ashburnham 26v. Venturi (1919), pp. 80–81, considers such notes as "astrattismi inutili." See Alberti, ii, 90 (Spencer:74), and Mallè's footnote: "Leonardo giunge a particolarismi ignoti all'Alberti e che rappresenterebbero nella pittura la morte dell'arte; ma ciò va visto nella peculiare spiritualità leonardesca tenendo conto poi della meravigliosa libertà che l'artista sapeva mantenere devanti alle sue tele." Leonardo's precept must be considered as a device for memorizing physiognomies, a basic scheme for the study of expression. Such a method was developed by Charles Le Brun, *Le Méthode pour apprendre à dessiner les passions* (Paris, 1696). Cf. Gombrich (1960), pp. 347–348. For the chronology of this chapter see the Introduction, p. 21.

33. Codex: ". . . o di sopra concauo, o' conuesso, 6ª." Ludwig's interpretation is accepted.

ha tre varietà,[34] o che l'è piana, o che l'è concava, o che l'è colma. La piana si divide in quattro parti,[34] cioè o che l'è convessa nella parte di sopra, o che l'è convessa nella parte di sotto, ovveramente ell'è convessa di sopra e di sotto, ovveramente piana si sopra e di sotto.

head has three variations: [34] it is flat, or concave, or it is round. Flat foreheads are divided into four kinds; [34] that is, convex on the part above, or convex on the part below, or else convex above and below, or flat above and below.

CARTA 23

CU 108v, LU 289, MCM 416; RIG 23]

30. Del fare una effige umana di profilo solo col sguardo d'una sola volta [35]

30. On Making a Man's Portrait in Profile after Having Seen Him Only Once [35]

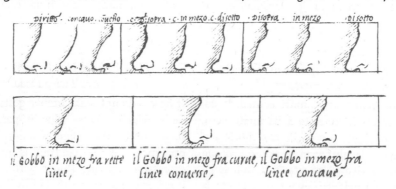

In questo caso ti bisogna mettere a mente le varietà di quattro membri diversi in profilo, come sarebbe naso, bocca, mento e fronte. Diremo prima de' nasi, li quali sono di tre sorti, cioè diritto, concavo e convesso; de' diritti non v'è altro che quattro varietà, cioè lungo, corto, alto, con la punta in basso; i nasi concavi sono di tre sorti, delli quali alcuni hanno la concavità nella parte superiore, alcuni nel mezzo ed altri nella parte inferiore. Li nasi convessi ancora si variano in tre modi, cioè alcuni hanno il gobbo nella parte di sopra, alcuni in mezzo ed altri nella parte di sotto; li sporti [36] che mettono in mezzo il gobbo del naso si variano in tre modi, cioè o sono diritti o sono concavi ovveramente sono convessi.

In this case it is necessary to commit to memory the varieties of the four different features in profile, which would be the nose, mouth, chin, and forehead. We shall speak first of noses, which are of three kinds, that is, straight, concave, and convex. Of the straight there are only four kinds, that is, long, short, high, and pointed at the bottom. Concave noses are of three kinds, of which some have the concavity on the upper part, others in the middle, and still others on the lower part. Convex noses also vary in three ways; some have a projection on the upper part, some in the middle, and others on the lower part. Those which have a projection [36] in the middle of the nose vary in three ways, that is, they are straight, or concave, or else convex.

34. Codex: "La fronte ha due varietà . . ." and ". . . la piana si diuide in due, parti. . . ." Ludwig's corrections are accepted.

35. Gombrich (1954), p. 209, states that this passage looks like a deliberate elaboration of Alberti's precepts; cf. Alberti, ii, 106: "Vedrai a chi sarà il naso rilevato e gobbo, altri aranno le narici scimmie o arrovesciate aperte, altri porgerà

labri pendenti, alcuni altri avranno hornamento di labrolini magruzzi et così examini il pittore qualunque cosa" (Spencer:92).

36. As specified at the beginning of the preceding chapter, the "sporti" (projections) correspond to the "parti che mettono in mezzo il gobbo del naso."

See note 32, above.

CU 228, LU 779, MCM 782]

31. *De lustro* [37]

Il lustro fia sopra li obbietti trovato in tanti vari siti, quanto son vari i lochi dond'esso è veduto.

31. *On Highlights* [37]

Highlights may be seen on objects in as many different locations as there are points of view.

CARTA 24

CU 32, LU 55, MCM 68; RIG 27]

32. *Studio del pittore giovane* [38]

Il pittore debbe studiare con regola e non lasciare cosa che non si metta alla memoria, e vedere che differenza è infra le membra delli animali e loro giunture.[39]

32. *Study of the Young Painter* [38]

The painter ought to study methodically and leave nothing unmemorized; and he must observe how limbs and joints vary from one animal to another.[39]

CU 125–125v, LU 376, MCM 403]

33. *Che se le figure non isprimeno la mente sono due volte morte* [40]

Se le figure non fanno atti pronti e quali [41] co' le membra isprimino il concetto della mente loro, esse figure son due volte morte. Perchè morte son principalmente chè la pittura in sè non è viva ma isprimitrice di cose vive senza vita, e se non se gli aggiunge la vivacità dell'atto essa riman morta la seconda volta. Sicchè dilettatevi studiosamente di vedere in quei che parlano insieme co' li moti

33. *How Figures Not Expressive of the Mind Are Twice Dead* [40]

If figures do not make lifelike gestures [41] with their limbs which express what is passing through in their minds, these figures are twice dead—dead principally because painting is not alive, but only expressive of living things without having life in itself, and if you do not add liveliness of action, it remains a second time dead. Therefore take delight in studying carefully people who gesticulate

---

37. This is the seventh paragraph of McM 782. The other paragraphs were probably copied from other manuscripts. Ludwig referred the mark *L° A* erroneously to the second paragraph. A similar note is found in MS E 31v (McM 780): "The lights which are created on the polished surfaces of opaque bodies will be immobile on immobile bodies, even though the eye of the observer moves. But the luster will be seen on these bodies in as many places on the surface, as there are places to which the eye moves." Cf. also the earlier note in MS H 90 (42)v (Mac-Curdy:II.285).

38. The title was added later by Manus 3.

39. McMahon translates literally: ". . . what difference there is between the limbs of animals and their joints." Leonardo undoubtedly refers to comparative anatomy, studies on which are found in his manuscripts *ca.* 1504–1508; cf. MS K 102r and 109v, and Windsor 12,625. See also *Libro A* 70, and Lu 79 (McM 96) from MS G 5v, *ca.* 1510: ". . . all terrestrial animals have a certain resemblance in their parts, that is, their

muscles, sinews, and bones, and these do not vary, except in length or in breadth, as will be shown in the book on anatomy."

40. For Leonardo's theory of *Decorum* see Blunt (1959), pp. 35–36: "In the hands of Leonardo decorum is simply an element in the complete rendering of the outside world, without which history painting would be incomplete and unconvincing." Venturi (1919), p. 85: "Convenienza e decoro sono sinonimi nella retorica del Rinascimento. Partono ambedue da una necessità di estrinsecazione dell'opera d'arte e finiscono in astrazioni di dubbio gusto." That Leonardo was still concerned with the theory of *Decorum* during his second Milanese period is proved by a note in Codex Atlanticus 345 v-b (plate 25), *ca.* 1508 (studies for the canalization of the Adda River): "Let the movements of men be such as are in keeping with their dignity or meanness" (McCurdy:II.279). See also note 69.

41. Codex: ". . . pronti, equali co' le membra et esprimino. . . ." Ludwig's interpretation is accepted.

delle mani, se persone, d'accostarvi a quelli ed udire che causa gli fa fare tali movimenti che per loro si fanno. Molto bene fia vedute le minuzie delli atti particulari appresso de' muttoli, li quali non sanno disegnare, benchè pochi sieno che non s'aiutino e che non figurino col disegno; imparate dunque da' muti a fare li moti delle membra ch'isprimino il concetto della mente de' parlatori. Considerate quelli che rideno e quelli che piangono, guardate quelli che con ira gridano, e così tutti li accidenti delle menti nostre. Osservate il decoro e considerate che non si conviene, nè per sito nè per atto, operare il signore come il servo, nè l'infante co' l'adolescenza, ma equale al vecchio che poco si sostiene; non faccia l'atto il villano che si deve ad un nobile accostumato, nè il forte come 'l debole, nè gli atti delle meretrici come quelli delle oneste donne, nè de' maschi come delle femmine.

as they talk together. If possible, get close enough to hear what causes them to make the particular gestures that they make. Observe well the details of particular gestures among the mute—those who do not usually know how to draw, although there are few who do not help themselves by representing things in drawing—thus you will learn from the mutes to depict gestures which express the ideas of the speaker. Consider those who laugh and those who cry; watch those who scream in anger and, by means of this, all that happens in our minds. Observe decorum and consider that it is not proper, either as regards rank or action, to make the master act like a slave, nor the infant like an adolescent, or else an old man who can hardly stand; do not depict the peasant making a gesture which, by custom, is appropriate for a nobleman; do not make the strong like the weak, nor the gestures of prostitutes like those of honest women, nor those of men like those of women.

CU 182v, LU 591, MCM 625]

34. *Che l'ombre derivative sono di tre speci*

34. *Derivative Shadows Are of Three Kinds*

L'ombre derivative sono di tre speci, cioè o e' sarà maggiore il tagliamento suo nella parete ove percote che non è la basa sua, o ella sarà minore d'essa basa, o ella sarà equale. E se sarà maggiore è segno che 'l lume che allumina il corpo ombroso è minor d'esso corpo. E se sarà minore, il lume fia maggior del corpo, e se sarà equale, il lume fia equale a esso corpo.

Derivative shadows are of three kinds; that is, its size on the wall where it strikes will be either larger than its base, or smaller than the base, or equal to it. If it is larger, that is a sign that the light which illuminates the ⟨opaque⟩ object is smaller than that body. If it is smaller, the light is larger than the object; and if it is equal, the light is equal to the object in size.

CARTA 25

CU 75–75v, LU 251, MCM 147, nig 211]

35. *Delle cose poste in campo chiaro e perchè tale uso è utile in pittura*

35. *On Objects Placed against a Light Background and Why This Practice Is Useful in Painting*

Quando il corpo ombroso terminerà in campo di color chiaro e alluminato, allora per necessità parrà spiccato da esso campo.

Quel ch'è detto accade perchè i corpi di curva superfice, per necessità, si fanno ombrosi dalla parte opposta donde sono percosi dalli razzi luminosi, per essere tale loco privato di tali razzi, per

When an ⟨opaque⟩ object is outlined on a clear and illuminated ground, it will naturally appear detached from that ground.

This happens because bodies with a curved surface become, of course, dark on the parts opposite those struck by rays of light, since they are cut off from such rays and thus contrast strongly with

la qual cosa molto si varia dal campo. E la parte d'esso corpo alluminata non termina mai in esso campo alluminato, con la sua prima chiarezza,

the background. The lighted part of the object in its greatest brilliance never borders on the light background, since between the background and

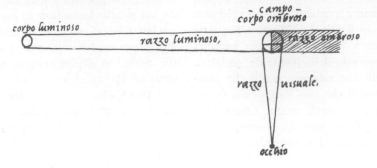

anzi infra 'l campo e 'l primo lume del corpo s'interpone un termine del corpo che è più oscuro che 'l campo, o che 'l lume del corpo rispettivo.

the highlight of the object there is an intervening area that is darker than either the background or the lighted part of the object.

CARTE 25–26

CU 127v, LU 388 & 389, MCM 378]

36. Del rizzarsi l'uomo da sedere di sito piano [42]

Stando l'uomo a sedere nel pavimento, la prima cosa che fa nel suo levarsi, è che tra' da sè il piede

36. On a Man's Rising-Up from Sitting on Level Ground [42]

When a man is seated on the floor, the first thing he does in rising is to pull in the leg and place the

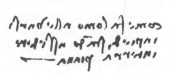

A draft of *Libro A* 36 in Windsor 19,070 (*author's tracing*)

---

42. At the end of this chapter the transcriber has written: "Trouo scritto apresso al capitolo di sopra il suggeitto del suo contrario ma poi non ne parla niente, et, è questo: Del cadere l'huomo a' sedere in, sito piano" (After the chapter above I find written the heading only for a chapter on the opposite action. The heading reads: On a Man's Falling into a Seated Position on The Flat Ground). The mark "Lº A car. 26" is written near the transcriber's note, but it probably refers to the chapter of which Leonardo wrote only the title. The anatomical sheet Windsor no. 19,070 (C I 13) contains a small drawing of a man rising from ground level, illustrating a note on movement: "Come fa l'omo alevarsi in piedi stando a sedere in terra piana" (How a man lifts himself to his feet from a seated position on level ground). This is obviously a draft of the unwritten chapter of *Libro A*, providing further evidence for dating the lost notebook. Melzi's remark about the omitted description of the opposite action is useful in suggesting the late date of a chapter the original of which is unknown, namely McM 386, "On a figure alone outside of history ["istoria"]," in which the "change of motion" in the limbs of a man on sitting down is discussed. Cf. Pedretti (1957*b*), pp. 152–157, and pp. 171–182.

Aristotle's *Mechanical Questions*, XXX, deals with the center of gravity of a man rising from a sitting position. Cf. Marcolongo (1937), pp. 182–183 and note 60.

e posa la mano in terra da quel lato che si vuol levare e gitta la persona sopra il braccio che posa, e mette il ginocchio in terra da quel lato che si vuol levare.

hand on the ground on the side on which he wishes to rise, then throwing the weight of his body on that arm, he puts his knee to the ground on the side on which he wishes to rise.

CARTA 26

Ibid.]

37. *Del cadere l'uomo a sedere in sito piano* [43]

37. *On a Man's Falling into a Seated Position on the Flat Ground* [43]

CU 156v, LU 497, MCM 458; RIG 206]

38. *Del far che le cose paiano spiccate da loro campi, cioè dalla parete dove sono dipinte*

38. *On Making Objects Appear Detached from Their Backgrounds, That Is, from the Walls on Which They Are Depicted*

Molto più rilievo dimostreranno le cose nel campo chiaro e alluminato che nell'oscuro.

La ragione di quel che si propone è che se tu vuoi dare rilievo alla tua figura tu le fai che quella parte del corpo ch'è più remota dal lume, manco partecipa d'esso lume, onde viene a rimanere più oscura; e terminando poi in campo oscuro viene a cadere in confusi termini, per la qual cosa, se non vi accade riflesso, l'opera resta senza grazia [44] e da lontano non apparisce se non le parti luminose, onde conviene che l'oscure paino essere del campo medesimo onde le cose paiono tagliate, e rima nere [45] tanto men che 'l suo dovere quant'è l'oscuro.

Objects against a bright and illuminated background display much more relief than against a dark one.

The reason for this proposition follows: if you wish to show relief in a figure, you must depict it so that the part of the body farthest from the light partakes least of that light, and thus will be darker, and since it terminates against a dark background, its outlines become indistinct. For this reason, if no reflected lights fall on it, the work remains without grace,[44] that is, from a distance nothing will show but the light parts. It is correct, therefore, that the other parts be of a darkness similar to the background from which the figure has to appear detached, but keep [45] them less dark than they should be on that background.

---

43. See note 42.
44. "L'opera resta senza grazia" is translated by McMahon as "the work remains unattractive." Rigaud uses the word "grace" in addition to "roundness and effect," which are not in Leonardo's text. The word *grazia* in this passage, as well as in *Libro A* 44, refers to smooth transition from light to shade. It is revealing to find such a word in Leonardo's notes of his late period. This confirms what Sir Kenneth Clark says about Leonardo as being in sympathy with the aim that had occupied Florentine artists in the preceding fifty years: the rendering of movement through style as a visible expression of grace. "Although Renaissance writers left no formal definition of that word, they would all have agreed that it implied a series of smooth transitions" (Clark [1952], p. xiv). Leonardo analyzes the transition

from light to shade as a process of continuity. To this process, being the same as in every other movement in nature, he applies the traditional word *grazia*, thus charging it with a meaning that never appears again in Renaissance writers. *Grazia* becomes the visible equivalent of the abstract principles of "continuous quantity," but only for Leonardo. In Baldinucci's *Vocabolario Toscano dell'Arte del Disegno* (Florence, 1681) *grazia* is defined as "piaceuolezza di mouimento, la quale accresce la bellezza."
45. Ludwig suggests: ". . . e rileuate tanto." The Codex has the word "rimanere," which changes the meaning of the sentence into a recommendation to the painter, directly related to the preceding sentence, "onde conviene. . . ." McMahon translates "onde conviene" with "whence it comes about"; but Leonardo says

CU 104, LU 269, MCM 359; RIG 87]

39. *Delle spalli* [46]

Quattro sono li moti semplici [47] principali del piegamento fatto dalla giontura della spalla, cioè quando il braccio a quella appicato si move in alto o in basso, o innanzi o in dietro, benchè si potrebbe dire tali moti essere infiniti, perchè se si volterà la spalla a una parete di muro e si segnerà col suo braccio una figura circulare, si sarà fatti tutti i moti che sono in essa spalla. E perchè ogni quantità continua è divisibile in infinito e tal cerchio è quantità continua fatta dal moto del braccio, il qual moto non produce quantità continua s'esso continuamente non la conduce,[48] adunque il moto d'esso braccio è stato per tutte le parte del cerchio: essendo esso cerchio divisibile in infinito, infinite sono state le varietà della spalla.

39. *On Shoulders* [46]

Four in number are the principal, simple bending movements [47] of the shoulder joint, namely when the attached arm moves up or down, or forward or backward, although one might say that such movements are infinite, because if you turn your shoulder toward a wall and trace with your arm a circular figure, you will have made all the movements possible in that shoulder. And because every continuous quantity is infinitely divisible, and such a circle is a continuous quantity made by the movement of the arm—which motion does not produce a continuous quantity unless it pushes the arm continuously [48]—therefore the movement of the arm has been through every part of the circle; thus this circle being infinitely divisible, infinite are the variations in position of the shoulder.

CARTE 26–27

CU 107, LU 281, MCM 358; RIG 86]

40. *Delle gionture delle membra*

Delle gionture delle membra e varietà delle loro piegature, è da considerare come del crescere della carne da un lato è mancamento dall'altro, e questo s'ha a ricercare nel collo delli animali, perchè li loro moti sono di tre nature, delle quali due ne sono semplici ed una composta che partecipa dell'uno e dell'altro semplice; de li quali moti semplici l'uno è quando si piega all'una o all'altra spalla, o quando esso alza o abbassa la testa che sopra se gli

40. *On the Joints of Parts of the Body*

Concerning the joints of the parts of the body, and the various ways in which they bend, you should notice how the flesh increases on one side and diminishes on the other. This may be studied in the necks of animals, as their motions are of three kinds, two of which are simple, and the third compounded of the two simple ones. Of the simple movements one is when the neck bends toward one or the other shoulder, or when it raises

---

"che [le parti] oscure paino," not "paiono" (he uses "paiono" in the same sentence with the meaning that McMahon attributes to "paino"); thus the sentence implies advice: "It is correct, therefore, that the other parts *be* of a darkness similar to. . . ." "Similar," however, does not mean "identical." In fact, the last sentence, which is actually a subordinate clause, "e rimanere tanto men . . . ," explains how convenient it would be that the parts in shade "remain," that is, "be left" or "be kept" less dark than they should be.

46. Cf. Panofsky (1940), p. 127. See also *Libro A* 85. For chapters 39 and 40 of *Libro A* cf. MS E 17r, quoted above, p. 17, and Windsor

19,005v (*Fogli A dell'Anatomia* 6v): "Represent the arm from the shoulder to the elbow when it makes a circular movement by fixing the shoulder against the wall, and making the hand with a piece of charcoal turn around the shoulder, the arm being extended; and it will make in this circumduction all the actions of the muscles which move the shoulder."

47. Codex: "sono li moti semplici. . . ." Ludwig's addition and correction are accepted.

48. Codex: ". . . se' esso continua non la conduce. . . ." Owing to a mistake in his transcription, Ludwig has altered the meaning of the last section of the paragraph.

posa; e 'l secondo è quando esso collo si torce a destra od a sinistra senza incurvamento, anzi resta diritto, ma avrà il volto in verso l'una delle spalli; e 'l terzo moto, ch'è detto composto, è quando nel piegamento suo s'aggionge il suo torcimento, com'è quando l'orecchio s'inclina in verso l'una delle spalli e 'l viso si volta in verso la medesima parte o alla spalla opposita, col viso volto al cielo.[49]

or lowers the head poised on it. The second is when the neck twists to the right or to the left without bending so that it remains upright, but the face will be turned toward one of the shoulders. And the third, which is called compound, occurs when twisting is added to the bending motion, as when the ear is inclined toward one of the shoulders and the face turned to the same side or toward the opposite shoulder with the face turned skyward.[49]

CARTA 27

CU 51, LU 139, MCM 277]

41. *De bellezze e bruttezze* [50]

Le bellezze con le bruttezze paiono più potenti l'una per l'altra.

41. *On Beauty and Ugliness* [50]

Beauty and ugliness seem more effective through one another.

CU 75v, LU 252, MCM 153; Rig 210]

42. *Campi* [51]

De' campi delle figure, cioè la chiara nella oscura e la scura nel campo chiaro.

Del bianco co 'l nero, o nero co 'l bianco, pare più potente l'uno per l'altro, e così i contrari l'un per l'altro si mostra sempre più potente.

42. *Backgrounds* [51]

On backgrounds of objects, that is light against dark, and dark against a light background.

Concerning white with black or black with white, each seem stronger because of the other, and thus opposites always appear to intensify one another.

CU 75v, LU 253, MCM 182]

43. *De' colori* [52]

I colori che si convengano insieme, cioè il verde col rosso o pagonazzo, o biffa, e il giallo coll'azzurro.

43. *On Colors* [52]

Colors which go together harmoniously are green with red or purple or violet, and yellow with blue.

---

49. This chapter is chronologically related to the note in Windsor 19,003v (*Fogli A dell'Anatomia* 4r): "The neck has four movements of which the first is raising, the second lowering the face, the third turning to the right and left, the fourth bending the head to the right and left. The [others] are compound motions, that is, raising or lowering the face with one ear near the shoulder, and likewise raising or lowering the face when turned to one of the shoulders with one eye lower or higher than the other, and this is called twisting motion." The subject of the note from *Libro A* is outlined in Codex Atlanticus 305 r-a. Cf. Pedretti (1960a), p. 91.

50. Cf. Blunt (1959), p. 31, and Gombrich (1954), p. 205.

51. The mark *L⁰ A* is repeated before the second paragraph.

52. Cf. Alberti, ii, 101–102: ". . . et truovasi certa amicitia de' colori, che l'uno giunto con l'altro li porge dignità e grazia. Il colore rossato presso al verde et il cilestro si danno insieme honore et vista" (Spencer:85). Lomazzo (1584), bk. vi, chap. vii, suggests that harmonious effects of color be obtained, ". . . sì che non vi si scorga alcuna dissonanza la quale risulterebbe per esempio se si vedesse un verde vivo tanto soave accanto ad un rosso infiammato tutto acuto e fiero."

CU 154, LU 487, MCM 468; RIG 246]

44. Delle incarnazioni e figure remote dall'occhio

Debbesi per lo pittore porre nelle figure e cose remote dall'occhio solamente le macchie,[53] ma non terminate, ma di confusi termini. E sia fatta la elezione di tale figure quando è nuvolo o in sulla sera e sopra tutto guardarsi, come ho detto, di lumi od ombre terminate, perchè paiono poi tinte quando tu le vedi da lontano e riescono opere difficili sanza grazia. Ed ha'ti a ricordare che mai l'ombre sieno di qualità che per la loro oscurità tu abbia a perdere il colore ove si causano, se già il loco dove li corpi sono situati non fusee tenebroso. E non fare profili, non disfilar capegli,[54] non dare lumi bianchi se non nelle cose bianche. E ch'essi

44. On Flesh Tones and Figures Distant from the Eye

The painter, depicting figures and objects distant from the eye, should put in only the mass,[53] not detailed but with indistinct outlines. Choose these figures when it is cloudy or else toward sunset; and, as I have said before, above all avoid sharply defined lights and shadows, because the figure would appear tinted when seen at a distance; and your work would be crude, that is without grace. And remember that the shadows should never be so dark that you must lose color in the area where they are found, unless the place where the objects are situated is already in the dark. And do not make sharp outlines, do not cause hair to shine,[54]

53. "Macchie" is translated by McMahon as "stains," and more accurately by Rigaud as "generally undetermined masses." Leonardo is perhaps the first to use the word "macchia" as a reference to a painting technique that was to become a characteristic of the Venetians. According to Eastlake (1869), II, pp. 355–357, the word "macchia," literally a blot, was used by the Italian writers of the sixteenth century to indicate the blocking-out of the masses of light and shade. Cf. Boschini (1660), p. 300: "Coloring (as practiced by the Venetians) comprehends both the macchia and drawing"; and (p. 328): "By macchia I understand that treatment by which the figures are diminished from each other by different tones lighter or darker." See also Eastlake (1840), pp. 415 ff., and Baldinucci (1681), sub voce.

In a passage in Codex Atlanticus 199 v-a (ca. 1505; see plate 24 of this volume, upper part) (Richter [1883], I, 548) Leonardo refers to the painter's practice of reproducing cose infuscate at a distance, thus proving that the macchia technique was already in use in his time. But Leonardo was not satisfied with that technique. He considered light and shade and color as having infinite gradations because the surface on which they are found is a "continuous quantity" and therefore is in itself infinitely divisible: "Although painters in practice give to all smoky looking objects (cose infuscate)—trees, fields, hair, beards, and furs—four degrees of darkness in each colour they use: that is to say first a dark foundation, secondly a spot of colour (macchia) somewhat resembling the form of the details, thirdly a somewhat brighter and more defined portion,

fourthly the lights which are more conspicuous than other parts of the figure; still to me it appears that these gradations are infinite upon a continuous surface which is in itself infinitely divisible." Leonardo's advice is echoed by Cristoforo Sorte's Osservazioni nella pittura (1573) in Barocchi (1960), I, p. 287: "In representing figures in a landscape make a delicate macchia to indicate the more remote ones, and, as they come closer make them more distinct; that is, objects seen at a distance are to be only sketched and left unfinished, and with delicate colors; and the objects that are close to the observer must show firm color."

54. "Non disfilar capegli" is translated by Rigaud as "one ought not to make the hair stringy," and by McMahon as "do not cause each hair to stand out." Again Leonardo refers to a "macchia" effect, and explains how hair should be represented when seen from a distance: "non disfilar capegli" (literally, do not represent hair as threads) means "do not highlight hair" but render it in painting as a mass of color. In fact, figures at a certain distance do not show sharp outlines, and "white lights," that is, highlights, occur only on white objects. Eastlake (1869), II, pp. 355–356, explains the macchia technique used by the Venetians: "The effect of the minuter shades or dark colours (or eyes, brows, beards, &c.) is, as Leonardo observes, to colour the whole mass—to make it darker and warmer. . . . There is also no shine on dark hair at a certain distance."

Leonardo's late drawing of a pointing lady (see frontispiece) shows hair represented accord-

lumi abbino a dimostrare la prima bellezza del colore, dove si posano.

do not make white lights except on white objects, and notice that those lights must show the highest beauty of the color on which they are placed.

CARTA 28

CU 44V–45, LU 109, MCM 87; Rig 128]

45. Precetti, che 'l pittore non s'inganni nella elezione della figura in che esso fa l'abito

45. Precepts: The Painter Should Not Make a Mistake in Selecting the Figure of Which He Makes a Specialty

Debbe il pittore fare la sua figura sopra la regola d'un corpo naturale il quale comunemente sa di proporzione laudabile. Oltre di questo, far misurare sè medesimo e vedere in che parte la sua persona varia, assai o poco, da quella antidetta laudabile. E fatta questa notizia, debbe riparare con tutto il suo studio di non incorrere nei medesimi mancamenti, nelle figure da lui operate, che nella persona sua si trova. E sappi che questo vizio ti bisogna sommamente pugnare, conciossiachè egli è mancamento ch'è nato insieme col giudizio; perchè l'anima, maestra del tuo corpo, è quella che [fe'] [55] il tuo proprio giudizio; e volentieri si diletta nelle opere simili a quella ch'ella operò nel comporre del suo corpo.[56] E di qui nasce che non è sì brutta figura di femmina che non trovi qualche amante, se già non fussi mostruosa. Sì che ricordati de intendere i mancamenti che sono

The painter should make his figure according to the rules for a body in nature, which is commonly known to be of correct proportions. Besides, he should have himself measured to see where his own person varies much or little from the aforesaid proportions. With this information, he must studiously oppose, in the figures which he makes, falling into the same shortcomings which are found in his person. Be advised that you must fight your utmost against this vice, since it is a failing that was born together with judgment, because the soul, mistress of your body, is that which makes [55] your judgment, and she naturally delights in works similar to that which she created in composing her body.[56] And from this it comes about that there does not exist a woman so ugly that she does not find a lover, unless she is a monster. So remember to understand the shortcomings that

ing to Lu 404 (McM 442): "Depict hair which an imaginary wind causes to play about youthful faces." This does not contradict the passage in *Libro A*, because it refers to a foreground figure. Throughout his career Leonardo dedicated special care to the representation of hair. (According to Vasari, he employed Salai as a model because of his fine curly hair.) Several of his drawings seem to illustrate a passage in Alberti's *della Pittura*, ii, 97 (Spencer:81): "The seven movements are especially pleasing in hair where part of it turns in spirals as if wishing to knot itself, waves in the air like flames, twines around itself like a serpent, while part rises here, part there." In his late drawings of men's heads Leonardo represents hair as "waves in the air like flames" (cf. Popham 147) or even turning in spirals like wind and smoke as in the drawings of the Deluge (cf. Popham 146, 148, 149). In a note on Windsor 12,579, *ca.* 1513 (see above p. 13, and plate 1), Leonardo compares the movement of hair

to that of water. In Windsor 12,659v the stream swirling around an obstruction forms waves like plaited hair (Clark). The hair of the "St. John" in the Louvre is represented in the same way as the water in the Windsor drawing. Cf. Hours (1954), pl. XXXIII (special monochromatic photograph).

55. Codex: ". . . è quella che il tuo proprio giudizio." It must be completed as such: ". . . è quella che [fe'] il tuo proprio giudizio." Cf. *Libro A 11*, and Lu 108: ". . . si è quella che fa il nostro giudizio."

56. Cf. Accolti, p. 146: "Et con questo vizio, et difetto persuadesi pure ciascuno di dover lungo tempo contrastare, et combattere; perciò che, si come è natural in lui tal mancamento, così si desta sempre, o inclinazione, o senso, o giudizio, il quale si diletta, et confà nelle opere simili a quelle, che la natura ha operate nel comporre, et organizzare il proprio suo corpo."

Compare note 11, above.

nella tua persona e da quelli ti guarda nelle figure che da te si compongono.

CU 107, LU 282, MCM 438; RIG 13]

46. De la membrificazione de l'uomo

Misura in te la proporzione della tua membrificazione, e se la trovi in alcuna parte discordante, notela, e forte ti riguarderai di non l'usare nelle figure che per te si compongono; perchè questo è comun vizio de' pittori di dilettarsi e far cose simili a sè.

CU 127, LU 385, MCM 421; RIG 172]

47. Del ridere e piangere [57]

Non farai il viso di chi piange con equali movimenti di quel che ride, perchè spesso si somigliano e perchè il vero modo si è di variare, sì com'è variato l'accidente del pianto dall'accidente del riso; imperocchè per piangere, le ciglia e la bocca si varian nelle varie cause del pianto, perchè alcuno piange con ira, alcuno con paura ed alcuni per tenerazza ed allegrezza, alcuni per sospetto, ed alcuni per dogli e tormento, ed alcuni per pietà e dolore delli parenti e amici persi; delli quai pianti, alcuno si dimostra disperato, alcuno mediocre, alcuni sono lacrimosi, ed alcuni gridano, alcuni col viso al cielo e con le mani in basso avendo le dita di quelle insieme tessute, altri timorosi, con le spalli innalzate agli orecchi; e cosi seguono secondo le predette cause. Quel che versa il pianto alza le ciglia nelle loro gionture e le stringe insieme e compone grinze di sopra ed in mezzo, li canti della bocca in basso; e colui che ride gli ha alti e le ciglia aperte e spaziose.

exist in your own body, and be on guard against them in the figures which you compose.

46. On the Parts of the Body in Man

Measure on yourself the proportion of the parts of your body, and if you find any discordant part, note it and take great care not to use it in the figures you compose, because it is a common vice of painters to delight in making figures similar to themselves.

47. On Laughing and Weeping [57]

Do not depict the face of one who weeps with the same expression as that of one who laughs, because they often resemble one another. The right way is to vary expressions, since the character of weeping differs from that of laughter. In weeping the eyebrows and the mouth change with various causes for tears. One weeps from anger, another from fear, some from tenderness and joy, some from suspicion, some for pain and torment, and some for pity and sorrow for lost friends or relatives. As to types of weeping, one shows despair, another is moderate; some are tearful and some shout, some weep their face to heaven with their hands held low, their fingers intertwined; others are fearful with shoulders raised to their ears, and so on, in accordance with the above-mentioned causes. He who sheds tears raises his eyebrows at their juncture and draws them together, producing wrinkles between and above them, the corners of his mouth are turned down, but he who laughs has the corners of the mouth turned up and his brows are open and relaxed.

CARTA 29

CU 25–25V, LU 41, MCM 57]

48. Equiparazione da pittura a scultura [58]

Manca la scultura della bellezza de' colori, manca della prospettiva de' colori, manca della prospet-

48. Comparison of Painting and Sculpture [58]

Sculpture lacks beauty of color, it lacks the perspective of color, it lacks the perspective and

_____

57. This chapter has the heading "Del medemo" (Of the same) as a reference to the subject of the preceding chapter of the *Trattato*

(Lu 384), also copied from *Libro* A (chapter 63).
58. Ludwig refers to the mark *L⁰* A only in his "Errata-Corrige." On the chronology of Leo-

tiva e confusione de' termini delle cose remote dall'occhio, imperocchè così farà cognito li termini delle cose propinque come delle remote; non fà l'aria interposta infra l'obbietto remoto occupare più esso obbietto che l'obbietto vicino, non farà i corpi lucidi e trasparenti, come le figure velate che mostrano la nuda carne sotto i veli a quella anteposti, non farà la minuta giara di vari colori sotto la superfice delle trasparenti acque.

blurred outlines of objects distant from the eye, for it records the outlines of things nearby in the same way it does those that are distant. It cannot show that the air lying between the distant object and the eye envelops that object more than a nearby object. It cannot represent luminous and transparent bodies, such as veiled figures which show the nude flesh beneath the veils covering them, and it cannot show small pebbles of various colors beneath the surface of transparent waters.

CU 27, LU 43, MCM 52]

49. *Risposta allo scultore* [59]

Dirà lo scultore far opere più eterne che 'l pittore. Qui si risponde esser virtù della materia sculta e non dello scultore che la sculpisce. E se 'l pittore dipinge in terra cotta con vetri, essa sarà più eterna che la scultura.

49. *Answer to the Sculptor* [59]

The sculptor will say that he makes works that are more enduring than the painter's. Here the reply is that this is a virtue of the material and not of the sculptor who carves it. If the painter paints on terra cotta with glazes, his work will be even more durable than sculpture.

---

nardo's discussions on the comparison of painting and sculpture see below, pp. 121–128. In his late period Leonardo added to his "Paragone" new arguments in favor of painting. Cf. Codex Atlanticus 277 v-a (*ca.* 1508)—a discussion on Light and Shadow, quoted above, p. 16. Galileo favored painting in a way similar to Leonardo's. In his letter to Lodovico Cigoli, June 26, 1612, Galileo states: "By 'painting' one understands the faculty of imitating Nature by means of light and dark. Now, sculptures will have relief only to the extent that they have shadows, that is that they are light in one part, and dark in another. And that this is true is demonstrated by experience; for if we were to expose a sculptured figure to the light and were then to proceed to color it in such a way that we paint it dark wherever it is light until its tone is completely unified, the figure would appear devoid of relief altogether" (Panofsky [1954], p. 8). Panofsky had already pointed out the similarities between Galileo's letter and Leonardo's "Paragone." Pietro Accolti, a contemporary of Galileo's, alludes to Leonardo's standard definition of painting as a combination of light and shadow, and refers to an anecdote that might well be considered as the source of Galileo's experiment. Cf. Accolti, p. 95: ". . . non sono mancati chi molto auuedutamente habbia stimato non esser altro la Pittura, che una varia rappresentazione d'ombre, e di lumi; onde può anche reputarsi douer questo essere il principale studio di chiunque desidera auanzarsi sopra gl'altri nella

Pittura. Nobilissimo testimonio ce ne lasciò la disputa, et gareggio di Apelle (come vogliono alcuni) con Praxitele scultore celeberrimo de gl'antichi secoli, à chi volendo far apparire non meno l'eminenza della Pittura, che l'eccellenza della sua Arte, ad una delle statue di Praxitele si accostò, e di quella tutti i lumi ombreggiando, e tutte l'ombre proportionatamente lumeggiando, fece in guisa, che quello, che era rilieuo, non più tale à riguardanti appariua, ma una pura semplice piana superficie, et potè con l'artificio del pennello, annichilire l'opera dell'Emulo suo."

Leonardo's later ideas in the "Paragone" are echoed by Castiglione (1528), bk. i, chap. 52. And of course Michelangelo knew of them, as he alludes to them in 1549 in his well-known reply to Benedetto Varchi's questionnaire. See p. 241 below.

59. This is the last paragraph of McM 52. In Leonardo's notebook this paragraph probably followed McM 57 (*Libro A* 48). Lu 43 does not reproduce the mark *L⁰ A*, and does not show this as being a separate paragraph. On the subject of the indestructibility of sculpture see Galileo's letter to Cigoli in Panofsky (1954), p. 37: "The argument of eternity [indestructibility] counts nothing because it is not sculpture that eternalizes the marble block; rather the marble block eternalizes the sculpture. This prerogative belongs, not to sculpture, but to coarse rock—although perhaps sculptures and painting are [in fact] equally subject to annihilation."

CU 27, LU 44, MCM 46]

50. Dell'obbligo che ha la scultura
col lume e non la pittura

Se la scultura avrà il lume di sotto parrà cosa mostruosa e strana. Questo non accade alla pittura, che tutte e' parti porta con seco.

50. How Sculpture Is Indebted to Light
but Painting Is Not

If sculpture is lighted from below, it will seem monstrous and strange, but this does not happen with painting, which contains within itself all its elements.

CU 75v–76, LU 254, MCM 176; RIG 227]

51. De' colori che risultano dalla
mistione d'altri colori li
quali si dimandano spezie seconda

I semplici colori sono sei,[60] de' quali il primo è il bianco, benchè alcuni filosofi non accettino il bianco nè 'l nero nel numero de' colori, perchè l'uno è causa de' colori e l'altro n'è privazione. Ma pure, perchè il pittore non può fare senza questi, noi li metteremo nel numero degli altri e diremo il bianco in questo ordine essere il primo ne' semplici, ed il giallo il secondo, e 'l verde n'è 'l terzo, l'azzurro n'è 'l quarto, e 'l rosso n'è 'l quinto, e' l nero n'è 'l sesto.

E il bianco metteremo per la luce, senza la quale nessun colore vedere si può, e 'l giallo per la terra, il verde per l'acqua, e l'azzurro per l'aria, e 'l rosso pe'l fuoco, e 'l nero per le tenebre che stan sopra l'elemento del foco, perchè non v'è materia o grossezza dove i razzi del Sole abbino a percotere [61] e per conseguenza a illuminare.[62]

51. On Colors That Result from the
Mixture of Other Colors,
Which Are Called Secondary

The simple colors are six,[60] of which the first is white, although some philosophers do not accept white or black in the number of colors, because one is the origin of all colors and the other is their absence. But as painters cannot do without them, we include them in the number of the others, and say that in this order white is the first among the simple, and yellow is second, green is third, blue is fourth, red is fifth, and black is the sixth.

White we designate for light without which no color can be seen; yellow for the earth; green for water; blue for air; red for fire; and black for darkness, which is stronger than the element of fire, for in it, there is no material or substance for the rays of sun to strike,[61] and thus illuminate.[62]

---

60. Codex: "I semplici colori sono de qua il primo. . . ." Ludwig's interpretation is accepted.

61. Codex: ". . . doue i razzi del sole habbino a penetrare." "Penetrare" is corrected and changed to "percotere."

62. Cf. Alberti, i, 63: "Fia il colore di fuoco il rosso, dell'aere cilestrino, dell'acqua il verde et la terra bigia e cinericcia . . . 'l bianco e 'l nero non sono veri colori ma sono alterazione de li altri colori; pero che il pittore truova cosa niuna con la quale elli ripresenti l'ultimo lustro de lumi altro che il bianco et così solo il nero a dimostrare le tenebre" (Spencer:50). See also Accolti, p. 151. Spencer, pp. 104–105, n. 23, points out Alberti's omission of yellow from the basic colors of the painter's palette as most striking, since Alberti clearly refers to yellow as a part of his color chords. Filarete, pp. 635–637, includes yellow in a passage that is a paraphrase of Alberti's, but he

deviates from Alberti in the medieval identification of colors with the elements. Thus green is for Filarete to be taken for grass, whereas for Alberti and Leonardo it is to be taken for water. Filarete does not associate yellow with any element, but he states that it is used to represent gold. It is illuminating that Leonardo associates yellow with earth (see also Libro A 96: ". . . wet streets are more yellowish than are dry ones. . . ."), whereas for Alberti earth is represented by gray ("et la terra bigia e cinericcia"). Recipies for the composition of yellow are found in Leonardo's writings dating from his early Florentine period, ca. 1478–1480; e.g., Codex Atlanticus 71 v-a (Richter [1883], I, 621): "A fine yellow—dissolve realgar or orpiment with aqua fortis." Cennini, chap. xlviii, refers to yellow made from realgar as being poisonous.

Aristotle's De Coloribus, 791a, is the possible

CARTE 29-30

Se vogli con brevità vedere le varietà di tutti i colori composti, togli vetri colorati e per quelli guarda tutti i colori della campagna che dopo quello si veggono; e così vedrai tutti i colori delle cose che dopo tal vetro si vedono, essere tutte miste col colore del predetto vetro, e vedrai quale fia il colore che con tal mistione si racconci o guasti.

If you wish to see briefly all the varieties of composite colors, take pieces of colored glass and look through them at all the colors of the country-side. There you will see that all the colors of objects seen through the glass blend with the color of the glass, and you will see which color is strengthened or impaired by such a mixture.

CARTA 30

Come: sia il predetto vetro di color giallo; dico che le spezie delli obbietti che per tal colore passano all'occhio possono così peggiorare come migliorare; e questo peggioramento in tal colore di vetro accaderà alli azzurri e nero e bianco sopra tutti gli altri,[63] e lo meglioramento accaderà nel giallo e verde sopra tutti gli altri; e così andrai scorrendo con l'occhio le mistioni de' colori, le quali sono infinite, ed a questo modo farai elezione de' colori di nove invenzioni di misti e composti. E 'l medesimo si farà con due vetri di vari colori anti-posti all'occhio, e così per te potrai seguitare.

For example, if the glass is yellow, I say that the visual images of objects which pass through that color to the eye can be impaired as well as im-proved. Deterioration will take place with blue, black, and white more than with all the others,[63] and improvement will occur with yellow and green more than with all the others. Thus with the eye you will consider color mixtures which are infinite in number, and in this way you will make a choice of colors for innovations of mixed and composite colors. You will do the same with two glasses of different colors held before the eye, and thus you will be able to continue by yourself.

---

source of the concept that all the colors come from a mixing of black and white. Leonardo must have read Aristotle's *De Coloribus* in 1508 when he wrote the note on white in MS F 75 (Lu 247; McM 204). In MS F 84v and 96v Leonardo quotes Aristotle's *De Physica*. In Codex Atlanticus 83 v-b, *ca.* 1508, Leonardo transcribes a Latin passage "in 2 de 80 fisicorum." Cf. Solmi (1908), p. 75; Uccelli (1940), pp. xxxv ff.; Pedretti (1957a), pl. 6.

In the last paragraph of *Libro A* 51 Leonardo suggests looking at objects through a yellow glass. Yellow stained glass is mentioned by Vasari, *On Technique*, p. 270, as being made with a red hue, which when fused stains the glass yellow (normally, of course, the yellow stain on glass is produced by silver), but Vasari does not say what his composition is. Cf. the recipe for "vetro giallo" in Codex Atlanticus 244 v-b, written from left to right (if by Leonardo, *ca.* 1504). See also Codex Atlanticus 270 r-a, *ca.* 1508–1510, in which Leonardo develops a study of the move-ments of the flame: "We are not concerned here with the science of the heat and color of fire,

neither with its nature, nor with the method of staining glasses and other objects by means of fire; but we are concerned with the motion of fire. . . ."

In *Libro A* 51 Leonardo lists green and blue among the simple colors, whereas in *Libro A* 52 he states that they are compound. As Solmi (1905), p. 193, points out, this is only apparently a contradiction: "Leonardo observes that on mix-ing together the colors of the painter's palette one can obtain a blue and a green that are compound, although they are less brilliant than the primary green and blue; thus Leonardo could well speak of blue and green as both primary and compound colors."

63. Codex: ". . . acchadera alli azuri sopra e' nero e' biancho, tutti gli altri. . . ." Ludwig's interpretation is accepted. It is possible that Leo-nardo had written the words "e nero e biancho" in the space between the lines, above the word "azuri":

CU 76–76v, LU 255, McM 177; Rig 248]

52. De' colori

L'azzurro e 'l verde non è per sè semplice, perchè l'azzurro è composto di luce e di tenebre,
com'è quel dell'aria, cioè nero perfettissimo e
bianco candidissimo.

Il verde è composto d'un semplice e d'un composto, cioè si compone d'azzurro e di giallo.

52. On Colors

Blue and green are not in themselves simple colors,
because blue is composed of light and darkness,
as in the case of the air; that is, it is composed of
most perfect black and purest white.

Green is composed of a simple and a compound
color, that is, it is composed of blue and yellow.

CU 136, LU 423, McM 456; Rig 199]

53. Del dividere e spiccare le figure dalli loro campi

Tu hai a mettere la tua figura scura in campo
chiaro e se la figura è chiara mettila in campo
scuro. E s'ell'è chiara e scura, metti la parte scura
nel campo chiaro e la parte chiara nel campo
scuro.[64]

53. On Separating and Detaching Figures from Their Backgrounds

You must place your dark figure against a light
background, and if your figure is light, place it
against a dark background, and if it is both light
and dark, put the dark side against a light background and the light side against a dark background.[65]

CU 137, LU 429, McM 463; Rig 197]

54. Delle nature de' termini de' corpi sopra gli altri corpi

Quando li corpi di convessa superfice
termineranno sopra altri corpi d'equal
colore, il termine del convesso parrà più
oscuro che 'l corpo che col convesso termine
terminerà.[65]

Il termine dell'aste equigiacente parrà in campo
bianco di grande oscurità e in campo scuro parrà
più che altra sua parte chiarissimo, ancora che il
lume, che sopra l'aste discende, sia sopra essa aste
d'equal chiarezza.

54. On the Nature of Contours of Bodies upon Other Bodies

When bodies with a convex surface are
seen against other bodies of the same
color, the edge of the convex body will
seem darker than the body contiguous to it.[65]

An upright pole placed parallel to a wall will
appear to have a very dark outline when the background is white, and when the background is dark
this outline will appear very much brighter than
any other part of the pole, even though, in each
case, the light which descends onto the pole is
equally brilliant.

---

64. Cf. MS E 4 (Lu 246, McM 146): "On
Background of Shapes of Bodies in Painting—
The background surrounding the form of any
painted thing should be darker than the illuminated side of that form, and brighter than the
side in shadow." See also Accolti, p. 149: "Metta
in quanto può il Pittore la sua figura in campo
chiaro, se ella sarà oscura; et se sarà chiara, et
vicina a gran lume, campeggi ella nello scuro."

65. Codex: ". . . parrà più oscuro che col conuesso termine. . . ." Ludwig's interpretation is
accepted. Cf. MS G 23v (Lu 482, McM 464):
"A most important part of painting is the back-

ground of painted objects. Backgrounds in which
the outlines of natural bodies have a convex
curvature are always recognizable as forms, even
when the colors of those bodies are the same as
the background. This comes about because the
convex outlines of bodies are not illuminated in
the same way as the background, since such an
outline is often brighter or darker than the background. But if the outline is the color of the background, doubtless there can be no clarity in painting the outline of such a form. This composition
in painting is to be avoided by painters of intelligence."

CARTA 31

CU 136–136v, LU 425 & a, MCM 499; RIG 127]

55. *Del fuggire la improporzionalità delle circostanze*

Grandissimo vizio si dimostra appresso di molti pittori, cioè di fare le abitazioni delli uomini ed altre circostanze in tal modo che le porte delle città non danno alle ginocchia de' loro abitatori, ancora ch'elle sieno più vicine all'occhio del riguardatore che non è l'uomo che in quella mostri volere entrare. Abbiam veduto li portici carichi d'uomini e le colonne di quello sostenitrici essere nel pugno a un uomo, che a quella s'appoggiava ad uso di bastone.[66] E così altri simili cose sono molto da essere schifate.

⟨Corrispondino i corpi sì per grandezza come per ufficio alla causa di cui si tratta.⟩ [67]

55. *On Avoiding Lack of Proportion in Settings*

A very great vice is found in many painters, that of depicting men's houses and surroundings in such a way that the gates of the city do not come up to the knees of its inhabitants, even though they are nearer to the eye of the observer than is the man who indicates that he wishes to enter. We have seen porticoes loaded with men, with its sustaining column held in the fist of a man who leaned against it as on a thin cane.[66] Other like things are greatly to be avoided.

Bodies should correspond in size as well as in function to the matter concerned.[67]

CARTA 32

CU 61, LU 183, MCM 268; RIG 137]

56. *Della varietà nelle istorie* [68]

Dilettisi il pittore ne' componimenti dell'istorie della copia e varietà e fugga il replicare alcuna parte che in essa fatta sia, acciocchè la novità e abbondanza attragga a sè e diletti l'occhio d'essa risguardatore. Dico che nella istoria si richiede, ed ai loro lochi accadendo, misti li omini di diverse effigi con diverse età e abiti, insieme misti con donne, fanciulli, cani, cavagli, edifici, campagne e colli.

56. *On Variety in Narrative Paintings* [68]

Let the painter composing narrative scenes take pleasure in abundance and variety, and avoid repetition of any part that occurs in it, so that novelty and abundance attract people to it and delight the eye of the observer. I say that a narrative painting requires, depending on the scene, in the appropriate places a mixture of men of various appearances, of different ages, and costumes, and also mixed with women, children, dogs, horses, buildings, fields, and hills.

---

66. Leonardo's criticism was probably directed to Taddeo Gaddi's frescoes in Santa Croce, Florence. Cf. White (1957), fig. 27b. Similar criticism is found in Alberti, ii, 91: ". . . quello che spesse volte veggo, ivi fusse huomo alcuno nello hedifitio quasi in uno scrigno inchiuso, dove apena sedendo vi si assetti" (Spencer:75). See also Filarete, p. 621: ". . . guarda a quegli casamenti; chè alcuna uolta erano quasi maggiori le figure che le case."

67. The last paragraph is preceded by the words "al medesimo" (at the same), which means that this paragraph was copied from the same folio of *Libro A* as the preceding one. At the end of the chapter the transcriber noted: "Questa propositione è prima definita che proposta adunque leggierai di sopra" (This proposition is first discussed, and then stated; therefore read above).

68. Cf. Alberti, ii, 91–92: "Quello che prima dà voluptà nella istoria viene dalla copia e varieta delle cose; come ne' cibi et nella musica sempre la novità et abondanza tanto piace quanto sia differente dalle cose antiche e consuete, così l'animo si diletta d'ogni copia e varietà; per questo in pittura la copia et varietà piace. Dirò io quella istoria essere copiosissima in quale, a suoi luoghi, siano permisti vecchi, giovani, fanciulli, donne, fanciullini, polli, catellini, ucciellini, cavagli, pecore, hedifici, provincie e tutte simili cose" (Spencer:75).

CU 61, LU 184, MCM 272; Rig 137]
57. Della istoria [69]

sia osservata nella istoria la degnità e decoro del principe o del savio che nella istoria si propone, con la separazione e interamente privata del tumulto del vulgo.

CU 61, LU 185, MCM 269]
58. Convenienze de parti delle istorie [70]

Non misterai i malinconiosi e lacrimosi e piangenti colli allegri e ridenti, imperocchè la Natura dà che colli piangenti si lacrimi e colli ridenti si allegri, e si separa li loro risi e pianti.

CU 115–115v, LU 325, MCM 399; Rig 133]
59. Dell'attitudine delli omini

Siano l'attitudini delli uomini con li lor membri in tal modo disposti, che con quelli si dimostri la intenzione de' loro animi.

57. On Narrative Painting [69]

In a narrative scene the dignity and decorum of a prince or sage which the story propounds should be evident; it may be shown by separating him and setting him entirely apart from the tumult of the crowd.

58. Conformity in the Parts of Narrative Paintings [70]

Do not mix the melancholy, those who weep and lament, with the cheerful and those who laugh, for Nature decrees that with those who weep, one sheds tears, and with those who laugh one becomes happy, and their laughter and tears are separate.

59. On Postures of Men

Let the postures of men and the parts of their bodies be so disposed that these display the intent of their minds.

---

69. Cf. Alberti, ii, 92: "Suole ad i principi la carestia delle parole tenere maestà dove fanno intendere suoi precepti; così in istoria un certo competente numero di corpi rende non poca degnità" (Spencer:76). Leonardo seems to follow the Latin text of Alberti's della Pittura: "Meo quidem iudicio nulla erit usque adeo tanto rerum varietate referta historia quam novem aut decem homines non possint condigne agere ut illud Varronis hoc pertinere arbitror in convivio tumultum evitans non plusquam novem accubantes admittebant" (Spencer:76). See also note 40.

70. Cf. Alberti, ii, 93: "Interviene in natura, quale nulla più che di lei si trova capace di cose ad sè simile, che piagniamo con chi piange et ridiamo con chi ride et dolianci con chi si duole" (Spencer:77). The next sentence, "ma questi movimenti d'animo si conoscono dai movimenti del corpo," is echoed in Leonardo's next note of Libro A. Clark (1944), p. 17, states that in compiling the Codex Ashburnham 2038 (ca. 1492) Leonardo had "a copy of Alberti's Della Pittura beside him." Leonardo also looked through Alberti's book during the compilation of Libro A. Chapters 55 to 58 of Libro A follow Alberti's

arguments even in their sequence. It is usually assumed that Leonardo used Alberti's book only during the Sforza period, ca. 1492. Cf. Zoubov (1960), pp. 1–14. The proof that Leonardo was still following Alberti's della Pittura after 1500 is found not only in the reconstructed Libro A but also in a passage in MS G 19 (Lu 483, McM 428): "On the Judgment that You Must Make of a Painter's Work. . . . The second thing is that the distribution or grouping of figures should be made according to the episode in the story you have selected. The third is that the figures should, in lifelike fashion, be intent on their particular concern." Cf. Alberti, ii, 91: "Adunque tutti i corpi per grandezza et suo officio s'acconfaranno a quello che ivi nella storia si facci" (Spencer:75).

The word "convenienze" in the title of this chapter is translated by Ludwig as "Passende Zusammenstellung," and by McMahon as "Consistency." Either rendering is correct, but it would seem that "conformity" is closer to the concept of fitness or aptness as implied in the Italian word. "Convenienza" is in fact the equivalent of the Latin Concinnitas.

CU 136V, LU 426, MCM 511; Rig 114]

60. De' termini de' corpi
detti lineamenti ovver dintorni

Sono i termini de' corpi di tanta minima evidenza
che in ogni piccolo intervallo che s'oppone infra
la cosa e l'occhio, esso occhio non comprende la
effige dell'amico o parente e nol conosce se non
per l'abito, e pel tutto riceve notizia del tutto
insieme colla parte.

60. On the Boundaries of Bodies
Called Outlines or Contours

Outlines of bodies are so little conspicuous that at
each small interval lying between the object and
the eye, the eye does not grasp the image of friend
or relative, and does not recognize him, unless it
be by his clothing, but gains knowledge of the
figure by means of the whole together with the
parts.

CU 235V, LU 802, MCM 831]

61. Dell'aria che infra
i monti si dimostra

Più si dimostra l'aria luminosa e chiara inverso la
parte del Sole che nelle parte opposite.

61. On the Air That Is Seen
in the Mountains

The air looks more luminous and bright toward
the sunny side than on the opposite side.

CARTA 33*

CU 115V, LU 326, MCM 389; Rig 134]

62. Varietà d'attitudini

Pronuncisi gli atti negli uomini secondo le loro
età e degnità e si varino secondo le spezie, cioè le
spezie de' maschi da quelle delle femmine.

62. Variety in Attitudes

Differentiate the actions of humans according to
their age and rank, and vary them according to
sex, that is, male and female.

CU 127, LU 381, MCM 420; Rig 172]

63. Del ridere e piangere
e differenze loro [71]

Da quel che ride a quel che piange non si varia nè
occhi, nè bocca, nè guance, ma solo la rigidità
delle ciglia che s'aggiongono a chi piange e levasi
a chi ride.

A colui che piange s'aggionge ancora le mani
stracciare li vestimenti e capegli e con l' unghie
stracciarsi la pelle del volto, il che non accade a
chi ride.

63. Of Laughing and Weeping and
the Difference between Them [71]

Between one who laughs and one who weeps
there is no difference in the eye, or mouth, or
cheeks, but only in the rigidity of the eyebrows,
which are drawn together by him who weeps and
are raised by him who laughs.

He who weeps also tears his garments and hair
with his hands, and scratches his face with his
finger nails, and this does not occur with a man
who laughs.

---

71. Cf. Alberti, ii, 94: "Et chi mai credesse,
se non provando, tanto essere difficile volendo
dipignere un viso che rida, schifare di non lo fare
piu tosto piagnoso che lieto?" (Spencer:77–78).
Cf. Zoubov (1960), p. 9.

See also *Libro A* 47.

In this chapter, as in *Libro A* 47 and 97, Leonardo is carrying out the program outlined in Lu
285 (McM 418): "First of laughter and weeping,
wherein the mouth, cheeks, and closing of the eyes

* The first chapter of carta 33 might have been that which in the present reconstruction comes as
fifth. Our chapter 66, in fact, is on the same subject as, and almost the continuation of, *Libro A* 61,
the last chapter of carta 32. In the Codex Urbinas the two chapters appear one after the other.

CU 175V, LU 552, MCM 584]

64. De l'ombre e sua divisione

L'ombre ne' corpi si generano dalli obbietti oscuri a essi corpi antiposti e si dividono in due parti, delle quali l'una è detta primitiva e l'altra derivativa.

CU 185V, LU 606, MCM 699]

65. Dove fia più scura l'ombra derivativa

Quell'ombra derivativa sarà di maggior oscurità la qual fia più vicina alla sua causa, e quelle che sono remote si faranno più chiare.

Quell'ombra fia più espedita e terminata che sarà più vicina al suo nascimento, e manco spedita è la più remota.

L'ombra si dimostra più scura inverso li stremi che inverso il mezzo suo.

CU 235V, LU 803, MCM 830]

66. De' monti e loro divisione in pittura

Dico che l'aria interposta infra l'occhio e 'l monte parrà più chiara in P che in A, e questo può accadere per diverse cause, delle quali la prima è che

64. On Shadow and Its Division

Shadows on bodies are created by dark objects placed in front of those bodies, and are divided into two parts, of which the first is called primary, and the other derivative.

65. Where the Derivative Shadow Is Most Obscure

That derivative shadow will be darkest which is nearest to its source, and those which are remote will be lighter.

That shadow is sharpest and clearest which is nearest to its origin, and the least sharp is the most remote.

A shadow looks denser toward its edges than toward its center.

66. On Mountains and Their Treatment in Painting

I say that the air lying between the eye and mountains seems brighter at P than at A, and this happens for different reasons, of which the first is

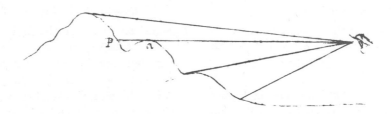

l'aria interposta infra l'occhio e 'l P è maggior somma che quella che s'interpone infra l'occhio e l'A, e per conseguente è più chiara. La seconda è che l'aria è più grossa in P valle che in A monte.

that the air lying between the eye and P is greater in quantity than that which lies between the eye and A, and is consequently brighter. The second is that the air is denser in the valley P than at A, the mountain.

---

are very similar, and only the eyebrows and the interval between them differ. All this will be discussed in the proper place. . . ." The second part of the chapter echoes Leonardo's early precept on how to represent a man in despair, Lu 382 (McM

423), from MS Ashburnham 29v, ca. 1492: "You will show the man in despair stabbing himself with a knife, having torn his garments with his hands. Let one of his hands be shown in the act of tearing open his wound. . . ."

CARTA 34

CU 137, LU 430, MCM 354; Rig 74]

67. *Della figura che va contro il vento*

67. *On the Figure Which Moves against the Wind*

Sempre la figura che si move infra 'l vento per qualunque linea, non osserverà il centro della sua gravità con debita disposizione sopra il centro del suo sostentaculo.

The figure which moves against the wind in whatever direction will not keep its center of gravity with the usual disposition of weight above its center of support.

CU 175v–176, LU 553 & a, MCM 590–591–592]

68. *Di due spezie d'ombre ed in quante parti si dividono*

68. *On Two Kinds of Shadows and into How Many Parts They Are Divided*

Le spezie de l'ombre si dividono in due parti, l'una delle quali è detta semplice e l'altra composta. Semplice è detta quella che da un sol lume e da un sol corpo è causata. Composta è quella che da più lumi sopra un medesimo corpo si genera, o da più lumi sopra più corpi. La semplice ombra si divide in due parti, cioè primitiva e derivativa. Primitiva è quella ch'è congionta nella superfice del corpo ombroso. Derivativa è quella ombra che si parte dal predetto corpo e discorre per l'aria e, se trova resistenza, si ferma nel luogo dove percote, con la figura della sua propria basa. E 'l simile si dice dell'ombre composte.[72]

The kinds of shadow are divided into two parts, one of which is called simple, and the other compound. That is simple which is caused by a single light and a single body; that is compound which is created by several lights on a single body or by several lights on several bodies. The simple shadow is divided into two parts; that is, primary and derivative. It is primary when it is attached to the surface of the body which casts the shadow; the derivative shadow is that which starts out from the same body and travels through the air, and meeting resistance, stops on the surface where it strikes with the shape of its own source.

The same can be said of compound shadows.[72]

---

72. The transcriber added to this chapter: "Sempre l'ombra primitiva si fa basa dell'ombra derivativa" (The primary shadow is always the base of the derivative shadow); "Li termini de l'ombre deriuatiue sono retti lineij" (The outlines of derivative shadows are straight lines from that base); "Tanto più diminuisce l'oscurità de l'ombra deriuatiua quanto essa è più remota da l'ombra primitiua" (The darkness of the derivative shadow diminishes the greater the distance from the primary shadow); and "Quell'ombra si dimostrerà più scura che fia circondata da più splendida bianchezza e' per contrario sarà meno euidente dou'ella sia generata in più oscuro campo" (That shadow looks darkest which is surrounded by the most brilliant whiteness, and, on the contrary, it appears least visible where it is placed against the darkest background). These added sections constitute the chapter Lu 553a, that is, McM chapters 613, 705, and 744. In McMahon's *Concordance*, chapters 613 and 705 are identified with MS E 32v. In the Codex Urbinas, however, they are not marked as having been copied from *Libro B* (i.e., MS E), so that it is possible that these sections were repeated on carta 34 of *Libro A*. The preceding sections are also similar to those in MS E 32v.

See also *Libro A* 69, 91, and 98.

Leonardo's texts on the classification of shadows in carte 33 and 34 of *Libro A* are in fulfillment of programs outlined in Codex Atlanticus 236 v-a and 277 v-a (blue paper, *ca.* 1513–1514). These programs are hints to Leonardo's later compilation (*Libro W*) on light and shade, now lost.

CARTA 35

CU 185v–186, LU 607, MCM 632]

69. *De l'ombre* [73]

Mai l'ombra avrà la vera similitudine del dintorno del corpo donde nasce, ancora che fusse sperica, se 'l lume non è della figura del corpo ombroso.

Se 'l lume è di lunga figura, la qual lunghezza s'astenda in alto, l'ombre de' corpi da quello alluminati s'astenderanno in latitudine.

Se la lunghezza del lume sarà traversale, l'ombra del corpo sperico si farà lunga nella sua altezza. E così, per qualunche modo si troverà la lunghezza del lume, sempre l'ombra avrà la sua lunghezza in contrario intersegata a uso di croce colla lunghezza del lume.

Se 'l lume sarà più grosso e più corto del corpo ombroso, la percussione dell'ombra derivativa fia più lunga e più sottile che l'ombra primitiva.

Se 'l lume sarà più sottile e più lungo che 'l corpo ombroso, la percussione dell'ombra derivativa sarà più grossa e più corta che la primitiva.

Se la lunghezza del luminoso sarà equale alla lunghezza e larghezza del corpo ombroso, allora la percussione della derivativa ombra fia della medesima figura, ne' suoi termini, che l'ombra primitiva.

69. *On Shadows* [73]

A shadow will never be truly identical to the contour of the body from which it derives, even if it is spherical, unless the light is of the same shape as the body casting the shadow.

If the light is long in shape and its length extends upward, the shadows of bodies illuminated by it will extend in breadth.

If the length of the light is crosswise, the shadow of a spherical body will become elongated in height. Thus, in whatever direction the light is longest, the shadow will always have its length in the opposite direction, intersecting crosswise the length of the light.

If the light should be broader and shorter than the body, the impact of the derivative shadow will be longer and narrower than the primary shadow.

If the light should be narrower and longer than the body which casts the shadow, the impact of the derivative shadow will be broader and shorter than the primary shadow.

If the length and breadth of the light source should be equal to the length and breadth of the body which casts the shadow, then the contours of the derivative shadow will be of the same shape as the primary shadow.

---

73. Each paragraph is marked with an asterisk. An asterisk is also placed before the mark *L° A* near the title.

Cf. *Libro B* (MS E) 32r (Richter [1883], I, 162): "If a spherical solid body is illuminated by a light of elongated form the shadow produced by the longest portion of this light will have less defined outlines than that which is produced by the breadth of the same light." Leonardo's experiments with elongated light sources resulted in the contradiction of his own rules. Cf. *Libro B* (MS E) 31v (Richter [1883], I, 197): "A luminous body which is long and narrow in shape gives more confused outlines to the derived shadows than a spherical light, and this contradicts the proposition next following: A shadow will have its outlines more clearly defined in proportion as it is nearer to the primary shadow or, I

should say, the body casting the shadow; the cause of this is the elongated form of the luminous body *a, c,* &c." It is on one of the diagrams illustrating this passage that Leonardo wrote: "Non si debbe desiderare lo impossibile" (One ought not to desire the impossible). See reproduction in Richter (1883), Vol. I, pl. XLI. Similar notes and diagrams are in Codex Atlanticus 258 v-a, blue paper, *ca.* 1513–1514.

It does not seem that before this time Leonardo had been experimenting with lights of elongated shape—and from the diagrams in MS E and Codex Atlanticus 258 v-a it appears that he was considering a light source in the form of a luminescent tube. In his early writings he may refer to a "lume lungo" as that of the flame of a candle. Cf. MS C 8r, 11v, and 18v. See also Codex Arundel 103v (*ca.* 1490–1495), quoted below, p. 237n.

CARTA 36

CU 104–104V, LU 270, MCM 291; RIG 7]

70. *Delle misure universali de' corpi*

Dico: le misure universali si debbono osservare nelle lunghezze delle figure e non nelle grossezze, perchè delle laudabili e maravigliose cose che appariscono nelle opere della Natura è che nissuna sua opera, in qualunche spezie per sè, l'un particolare con precisione si somiglia l'un all'altra. Adunque tu, imitatore di tal Natura, guarda ed attende alle varietà de' lineamenti. Piacemi bene che tu fuggi le cose mostruose, com'è le gambe lunghe e busti corti e petti stretti e braccia lunghe. Piglia adonque le misure delle gionture e le grossezze in che forte varia la Natura, variale ancora tu.[74]

⟨E se tu pure vorrai sopra una medesima misura fare le tue figure sappi che non si cognosceranno l'una dall'altra, il che non si vede nella Natura.⟩

70. *On General Measurements of Bodies*

I say that general measurements should be observed in the length of figures, and not in their thickness. Among the praiseworthy and marvelous things that appear in the works of Nature is the remarkable fact that none of its works in any species precisely resembles any other in detail. Therefore, you imitator of Nature, note and be attentive to the great variety of lineaments. I would be well pleased to have you avoid monstrous things, such as long legs with short torsos, narrow chests with long arms. So take the measurements of length in the joints as constants, and when it comes to the thicknesses in which Nature varies greatly, vary them, you, too.[74]

But if you wish nevertheless, to make your figures on the basis of one and the same measurement, be aware that they cannot then be distinguished one from another, a thing which is never seen in Nature.

---

74. Codex: ". . . in che forte uaria uariale anchora tu." Ludwig's interpretation is accepted. It is possible however that the compiler transcribed the original text correctly, with the exception of mistaking an *s* for an *f* in the word *forte*, and neglecting a possible abbreviation of *n* in the word *uaria*[*n*]. The sentence "Piglia adonque le misure delle gionture e le grossezze in che sorte uaria[n], variale ancora tu" can be translated thus: "Consider therefore the measurements and thickness of the joints in the way they vary, and vary them, you, too." (In the Codex Urbinas this text is followed by *Libro A* 108, which is in fact on this subject.) The mark *L° A* is repeated before the second paragraph. Cf. MS E 6v (Lu 375, McM 287): "Make each part proportionate to the whole, so that when a man has a thick, short figure, his every part is also thus. . . ." See also MS G 5v (Lu 78, McM 97): ". . . And he who takes no account of these differences makes his figures as if they had been turned out by a press, so that they all seem sisters. Such a thing merits grave reproof." Cf. Alberti, iii, 107 (Spencer:93); Panofsky (1952), p. 34.

On Codex Atlanticus 375 r-c, a folio in blue paper dating from 1508–1513, is a note not in Leonardo's handwriting, translated by MacCurdy (II:286): "We consider as a monstrosity one who has a very large head and short legs, and as a monstrosity also one who is in great poverty and has rich garments; we should therefore deem him well proportioned in whom the parts are in harmony with the whole." This handwriting is also found in a note on the saltiness of the sea in Windsor 19,089 (C II 19 and 20; blue leaves), *ca.* 1513. Clark states that this writing is in the same hand as the notes in Codex Atlanticus 342v, which Calvi has identified as that of Melzi. In my opinion this writing is not Melzi's but that of an unidentified pupil (Salai?) who wrote the draft of a letter dated 5 July 1507 in Codex Atlanticus 132 r-a, as well as the list of expenses in Codex Atlanticus 202 r-a. Cf. Pedretti (1960d), p. 542. The characteristic form of the *F*, which occurs in the words "laFacenda" and "inFeratura" on both folios, is to be seen in the word "seFacessi" in the Windsor note. On the handwriting of Francesco Melzi see below, pp. 97 ff.

CARTA 37

CU 40v–41, LU 87, MCM 136; RIG 190]

71. Delle qualità del lume per ritrarre rilievi naturali o finti

Il lume tagliato dalle ombre con troppa evidenza è sommamente biasimato ⟨appresso de' pittori⟩; onde per fuggire tale inconveniente, se tu depingi li corpi in campagna aperta, farai le figure non alluminate dal Sole, ma fingi alcuna quantità [75] di nebbia o nuvoli trasparenti essere interposti infra l'obbietto e 'l Sole; onde, non essendo la figura del Sole espedita,[76] non saranno espediti i termini dell'ombre co' termini de' lumi.

71. On the Quality of Light in Which to Represent Relief, Natural or Simulated

Light separated too obviously from shadow is severely condemned by painters. Therefore to avoid such unpleasantness, if you portray figures in the open country, you should not paint their forms as though illuminated by the sun, but pretend that there is some sort of mistiness [75] or transparent clouds which come between the object and the sun. As the image of the sun [76] is not sharply defined, so the edges of the shadows and the luminous parts of the figure will not be sharply defined.

CU 61, LU 186, MCM 273; RIG 139]

72. Del diversificare l'arie de' volti nelle istorie

Comune difetto ne' pittori italici [77] il ricognoscersi l'aria e figura dell'operatore [78] mediante le molte figure da lui depinte. Onde, per fuggire tal errore, non sieno fatte o replicate mai, nè tutto nè parte della figura,[79] che uno volto si veda nell'altro nella istoria.

72. On Diversifying the Expression of Faces in Narrative Paintings

It is a common defect of Italian painters [77] that one recognizes the expression and figure of the author [78] in the many figures painted by him. Therefore, to avoid such an error, do not make or repeat either the whole figure or a part of it, so that one face [79] is seen elsewhere in the painting.

CU 136v, LU 427, MCM 505; RIG 121]

73. De li accidenti superficiali che prima si perdono per le distanze

Le prime cose che si perdono nel discostarsi dalli corpi ombrosi sono i termini loro; secondariamente

73. On the Parts of Surfaces Which First Are Lost through Distance

As you go away from ⟨opaque⟩ figures the first thing to be lost is their outlines; second, with

---

75. Ludwig suggests: ". . . ma fingi alcuna qualità di nebbia," instead of "quantità" as in the codex. Sometimes Leonardo expressed a preference for the "lume particulare." Cf. MS E 32v (Lu 790, McM 855) concerning landscape, and Lu 784 concerning the human figure.

76. McMahon: ". . . As the figure is not sharply illuminated by the sun." Rigaud's translation is closer to the meaning of Leonardo's sentence: ". . . so that the sun not being visible." Leonardo refers to the sun as a screened source of light of the kind described in Libro A 75. "Figura" refers to the sun, not to the object illuminated by it; hence it can be translated "image."

Cf. Codex Atlanticus 270 v-b, ca. 1490: "Il sole ha corpo, figura, moto. . . ."

77. Ludwig: "Comune diffetto è ne' dipintori. . . ."

78. In almost all the abridged compilations of the Trattato della Pittura the word "operatore" is altered to "Imperatore"; Steinitz (1958), pp. 32–33. Only the Codex Vaticanus Ottobonianus 2984, chap. 98, and the Codex Casanatense 5018, fol. 28v, have the correct word; see Pedretti (1959a), p. 449. For a possible indirect reference to Flemish painters see Venturi (1919), pp. 39–40.

79. Ludwig: ". . . ne' parte delle figure. . . ."

in più distanza si perde li intervalli [80] ombrosi che divideno le parti de' corpi che si toccano; terza le grossezze delle gambe da pie'; e così successivamente si perde le parte più minute in modo che a lunga distanza sol rimane una massa ovale di confusa figura.[81]

greater distance one loses the intervening shades [80] that separate parts of bodies that touch one another; third, the breadth of the legs beginning at the feet; and thus the more minute parts are lost in succession, until at a great distance there remains only an oval mass of indistinct shape.[81]

cu 193v, lu 656, mcm 685]
74. *De' termini insensibili de l'ombre*
Quella parte de l'ombre sarà più scura che con men somma di lume s'infonde.

74. *On the Imperceptible Outlines of Shadows*
That part of the shadow will be most dark which is suffused with the least amount of light.

CARTA 38

cu 41v, lu 92, mcm 132; rig 184]
75. *Del ritrarre l'ombre de' corpi al lume di candela o di lucerna*
A questo lume di notte [82] sia interposto il telaio con carta lucida o senza lucidarla, ma solo uno intero foglio di cancellcresca. E vedrai le tue ombre

75. *On Representing the Shadow of Bodies by the Light of a Candle or Lamp*
In front of this night light [82] place a frame on which paper, made transparent or not, has been stretched, but use only one whole sheet of chancel-

---

80. Codex: ". . . in più distantia si perde li [a space is left] ombrosi. . . ." Ludwig's interpretation is accepted.

81. Cf. MS G 53v, the last section of a note on painting (Brizio [1952], pp. 447–448; MacCurdy.II.377). "In every figure placed at a great distance you lose first the knowledge of its most minute parts, and preserve to the last that of the larger parts, losing, however, the perception of all their extremities; and they become oval or spherical in shape, and their boundaries are indistinct." In Lu 489 Melzi copied only the first section of the note on painting in MS G 53v. See also a note on the same subject in MS E 80v (Brizio [1952], p. 459; MacCurdy:II.375).

82. "Lume di notte" is translated "artificial light" by Rigaud and "Licht bei Nacht" by Ludwig. McMahon considers "notte" as an indication of time ("At night place in front of this light . . .") probably because of a note in MS A 1v, ca. 1492 (Richter [1883], I, 524): "A Method of Drawing an Object in Relief at Night—Place a sheet of not too transparent paper between the relievo and the light and you can draw thus very well." However, "lume di notte" can be interpreted as "lume da notte," that is, "light to be used during the night"; therefore it can be translated simply as "lamp." That both interpretations are correct is proved by two passages in Codex

Atlanticus 138 r-b, ca. 1490: "se metti uno lume di notte intra due specchi . . ." (If you place a night lamp between two mirrors . . .) and "se metterai ᴧdi notteᴧ [word added later above the line] un lume infralle pariete . . ." (If you place at night a lamp between two walls . . .). A passage in Codex Atlanticus 126 v-b, ca. 1490–1495 (Richter [1883], I, 243) seems to favor the interpretation of "lume di notte" as "night lamp": ". . . e così fa il sole di dì come la luna . e li altri mortali [Richter transcribes incorrectly "immortali"] lumi di notte" (Thus it is with the sun by day, as well as the moon and the extinguishable night lights).

In his late period Leonardo shows again his preference for "smoky shadows," which are the essence of his *sfumato* technique. The indoor experiment with a light screened by paper reproduces the effect of clouds screening the sun. (Cf. *Libro A* 71, 76, 79.) In MS G 3v (Richter [1883], I, 118) Leonardo refers again to this type of light source: ". . . and there is a 4th [kind of light] which is that which pass through [semi-]transparent bodies, as linen or paper or the like." See also Windsor 19,076r, ca. 1513 (Richter [1883], I, 292): "Of the edges [outlines] of shadows. Some have misty and ill defined edges [*termini fumosi*], others distinct ones." See also notes 53 and 54, above.

fumose, cioè non terminate. ⟨E 'l lume sanza interposizione di carta ti facci lume alla carta ove
disegni.⟩

lery size. You will see the shadows appear smoky,
that is, not sharp at the edges, and the light,
where it is not cut off by the paper, will illuminate
the paper on which you are drawing.

CU 42, LU 95, MCM 143; RIG 249]

76. Del lume dove si ritrae le incarnazioni delli volti o ignudi

Questa abitazione vuol essere scoperta all'aria colle
pareti del colore incarnato, e li ritratti si faccino di
state, quando li nugoli copreno il Sole. Ossia
veramente farai la parete meridionale tanto alta
che i razzi del Sole non percotino la parete set-
tentrionale, acciocchè i suoi razzi reflessi non
guastino l'ombre.

76. On the Light in Which to Represent the Flesh Tones of Faces or Nudes

This room should be open to the air, with walls of
flesh color. Portraits should be made in summer
when clouds cover the sun; or else you can make
the south wall so high that the rays of the sun do
not reach the north wall, so that its reflected rays
will not spoil the shadows.

CU 76v, LU 256, MCM 211; RIG 248]

77. De li colori specchiati sopra cose lustre di vari colori

Sempre la cosa specchiata partecipa del colore
del corpo che la specchia.

Lo specchio si tinge in parte del colore da lui
specchiato e partecipa tanto più l'un dell'altro,
quanto la cosa che si specchia è più o men potente
che 'l colore dello specchio. E quella cosa parrà
di più potente colore nello specchio che più partecipa del colore d'esso specchio.

77. On Colors Reflected on Lustrous Objects of Varied Colors

A reflected object always takes on the color of the
body on which it is reflected.

The mirror is tinted in part with the color reflected in it, and each partakes of the color of the
other, as the object reflected is stronger or less
strong than the color of the mirror. That will appear of the strongest color in the mirror which
most resembles the color of the mirror.

CU 136v–137, LU 428, MCM 522; RIG 291]

78. De li accidenti superficiali che prima si perdono nel discostarsi de' corpi ombrosi

La prima cosa che de' colori si perde nelle distanza
è il lustro loro parte minima, ed è il lume de'
lumi. Secondariamente è il lume, perchè minor
dell'ombra. Terza è l'ombre principali. E rimane,
nell'ultimo, una mediocre scurità confusa.

78. On Surface Conditions That Are Lost First in Receding from ⟨Opaque⟩ Bodies

The first characteristic of color to be lost with distance is the highlight, which is its smallest part,
and is a light within lights. The second is the light
area because it is smaller than the shadow. Thirdly,
the principal shadows are lost, and at last there
remains an intermediate, indistinct shade.

CU 137–137v, LU 431, MCM 451; RIG 250]

79. Delle finestre dove si ritrae le figure

Sia la finestra delle stanze de' pittori fatta d'impan-
nate, sanza tramezzi ed occupata di grado in grado
inverso li suoi termini di gradi di scurito di neri,

79. On the Windows of Rooms in Which Figures Are Drawn

The window of the painter's rooms should be
made of linen, without crossbars, and gradually
covered toward its edges with increasing values of

in modo che 'l termine del lume non [83] sia congionto col termine della finestra.

black, in such a way that the edge of the light does
not [83] coincide with the edge of the window.

CARTA 39

cu 58–58v, lu 170, mcm 175; rig 282]
80. *De reflessione*

Quel colore che sarà più vicino al reflesso più
tingerà di sè esso reflesso, e così de converso.

Adunque tu, pittore, fa di operare nei riflessi
delle effigi delle figure il colore delle parte de' vestimenti che sono presso alle parti della carne che li
son più vicine, ma non separare con troppa loro
pronunciazione, se non bisogna.[84]

80. *On Reflection*

That color which is closest to the area illuminated
by reflected light will tint it most, and vice versa.

Therefore, painter, see that in the faces of your
figures such areas be worked in with the color of
the garments which are closest to the flesh, but do
not separate sharply the color of the flesh from
that reflected from the garments, if there is no
need for it.[84]

cu 113v–114, lu 318, mcm 336; rig 78]
81. *Del bilico delle figure*

Se la figura posa sopra un de' suoi
piedi, la spalla di quello lato che posa
fia sempre più bassa che l'altra e la
fontanella della gola sarà sopra il
mezzo della gamba che posa. E 'l medesimo accaderà per qualunche linea
noi vederemo essa figura, essendo senza braccia
sportanti non [85] molto fuori della figura, o senza
peso addosso, o in mano, o in spalla, o sporta-
mento, della gamba che non posa, inanzi o indietro.[86]

81. *On Balance of Figures*

If a figure balances on one foot, the
shoulder on the side on which its
weight rests will always be lower than
the other, and the hollow of the throat
will be above the middle of the leg
on which the weight rests. The same
thing will happen along whatever line we view that
figure, provided it is without arms extending very
far beyond the figure,[85] or without a weight on its
back, in the hand, or on the shoulder, or extension forward or backward of the leg on which the
weight does not rest.[86]

---

83. Codex: ". . . ch' el termine de lumi
neri. . . ." Ludwig's interpretation is accepted.
In Leonardo's handwriting, especially that of his
late period, the word "non" can be easily read
as "neri":

non; neri.

84. In *Libro A* 76 Leonardo had already advised the painter to avoid direct light in portraits
so that "reflected rays will not spoil the shadows."
Cf. Venturi (1919), p. 60. Leonardo attaches
great importance to reflected light because it
gives relief to objects, but he is also careful about
it because it carries colors that can "spoil" the
actual color of the shadows. It is again his sense
of *grazia* that prevents him from accepting spots
of reflected color in the shadows; although he
does not deny them, he recommends smooth
transition in blending them with the actual color
of the shadow. This approach is demonstrated by
Leonardo's treatment of the head of the Virgin

in his "Virgin and Child with St. Anne" (*ca.*
1508–1510): the garment of the Virgin's left leg
sends the reflection of its greenish color to the
Virgin's throat, which is a shaded part above it.
This greenish hue, which is perceptible in good
reproductions, blends harmoniously with the redness and yellowness reflected in the same part
from the garment on the Virgin's right shoulder
and arm. Cf. Goldscheider (1959), pls. 68–69.

85. Ludwig suggests: ". . . essendo senza braccia sportanti molto fuori . . . ," omitting the
word "non" that is in the codex.

86. Cf. Accolti, p. 147: ". . . et se poserà, la
spalla di quel lato che posa sarà parimente più
bassa che l'altra, et la fontanella della gola piom-
berà sopra il mezzo del collo del piede che posa:
il che accaderà per qualunque veduta rimireremo
essa figura, se da esterno non sarà traviata e re-
mossa."

Favaro (1926–1927), pp. 241–242, notices that

CU 137V, LU 432, MCM 496; RIG 347]

82. *Perchè misurando un viso
e poi dipingendolo in tale grandezza egli
si dimostrerà maggiore che 'l naturale* [87]

82. *Why, when Measuring a Face and
then Painting It Life Size,
It Will Appear Larger than Nature* [87]

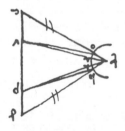

A B è la larghezza del viso ed è posta nella distanza della carta C F dove son le guance; ed essa arebbe a stare indietro tutto A C, ed allora le tempie sarebbono portate nella distanza O R delle linee A F e B F, sì che c'è la differenza C O e R D. Sì che si conclude che la linea C F e la linea D F, per essere più corte ad andare a trovare la carta dov'è disegnata l'altezza tutta che le linee A F e B F dov'è la verità, e' si fa la differenza, com'è detto, di C O e di R D.

A B is the breadth of the face which is represented on the paper C D facing the cheeks. C F is the distance of this paper from the eye of the observer. The breadth A B must be back of C D by the distance A C, and then the temples A B would be transferred to O R in the paper C D by the lines A F and B F, so that there would be the differences C O and R D. Therefore one concludes that the lines F C and F D, being shorter in reaching the paper C D than the lines F A and F B in reaching the actual breadth of the face A B, produce the differences C O and R D. [Thus C D painted according to the dimension A B appears larger than O R painted according to perspective.]

---

in the second sketch the vertical line is slightly inclined toward the right, so that the shoulders appear to be almost on a horizontal line. However, Favaro uses the reproduction from the Roman edition of the *Trattato della Pittura* (1890), p. 112, in which the entire figure is inclined toward the right. This reproduction is taken from the first edition of the *Codex Urbinas* (Rome, 1817), Pl. III, fig. 13, in which the right shoulder of the standing man is slightly emphasized, while the vertical line is correct. In Melzi's sketch the right shoulder is represented slightly lowered. Ludwig 318 has a badly redrawn figure in which the right shoulder is exaggeratedly lowered. Ludwig gives a completely wrong interpretation of the other figure. Cf. Pedretti (1957*b*), p. 158, for a similar example of a figure altered by copyists—the figure in Lu 173 copied from MS Ashburnham 27v. In the original manuscript it represents a seated man, but after two transcriptions of the note it became a running man!

87. This problem of perspective is related to Leonardo's experiment of *ca.* 1508 to prove that artificial perspective does not reproduce objects as they are seen according to optics. See MS D 2r (*ca.* 1508): "The rectilinear course of the visual rays bends in entering the eye, and that is why the eye judges the size of an object as being larger than that which is shown by artificial perspective (*prospectiva de pictori*). The cause of

this is that the image *a b* comes into the eye through *o p*, whereas the perspectivist who believes that visual rays come straight into the eye cuts these rays in *r t*; therefore the image reproduced by means of perspective is somewhat smaller than that seen by the eye." Leonardo had already set this problem as early as 1492. Cf. MS A 64v: "Why the eye sees distant objects larger than they result from artificial perspective." But only around 1508 did he resume it and explain it in MS D and *Libro A*. See also Codex Arundel 220v (Richter [1883], I, 84), *ca.* 1508: "Pictorial perspective can never make an object at the same distance look of the same size as it appears to the eye." Richter's translation is incorrect in the last paragraph: what Leonardo calls "filo de pictorj" is not the "painter's plumb-line" but the actual threads used by painters to join the extremities of an object to a point representing the eye. In terms of artificial perspective these "threads" represent what Leonardo also calls "linee essentiali," that is, the lines F A and F B in the *Libro* A diagram, as opposed to the "visual lines" of optics, which enter the eye through the extremities of the

[*Author's tracing*]

CU 140V, LU 439, MCM 436]

83. *Pittura e sua definizione*

La pittura è composizione di luce e di tenebre insieme mista con le diverse qualità di tutti i colori semplici e composti.

83. *Painting and Its Definition*

Painting is a composition of light and shade, combined with all the various kinds of simple and compound colors.

CARTA 40

CU 125V, LU 378, MCM 393; RIG 138]

84. *Dell'età delle figure*

Non mischiare una quantità di fanciulli con altrettanti vecchi, nè giovani con infanti, nè donne con uomini, se già il caso che vuoi figurare non li legassi insieme mischi.

84. *On the Age of Figures*

Do not mix a group of boys with the same number of old men, nor young men with infants, nor women with men, unless the subject which you wish to represent requires you to mix them.

CU 130–130V, LU 402, MCM 363; RIG 100]

85. *Che gli è impossibile che alcuna memoria riservi tutti gli aspetti e mutazioni delle membra* [88]

85. *That It Is Impossible to Memorize All the Aspects and Changes of the Parts of the Body* [88]

Impossibil è ch'alcuna memoria possa riservare tutti gli aspetti o mutazione d'alcuno membro di qualunque animale si sia. Questo caso esemplificheremo con la dimostrazione d'una mano. E perchè ogni quantità continua è divisibile in infinito, il moto

It is impossible for anyone to memorize all the aspects or changes of each member of any animal whatsoever. This we shall demonstrate by analyzing the movement of a hand. Because every continuous quantity is infinitely divisible, the motion of

---

pupil, so that they have to bend in order to converge at the point of vision. In the *Libro A* diagram the line C D represents the "pariete" mentioned in Codex Arundel 220r, the lines F C and F D being the "visual lines." The diagram in MS D 2r explains the nature of these "visual lines" according to Leonardo's theory of optics.

For further observations on Leonardo's discussions on the optical effect of relief in painting see in this volume, pp. 138–139. See also page 164 for the comparison of this chapter with notes in MSS Ashburnham 19r and D 3r.

88. Cf. Panofsky (1940), pp. 127–128. See also *Libro A* 39. In Codex Atlanticus 45 v-a, *ca.* 1509–1510, Leonardo writes a memorandum on the movement of the hand (Richter, I, 353): "The principal movements of the hand are ten; that is forward, backward, to right and to left, in a circular motion, up or down, to close and to open, and to spread the fingers or to press them together." The folio containing this note is chrono-

logically related to *Libro A* also because of the notes it contains on reflected colors and on the flight of birds. It is in this folio that Leonardo mentions beginning his book "De ludo geometrico," the book on the geometrical process of transformations *ad infinitum*. The note on the circular movement of the hand is developed in Windsor 19,013 (*Fogli A dell'Anatomia*), *ca.* 1510: "The circular motion of the hand, showing first the four principal ones A D [Flexing], D A [Opening], B C [Adduction], and C B [Abduction], and in addition to these four principal movements, one should mention the subordinate motions which are infinite." (The interpretation of the movements is given by O'Malley and Saunders

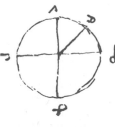

[*Author's tracing*]

dell'occhio che riguarda la mano e si muove da A a B, si muove per uno spazio, A B, il quale è ancora lui quantità continua e per consequente divisibile in infinito; ed in ogni parte di moto varia l'aspetto e figura della mano nel suo vedere, e così farà movendosi in tutto 'l cerchio. Ed il simile farà la mano che s'inalza nel suo moto, cioè passerà per ispazio ch'è quantità continua.[89]

the eye which looks at the hand as it moves from A to B moves through the space A B which is also a continuous quantity and consequently infinitely divisible, and in each part of its motion changes the aspect and shape of the hand as it is seen, and thus it moves through the whole circle. The hand which rises in its motion does likewise; that is, it will pass through space, which is a continuous quantity.[89]

[1952], p. 42.) See also Windsor 19,009v (*Fogli A dell'Anatomia* 10v), *ca.* 1510: "After these movements, designate the compound movements, which I call compound because they partake of two of the above movements, and these are infinite for they are produced in the whole of space, a continuous quantity, interposed between the said four principal movements."

Panofsky (1954), pp. 26–28, pointed out that Galileo reduces all human movements to a system of circles and epicycles, in a way that is exactly the same as that suggested by Leonardo in his *Trattato della Pittura* (i.e., in the notes from *Libro* A), and which is systematically elaborated in the Codex Huygens. The hypothesis that Galileo was acquainted with Leonardo's theory is not to be excluded. Despite the fact that Leonardo's *Trattato* was not published until 1651, Galileo could have seen a manuscript copy of it. (Cf. Galileo, *Opere*, VII, 60: ". . . altri posseggono tutti i precetti del Vinci e non saprebbero poi dipingere uno sgabello.") Moreover, Pietro Accolti published in 1625 a treatise on perspective containing a section on Drawing which is nothing but a compilation from the abridged version of Leonardo's *Trattato*.

According to Panofsky, it is only in Leonardo's writings that the theory of human movement is based on the idea of continuity or, what amounts to the same thing, *infinity*. Aristotle's concept of "continuous quantity" must have been well known to Renaissance theorists. Ghiberti, for example, refers to it in a passage of his *Commentari* (III, 11), taken from Roger Bacon's *Opus Majus*, II, 455: "Every object can be divided *ad infinitum* because according to Philosophy, and as Aristotle has proven in the 6th Book of his *De Physica*, what results from the division of a quantity does not represent an indivisible quantity." Leonardo's concept of "infinity" applied to human motion seems to be echoed by Castiglione's famous statement about Leonardo's philosophical "chimeras." Almost a century after Leonardo, Federico Zuccaro in his *Idea de' Pittori, Scultori, e Architetti*

(Turin, 1607) specifically referred to Leonardo's theory of infinity applied to human movement. Zuccaro alludes to some original Leonardo writings now lost, probably those on which the compilation of the Codex Huygens was based: "Equally fruitless and lacking in substance was the other work which was left of drawings together with writings in mirror script, by another man of our profession but too cunning, using merely mathematical precept for the motion and twisting of the human figure, by means of perpendicular lines, square and compass; certainly ingenious things but fantastic, without profit and substance. . . . I say that these mathematical rules should be left to such sciences and speculative disciplines as geometry, astronomy, arithmetic, and the like, which, by giving proof, satisfy the mind. But we teachers of drawing do not need such rules, but only those which Nature herself gives us in order to imitate her." Zuccaro must presumably have seen a lost book on human motion written by Leonardo himself. If he had known the Codex Huygens he would not have referred to "writings in mirror script." We can exclude the possibility that he was referring to Leonardo's *Trattato*. In his reply to Zuccaro's statement, Lodovico Antonio David, referring to the *Trattato*, affirms: ". . . [cose] mai sognate da Lionardo ne in esso libro, ne altrove." Cf Bassoli (1954), p. 300.

As the present book went to press I found the evidence that a selection of nine folios of the Codex Huygens was published in London in 1720 by Edward Cooper, along with an English translation of the Italian text. (This publication is so rare that it is known only through eighteenth-century descriptions.) I hope to publish this evidence soon.

Leonardo's interest in the problem of the "two infinites" is fully discussed by Duhem (1903–1913), Vol. II, pp. 3 ff.; see also the recent contributions by Michel (1952), pp. 31–42, and by Hooykaas (1952), pp. 163–169.

89. The last word is added, following Ludwig's suggestion.

CU 137v–138v, LU 433, MCM 469; RIG 247]

86. *Se la superfice d'ogni corpo opaco partecipa del colore del suo obbietto*

Tu hai da intendere, se sarà messo un obbietto bianco infra due pareti delle quali l'una sia bianca e l'altra nera, che tu troverai tal proporzione infra la parte ombrosa e la parte luminosa del detto obbietto, qual fia [90] quella delle predette pareti; e se l'obbietto sarà di colore azzurro, farè il simile. Onde, avendo da dipingere, farai come seguita: togli il nero per ombrare l'obbietto azzurro che sia simile al nero ovvero ombra della parete che tu fingi ch'abbia a riverberare nel tuo obbietto, e così fara' volendolo fare con certa e vera scienza, userai fare in questo modo. Quando tu fai le tue pareti di quel colore si voglia, piglia un piccolo cucchiaro,[91] poco maggiore che quello da orecchie e maggiore o minore secondo le grandi o piccole opere in che tale operazione s'ha a esercitare; e questo cucchiaro abbia li suoi estremi labbri d'equale altezza, e con questo misurerai li gradi delle quantità de' colori che tu adopri nelle tue mistioni; come sarebbe quando nelle dette pareti che tu avessi fatto la prima ombra di tre gradi d'oscurità e d'un grado di chiarezza, cioè tre cucchiari rasi, come si fa le misure del grano, e questi tre cucchiari fussino di semplice nero ed un cucchiaro di biacca, tu aresti fatta una composizione di qualità certa senza alcun dubbio. Ora tu hai fatto una parete bianca ed una oscura e hai a mettere uno obbietto azzurro infra loro, il quale obbietto tu vogli ch'abbi le vere ombre e lumi che a tale azzurro si conviene. Adunque poni da una parte quello azzurro che tu vuoi che resti sanz'ombra, e poni da canto il nero. Poi togli tre cucchiari di nero e componlo con un cucchiaro d'azzurro luminoso, e metti con esso la più oscura ombra. Fatto questo, vedi se l'obbietto è sperico o colunnale o quadrato, o come e' si sia. E s'egli è sperico,

86. *Whether the Surface of Every Opaque Body Takes on the Color of the Opposite Object*

You must understand that if a white object is placed between two walls, one of which is white and the other black, you will find that the proportion between the parts of the object in shadow and those in the light is similar to that of the walls,[90] and if the object is blue in color instead of white, the same is true. Therefore, when you are about to paint it, do the following: choose a black to darken the blue object, similar to the black or rather the shadow of the wall from which the reflections come to your object, for, if you would work according to certain and true science, you will work thus. When you paint walls choose whatever color you wish, and take a little spoon,[91] hardly larger than an ear-spoon, but larger or smaller according to whether the works to be painted are large or small, and this spoon's outer edges should be even, and with this, measure the amounts of the colors with which you will effect your combinations. If on the said walls which you have made, the first shadow should be three parts dark and one part light, that is three level spoonfuls—just as if you were measuring grain—of pure black and one spoonful of white, you would have made a mixture of definite value without any possibility of error. Now you have made one wall white and one dark and are going to place a blue object between the two and you wish this object to have the true shadows and lights that are appropriate to such a blue. Then put aside that blue which you wish to leave without shadow and place the black alongside it. Then take three spoonfuls of black and mix these with one spoonful of luminous blue to make the darkest shadow. Having done this, observe whether your object is spherical, cylindrical, square, or whatever it may

---

90. Codex: ". . . obbietto qual fu quella. . . ." Ludwig's correction is accepted. In Leonardo's handwriting of his late period the word "fia" could be easily read as "fu": ∿ꟼ = fia; ∿ꟼ = fu.

91. A figure of such a spoon for measuring colors appears in Lu 756 (McM 869) on folio 224 of the Codex Urbinas:

tira le linee dalli stremi della **parete oscura al** centro d'esso obbietto sperico, e dove esse linee si tagliano nella superfice di tal obbietto quivi infra tanto [92] terminano le maggiori ombre infra equali angoli. Di poi comincia a rischiarare, come sarebbe in N O [93] che lascia tanto de l'oscuro quanto esso partecipa della parete superiore A D; il qual colore mischierai colla prima ombra di A B con le medesime distinzioni.

be. If it is spherical, draw lines from the extremes of the dark wall [A B] to the center of the spherical object. The darkest shadow will be in the area [N] between the equal angles formed by the lines intersecting the surface of the object.[92] Then begin to lessen the intensity of the shadow as you move from N to O [93] because the object begins to partake of the color of the upper wall A D; this is a color which you will mix with the first shadow of A B, making the same gradations.

CARTA 41

CU 113V, LU 406, MCM 439; RIG 364]

87. *Del giudicare il pittore le sue opere e quelle d'altrui*

87. *On the Painter's Judgment of His Own Work and That of Others*

Quando l'opera sta pari col giudizio quello è tristo segno in tal giudizio; e quando l'opera supera il giudizio questo è pessimo, com'accade a chi si maraviglia d'avere sì bene operato; e quando il giudizio supera l'opera questo è perfetto segno, e s'egli è giovane in tal disposizione, senza dubbio questo fia eccellente operatore. Ma fia componitore di poche opere; ma fieno di qualità che fer-

When one's work is equal to one's judgment, that is a bad sign for one's judgment; and when one's work surpasses one's judgment, that is worse, as happens when a painter is amazed at having done so well; and when judgment exceeds the work, that is a very good omen and a young man so endowed will without doubt produce excellent work. He will compose few works, but they will be of a

92. Codex: ". . . quiui infra tante terminano. . . ." The meaning of "in frattanto" is accepted following Ludwig's suggestion.

93. Ludwig: ". . . come sarebbe in M O." In Ludwig's diagram the M is added.

These painstaking, almost tedious experiments with pigments are typical of Leonardo's late notes on light and shade. According to M. Rzepinska (1962*a*), p. 260, pedagogic suggestions become less and less frequent in Leonardo's writings after 1505: "His theoretical study, now very vast, distinctly overbears his practical interest. Some of the passages that occur from time to time in his notes are very much like an exercise meant to be tried out technically, like a laboratory experiment —artistically those paragraphs have not much meaning and we do not know whether Leonardo ever tested those experiments; however, they should be appreciated as one more proof of his effort toward a possibly more accurate means of grading the color values on geometrical figures, as an effort of an empirical and technical character. He suggests here [that is, in the present passage of *Libro* A] that when trying to fix shadow and

light one should successively administer definite quantities of white and black pigment, measured out with a little spoon. (Trat. 756, Trat. 433, both according to Pedretti from the years between 1508–10.) 'If you want to proceed in a truly scientific fashion' says Leonardo. It is amazing that he not even once refers to the keenness of his eye, or to his exceptional sensitiveness to differences of value, that he never relies on his artistic intuition. His artistic ambition tends exclusively toward attaining objective truth in presenting the essential condition of things. This is perhaps what in his theory of art strikes us as something quite alien to the contemporary mind." A study on "The Basic Notions and Elements of the Theory of Painting in the Writings of Leonardo da Vinci" has been developed by M. Rzepinska in an impending publication. She announces that "in my study I endeavored to follow the appearance of those elements in the *sequence of time*, and the changes in Leonardo's approach to those elements." She has already published a critical edition of the Codex Urbinas in Polish translation (*see* Bibliography: Rzepinska [1961]).

meranno gli uomini con admirazione a contemplar le sue perfezioni.

kind to make men stop and contemplate their perfection with admiration.

cu 263v–264, lu 912, mcm 967]

**88. De' paesi nelle nebbie,
o nel levare o nel porre del Sole**

**88. On Landscapes in the Mist
at Sunrise or at Sunset**

Dico de' paesi all'occhio tuo orientali.[94] Nel levare del Sole ovvero colle nebbie od altri vapori grossi interposti infra 'l Sole e l'occhio, dico che essi saranno molto più chiari inverso il Sole e manco splendidi nelle parti opposite,[95] cioè occidentali. Ma s'egli è senza nebbia o vapori, le parti orientali, ovvero quella parte che s'interpone infra 'l Sole e l'occhio, sarà tanto più oscura quant'ell'è all'occhio più vicina. E tale accidente accaderà in quella parte che fia più vicina al Sole, cioè che parrà più sotto il Sole; e nelle parti opposite farà il contrario a tempo chiaro. Ed a tempo nebuloso farà il contrario de' tempi belli.

Of landscapes to the east of your eye,[94] I say that at the rising of the sun, or indeed with mists, or other thick vapors lying between the sun and the eye, these will be much brighter toward the sun and less splendid on the opposite side,[95] that is, the western side. But if they are without mists or vapors, the eastern side, or rather that side which lies between the sun and the eye, will be darker in proportion as it is closer to the eye. This accidental condition will occur on that side which is nearest the sun, that is, which seems to be more directly under the sun; and on the opposite side in clear weather it will do the contrary. In misty weather it will do the contrary of what it does in fine weather.

CARTA 42

cu 58v, lu 171, mcm 162; rig 273]

89. De' colori de' riflessi

89. On the Color of Reflected Lights

Tutti i colori reflessi sono di manco luminosità che 'l lume retto, e tale proporzione ha il lume

All the colors of reflected lights are less brilliant than those of direct light. The brilliance of direct

---

94. Codex: ". . . all'occhio tuo orientale nel leuare del sole. . . ." Ludwig's correction is accepted.

95. Codex: ". . . mancho splendidi che nelle parti opposite. . . ." "Che" is omitted following Ludwig's suggestion. However, the possibility remains that the original passage was actually as it appears in Melzi's copy: "[i paesi] saranno molto più chiari inverso il sole e manco splendidi che nelle parti opposite, cioè occidentali." This would imply that when looking toward the rising sun one sees the elements of landscape, such as houses, trees, etc., through the brightness of mist, and therefore these elements appear less splendid (in color) than those on the opposite side. In Codex Atlanticus 176 r-b, a folio that is chronologically

related to the Foglio Resta in the Ambrosiana, *ca.* 1508–1510, Leonardo considers landscapes at the first hour of the day in the south, east and west: "The atmosphere in the south near to the horizon has a dim haze of rose flushed clouds; toward the west it grows darker, and toward the east the damp vapor of the horizon shows brighter than the actual horizon itself, and the white of the houses in the east is scarcely to be discerned, while in the south, the farthest distant they are, the more they assume a dark rose-flushed hue, and even more so in the west; and with the shadows it is the contrary, for these disappear before the white." Similar notes dating from the time of *Libro A* are gathered in MacCurdy's section on "Landscape," Vol. II, pp. 303–320.

incidente col lume reflesso quale è quella che hanno infra loro le luminosità delle loro cause.

light and of reflected light is in direct proportion to the luminosity of their sources.

CU 139–139V, LU 436, MCM 498; RIG 345]

90. *Per fare una figura che si dimostri essere alta braccia quaranta in ispazio di braccia venti ed abbia membra corrispondenti e stia diritta in piedi* [96]

90. *To Make a Figure Which Appears to Be Forty Braccia High in a Space of Twenty Braccia, with Corresponding Members, the Figure to Stand Erect on Its Feet* [96]

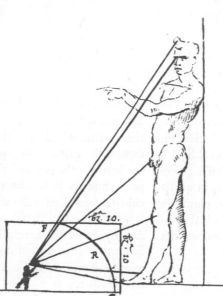

In questo caso ed in ogni altro caso non de' dar noia al pittore come si stia il muro ovver parete dov'esso dipinge, e massime avendo l'occhio riguardatore di tale pittura a vederla da una finestra o altro spiraculo; perchè l'occhio non ha ad attendere alla planizia o curvità d'esse pareti, ma solo alle cose che di là de tale parete s'hanno a dimostrare per diversi lochi della finta campagna.

In this and every other case, the painter should not be annoyed about the condition of the wall or surface on which he paints, most especially if the eye of the observer is to see it from a window or rather an opening, because the eye is not to attend to the evenness or curvature of that wall, but only to what is to be represented as beyond that wall such as the various places of an imagined countryside.

Ma meglio si farebbe tal figura nella curvità F R G perchè in essa non è angoli.

But this figure would be executed better on the curved surface F R G because it has no angles.

CU 193V, LU 657, MCM 683]

91. *Delle qualità de' lumi e ombre ne' corpi ombrosi*

91. *On the Qualities of Lights and Shadows on ⟨Opaque⟩ Bodies*

Dico che l'ombre sono di poca potenza nelle parti de' corpi che son volte inverso la causa del lume, e così sono l'ombre infra l'ombre volte alla causa d'esse ombre. Dimostrasi di gran potenza l'ombre e lumi che sono infra la causa de l'ombre e la causa del lume.[97]

I say that shadows have less strength on the sides of bodies [e.g., a sphere] which are turned toward the light source, and so also the shadows within shadows facing the cause of those shadows. Those shadows and lights are shown to be of great strength which are within the cause of the shadows and within the source of the light.[97]

96. A similar subject is treated in MS A 38v (Lu 437, McM 497). The note from *Libro A* is chronologically related to the note in Codex Arundel 62, *ca.* 1508: "Della prospettiva naturale mista colla prospettiva accidentale." Lomazzo (1584), pp. 335–336, states that Leonardo had made an anamorphic representation of a fight be-

tween a lion and a dragon, as well as a representation of horses for Francis I. Cf. Pedretti (1957*b*), pp. 68–76. See also Baltrušaitis (1955), pp. 18–21.

97. This chapter is apparently senseless. To say, in literal translation, that "shadows have little strength on the sides of bodies which are turned to the cause of the light" may seem ab-

CU 193V–194, LU 658, MCM 747]

| 92. *Delle dimostrazioni de'* | 92. *On the Appearance of* |
| *lumi e dell'ombre* | *Lights and Shadows* |

Quell'ombra si dimostrerà più oscura che sarà più vicina alla più luminosa parte del corpo, e così de converso, si dimostrerà meno oscura che sarà più vicina alle più oscure parti de' corpi.

That shadow will appear darkest which is nearest the lightest part of the body, and thus, conversely, that will look least dark which is nearest the darkest parts of bodies.

CARTA 43

CU 194, LU 659, MCM 748]

| 93. *De' lumi* | 93. *On Lights* |

Quel lume si dimostrerà più chiaro che s'accosterà più all'oscuro, e parrà men chiaro che fia più vicino alle parti più luminose del corpo.

The light will look brightest which is nearest to darkness, and the light will look least bright which is nearest the brightest parts of bodies.

CARTA 44

CU 51V, LU 140, MCM 278]

| 94. *Delle bellezze* | 94. *On Beauty* |

Le bellezze de' volti possono essere in diverse persone di pari bontà, ma non mai simili in figura, anzi fieno di tante varietà quant'è il numero a chi quelle sono congionte.[98]

Beauty of face may be equally fine in different persons, but it is never the same in form, and should be made as different as the number of those to whom such beauty belongs.[98]

---

surd, considering that the sides of a body which are turned to a light should not have shadow at all. But this is not so. Leonardo is certainly referring to a sphere as a body having "sides" that are not impinged upon directly by the light source. See for example the diagram in Codex Urbinas, folio 213 (from MS Ashburnham 2038, fol. 13v). These "sides" of a sphere are actually in shadow, and this shadow gradually diminishes in strength as it approaches the "side" facing the light.

The second part of the first sentence of this chapter is no less obscure (in literal translation): "and so also the shadows among shadows turned to the cause of these shadows." This can be interpreted as referring to those parts of a shadow ("shadow within a shadow") that appear less conspicuous when adjacent to a darker shadow, as explained in *Libro A* 92 and 93. (See also *Libro B* [MS E] 32r: "A shadow looks darkest against a light background.") "Infra" is translated by Mc-Mahon as "among," but it probably means "within." Such a meaning must also be attached to the word "infra" in the last sentence of the chapter; otherwise this sentence seems to refer to lights and shadows of great strength occurring "between" the light source and the opaque object.

This last sentence, however, might imply a concept that is clearly expressed in *Libro B* (MS E) 17r (Lu 472, McM 448): "Le cose vedute infra 'l lume e l'ombre si dimostreranno di maggiore rilievo che quelle che sono nel lume o nell'ombre" (Objects seen between light and shadow will appear in greater relief than those which are in the light or in the shadow).

The chapters on light and shade in *Libro A* are related to the notes in *Libro B* (MS E), fols. 31v and 32r (Richter [1883], I, 159, 161–162, 197–198). They show Leonardo's mind at work in developing an idea as if he were "thinking aloud." This may account for our difficulty in following the thread of his thoughts. Sometimes one statement contradicts another, as in *Libro B* (MS E) 31v. See note 73, p. 64 above.

Libro A 93 was first marked "L.° A. car. 42," and then the 2 was corrected to 3.

98. Codex: ". . . di tante uarieta quanto il numero a chi. . . ." Ludwig's interpretation is accepted. The meaning of the sentence is rendered better in the English translation. Cf. Alberti, iii, 107 (Spencer:93), and Alberti's *De re aedificatoria*, bk. vi, chap. ii. See also Venturi (1919), p. 86.

CU 51V, LU 141, MCM 279]

95. De' giudicatori di varie bellezze in vari corpi e di pari eccellenza

Ancora che in vari corpi sia varie bellezze e di grazia equali, li vari giudici di pari intelligenza le giudicheranno di gran varietà infra loro; e sarai [99] tra l'un l'altro delle loro elezioni.

95. On Judges of Various Beauties of Equal Excellence in Various Bodies

Although in different bodies the various types of beauty have equal attraction, different judges of like intelligence will show great variety among themselves in their judgments. And you, in your selection, will be somewhere in between.[99]

CARTA 47

CU 207V, LU 710, MCM 802]

96. Dell'ombre de' visi che passando per le strade molli non paiono compagne delle loro incarnazioni [100]

Quello che si dimanda accade che spesse volte un viso fia colorito o bianco e l'ombre gialleggiaranno. E questo accade chè le strade bagnate più gialleggiano che le asciutte e che le parti del viso che sono volte a tali strade sono tinte della giallezza ed oscurità delle strade che gli stanno per obbietto.

96. On Shadows on Faces Passing along Wet Streets Which Do Not Seem Compatible with Their Flesh Tones [100]

What you are asking about often happens when the face is high in color or white, and its shadows make it yellowish. This occurs because wet streets are more yellowish than are dry ones, and the parts of the face nearest those streets are tinted by the yellow tones and shadows of the streets which reflect on them.

CARTA 48

CU 115V, LU 327, MCM 404; RIG 156]

97. Delle attitudini delle figure

Dico che 'l pittore debbe notare l'attitudini e li moti delli uomini nati da qualunche accidente, immediate sieno notati o messi nella mente, e non aspettare che l'atto del piangere sia fatto fare a uno in prova sanza gran causa di pianto e poi ritrarlo, perchè tale atto, non nascendo dal vero caso, non sarà nè pronto nè naturale; ma e ben

97. On the Attitudes of Figures

I say that the painter should note the attitudes and the gestures of men which come from some particular emotion. Note them at once and fix them in your mind, and do not wait until the action of weeping has to be copied from one who poses as if weeping, but without great cause for grief, and then draw it, because such an action,

99. Codex: ". . . di gran uarietà infra loro esserui tra l'un, l'altro delle loro ellettioni." Ludwig suggests: ". . . tra l'un l'altro i membri delle loro ellettioni." It is possible that in Leonardo's original manuscript Melzi read "esserui" for what was actually "essarai":

$$\mathit{1A \tau \tau i}\,]\!]\!\cdot = \text{esserui}; \quad \mathit{1A \tau A}\,]\!]\!\cdot = \text{essarai}.$$

In this case the last sentence would be an exhortation to objectivity in selecting a model of beauty ("e sarai tra l'un l'altro delle loro ellettioni"). The same concept is found in Lu 114–115 (McM 90, 250). These chapters are stylisti-

cally close to the contents of Libro A and may therefore be dated in a late period. See also Lu 159 (McM 163).

100. The number 46 after the mark L° A has been corrected and changed to 47. Cf. Alberti, i, 64, a passage that Zoubov (1960), p. 8, compares to Leonardo's note in MS Ashburnham 20 (Lu 785; McM 786), ca. 1492. Alberti says: "Ma basti qui che questi razzi flessi seco portano quel colore, quale essi truovano alla superfitie. Vedilo che chi passeggia su pe' prati al sole, pare nel viso verzoso" (Spencer:51). See also Libro A 24 and the Introduction, p. 19.

buono averlo in prima notato dal caso naturale e poi far stare uno in quell'atto per vedere alcuna parte al proposito e poi ritrarlo.[101]

having no real cause, will be neither lifelike nor natural. But it is very good to have noted it first as it occurs naturally, and then pose somebody in that act, in order to see any necessary detail and draw it.[101]

CU 194, LU 660, MCM 604]

98. De' lumi e ombre

Ombra è diminuzione o privazione di luce. L'ombra sarà di maggiore quantità sopra il suo corpo ombroso che da minor quantità di luce sarà alluminato.[102]

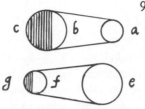

[See note 102 below]

Da quanta maggior somma di luce il corpo sarà alluminato, tanto minor fia la quantità dell'ombra che sopra esso corpo rimane: A è il corpo luminoso, B C è il corpo ombroso, B è la parte del corpo che s'allumina, C è quella parte rimanente privata di luce, ed in questa è maggior l'ombroso che 'l luminoso. E [103] è il corpo luminoso maggior che l'ombroso a sè opposito; F G [103] è il corpo ombroso ed F è la parte alluminata e G è la parte ombrata.

98. On Lights and Shadows

Shadow is the diminution or absence of light. That shadow will be largest on an ⟨opaque⟩ object, which is illuminated by the smallest light.[102]

It follows that the greater the quantity of light by which the body is illuminated, the less is the quantity of shadow which remains on that body. A is the luminous body, B C is the ⟨opaque⟩ body, B is the side of the body which is illuminated, C is that which remains without light, and the shaded area is greater than the luminous. E [103] is the luminous body greater than the ⟨opaque⟩ object opposite it, F G [103] is the ⟨opaque⟩ body, F is the illuminated side, and G is the shaded side.

CARTA 49

CU 58v, LU 172, MCM 173; RIG 219]

99. De' termini de' riflessi
nel suo campo

Il termine de' reflessi, nel campo più chiaro d'esso reflesso, fia causa che tale reflesso [104] terminerà in

99. On the Edges of Reflected Lights
against Their Background

The edges of reflected light, which are the brightest portions of such a light,[104] will cause the re-

101. This passage is paraphrased by Accolti, p. 148.

102. The first paragraph has the note: "segue Lº .A. 48."
The diagram is missing but it has been restored from the description. It was presumably similar to those of chapters 638 and 639 on Codex Urbinas 190v.

103. Codex: "F, è il corpo . . ." and "f, è, il corpo ombroso. . . ." Ludwig's corrections are accepted.

104. Ludwig: ". . . fia causa che tale reflesso mostri poca euidenza." McMahon accepts this interpretation. Although Ludwig's interpretation is acceptable, one cannot exclude the possibility that Leonardo's sentence was actually as it appears in Melzi's copy. In this case the meaning

could be restored by appropriate punctuation. The word "campo" would indicate first the edges of the reflected light, and then the background of such a light, that is, the surface on which the reflected light falls. Leonardo would have considered the reflected light as a spot of light brighter at its edges than in its central portion. He describes a similar phenomenon in considering a spot of color transmitted into a camera obscura. Cf. Codex Atlanticus 190 r-b, ca. 1508 (MacCurdy:II.325): "The boundaries of the images of any colour which penetrate through a narrow hole into a dark place will be always of a more powerful colour than its centre"; also Codex Atlanticus 195v, ca. 1508 (MacCurdy:II.325): "And the colours are more sharply defined at their edges than in any other part."

campo più oscuro di lui; allora esso reflesso sarà sensibile, e tanto più si farà evidente quanto tal campo fia più oscuro, e così di converso.

flection to end against a darker background. The reflected light will be perceptible, making itself all the more apparent, the darker the background is, and vice versa.

CARTA 50

cu 61–61v, lu 187, mcm 271; Rig 139]

100. *Del variar valetudine, età, complessione di corpi nelle istorie* [105]

⟨Dico anco che nelle istorie si debbe mischiare insieme vicinamente i retti contrari, perchè danno gran paragone l'uno all'altro e tanto più quanto saranno più propinqui, cioè⟩ il brutto vicino al bello, il grande al piccolo, il vecchio al giovane, il forte al debole, ⟨e così si varia quanto si può e più da vicino.⟩

100. *On Varying the Vigor, Age, and Complexion of Figures in Narrative Paintings* [105]

I say also that in narrative paintings one ought to mingle direct contraries so that they may afford a great contrast to one another, and all the more when they are in close proximity; that is, the ugly next to the beautiful, the big to the small, the old to the young, the strong to the weak; in this way you will vary as much and as close together as possible.

cu 107v, lu 284, mcm 288]

101. *Delle membrificazioni delli animali* [106]

Sia fatto le membra alli animali convenienti alle loro qualità.

Dico che tu non ritraghi una gamba d'un gentile, o braccio, o altre membra e l'appichi ad un grosso di petto o di collo, e che tu non mischi membra di giovani con quelle di vecchi, e non membra prosperose e muscolose con le gentili e fievoli, e non quelle de' maschi con quelle delle femine.

101. *On Composition of Limbs of Creatures* [106]

Let the parts of living creatures be in accordance with their type.

I say that you should not make the leg of a delicate figure, or the arm, or other limb, and attach it to a figure with a thick chest or neck. And do not mix the limbs of the young with those of the old, nor limbs that are vigorous and muscular with those that are delicate and fine, nor those of males with those of females.

cu 138v, lu 434, mcm 352; Rig 73]

102. *De' moto e corso degli animali*

Quella figura si dimostrerà di maggiore corso la quale stia più per rovinare innanzi.[107]

102. *On the Movement and Running of Animals*

That figure will appear swiftest in its course, which is about to fall forward.[107]

105. This chapter is related to *Libro A* 41. Leonardo's drawings representing a stern warrior juxtaposed with a handsome youth may be considered as examples of "retti contrari." Cf. Gombrich (1954), pp. 205–206.

106. Cf. Leonardo's crossed-out notes in Codex Atlanticus 345 v-b (plate 25 of this volume)—a folio of *ca.* 1508–1510 containing studies for the canalization of the Adda River: "Painting. All the limbs of every kind of animal should correspond with its age, that is, the young should not show their veins or nerves as most [painters] do in order

to show their dexterity in art, spoiling the whole by mistakes in the limbs"; "Painting. All the parts of an animal should correspond with the whole, that is, when a man is short and thickset you must see that each of his limbs is short and thickset. Let the movements of men be such as are in keeping with their dignity or meannes" (MacCurdy:II. 279). See also Alberti, ii, 90 (Spencer:74). Cf. Zoubov (1960), pp. 5–6. Similar crossed-out notes occur on Windsor 19,121r (plate 26).

107. This passage is paraphrased by Accolti, p. 148.

CARTA 51

CU 115, LU 323, MCM 330; RIG 64]

103. Del bilicare il peso intorno al centro della gravità de' corpi

La figura che senza moto sopra li suoi piedi si sostiene, darà di sè equali pesi opposti intorno al centro del suo sostentaculo.

Dico che se la figura senza moto [108] sarà posata sopra li suoi piedi, che se gitta un braccio innanzi al suo petto, che gitti tanto peso naturale indietro, quanto egli ne gitta del naturale e accidentale innanzi. E quel medesimo dico di ciascuna parte che sporta fuori del suo tutto oltra 'l solito.

CU 115, LU 324, MCM 341; RIG 65]

104. Delle figure che hanno a maneggiare o portare pesi [109]

Mai si leverà o porterà peso dall'uomo che non mandi di sè più d'altrettanto peso che quello che vuol levare e lo sporti in opposita parte a quella dove esso leva il detto peso.

CU 138v–139, LU 435, MCM 353; RIG 73]

105. De' corpi che per sè si muovono o veloci o tardi [110]

Il corpo che per sè si move, sarà tanto più veloce quanto il centro della sua gravità è più distante dal centro del suo sostentaculo. Questo è detto pel moto delli uccelli, li quali sanza battimento d'alie o favore di vento per sè medesimi si movono,

103. On Balancing the Weight about the Center of Gravity in Bodies

The figure which sustains itself motionless on its feet will automatically place equal weight on opposite sides about its center of gravity.

I say that if the motionless figure [108] is poised on its feet, and his arm is extended in front of the chest, he will throw backward as much natural weight as the natural and accidental weight which he thrusts forward. And I say the same of each part that projects more than usual beyond the whole.

104. On Figures That Have to Handle or Carry Weights [109]

Never will a weight be lifted and carried by a man without his extending outside himself more than as much weight as that which he wishes to lift, and he thrusts it on the side opposite the one where he lifts the weight.

105. On Bodies Which Move by Themselves, Either Quickly or Slowly [110]

A body which moves by itself will be faster, the more its center of gravity is distant from the center of its support. This is said with regard to the motion of birds, which, without beating their wings or without favor of the wind, move by

108. Codex: "Dico che se la figura, e' sanza moto. . . ." Ludwig's correction is accepted. The mark *Lº A* is repeated before the second paragraph.

109. This passage, as well as the preceding one, is paraphrased by Accolti, p. 147.

110. For Jean Baptiste Villalpand's paraphrase of this chapter see note 37 to page 22 above.

In the original manuscript this chapter was probably illustrated with a diagram of a bird showing the position of the centers of gravity and resistance. If so, the missing diagram may be restored by using the one accompanying a note in the *Codex on the Flight of Birds* (*ca.* 1505), fol.

16 (15)v: "When the bird drops down its center of gravity is outside the center of its resistance, as if the center of gravity were on the line *a b* and the center of resistance on the line *c d*." *See* Giacomelli (1936), pp. 227–228; MacCurdy:I.438.

This passage on the flight of birds in *Libro A* suggests the year 1505 as a *terminus a quo* for the dating of the lost notebook. See also MS L 56r (1502), MS K 11v (*ca.* 1505), Codex Atlanticus 220 v-c (1505–1508), MS F 41v, and Codex Arundel 277, all quoted by Giacomelli (1936), pp. 248 ff. See also the notes on the flight of birds in Codex Atlanticus 214 r-d; this folio, which contains the note used as a motto at the beginning

e questo accade quando il centro della sua gravità [a, b] è fori del centro del suo sostentaculo, cioè fori del mezzo della resistenza delle sue ali [c, d]. Perchè s'esso mezzo delle ali fia più indietro che 'l mezzo ovver centro della gravità di tutto l'uccello, allora esso uccello si moverà innanzi ed in basso, ma tanto più o meno innanzi che in basso, quanto il centro della detta gravità fia più remoto o propinquo al mezzo delle sue ali; cioè che 'l centro della gravità remoto dal mezzo de l'ali fa il discenso dell'uccello molto obliquo, e s'esso centro sarà vicino al mezzo delle ali il discenso di tale uccello sarà di poca obliquità.

Codex on the Flight of Birds, 16 [15]v

themselves, and this happens when their center of gravity [a b] is outside the center of their support, that is, outside the middle of the resistance of their wings [c d]. If the middle of the wings [c d] is behind the middle or center of gravity of the whole bird [a b], then that bird will move forward and down; but it will move forward rather than down depending on how far the center of gravity [a b] is from the center of the wings [c d], that is to say, if the center of gravity is far from the center of the wings the descent of the bird will be very oblique, whereas if the center of gravity is close to the center of the wings the descent of the bird will be less oblique.

CARTA 54

LEICESTER 28v]

106.

Nasce il vento da umidità vaporata.[111] In 54 in A.

106.

The wind is created by vaporized humidity.[111] In 54, A.

---

of the present book, can be dated *ca.* 1508, because on its verso is the well-known draft of a letter concerning Leonardo's litigation with his brothers. Cf. Brizio (1952), p. 642, and Mac-Curdy:II.538. At that time Leonardo was compiling the Codex Leicester and the first part of the Codex Arundel.

111. Cf. Codex Atlanticus 279 r-b, *ca.* 1515: "The movements of the air originate from the changes in humidity in the atmosphere." In his studies on the wind Leonardo discussed scholastic opinions such as the ones contained in the works of Alberto Magno, Alberto of Saxony, and in the medieval translations of Aristotle's *De Physica.* Cf. Codex Atlanticus 169 v-a (Brizio [1952], p. 575)—a passage taken from Alberto Magno's *Metheorum libri*—and folio 97 v-a: "See Aristotle *De Cielo e Mundo.*" See also the note in folio 279 r-b, *ca.* 1515, from which Lu 928 is developed: "Again we shall say: wind moves along a straight line, and not in a circle as Aristotle maintains . . ."; and folio 200 v-a, *ca.* 1515: "wind does not move along a straight line; on the contrary, it always moves in a circle. . . ." One of Leonardo's greatest talents was undoubtedly his ability to combine scholastic knowledge and visual

experience. The writings in Windsor 12,671 r-v and 12,672 are a discussion on Alberto Magno's theory on steam and wind. About 1505 Leonardo increased his observations on this subject. Thus, in Codex Leicester 28 he notes: "And lately over Milan toward Lake Maggiore I saw a cloud in the form of an immense mountain . . ." (Brizio [1952], p. 581); in Codex Leicester 30: "And once I saw the wind dig out the ground . . ." (Brizio [1952], p. 579); in MS F 37v: "I have seen such furious movements of the air . . ." (Brizio [1952], p. 578); in Codex Arundel 129v: "I have seen sand carried away by wind . . ." (Brizio [1952], p. 576). In Codex Atlanticus 79 r-c (plate 11), *ca.* 1515—the folio containing notes and sketches related to the Windsor drawings of the "Deluge"—Melzi wrote several notes from Leonardo's dictation. In one of them Leonardo suggests a device for observing the movement of the wind in the air: "In order to see the swirling movements of the wind within the air, have a tube made out of a reed and put cotton well compressed at one end of it; and from the other end blow smoke through it. The smoke, coming out of the tube, will show how wind whirls in the air." See also below, pp. 156–157.

CARTA 61

107.

L'acqua che risalta da l'una al-
l'altra riva, seguirebbe infine il
moto da essa riva se non fussi
chiamata in loco di maggiore
bassezza. La qual bassezza fu
causata quando il fiume era nella
sua inondazione; la quale inon-

[*Author's tracing*]

dazione superava il colle della ghiara da lei con-
dotta; dopo la qual superazione fece concavità nel
fine d'esso colle, dove, poichè 'l colle rimarrà
scoperto dall'acqua, e' resterà la predetta concavità che attrarrà a sè l'acqua di qualunche parte
essa si troverà più alta di lei; come: se l'acqua si
movessi di A N e corressi e empissi tutto il fondo
A C N M, l'acqua che nel fondo percosse l'obbietto A perse impeto, e fece il colle A B tutto di
giara gittata fori della corrente A D B M; e l'acqua
che lì la condusse, quando li mancò l'impeto,
lì la lasciò, e attese poi a discenderne, ripigliando
nuovo impeto, col quale cavò il fondo C dove,
poichè il fiume s'abbassò, l'acqua quivi di tutto il
fiume discese, come loco più basso.

[Figura] N D M B A C
61, in A.

107.

Water which bounces from one
bank to the other would finally
follow the flow along the latter
bank if it were not drawn to a
deeper place in the river. This
deep place was caused when the
river was in flood, because the
current kept flowing over the heap of gravel
brought down by it, and after passing over it,
would make a concavity at the far end of the heap.
When the inundation was over, the heap emerged
from the water, and this concavity at its foot at-
tracted water from wherever it was at a higher
level. So that, if the water moved from A N and
rushed and filled the whole bottom A C N M, the
water which on the bottom struck object A lost
impetus and made the heap A B, which was
formed by gravel carried by the current A D B M;
and when the water which brought it there, since
it lacked impetus, had dropped it there, it paused
before descending, taking new impetus and carrying out the bottom C. Now that the river has
receded, the water from the whole river comes
down there because it is the lowest spot.

[Figure] N D M B A C.
61, in A.

Beginning with carta 54, the present reconstruction of *Libro A* includes notes on water and
atmosphere from the Codex Leicester, as well as
two notes on painting from the Codex Urbinas.
The latter, which were on carte 64 and 65, can
be considered as pertaining to anatomy rather
than painting. They are in fact on bone structure
and on the foot, and are both related to notes in
the *Fogli A dell'Anatomia* at Windsor, dating
from 1510. (The notes on the human figure and
its movement on carte 48, 50, and 51 are also related to programs outlined in the *Fogli* A.) Thus
the overlapping of the two sections of *Libro A*
(painting and hydraulics) can be considered as
only apparent. Carte 54 to 96 in the original manuscript would include almost three signatures of
sixteen folios each—such being the number of
folios in each signature of *Libro B* (MS E). Three

signatures make up 48 folios, exactly half the total number of folios in the manuscript. The considerable amount of gaps in the second section of
our reconstruction of *Libro A* indicates that the
original manuscript contained more material other
than painting and hydraulics. *Libro B* gives us an
idea of the missing contents of *Libro A*: mechanics, geometry, optics, perspective, flight of birds,
and personalia. *Libro A* was structurally similar
to the early MS A, which is also composed of two
sections (painting and hydraulics), and contains
notes on optics, perspective, geometry, and mechanics as well. But the impression we get from
the present reconstruction of *Libro A*, especially
in this last section from carta 54 on, is definitely
that of a notebook of the same type as MSS E, F,
and G, which are all alike both in format and in
contents.

CARTA 64

CU 104V–105, LU 271, MCM 296; RIG 30]

108. *Delle figure del corpo umano e piegamenti di membra*

Necessità costringe il pittore ad avere notizia de li ossi sostenitori e armatura de la carne che sopra essi si posa, e delle gionture che acrescano e diminuiscano ne li loro piegamenti; per la qual cosa la misura del braccio disteso non confà con la misura del braccio piegato.

Cresce il braccio e diminuisce infra la varietà de l'ultima sua astensione e piegamento la ottava parte della sua lunghezza.[112]

L'accrescimento e raccortamento del braccio viene dall'osso che avanza fuora [113] de la giontura del braccio, il quale, come vedi nella figura A B, fa lungo tratto della spalla al gomito, essendo l'angolo d'esso gomito minore [114] che retto, e tanto più cresce quanto tal angolo diminuisce, e tanto più diminuisce quanto el predetto angolo si fa maggiore.

Tanto più cresce lo spazio della spalla al gomito, quanto l'angolo della piegatura d'esso gomito si fa minore che retto, e tanto più diminuisce quant'esso è maggior che retto.

108. *On Measurements of the Human Body and Flexing of the Limbs*

Necessity requires the painter to take note of the sustaining bones which serve as an armature for the flesh that rests on them, and of the joints that increase or diminish as they bend, on which account the measurement of the extended arm is not the same as that of C, the arm which is bent.

The arm increases and diminishes by one-eighth of its total length between its farthest extension and its bending.[112]

The lengthening and shortening of the arm comes about through the bone which extends beyond [113] the elbow joint, which, as can be seen in the figure, A B, increases the length from the shoulder to the elbow when the angle of the elbow is less than a right angle,[114] and increases the more as that angle diminishes, and diminishes as that angle becomes greater.

The length from the shoulder to the elbow increases as the angle of the bend of the elbow becomes less than a right angle, and decreases as that angle becomes greater than a right angle.

112. This passage is paraphrased by Accolti, p. 146. Cf. Windsor 19,004 (*Fogli A dell'Anatomia* 5r) and Windsor 12,614. See also *Libro A 10* and note 10. As Panofsky pointed out (1955; p. 98, n. 87), Alberti had already observed that the breadth and thickness of the arm change according to its movements; but he had not as yet attempted to measure the extent of these changes. Cf. Alberti's *De Statua*, p. 203: "Brachii latitudines et crassitudines motibus inconstantes sunt." Accolti, p. 146, follows Leonardo's text almost literally.

It is possible that in the original manuscript the three figures were not one above the other, but next to one other. In *Fogli A dell'Anatomia* 5r

similar figures are in fact next to one other. Moreover, the copyist had actually begun to draw the second figure with black chalk on the left of the first one (this is visible in our plate 7), and then he changed his mind and went over the chalk trace with the text of the chapter. See below, p. 140, for the style and chronology of Leonardo's drawings of bones.

113. Codex: ". . . del braccio dell'osso che auanza fuora. . . ." Ludwig's interpretation is accepted.

114. Codex: ". . . e' tanto piu cresse quant'esso e' maggior che retto." Ludwig's interpretation is accepted. The mark *L*o A is repeated before the third paragraph.

CARTA 65

CU 107V, LU 283, MCM 317; RIG 109]

109. *Del piede* [115]

Che 'l piede che riceve il peso de l'uomo sia schiacciato e non con dita scherzanti, se già non posassi sopra il calcagno.

109. *On the Foot* [115]

A foot that receives the weight of a man's body should lie flat, without movement of the toes, unless the weight rests on the heel.

CARTA 74

LEICESTER 15]

110.

[Figura] Mugnone. Arno.[116]
Ma se 'l fiume minore versa nell'acque ringorgate del maggiore,[A.74] allora il fiume minore manderà le sue acque a diritta linea inverso il mezzo del fiume maggiore.

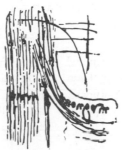

[*Author's tracing*]

110.

[Figure] Mugnone. Arno.[116]
But if the smaller river pours into the dammed-up waters of the larger,[A.74] then the smaller river will send its water along a straight line toward the center of the larger river.

---

115. The mark *L° A* is placed at the beginning of folio 107v, but the chapter begins on folio 107: "De membri. Tutti li membri essercittino quel ufitio al quale furono destinati. Ne morti e dormienti nessun membro aparisca uiuo, o' desto" (Of parts of the body. All parts of the body should exercise that function for which they were destined. In the dead or the sleeping no part should appear alive or awake). This note was probably copied from another manuscript. Cf. Alberti, ii, 89 (Spencer:73); Accolti, p. 148.

The note on the foot from *Libro A* can be compared to that in the first folio of *Libro B* (MS E) (folio dated September 24, 1513, the day Leonardo left Milan for Rome), which has not been translated in previous Leonardo studies: "The foot that receives weight is always flatter and more spread out than that which does not receive weight; and this expansion and flatness occurs in the flesh that intervenes between the bones of the foot and the ground on which that foot rests." Cf. Favaro (1926–1927), p. 242.

116. The names of the rivers, "Mugnone" and "Arno," are written within the figure. Cf. Codex Arundel 29v: "[With drawing] Solid rock of Mugnone hollowed out by the water in the form of vessels. It seems a work done with the hand, be-

cause it is so exact" (MacCurdy:I.387). See also Codex Leicester 18v, and Windsor 12,677 and 12,678.

The reference "A. 74" is written on the left margin of the folio in correspondence with the word "maggiore," that is, at the end of the first sentence, and not in correspondence with the word "maggiore" at the end of the second sentence. It might be that Leonardo intended to write the reference at the end of the passage, as he always does, and that he had mistaken the first "maggiore" for the second. But since the passage begins with a "ma" (but), it might be that he intended the reference "A. 74" also for the preceding passage, which ends on the line indicated as copied from *Libro A*. The preceding passage is translated by Richter (1883), II, 972: "When the smaller river pours its waters into the larger one, which runs across the current at the mouth of the smaller river, its waters will bend with the downward movement of the larger river." In the second passage, which comes from *Libro A*, Leonardo explains how a smaller river entering a larger one maintains its current along a straight line, providing that the waters of the larger river be "*ringorgate*," that is, dammed-up so as to reduce their current to a minimum. For the meaning of the

LEICESTER 16]

111.

Sempre, dinnanzi all'ostaculo, l'acqua si tarda e la rena del fondo s'inonda. 74 in A.

LEICESTER 16]

112.

Un piccol palo, fitto nel fondo della corrente, farà concavare il fiume per lungo spazio dalla predetta corrente. In A a 74.

111.

Water always slows down before an obstacle, and the sand in the bottom becomes wavy. 74 in A.

112.

A little pole fixed at the bottom of a stream will cause a current to hollow out the riverbed for a considerable distance. In A, 74.

CARTA 75

LEICESTER 16]

113.

Quando l'onde reflesse dalle rive si scontran nel mezzo della corrente, esse partoriranno un terzo moto reflesso, il quale risalta in alto e, nel ricadere, cade in moto participante della lunghezza e latitudine del fiume. In A a 75.

LEICESTER 16]

114.

Ma quando i moti reflessi che risaltano dalle rive si varian, come nel continuo accade, cioè da maggiore o minore potenza, allora il terzo suo moto reflesso che si fa nel mezzo del fiume caderà ora a destra e ora a sinistra, cioè sempre inverso l'antecedente reflessione più debole. In A 75.

113.

When the waves reflected from the banks meet in the middle of the stream, they produce a third reflected motion, which rises high and, in falling back, falls into a motion consonant with the length and width of the river. In A, 75.

114.

But when, as continually happens, the reflected motions from the banks vary, that is, when one of the motions has greater or lesser strength, then the third reflected motion, which is made in the middle of the river, will at times fall to the right and at others to the left, namely, always toward the weaker preceding reflection. In A, 75.

CARTA 85

LEICESTER 13]

115.

Sempre dove il moto reflesso che indirieto si rivolta si scontra nella corrente, quivi sarà poca profondità d'acqua, perchè in tal sito si crea il colle della rena, tagliente nel suo culmine, del

115.

Where the reflected current meets its own waves in the stream, the water will always be shallow, because in such a spot a sharp-crested heap of sand is created, the slopes of which are affected

---

word *ringorgato* or *ringorgazione* cf. Codex Leicester 15v ("come si faranno i sostegni navigabili che ringorgan l'acque d'essi canali") and 17v ("e l'acque di tali ruine [i.e., mountain slides] ringorgate fanno i gran pelaghi"). A diagram of a system

of *ringorgame nti* in a river is in Codex Leicester 6r. See also Leonardo's instructions for the canalization of the Saudre river at Romorantin, Codex Atlanticus 336 r-b, *ca.* 1517, and 217 v-c, also *ca.* 1517 ("ringorgazione dei mulini").

quale le spiagge son confregate da due moti contrari. In 85 in A.[117]

by the friction of two contrary motions. In 85, A.[117]

CARTA 86

LEICESTER 13]

116.

Quando la circonvolubile onda reflessa dall'obbietto ove percote inverso il fondo del fiume e che, nel processo della sua revoluzione, si scontra nell'onda incidente, che di sopra le passa, parte di lei seguita la già principiata revoluzione e parte se ne gitta in opposita revoluzione e percote la spiaggia, onde discende la rena dell'antiposto colle. Come se l'acqua che percote l'obbietto venissi per la linea B A e percotessi nell'obbietto A: dico che subito si rigirerà inverso il fondo D c, quel percosso, si rigirerà in alto con moto circulare e percoterà nella corrente che sopra le passa in C, onde, in tal percussione, si dividerà sì com'ella fece nello obbietto A, e parte ne rigirerà inverso la corrente F E, e così seguirà suo moto. 86 in A.

[Figura] H A C B G F E D.
[Figura] Obbietto.

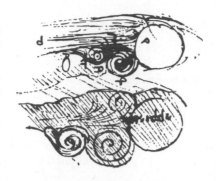

[Author's tracing]

116.

When a circumvoluted wave, by hitting an object, is deflected toward the bottom of the river and in revolving encounters the incidental wave which is passing above it, part of the wave will continue in the revolution already begun and part will be thrown by it into a contrary revolution and strike bottom, and sand will come down from the slope in front of it. As if the water, which strikes the object, came along the line B A and struck object A: I say that immediately it will whirl toward the bottom D, and having hit that, will whirl upward with a circular motion, and will strike the current, which passes above, in C; so that, with such an impact, it will divide itself as it had done before in its impact against the object A—part of it whirling along with the current F E, and its motion thus will continue. 86 in A.

[Figure] H A C B G F E D.
[Figure] Object.

LEICESTER 14]

117.

La pioggia che discende dal nugolo non discende integralmente intera, ma vapora in gran parte e s'infonde coll'aria per la confregazione che essa ha con lei.[118] 86 in A.

117.

The rain, which descends from a cloud, does not descend in its entirety, but vaporizes in large quantity and diffuses in the air because of friction with the air.[118] 86 in A.

---

117. Underlined in the original.
On top of the folio Leonardo writes: "Vedi de navi di messer Battista. . . ." This is a reference to Leon Battista Alberti's lost treatise *De Navis*, which is mentioned by Alberti himself in his *De Re Aedificatoria*, Book V, chap. xii. Leonardo refers to Alberti's *De Navis* in MS F 82r and in MS G 54r, and he might have used it also when he was writing the notes on water in *Libro A*. More-

over, there are passages in Alberti's *De Re Aedificatoria* which are echoed by notes in this section of *Libro A*. See for example the long passage in Book X, chap. x, which ends: "These whirls and eddies in a river seem to have somewhat of the nature and force of a screw, which no strength or solidity can long resist."
118. Cf. Windsor 12,661, *ca.* 1508: "Quando più l'acqua discende infra l'aria tanto più si dis-

LEICESTER 14]
118.

Quando l'acqua reflessa si scontra, nel fondo del fiume, coll'onda incidente, ciascuna di lor torna indietro lasciando una rilevata cresta nel sito della lor percussione. 86 in A.

118.

When the reflected and incidental waters meet at the bottom of the river, each of them turns backward, leaving a raised crest on the site of their impact. 86 in A.

CARTA 87

LEICESTER 14]
119.

E se l'acqua caderà nel pelago dallo stremo d'un de' sua lati, tutta l'acqua tornerà indietro, a uso di retroso, e si sommergerà sotto il fine del moto incidente, e lascerà il fondo di men profondità infra la congiunzione della corsia col retroso. 87 in A.

119.

And if water falls into a pool from the edge of one of the sides, all the water will turn back, like a whirlpool, and be submerged beneath the end of the incoming stream; and the bottom will be, less deep at the point where the stream meets the whirlpool. 87 in A.

LEICESTER 14]
120.

Quando la corrente che porta materia giugnie nel pelago morto essa manca di suo corso, onde scarica la materia portata vicino all'entrata d'esso pelago. 87 in A.

120.

When a current which carries foreign matter reaches a stagnant pool it loses strength, so that it unloads the material at the entrance of that pool. 87 in A.

LEICESTER 16]
121.

Quando due correnti insieme si scontrano e che l'una, avanti esso scontro, abbia percosso nell'argine del fiume, la profondità fatta nel detto scontro sarà sotto il lato che non percosse la riva. In A 87.

121.

When two currents encounter one another, and one, before that meeting, has struck the bank of the river, the hole produced in the bottom by that meeting will be beneath the side where the bank was not struck. In A, 87.

---

grega e diminuisce." Cf. Clark (1935), *sub numero*. See also MS F 35r, 1508 (MacCurdy:II.46–47): "Book 42nd. On Rain. The water that falls from the cloud is sometimes dissolved into such minute particles that by reason of the friction that it has with the air it cannot divide the air but seems to change itself into air . . ."; Codex Atlanticus 75 v-a, *ca.* 1508 (MacCurdy:I.394): "And this is the reason why after it has penetrated the whole of the cloud in every stage of descent its pace will become slower, and there will be many occasions when these particles will not arrive at the ground"; Codex Atlanticus 292 r-a, *ca.* 1505–1508 (MacCurdy:I.405): "But unless the drops are so formed as to be of considerable size they are consumed by the friction they make with the air as they traverse it." See also *Libro A 129*. In Codex Atlanticus 75 v-a Leonardo meditates further on the nature of the drops of rain: "Why if two spherical liquids unequal in quantity come to the beginning of contact with each other does the greater draw to itself the lesser and incorporate it immediately without destroying the perfection of its own roundness? . . . I do not perceive that the human intellect has any means to acquiring perception of this except by saying as one says of the action of the magnet when it draws the iron, that such virtue is a hidden property of which there are in nature an infinite number." (Cf. Leonardo's famous *dictum* in MS I 18r, quoted below, p. 168.)

CARTA 88

LEICESTER 16]

122.

L'isole de' fiumi aran sopra di loro le più grave cose di verso l'avvenimento dell'acque che nel contrario sito. In A 88.

122.

The islands [formed] in rivers will have the heaviest things at the end that faces the incoming waters rather than at the opposite end. In A, 88.

LEICESTER 16]

123.

Ma se l'isola che si scopre infra 'l fiume scolerà le sue acque in pelaghi morti, allora la rena e terra da esse acque portate si fermeranno i' ne' predetti pelaghi e riempiranno le lor profondità. In A 88.

123.

But if the island, which emerges from the river, drains its waters into stagnant pools, the sand and earth carried by such water will stop in these pools and will fill them up. In A, 88.

CARTA 89

LEICESTER 16]

124.

Quando i tomoli [119] delle acque son fatti nelle rive de' fiumi con equal potenza, e' sarà segno che in tal parte il fiume è diritto, e la sua massima profondità fia nel mezzo della larghezza sua, cioè sotto la principal corrente delle sue acque. In A 89.

124.

When water breaks [119] with equal force on either bank of a river, it is evidence that the river is straight, and that its maximum depth is in the middle of its width, namely, under the main current of its water. In A, 89.

LEICESTER 16]

125.

La massima profondità de' fiumi fia sotto la corrente fatta alli moti reflessi. In A 89.

125.

The greatest depth of rivers is under the current produced by reflected motions. In A, 89.

LEICESTER 16]

126.

Le correnti de' fiumi minori che entran ne' maggiori son causa di rompere l'argini opposite d'essi maggior fiumi. In A 89.

126.

The current of smaller rivers which enter larger ones is the cause of breaking the opposite banks of the larger rivers. In A, 89.

LEICESTER 21]

127.

Le strette e veloce acque tolgan tutta la materia che le larghe e pigre acque alla lor congiunzione conducano. 89 in libro A.

127.

The narrow and rapid waters carry away all the material which the wide and slow waters bring to their joining. 89 in Libro A.

119. "Tomolo," leap of water. Cf. Codex Leicester 26v (Brizio [1952], p. 519, n. 1). See also in Codex Atlanticus 74 r-a the heading of one

of the projected notes on hydraulics: "Del tomolo de' liti marittimi"; as well as Codex Atlanticus 330 r-b: "tomolo del lito."

LEICESTER 21]

128.

Dove l'ostaculo s'interpone al corso dell'acque infra la superfice e 'l fondo, il quale non sia di molta latitudine, dopo tale obbietto il fiume farà la sua corrente sopra la maggiore sua profondità; e questo accade perchè l'acqua che cade di tale ostaculo cava il fondo ove percuote, e l'acqua laterale che cigne tale obbietto viene a correre in tal bassezze, e s'accompagnano insieme e cavano il fondo, nella lunghezza del lor concorso, in figura navale. In A 89.

128.

If an obstacle is placed between the surface and the bottom of a not very wide stream, after passing such an object the river creates a current above its deepest part; and this occurs because the water which falls from that obstacle digs out the bottom where it strikes, and the lateral currents of water which surround the object rush to that depth; and they join each other and excavate the bottom, along the length of their concurrence, in a shiplike form. In A, 89.

CARTA 92

LEICESTER 19]

129.

La veloce confregazione o percussione dell'acqua coll'aria, quando piove, fa vaporare e consumare gran parte dell'acqua piovana; e questo si prova perchè si vede el vento che si confrega colle cose umide che subito l'asciuga col consumare tale umidità; e perchè tanto è a mover l'acqua contro all'aria ferma, quanto l'aria ovver vento contro all'acqua ferma; ancora, se vapori colle labbra strette un peso noto [120] d'acqua infra l'aria, e la lasci cadere sopra un lenzuolo [121] del quale il peso ti sia noto, tu troverai, al conto del peso del lenzuolo esser discesa poca acqua sopra di lui, e 'l rimanente è vaporato in aria. 92 in A.

129.

The swift friction or impact of the water with the air, when it rains, makes a great part of the rainwater vaporize and be consumed; and this is proved, because one sees the wind, which hits against wet things, that immediately dries them by consuming that humidity; and because it takes as much to move water against still air, as air or wind against still water; yet, if you blow out with tight lips a known weight [120] of water into the air, and you allow it to fall above a sheet,[121] the weight of which is known to you, you will find, when you weigh the sheet, that little water has descended upon it, and the rest has evaporated into air. 92 in A.

LEICESTER 21]

130.

[Figura] A B C D F E N
M.[122]
Vento in A 92.

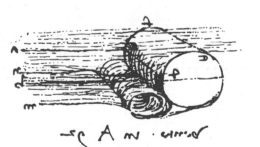

[Author's tracing]

130.

[Figure] A B C D E F N
M.[122]
Wind in A 92.

---

120. Calvi transcribes "peso nato."

121. Leonardo used a piece of cloth also to weigh two different samples of water; cf. MS G 37v (MacCurdy:II.155). See also the early note in Codex Atlanticus 80 r-b: "Del saggiare le qualità dell'acque per peso, con due panni bagnati." Leonardo could have learned this experiment from Vitruvius, De Architectura, VII, i, or Piero Crescentio, Della Agricoltura, I, iv.

122. Leonardo omitted the note that accom-

CARTA 95

131.

L'acqua che spira pel picolo spiraculo del vaso ov'ella bolle, soffia con furia e tutta si converte in vento; con questa si volta l'arrosto.[123] In A a 95.

131.

The water, which spurts out through the little opening of the vessel in which it is boiling, blows with fury, and is all converted into wind; with this, one may turn the roast.[123] In A, 95.

---

panied this figure. The diagram, which illustrates a stream of wind against a cylindrical object, can be referred to the note in *Libro A* 116. A note in MS G 69r can be used as a further explanation of this figure: "Reflex course of wind and water. The reflex wind as it turns back upon its course sub-

[*Author's tracing*]

dues the oncoming wind until this reflex wind becomes enfeebled, and then it regains its force when it becomes joined with the falling movement; and such power springs from its condensation acquired at the place of the percussions, which condensation always penetrates into the falling wind up to the point at which it becomes separated and its speed of movement becomes less. The water does the same; not however by condensation but because it rises in the air and acquires weight" (MacCurdy:I.409). See also MS E 52v: "A current of air that impinges on an object always rebounds with a swirling movement." The invisible lines of force of the wind current are illustrated in the diagram from *Libro A* in the same way as the currents of the water in Leonardo's drawing in MS E 23v. Cf. Heydenreich (1954), p. 153 and fig. 235.

123. One of the headings in the list of notes on hydraulics in Codex Atlanticus 74 v-b (*ca.* 1505) refers to the subject of this note: "Water converts itself into wind, as one can see when boiling water spurts out through a small opening in a vase." Leonardo knew of the moving force of steam. Another heading in that list alludes to the so-called "architronito" of Archimedes: "Del trarre bombarde con acqua nelle bombarde di ferro infuocato." As Calvi (1909), p. 204, pointed out, folio 28r of the Codex Leicester is related to Codex Atlanticus 169 r-a, v-a, which contains Leonardo's discussions on the *Metheorum libri* of Alberto Magno (see n. 111 above). One of the notes on the verso of this folio of the Codex Atlanticus reads: "Cold attracts humidity and heat releases it. Take the example of a water container that has an air-tight closure: when you heat it the water evaporates, increasing in volume, and if the container has a small opening you will see the steam spurt through it as an impetuous current of air." See Reti (1956–1957), p. 21. Filarete (pp. 309–310) describes a similar device for blowing air into a fireplace.

In his discussion on the origin of the wind, in Windsor 12,671v, *ca.* 1512, Leonardo refers again to the experiment of steam escaping through the vent of a vessel in which water is boiling, but this time he does so with words that are almost the same as those of this last chapter of *Libro A*: ". . . nell'acqua bollente dentro alli vasi oue è rinchiusa che per li picholj spirachulj di tal uaso esse con furia in forma di vento" (. . . boiling water which is shut into vessels escapes through little vents of such a vessel with great force in the manner of wind). Compare the similar reference to vessels in Vitruvius' discussion of the origin of the wind in his *De Architectura*, I, vi, 2.

PART TWO

A CHRONOLOGY OF LEONARDO'S
Trattato della Pittura

In the citations to the "Treatise on Painting" the first number refers to the chapter-number of the Ludwig edition and the second (between parentheses) to the chapter-number of the McMahon edition.

Example:
202 (195) = Ludwig 202 (McMahon 195)

In the references to *Libro* A the italic numbers denote the chapter and the roman numbers the carta.

A *Chronology of Leonardo's* Trattato della Pittura

THE CODEX URBINAS 1270

The notes on painting in the Codex Urbinas 1270 were copied directly from Leonardo's original manuscripts when those manuscripts were still complete as their author had bequeathed them to his pupil, Francesco Melzi (*ca.* 1491–1570). Since Melzi owned all Leonardo's manuscripts it has been assumed that it was he who planned the compilation of the *Trattato della Pittura*. This codex was undoubtedly written during Melzi's lifetime. Leonardo, during his lifetime (d. 1519), may have worked out the outline of a book on painting as it was later carried out by Melzi, perhaps while he was Melzi's guest in the villa at Vaprio d'Adda, about 1513.[1] Leonardo's intention of collecting his own notes on painting would have led him to expand the material with new observations on plants and atmosphere, and to resume and develop his notes on light, shade, anatomy, and human movement which he had written during his Sforza period, from about 1487 to 1499. Even in his French period, 1517–1519, Leonardo continued to add to his notes on painting. Antonio De Beatis' report of 1517 gives us a hint on Leonardo's occupations in the Castle of Cloux in France: "He [Leonardo] has given good instructions to a Milanese pupil [Francesco Melzi] who works very well. And although the aforesaid Lunardo cannot color with the same sweetness as he used to, he is still able to make drawings and to teach others."[2] These instructions given to Melzi might also have included directions for compiling the "Treatise on Painting" and for the preparatory work of marking the notes on painting in Leonardo's manuscripts with little circles to be slashed through after transcription.[3]

The Codex Urbinas 1270 is a small folio volume, 20.4 × 15 cm. It contains 331 numbered folios including blanks (more precisely, 335 folios, as 4 folios are designated 242a, 242b, 242c, and 242d [*see* Appendix II]).

The history of the Codex Urbinas from the time it left Melzi's hands to enter the library of the Duke della Rovere is still unknown. Possibly Melzi had sent it to some influential person in the hope of finding a publisher. He was certainly aware of the fact, referred to by Vasari in 1568, that an anonymous Milanese

---

1. Cf. Windsor 19,077v, dated 9 January 1513: "chamera della torre da vaueri." Pedretti (1962c), pp. 66–76.
2. Pastor (1905), p. 143.
3. Cf. Carusi (1919), pp. 438–439; Marinoni (1954), p. 235.

painter had gone to Rome to arrange for publication of a book on painting by Leonardo, apparently an original manuscript.[4] It is possible that on learning this, Melzi hastened to publish the complete "Treatise on Painting" he had prepared.

Ludwig surmises that Melzi's codex might have come to Urbino along with the library of Pietro Bembo (1470–1547), who had been secretary to Leo X. This would mean that the codex was ready before Bembo's death in 1547. However, reliable records concerning this codex do not appear before 1640, when the manuscript was listed in the last catalogue of the Library at Urbino. Enrico Carusi,[5] in pointing this out, assumes that the manuscript was discovered at that time (1640), because in that catalogue it was given no number other than that of the crate in which it was placed when the new library of Castel Durante (which was formed by the last duke, Francesco Maria della Rovere [1548–1631]) was moved to the old library at Urbino. The two ducal libraries preserved their codices in two different ways—the old library at Urbino on shelves, and the new one at Castel Durante in twelve crates together with prints and drawings. Thus the Codex Urbinas belonged to the new library. The librarian who took care of the transportation of the codices from Urbino to the Vatican in 1657 specified the previous location of each codex: again the Codex Urbinas was listed with the number it had in the old crate according to the catalogue of 1640. It was not until later, probably in 1797, that it was practically rediscovered and catalogued in the Vatican Library with the number 1270. In 1808 the librarian of the Vatican Library, Abate Gaetano Luigi Marini, informed Giuseppe Bossi of his find.[6] In 1809 Bossi obtained in Milan a complete transcription of the Codex Urbinas, and in 1810 announced in his book on the *Cenacolo* that he planned to publish a complete new edition of Leonardo's "Treatise on Painting."[7] He would undoubtedly have prepared a critical edition of it, employing the same method of bibliographical research as that used in his book on the "Last Supper."

On March 26, 1809, in a letter to Bossi, Abate Marini wondered whether the word MELTIUS [*sic*] at the end of the second part of the Codex Urbinas could refer to Francesco Melzi.[8] He asked Bossi whether the eighteen books listed at the end of that codex could have been the ones Galeazzo Arconati had given to the Ambrosian Library. He also suggested that Bossi check to see whether the twelve manuscripts in the Ambrosian Library "had the marks by which they are there [i.e., in the list at the end of the Codex Urbinas] distinguished." Unfortunately, at that time the Leonardo manuscripts were no longer in the Ambrosian Library.

Basic for our knowledge of the Codex Urbinas is a study by Max Jordan pub-

---

4. See p. 24 above.
5. Carusi (1919), p. 430, n. 4. Carusi found this information in folio 5ov of the Codex 146 of the Biblioteca Nazionale in Rome (fondo Gesuitico), and in the Codex Vaticanus Latinus 9475, folio 31. These codices are respectively the last catalogue of the Library of the Duke of Urbino, 1640, and the cards that were written when the codices Urbinati were transferred to the Vatican Library, 1657.
6. Cf. Galbiati (1920), pp. 19 ff.   7. Bossi (1810), p. 52.
8. Cf. Galbiati (1920), p. 21.

lished in 1873 shortly before Ludwig's edition of the "Treatise on Painting."[9]
Jordan was the first to notice that the Codex Urbinas contains references to a lost
notebook, *Libro A.* In 1919 and 1921 Carusi and Pierantoni started research on
the several abridged versions of the "Treatise on Painting." They made the first
concordances between the Cordex Urbinas and the extant Leonardo manuscripts
(*see* Bibliography). The Codex Urbinas did not receive further substantial attention until 1956, when Anna Maria Brizio used another method of research.[10] Her
rigorous textual analysis revealed the first transcriber's system of compilation of
Leonardo's notes on painting and gave a clue to the chronology of those chapters
whose originals are lost.

Brizio assumes that the chapters in the Codex Urbinas are arranged in an approximately chronological order, because the compiler first used the notes edited
by Leonardo himself—that is, the notes of *ca.* 1490–1492—and then proceeded to as-
semble notes scattered in manuscripts written after 1500. Our list of concordance
confirms such an assumption. At the beginning the Codex Urbinas contains writings copied mainly from the early MS A (*ca.* 1492), whereas the chapters on
plants, clouds, and horizon at the end of the codex were copied from manuscripts
of a later date (*ca.* 1510 and after). Furthermore, after each section of the Codex
Urbinas the compiler left a certain number of blank folios to be filled with additional material. In the later sections of the codex these blank folios increase in
number. This can only mean that the compiler expected to find more material for
them. He knew that he could not find immediately all the notes on painting contained in Leonardo's late manuscripts, which deal mainly with other subjects. Thus
it seems reasonably certain that the chapters in the last parts of the Codex Urbinas
were copied from Leonardo's manuscripts of his late period.

THE HANDWRITING OF FRANCESCO MELZI

In 1925 Gerolamo Calvi dedicated several pages of his book on the chronology
of Leonardo's manuscripts to the study of notes written by a right-handed person
on folios of Leonardo's manuscripts datable from after 1505.[11] Some of these notes
are even found on folios of Leonardo's French period, 1517–1519.[12] They reveal
a person well acquainted with Leonardo's scientific studies, suggesting a pupil or
assistant who occasionally writes under dictation. In fact, his notes are often completed or corrected by Leonardo himself.[13] Calvi suggested identifying this handwriting as Melzi's after comparing it with Melzi's autograph notes on the Ambrosiana drawing dated 1510 (plate 13). This hypothesis is acceptable considering

---

9. See Bibliography.   10. See Bibliography.
11. Calvi (1925), pp. 254–262.
12. See for example Codex Arundel, fols. 270–263; Pedretti (1962c), fig. 82. See
also Codex Atlanticus 336 v-b; Calvi (1925), fig. 56.
13. Codex Atlanticus 79 r-c (plate 11, this volume): in the ninth line of the Melzi
note Leonardo enters the word "vnjta"; Codex Atlanticus 315 r-b (Pedretti, [1962c],
fig. 60): a note by Melzi is completed by Leonardo.

that this type of handwriting appears in notes written during Leonardo's French period. From Leonardo's will and other documents we learn that only two pupils accompanied Leonardo to France—Melzi and Salai.[14] We have no reason to believe that Salai ever took any interest in Leonardo's scientific studies. Therefore Melzi is the only one who can be identified as Leonardo's assistant.

Calvi did not include the Codex Urbinas in his analysis of Melzi's handwriting. Obviously, he left it out on purpose because of lack of evidence about Melzi's share in the compilation of this codex. We still have no information about Melzi's activities after Leonardo's death. From Vasari's and Lomazzo's reports we judge him to have been an aristocrat who painted for his own enjoyment, but no report is preserved of what he intended to do with the manuscripts Leonardo had bequeathed to him. Vasari says that he treasured them as "reliquie," and Lomazzo on one occasion states that he was allowed to read them thanks to Melzi's courtesy.[15] There is no real evidence, therefore, that Melzi had planned and carried out the compilation of the *Trattato della Pittura*. Circumstantial evidence, however, strongly favors the hypothesis that he did so.

When did the first copies of Leonardo's writings originate? As early as 1542 such copies were already available. Cellini reports that in that year he had acquired in Paris from an impoverished nobleman at the court of Francis I a manuscript copied from one of Leonardo da Vinci's, namely, a book on "the three great arts, sculpture, painting, and architecture," including a "discourse on perspective." [16] Unfortunately, both the original and the copy are lost. In 1523 Melzi was back in Milan (he is reported as being in his villa at Vaprio and as having the Leonardo manuscripts in his possession [17]); therefore, if he was responsible for the Cellini copy he should have made it before 1523, because it is unlikely that a copy made in Italy went to France to be sold by an impoverished nobleman in 1542. Since the Cellini manuscript included architecture and perspective, we may assume that it was independent of the plan of the *Trattato della Pittura*.

What, then, was Melzi's role in the planning and compilation of the Codex Urbinas? Melzi's figure has always appeared to be somewhat in the background. The identification of three different hands in the Codex Urbinas has suggested that Melzi employed helpers. One of these hands has been tentatively identified as Melzi's. According to Ravaisson-Mollien [18] it is the hand that wrote marginal notes, that is, the hand identified by Ludwig as Manus 3. Ludwig and Heydenreich [19] believe that Melzi's hand is Manus 2, the one that made spelling corrections on the first 33 folios of the Codex Urbinas. Thus, Melzi's role in the compilation of the Codex Urbinas is usually thought of as being limited to that of a supervisor or editor, while the hand designated Manus 1, which copied all the passages from Leonardo's manuscripts, is attributed to a professional scribe.

14. Beltrami (1919), documents nos. 241 and 244.
15. *Ibid.*, pp. 176, 205–206; see also Goldscheider (1959), pp. 18–19.
16. See below, pp. 167 ff.   17. Beltrami (1919), document 251.
18. Ravaisson-Mollien (1888), pp. 13 ff.
19. Ludwig (1882), II, pp. 388 ff.; Heydenreich (1956), p. xii, n. 4.

One cannot deny that Melzi employed helpers, for the same reason that Leonardo employed him. Although we do not have direct information about Melzi's entourage, Lomazzo gives us a glimpse of it when he mentions Leonardo's invention of the "tornio ovale" as being communicated by a "pupil" of Melzi to "Dionigi fratello del Maggiore." [20] That Melzi had pupils, however, does not prove that he employed scribes, and from our own paleographic analysis of the Codex Urbinas we draw a distinctly different set of conclusions, as follows: *Manus 1, the compiler's hand, is Melzi's; Manus 2 is that of a proofreading editor to whom the manuscript was entrusted before prospective publication; and Manus 3 is that of a scholar called in as an advisor after the work of compilation was completed.* Manus 3 could be tentatively identified either as the anonymous author of a note at the bottom of the Windsor anatomical folio 19,102v (plate 19) (the note at the top of the folio is by Melzi), or as the anonymous author of the Codex Huygens. We shall now examine in detail the elements leading to these conclusions.

The compilation of the entire Codex Urbinas is the work of one person, Manus 1. According to Ludwig, this person was a professional scribe. But such a person, even if instructed beforehand, would have needed constant assistance. Melzi was undoubtedly capable in calligraphy and certainly well trained in reading Leonardo's handwriting even without a mirror. It seems entirely reasonable to think that if he took the trouble to locate all the notes on painting in Leonardo's manuscripts and devised the plan of copying them according to a Trattato scheme, he might as well have carried out personally the entire work of transcription.

At first sight it may appear impossible that Melzi's free and fluent hand in the notes on Leonardo's folios (*see* plate 11) could turn into the highly controlled hand shown by Manus 1. But even a scratchy hand such as that of the Codex Huygens is able to write in an impeccable humanistic script. As Panofsky points out, the author of the Codex Huygens occasionally starts writing with formal script, which turns gradually into a personal, casual handwriting.[21] In the Codex Urbinas we have a similar occurrence. Folio 28v has a chapter added after the completion of the codex proper (plate 10, *b*). This added chapter is followed by a comment that reveals Melzi's hand as it gradually abandons the calligraphic style of the preceding paragraph. Thus, we suggest that Melzi, in common with many other writers, used two styles of handwriting: one style free and personal, used for annotations; and the other style more professional and calligraphic, used for copying Leonardo's writings.

This second style of Melzi's hand is found not only in the calligraphic text of the Codex Urbinas but also in the Windsor drawing 12,416 (plate 12). In this drawing two notes dated 1511 were written by Leonardo in red chalk and copied by Melzi in pen and ink.[22] This is actually the only example we have of notes written by Melzi in handwriting so controlled that it closely resembles the pro-

---

20. Beltrami (1919), p. 206.
21. Codex Huygens, fol. 2r. Cf. Panofsky (1940), pp. 14–15.
22. Cf. Gould (1947), pp. 239–242.

fessional calligraphy of Manus 1 in the Codex Urbinas. Melzi's hand is usually more fluent, with large decorative letters such as the Q with a characteristic curve of the tail and the Z similar to that of italic characters.[23] The degree of fluency, however, varies frequently. For instance, although the note on the Ambrosiana drawing dated 1510 (plate 13) is close in style to that on the Windsor drawing 12,416, dated 1511, in the note dated 1510 a word, *releuo*, is crossed out and re-written above the line with a broader pen and different speed, thus conveying the impression of a different hand.

Manus 1 shows similar changes of rhythm or speed. Toward the end of the Codex Urbinas Manus 1 loses control and becomes more cursive, denoting the compiler's haste to finish the work. It is here that we may see more frequent instances of Melzi's more personal style of handwriting. The "Memoria et Notta" at the end of the Codex Urbinas listing the marks of Leonardo's notebooks (plates 2 and 3) is written in calligraphy, but Melzi's style emerges in certain details, as, for example, in the words *pezzi* and *quali*.

The comments incorporated in the body of the Codex Urbinas were written by Manus 1 (plate 14, *a–c*).[24] One of them refers to chapter McM 396 on folio 124 of the Codex Urbinas: "But note, reader, that although Messer Leonardo promises to treat all the emotions mentioned above, he does not speak of them, I believe, through forgetfulness or some other accident, as can be seen in the original, for after this chapter he writes the heading of another, without writing the chapter, and it is the following: On Representing an Angry Man and into How Many Parts that Emotion Is Divided." A professional copyist would surely not have bothered to comment upon certain characteristics of Leonardo's manuscripts. Melzi would have to stay always on hand to dictate him such comments, which were certainly meant to be printed along with the Leonardo text.

One characteristic of Manus 1 does not appear in Melzi's handwriting: The g does not have the sinuous looped appendage as in Melzi's but it has a straight appendage similar to that of the *q*. Melzi's handwriting in Leonardo's manuscripts and in the Ambrosiana drawing always has a fluent g. This difference, however, can be explained as a possible development of style. In his early period Melzi adopted a chancellery style, which was standard in letter-writing at the beginning of the sixteenth century; later, his style must have undergone some development, especially considering that his handwriting as we know it from notes on Leonardo's folios is that of a young man of about twenty years of age. Since his early handwriting is in a

---

23. Calvi (1925), p. 256.

24. A comment on folio 28 (plate 14, *a*) justifies an error in transcription "which occurred because of the handwriting, which is left-handed." Another comment on folio 85 (plate 14, *b*) justifies a similar error as being caused by the "two different manners and colors of ink." See also McM 471 on folio 149v: "Below this chapter there was a cleft in the mountain, an opening within which played a flaming fire, drawn by pen and shaded with watercolor, an admirable and vital thing to see." And McM 552 on folio 158: "In the middle of this chapter there was a foreshortened view of a city, on which rain fell, illuminated here and there by the sun; touched with watercolor, a very beautiful thing to see, also by the author's own hand."

style that was common in the first decade of the sixteenth century, it is probable
that his mature handwriting had become closer to a style that was common in the
middle of the century, such as, for example, that of the handwriting of the Codex
Huygens, which in its turn still retains certain characteristics of earlier handwritings.
Unfortunately we have no sample of Melzi's handwriting that can be dated after
Leonardo's death. His letter to Leonardo's brothers is lost.[25] His notes written during his assistantship to Leonardo, preserved in Leonardo's manuscripts, date from
about 1508 to 1519. The earlier ones have a more decorative character than the
later, so that a development toward simplification (which is natural to everyone's
handwriting) is already perceptible in the few examples within the short period of
ten years. As we have seen, in the Windsor drawing 12,416 dated 1511 (plate 12),
only one year after the date of the Ambrosiana drawing (plate 13), Melzi's handwriting had already assumed the characteristics of Manus 1. Of course, Melzi could
have written the notes on the Windsor drawing much later than 1511, when the
red chalk of Leonardo's writing had started to fade away. In the Windsor note the
looped appendage of the *g* is not so fluent as in other notes by Melzi. Conversely, in
the Codex Urbinas one can still perceive Melzi's early form of the *g*: for example, in
the last word *seguente* in the note on folio 28v (plate 10, *b*) and in the words
compongano and *segnato* in the "Memoria et Notta" at the end of the Codex
Urbinas (plates 2 and 3).

A note in Codex Atlanticus 88 v-a, "Schizzi d'ogni sorte" (plate 15, *c*), is undoubtedly written by Manus 1. Besides the typical *g*, other letters are of the same
type as those of the calligraphic script of the Codex Urbinas, in particular the double *z* and the capital *S*. Since this folio, which has on the verso a drawing attributable to Melzi, was numbered 1, we may assume that it was the first of an unbound
file of sheets of a late manuscript dealing primarily with geometric studies on *lunulae*.
With the remark "Sketches of every type," Melzi thus indicated the contents of one
of Leonardo's latest manuscripts. This notation must have been made after the
compilation of the Codex Urbinas, in which Melzi had listed the Leonardo manuscripts used. Perhaps at the same time he also attempted a classification of all the
other manuscripts in his possession.

Melzi's later handwriting, which we would call post-*Trattato*, should be recognizable in those examples in which the *g* no longer has the sinuous looped appendage. On the covers of Leonardo's manuscripts in the Institut de France, we find
Melzi's collation notes specifying the number of folios of each manuscript (plate
16, *a-b*). They are undoubtedly by Manus 1, the same person, now aged, who wrote
in his youth the notes on Windsor 12,416 (plate 12).

The activities of Manus 1 were not limited to what appears to be the mere task
of transcribing Leonardo's notes in the Codex Urbinas. That this hand was also
responsible for the collation of Leonardo's manuscripts is most illuminating. Who
else besides the owner of those manuscripts could have carried out this collation?

---

25. Beltrami (1919), document 245. (For newly discovered evidence of Melzi's handwriting dating from 1546 see my "Post Scriptum," pp. 260–264.)

Manus 1 could hardly have been a professional hand employed by someone else who had planned the compilation of the "Treatise on Painting," because it did not work under dictation or according to a given outline. It went directly into Leonardo's manuscripts, searching for the notes to be copied, countersigning them, and finally copying them. During the work of transcription Manus 1 wrote in MS A 28v a title to be given to one of Leonardo's notes: "Del ritrar li nudi." With this title the note was copied on folio 41 of the Codex Urbinas. Only Melzi could feel free to write the draft of such a title directly on Leonardo's original. Melzi went through all of Leonardo's manuscripts searching for notes on painting; when a manuscript had no such notes he wrote on its cover "N[ul]^{la} di Pittura" (Nothing on Painting), as we can see, for example, on the last folio of MS Ashburnham 2037, the complement of MS B in the Institut de France (plate 15, *a*). The calligraphy of the word *Pittura* of this annotation is identical with that of the same word in the title of folio 154v of the Codex Urbinas (plate 14, *d*).

A note "N^{la} di Pit^{ra}" occurs also on Codex Arundel 93v (plate 15, *b*). This indication is sometimes limited to the initials *N. d. P.*, as one can see on folios 44r, 59v, and 235v of the Codex Arundel, and also on the cover of the *Codex on the Flight of Birds*. The notations in the Codex Arundel were originally on the outer folios of unbound files left loose by Leonardo himself pending a definitive grouping. Folios 44 and 59 form a single sheet that was originally the outer folio of a signature composed of sixteen folios. The signature of fourteen folios from folios 79 to 93 originally had a cover. Melzi wrote "Nulla di Pittura" on the inside of the cover. By closing the signature when the ink was still wet, this note left an imprint on folio 93v, over a figure drawn by Leonardo (plate 15, *b*). It is possible, however, that such an imprint was produced by the contact of the outer folio of another signature which was not inserted in the Codex Arundel.

The Codex Atlanticus, which was composed of similar files, does not contain Melzi's sign "Nulla di Pittura." None of the several notes on painting in that codex has the little circle that Melzi used for countersigning the notes on painting in Leonardo's original manuscripts. Therefore, none of the notes in the folios of the Codex Atlanticus was copied in the Codex Urbinas. One can assume that Melzi used solely notebooks like those in the Institut de France, and that none of the notebooks he listed at the end of the Codex Urbinas was taken apart by Leoni to form the Codex Atlanticus.

In the Codex Urbinas the name MELTIVS, written by Manus 1, appears twice as a catchword: the first time in the lower right corner of folio 78v (plate 17, *a*), with reference to the same name written at the beginning of folio 79r (not reproduced by McMahon); and the second time on the lower right corner of folio 86v (this time only MEL), with reference to the same name which was supposedly at the beginning of a missing signature (fols. 87–102).[26]

It may appear unlikely that Melzi would write his own name. However, since we do not know why his name has been used as a catchword we may well presume that he himself devised this reference system for his own use. It is usually assumed

---

26. See Appendix II.

that Manus 1, as that of an anonymous scribe, had used the name MELTIVS as a reference to signatures of blank sheets given to Melzi. And since one of these signatures, the twelfth, is missing it has been suggested that Melzi did not return it for some reason. But why, then, should he have returned the eleventh signature (fols. 79–86), which was not completed? In fact, only one folio of the eleventh signature is written on. Curiously enough, this is the penultimate folio (85) of the signature, so that six blank folios precede it and another blank follows it. This written folio contains the omitted portion of chapter 148 (282) in the second part (fols. 31–86) of the Codex Urbinas. Obviously, this addition had to be made at the end of the second part, on one of the folios left blank for this kind of emergency and for supplementary material. It is thus not surprising that the omitted portion of a chapter was copied at the end of a signature of blank folios: the preceding blank folios were reserved for the supplementary material. Thus the omitted paragraph defines the end of the second part (there is still a blank folio at the end of the eleventh signature, but this probably arose because the compiler did not feel sure that one folio was enough for the omitted paragraph). Consequently, the twelfth signature, which would have been the only one completely blank in the entire codex, was no longer necessary for additional notes pertinent to the second part of the Codex Urbinas; therefore, sooner or later it was decided not to keep it. The compiler did not care too much if the foliation jumped sixteen folios ahead. In the thirtieth signature the foliation is also wrong, this time because four folios were not numbered, so that they had to be indicated as folios 242a, b, c, and d.

This long digression is necessary in order to remove the last obstacle to the identification of Manus 1 as Melzi's. Melzi could well have used his own name as a catchword for the logical reason that this name does not catch anything but the same name at the beginning of a signature of blank folios. In fact, having to refer to a blank folio the compiler had to use a code word, so he used his own name, the first time complete, MELTIVS, the second time abbreviated, MEL.

Characteristics of Melzi's handwriting emerge from these names; for example the form of the *S* and the dotted capital *I*. The date 1510 in the Ambrosiana drawing (plate 13) is written with such a dot on the 1. As Calvi pointed out, this characteristic is always found in Melzi's notes and numbers on folios of the Codex Atlanticus.

The first 33 folios of the Codex Urbinas contain spelling corrections made by a heavy hand and broad pen, producing a disagreeable effect which spoils the beauty of the humanistic script of Manus 1. Ludwig, who calls this "supervisor's hand" Manus 2, suggests identifying it as Melzi's. But Manus 2 was probably a proofreader (Bembo?) to whom the manuscript was entrusted before the planned publication. However, the corrections are not made systematically and many errors remain. Since the corrections of Manus 2 stop on folio 33, we may assume that some obstacle halted the planned publication. Further evidence that the manuscript was prepared for publication is on folio 19r: the compiler suppressed a passage containing antidogmatic opinions that might have caused the revocation of ecclesiastical permission to print the book. The ink used for crossing-out the passage is the same as that used for the text. Curiously enough, the crossed-out passage contains four spelling corrections; this could mean that the editor wished to restore the crossed-out text. Apparently it was so interpreted by Guglielmo Manzi, since he included it in the first edition of the Codex Urbinas published in Rome in 1817.

In folio 5 the word *Dio*, as an attribute of the painter, is substituted by *creatore*. The author of such a correction is not Manus 2, but another one, Manus 3, which suggested modifications in the titles and arrangement of chapters and added observations about the originals. These suggestions for changes are always very cautious, often preceded by the phrase: "It would be better to say. . . ." Ludwig assumes that this was not a scribe's hand but that of an intellectual's—perhaps a scholar called in as a consultant by the compilers.

All the marginal notes in the Codex Urbinas were undoubtedly written by Manus 3, even though some of them appeared to Ludwig and others to be by Manus 1. For example, Ludwig distinguishes between the two marginal notes on folio 4r of the Codex Urbinas (plate 9) as being written by Manus 1 and by Manus 3, but both notes were undoubtedly written by the same hand. The word *Questo* in the note attributed to Manus 1 is identical in style with the same word in the note attributed to Manus 3 on folio 1v of the Codex Urbinas. Ludwig also records a Manus ?, the hand responsible for the note next to the description of a storm on folio 36r of the Codex Urbinas (plate 10, *a*): "Here I recall the admirable description of the deluge given by the author." Again it is the handwriting of Manus 3, a consultant scholar who had so intimate a knowledge of Leonardo's writings as to be able to recall Leonardo's description of the "Deluge." This description is undoubtedly the one on Windsor 12,665 r-v, a folio that was in the Melzi collection. A note on the "Deluge" also occurs on Codex Atlanticus 79 r-c (plate 11) (a folio containing sketches of rocks falling into the water), along with sixteen lines of Melzi's handwriting.

Who was this "consultant scholar" referred to as Manus 3? The contents of his notes give us some clue to his background. He is very familiar with Leonardo's manuscripts, since he is able to check the accuracy of the transcriptions. On one occasion, for example, he points out that a section is missing from a chapter copied from folio 18 of *Libro B*, that is, from the present MS E.[27]

Manus 3 cannot be Melzi's. Melzi would have made changes and corrections more directly, instead of suggesting them with a caution that is even reflected in the lightness and minuteness of the handwriting. Moreover, Manus 3 has characteristics that are alien to Melzi's handwriting: for example, a peculiar form of the *d*, with a looped appendage as opposed to Melzi's *d* with a straight appendage, and the *g* with the appendage looped directly backward, instead of Melzi's more humanistic *g* with a sinuous appendage.

Manus 3 might be the anonymous author of the Codex Huygens (see plate 18), for the *d* is the only letter that is not absolutely identical in both handwritings.

---

27. Codex Urbinas fol. 74, chap. 245 (193): "Seguita un cap.⁰ al L⁰ B. a questa car. 18" (Another chapter follows this folio 18 in Libro B).

Whoever he was, the author of the Codex Huygens was very close to Melzi and indeed very familiar with Leonardo's manuscripts. The system of transcribing Leonardo's notes is identical in both codices: the original passages were first countersigned with small circles to be slashed after transcription. Moreover, one codex does not include the material of the other; what was left out from one codex is usually found in the other.

However, the identification of Manus 3 as the anonymous author of the Codex Huygens cannot be indisputable. Even though circumstantial evidence strongly favors it, we cannot be absolutely certain, because the *d* of Manus 3 never appears in the Codex Huygens. But it does appear in a note on Windsor 19,102v (plate 19), one of Leonardo's anatomical drawings of *ca.* 1512. The handwriting of this note and that of Manus 3 are so similar in *ductus* that one feels certain they are identical, although the Windsor note was written many years before the compilation of the Codex Urbinas. (The Windsor note was certainly already written when Leonardo filled the page with his notes, because he went around it.) "It would be interesting," Sir Kenneth Clark says, "to identify the writer of the note at the bottom of the *verso*, as we have no other evidence that Leonardo's pupils made so deep a study of anatomy. It is not unlike the writing of Melzi, who is traditionally supposed to have been the pupil more interested in Leonardo's scientific studies." [28] The Windsor folio, however, contains four lines unquestionably by Melzi (on light and shade, not anatomy), so that Melzi can hardly be identified as the writer of the note on anatomy, which has a *ductus* completely different from that of the note at the top of the page. Obviously, someone else was deeply interested in Leonardo's scientific studies, although the hand of the Windsor folio never appears again on Leonardo's manuscripts. If this hand is one and the same with Manus 3 of the Codex Urbinas, we must think that Melzi, returned from France, had contacted this person who had worked with Leonardo in 1512.[29]

Having reached the conclusion that Manus 1 is most likely Melzi's and that Manus 3 is that of a supervisory scholar who had probably known Leonardo, we should now try to establish which of these two hands was responsible for the references to *Libro A* and *Libro B*. According to logic, this hand should be identified as Manus 1, that is, the compiler's, because to indicate the source while transcribing a chapter is easy, whereas to trace the copies back to the originals would have been very difficult, not only for the compiler of the Codex Urbinas, but for Leonardo himself.[30] And yet there is evidence that these references were added later by Manus

---

28. Clark (1935), *sub numero.*
29. On March 25, 1513, a few months before leaving for Rome, Leonardo was in Milan as a guest of Prevostino Viola, a consultant in the service of the Cathedral of Milan. Cf. Beltrami (1919), document 215. Nothing is known of Prevostino Viola besides the fact that his name appears a few times in the *Annali della Fabriceria.* We know that his house was in Porta Nuova (Cf. *Annali,* 1503, June 22). The "Porta Nova" is also mentioned in the Codex Huygens as being the address of a certain "Signora Ustina." Cf. Panofsky (1940), p. 84, n. 4.
30. Cf. Codex Arundel 1r: "O Reader, blame me not, because the subjects are many, and the memory cannot retain them and say 'this I will not write because I have already written it' . . ." (MacCurdy:I.62–63).

3. Although they are written in the same ink as the text, they are undoubtedly in the style of Manus 3. Chapter 425 (499) copied from *Libro A* 31 (Codex Urbinas 136 r-v) makes this identification indisputable: Manus 3, in fact, having written the source beside the title, specifies also that the second paragraph of the chapter comes from the same source, "al medesimo." The remark on the missing section of a chapter copied from *Libro B* also points to Manus 3 as being the author of the references to the originals.

One can consider further that if it was the compiler who made these references directly during his transcription, he would have made them with a certain consistency of method, providing, for example, proper space for them at the end of each paragraph, instead of placing them at random, near the title, on the right or left margins, and at the beginning or at the end of a paragraph. Moreover, it is certain that these reference marks were added later because frequently they are written on the pen-line with which Manus 1 closed the paragraphs.[31] Finally, Manus 1 would most likely have given the source of each chapter and not just that of the notes copied from *Libro A* and *Libro B*, although one cannot explain as yet why Leonardo himself did not indicate in the Codex Leicester all the other sources besides *Libro A*.

Another hint concerning the compilation of the "Treatise on Painting" can be obtained from an examination of the Codex Urbinas. The first impression is that of a work executed not many years after Leonardo's death, probably soon after Melzi had returned to Italy, from 1523 to about 1530. The paper is similar in size and quality to that of the first folios of the Codex Arundel. The modern binding does not permit a close examination of the watermark; however, it can be recognized as a bull's head (see figure), a type associable to paper produced in Lombardy, *ca.* 1525–1530.[32] The ink of Manus 1 does not have the corrosive quality of the black ink widely used after the middle of the sixteenth century; on the contrary, it has that soft, yellowish tone that characterizes many pages of Leonardo's manuscripts.

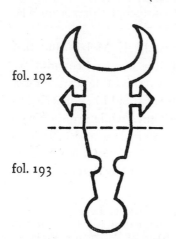

fol. 192

fol. 193

The marginal notes in the first part are usually in gray-brown ink. This kind of ink was used in some parts of the text, as for example at the end of the fourth part, in two chapters on drapery. One can assume that these chapters were added later, occupying the space left for such additions at the end of the part. In this case it is possible that such chapters were found by Melzi in manuscripts of a late period, as, perhaps, was the chapter added to the first part, that is, to the "Paragone" (plate 10, *b*). This chapter is also in gray-brown ink; and so

---

31. See, for example, Codex Urbinas 164r.
32. Cf. Briquet: 14,469 and 14,472. A few folios of the Codex Urbinas have a different type of watermark which is hardly recognizable. It represents either a rose or a vase of flowers, but nothing similar is found in Briquet. The folios in which this watermark appears more clearly are 82–83, 250–258, 270–271, and 285–288.

is the comment that follows it, with the exception of the last two lines, which are in a darker ink. Since the handwriting does not show substantial differences, we may assume that Melzi added these last two lines as an afterthought, using a different pen and ink.

The index of the chapters of the Codex Urbinas is also useful for the study of Melzi's compilation. When the index to the first part was completed, the chapter on folio 28v, "On Painting and Poetry," had already been added. In fact, the title of this chapter is listed on folio 301v between the titles of the chapters of folios 14 and 15. The marginal notes of Manus 3 are subsequent to the addition of that chapter because the new titles suggested by this hand are inserted in their proper places in the Index.

In the index to the fourth part the ink of the last two lines is different in tone. This confirms that the two corresponding chapters were added later on folios 239 and 241. The ink used in these added chapters is the same as that of the titles added to the index. In the index to the sixth part, on folio 327, the last six chapter titles were probably added later. The handwriting is slightly different and less careful. In the corresponding text on folio 266 the title "Precepts of Plants and Verdures" appears to have been inserted later between two lines.

However, in spite of all this evidence, we cannot expect Melzi's active, leading role in the compilation of the Codex Urbinas to be accepted as an indisputable fact until more is known about his other activities. We do not even know the dates of his life. The scanty information about him comes from Leonardo, Vasari, and Lomazzo, and from his own notes written on Leonardo's manuscripts. Because of this lack of documentation little can be added to what Calvi and Clark have already written about Melzi's handwriting and drawings.

The diagrams illustrating the "Treatise on Painting" were made by Manus 1, as they are in the same ink as that of the text of the chapters. The small sketches of human figures were made with brown-gray ink, but this does not exclude Manus 1 as the artist, since, as we have seen, this hand also used this kind of ink in certain parts of the text.

No Melzi drawing in pen and ink is identifiable with certainty among Leonardo's folios, or at least none of a type similar to that of the sketches in the Codex Urbinas. So far, only a few drawings in red chalk have been identified as Melzi's, by comparing them to the Ambrosiana drawing dated 1510. Diagrams and sketches in pen and ink are found in the pages written by Melzi in the Leonardo manuscripts, but unfortunately these are always too sketchy to be compared with the drawings in the Codex Urbinas. For example, Codex Atlanticus 335 v-e (plate 17, *b*) contains notes and sketches by Melzi of a "chamino all'antica." The Windsor folio 12,670v, which is identical to this in both the type of rough paper and the quality of ink, contains a drawing of a woman's head which is similar in style to that of the sketches in the folio of the Codex Atlanticus. The same type of woman's head is found in a few red chalk drawings at Windsor which have already been attributed to Melzi by Sir Kenneth Clark.[33]

---

33. Windsor 12,654 and 12,663v. Cf. Clark (1935), *sub numero*. The profile in

A careful examination of all the Leonardo manuscripts may reveal some other note or drawing by Melzi, although they can add nothing to our present knowledge of Melzi's activities. The only item worth considering is Windsor 12,684 (plate 20), the well-known topographical plan of the Gulf of Gaeta, because it has the names of cities and rivers in Melzi's handwriting. Perhaps the whole drawing was made by Melzi under Leonardo's directions, *ca.* 1515. The handwriting in the Windsor map resembles Manus 1 of the Codex Urbinas, although certain letters such as *z* and *h* are still of the earlier type of Melzi's handwriting. The letter *M* in the words *rio Martino* is the same as that of the "Memoria et Notta" at the end of the Codex Urbinas (plates 2 and 3).

Two other Windsor drawings,[34] not in the Clark catalogue but equally well-known—having been attributed to Leonardo as the first example of a map including the countries of the New World—can be recognized as the work of Francesco Melzi. Melzi executed the two hemispheres probably on Leonardo's instructions, *ca.* 1515. We can compare this map to a Leonardo sketch in Codex Atlanticus 279 r-a, *ca.* 1515. In the Windsor folios the names of countries and oceans, in capital and lower-case letters, are undoubtedly written by Manus 1 of the Codex Urbinas.

Finally, we may consider Windsor 12,641r (plate 21), which contains crossed-out notes on hydraulics by Leonardo, datable *ca.* 1506–1508. It also contains sketches of mountains which can be attributed to Melzi by comparing them with the background of the "Vertunno e Pomona" at Berlin.[35] This folio contains another clue that it was used by Melzi. To test the pen, Melzi wrote on the folio the phrase "Mag.ce p̄r. hoñ." ("Magnifice Presidente honorando"). This sentence reflects the activity of Melzi in 1508, when Leonardo employed him to write letters to Jaffredo Karly, the Presidente delle Acque in Milan.[36] A draft of a letter by Leonardo proves that the pupil assisted the master in the task of writing: "Good day messer Francesco. Why, in God's name, of all the letters I have written to you, have you never

---

Windsor 12,443r, cut from Codex Atlanticus 243 r-a, is also in this style of drawing (Pedretti [1957*a*], pls. 14 and 15). The sketches in red chalk of human figures in Codex Atlanticus 299 r-a are other examples of drawings by Melzi (Pedretti [1957*a*], pl. 19). This folio is the parent sheet of Windsor 12,485, which can be considered as a drawing by Melzi reflecting the style of Leonardo's drawing of about 1510. The draft of a letter on this folio of the Codex Atlanticus is also by Melzi, and can be compared to the note in Codex Atlanticus 188, which Carusi (1930), p. 467, had already compared with the handwriting of the Codex Urbinas.

34. Cf. Major (1866), pp. 1–40; see also Carusi (1941), pp. 27–34. The two drawings were mounted on the folios 232v and 233 of the Leoni album at Windsor. They were originally numbered 192 and 193.

35. Cf. Clark (1935), *sub numero.* Melzi was working on his "Vertunno e Pomona" about 1511. A drawing for the right foot of Pomona is on the Folio Resta in the Ambrosian Library; on the verso of the Folio Resta are notes on painting by Leonardo similar to those of MS G. The recto, prepared with red ground of the same type as that in Windsor 12,410–12,416, also contains a sketch of landscape made by Leonardo himself. Cf. Pedretti (1957*b*), pl. XVI.

36. Cf. Calvi (1925), p. 237; Bressy (1955), pp. 32–39.

answered one. Wait till I come, by God, and I shall make you write so much that perhaps you will become sick of it." [37]

THE ORIGINAL CONDITION OF LEONARDO'S MANUSCRIPTS

The Codex Urbinas was compiled prior to the dispersion and mutilation of Leonardo's manuscripts. Twelve of the eighteen manuscripts used in this compilation are lost. Moreover, some of the chapters of the "Treatise on Painting" were copied from missing folios of still extant manuscripts. The missing section of the MS A in the Institut de France was recovered in part, constituting the present MS Ashburnham 2038. We know that some folios of MS A are lost, because G. B. Venturi transcribed many passages from them when the manuscript was still complete.[38] Among Venturi's copies we find the notes on drapery that Melzi copied from MS A in chapters 534 (562) and 540 (560), as well as the notes on optics and color copied in chapters 555 (745) and 258a (186). All these were on the missing folios 67 and 79 of MS A.[39] There is no evidence of notes on painting copied by Melzi from the missing section (fols. 80–96) of MS E (*Libro B*). In fact, none of the notes marked *Libro B* in the Codex Urbinas has reference to folios 80 to 96.

The dispersion of Leonardo's manuscripts started some time after Melzi's death (*ca.* 1570). Although we do not have exact information about the number of Leonardo's manuscripts existing at that time, we can be certain that when Melzi died the "infinità di volumi et tutti in lingua volgare" seen by De Beatis at Cloux in 1517 were still all together in the villa at Vaprio.

In 1631 Ambrogio Mazenta wrote in his *Memorie* how thirteen manuscripts of Leonardo had come into his possession about fifty years before. Thus, around 1585 Mazenta became the first owner of a group of Leonardo's manuscripts previously kept in the Villa Melzi at Vaprio d'Adda. Unfortunately Mazenta does not describe the manuscripts he owned, but he certainly had some of those listed at the end of the Codex Urbinas. In fact, the manuscript he gave to Cardinal Borromeo was one of them.[40] Ten of the thirteen manuscripts in Mazenta's possession went to Pompeo Leoni, who took some of them apart in order to compile the Codex Atlanticus, the Windsor volume, and perhaps the Codex Arundel. At Leoni's death in Spain, *ca.* 1610, part of the Leonardo material in his possession returned to Italy and was bought by Galeazzo Arconati from Leoni's heir Polidoro Calchi. Besides the Codex Atlanticus, Arconati obtained eleven manuscripts: the notebooks now in the Bibliothèque de l'Institut de France, Paris, with the exception of MS C, which had been given to the Ambrosian Library by Cardinal Borromeo. Apparently Leoni did not take apart any of the Leonardo notebooks to form the Codex Atlanticus and

---

37. Codex Atlanticus 372v. J. P. Richter (1883), II, 335.
38. Cf. De Toni (1924), pp. 77–85; see also *Commissione Vinciana* (1938), pp. 1–11.
39. Cf. Pedretti (1962a), pp. 61–94.
40. The present MS C in the Bibliothèque de l'Institut de France.

other miscellaneous collections; for this purpose he must have used only those files that Leonardo himself had kept loose pending their definitive grouping.

The Leonardo manuscripts that Arconati gave to the Ambrosian Library are described in the deeds of donation, dated 1637. This document, which contains the earliest description of Leonardo's manuscripts, gives information on the size, foliation, type of binding, and contents of each manuscript, even recording the collation notes written on the covers, that is, the notes made by the compiler of the Codex Urbinas. Curiously enough, it has previously been believed that these notes were written by Baldassare Oltrocchi, Prefetto of the Ambrosian Library, at the end of the eighteenth century.[41]

The sixth manuscript of the Arconati donation is described as a notebook having on the cover the mark "B." This is the *Libro B* of the Melzi list in the Codex Urbinas, the notebook known today as MS E. We have already proved that Arconati did not have the *Libro A*,[42] but it is not proved that he gave the Ambrosian Library all the Leonardo manuscripts he owned. He could have kept some for himself. It is known that he had reserved the right to take home the donated manuscripts whenever he wished; from his correspondence with Cassiano dal Pozzo we learn that he even took them outside Milan.[43] Thus, we may assume that Arconati had kept for himself the present MS D, which he exchanged later for the fifth manuscript of his gift, the present Codex Trivulzianus.[44] It has always been believed that he even added sections to MSS H and I, but the discrepancies between the present number of folios of these manuscripts and that reported in their early descriptions are explained in Appendix V.

The compiler of the Codex Urbinas from time to time made remarks about the original manuscripts he was using. For example, at the end of chapter 470 (471), "On Smoke," the compiler writes: "Below this chapter there was a cleft in the mountain, an opening within which played a flaming fire, drawn by the pen and shaded with watercolor, an admirable and vital thing to see." This vivid description seems to refer to a drawing of Leonardo's late period, of the type of Windsor 12,404, which is probably a copy by Melzi, as Heydenreich suggests.[45] Considering the dispersion and mutilation of Leonardo's manuscripts, we may ask whether the

41. Cf. Ravaisson-Mollien (1881), p. 20, in the description of MS E (*Libro B*). See also Appendix V: General History of the Leonardo Manuscripts.

42. See above, pp. 23–24.

43. Cf. Uzielli (1884), p. 252: ". . . ad omnem requisitionem dicti Domini Arconati ei concedant usum dictorum librorum, etiam sui, et eius Domino Arconati domo, et tantùm viuente." See also the letter by Galeazzo Arconati to Cassiano dal Pozzo from Ornavaso (Val d'Ossola), July 31, 1639; reprinted by Steinitz (1958), p. 220.

44. Uzielli (1884), p. 240, n. 1. The Codex Trivulzianus is undoubtedly the fifth item of the Arconati donation. Its cover bears the number 5 and the collation mark "F," referring to the *Libro F* of the Melzi list (plates 2 and 3, this volume). Three folios are missing.

45. Heydenreich (1956), fig. 10.

drawing of a "cleft in the mountain" disappeared together with the notebook that contained it or whether such a notebook is still extant and just the drawing has disappeared.[46]

The drawing of a "cleft in the mountain" must have been stylistically and chronologically related to the one mentioned at the end of chapter 503 (522), a "foreshortened view of a city" during a storm. The subject of this drawing and its refined execution as described in the Codex Urbinas seems to imply a folio necessarily larger than that of the folios of late notebooks of the type of MSS E, F, and G. Heydenreich sees in Windsor 12,409 a preparatory study of this subject, which suggests that both chapters 470 and 503 may have been copied from a Leonardo manuscript of the first decade of the sixteenth century.

The format of Leonardo's notebooks and the way of arranging notes and drawings in their pages are valuable subsidiary elements in establishing the chronology of Leonardo's manuscripts. Since the chapters in the Codex Urbinas often reflect the physical character of the original manuscripts from which they were copied, this type of external evidence must be taken into account when attempting to date chapters no longer existing in the originals.

During his early period, *ca.* 1490, Leonardo's manuscripts are of the standard 8vo format, as used for MSS A, B, and Trivulzianus. The notes are seldom arranged in columns, with the exception of the list of *vocabula* in the Trivulzianus. The figures are placed haphazardly on the page.

About 1493 Leonardo started using pocket notebooks of the standard 24mo format, as used for MS H and the three Forster codices. He used this type continuously from the first through the second Milanese period, as the dates of MSS I, M, L, and K prove. The "librettini" listed at the end of the "Memoria et Notta" in the Codex Urbinas refer to this type of notebook. In fact, one of the "librettini" is identifiable as the present MS L.

After 1506 Leonardo adopted notebooks of medium size, 16mo, thus combining in a single notebook the characteristics of both types of notebooks previously used. He could carry such a book as a pocket notebook during his travels or use it as a normal notebook any time he had a chance to sit at a table. The lost *Libro A* was of this type, that is, a notebook similar to MSS E, F, and G. Because of the double function of this type of notebook, the media often change from red chalk to pen and ink, and sometimes to black chalk.

A last category of manuscripts used from after 1505 is that of large folios on which

---

46. Probably the entire notebook is lost. In a list sent to Cassiano dal Pozzo by Padre Gallo in 1639 the chapter on smoke is marked as having been checked against the original. This would indicate the source as one of the manuscripts now in the Institut de France, more precisely, either MS A or MS E, the only ones that are no longer complete as they were at the time of the Arconati donation. However, as we have seen (p. 23 above), the list sent to Cassiano is not reliable as a document concerning the original manuscripts because the chapters to be checked were not checked against the originals but against the Codex Pinellianus, an early copy of the abbreviated version of the "Treatise on Painting."

Leonardo started copying notes drafted in his notebooks; these in effect were files kept loose pending a definitive grouping. On this type of manuscript Leonardo started the compilation of his book on water, that is, the Codex Leicester, as well as books on mechanics and mathematics, fragments of which found their way into the Codex Atlanticus and the Codex Arundel. A lost compilation of notes on painting might have been written on this type of manuscript.

A characteristic of the manuscripts used by Leonardo in his late period is recognizable in the way of organizing the page. The notes in pen and ink are usually written in such a way as to leave ample space for marginal notes and for figures and diagrams. Codex Leicester (plate 4) and MSS E, F, and G contain several examples of this style of page layout. Chapter 507 (524) of the "Treatise on Painting" must have come from this type of page. The figure at the end of the text is accompanied by the note: "This figure should be put with the 24th section of the book on perspective; without it the explanation of transparent water is of no value." The compiler added at the end: "Taken from the margin." The last sentence of the preceding chapter has a similar note.

This type of analysis may increase considerably the possibility of dating lost chapters of the *Trattato*. Chapter 756 (869) is illustrated with the figure of a little spoon. In the Codex Urbinas the figure is placed in the center of the text, but in the lost original manuscript it must have been in the margin, because Leonardo writes, ". . . as is shown here in the margin." The spoon, indicated as a measure for color, is also mentioned in chapter 433 (469) from *Libro* A 40: ". . . take a little spoon, hardly larger than an ear-spoon." Chapter 233 (145), "On the Background of Painted Objects," also had a figure in the margin.

Transcriber's errors of the type that permitted us to detect the width of a line of writing in the lost *Libro* A are found in other chapters of the "Treatise on Painting." Such errors usually occur when in the original manuscript two lines end or begin with the same word or part of word, or when the same word is repeated in the same place in two consecutive lines. In both cases, the same amount would have been omitted.[47] These errors are important in establishing the width of line in two notes from the "Paragone" and in two notes from the second part.[48] We might well think that all four notes date from Leonardo's late period, 1505–1510, because we are able to establish that they were copied from manuscripts of large size.

As we shall discuss later, it is possible that in his late period Leonardo had developed in manuscript form his early notes on the "Paragone."

---

47. Cf. Codex Urbinas fols. 18–18v, chap. 32 (41); fol. 19, chap. 33 (19); fol. 47v, chap. 120 (135); fol. 63v, chap. 197 (207); fol. 64, chap. 198 (232).

48. Only in one instance are we able to check the cause of Melzi's lapsus. Chapter 149 (230) was copied from MS Ashburnham 2038 (the complement of the early MS A). In the third line of this chapter Melzi had started to write "elleuate *in alto*," instead of "elleuate e grandi," but, realizing immediately that he was on the wrong line, he corrected himself by crossing out the words "in alto." In Leonardo's manuscripts the words "elleuate in alto" are located in the middle of the line, just above the words "elleuate e grandi" in the following line.

AUTOBIOGRAPHICAL NOTES IN THE
Trattato della Pittura

Some notes of the "Treatise on Painting" contain autobiographical references which are useful for establishing the chronology, especially when Leonardo mentions his own paintings.

Chapter 25 (33), on the comparison between painting and poetry, contains one of the best known autobiographical notes:

If the poet says that he can inflame men with love, a principal concern of all kinds of living creatures, the painter has the power to do likewise, the more so in that he places before the lover the very effigy of the beloved, and the lover often kisses and speaks to the picture, which he would not do were the same beauties placed before him by the writer. The painter goes even further in affecting the minds of men, by inducing them to love and fall in love with a painting that does not represent any living woman. It once happened that I made a picture representing a divine subject, and it was bought by a man who fell in love with her. He wished to remove the emblems of divinity in order to be able to kiss the picture without scruples. But finally conscience overcame his sighs and desire and he was obliged to remove the painting from his house.

This passage has been referred interchangeably to the "Mona Lisa" and to the "Leda," but Leonardo specifically mentions a religious subject, probabably a Madonna with the symbols of her divinity removed. (It is not easy to think of the man who bought that painting as being one of the prominent patrons of Leonardo, because they were men who certainly did not need to resort to such a surrogate for their sexual desires.) It is impossible to date this chapter on the basis of the reference to an unknown painting by Leonardo. Only a textual analysis of the chapter can provide some element for its dating. Throughout his various periods Leonardo expressed his feeling and tastes as a painter in a manner that reflects the development of his art theory. Here in this passage Leonardo tells how astronomy is related to painting: "Astronomy cannot function without perspective, which is a principal element of painting. I mean mathematical astronomy and do not speak of false divination or popular astrology; let him who makes a living from fools by means of it forgive me." This can be associated with Leonardo's notes condemning astrology on anatomical folios at Windsor dating after 1500. Other elements of the chapter, however, are close to Leonardo's attitude during the Sforza period: "If I say: I shall describe hell or paradise, and other delights or horrors, the painter will surpass you because he will place before you things that, although silent, will tell you of delights, or will terrify. . . ." A note of similar feeling for fantastic representations is found in Windsor 12,591, *ca.* 1504, in a Polizianesque description of the mythical "Sito di Venere" at Cyprus.[49] In his late period Leonardo was still concerned with

49. Cf. Marinoni (1957), pp. 273–287.

this kind of fantastic description. Thus, in view of this uncertainty, the chapter must be placed at the end of the Quattrocento or the beginning of the Cinquecento.

The long chapter 27 (28), "Reply of King Mathias to a Poet Who Competed with a Painter," is undoubtedly datable in the Sforza period. The anecdote referred to contains subtle reasoning apparently aimed at gaining the approval of Leonardo's patron, Lodovico Sforza. Lodovico, like King Mathias, must have been the judge in some academic discussion among painters and poets. This chapter has the same character as Leonardo's tales written about 1494.

The well-known chapter 541 (574) on costumes may appear to be from a late period, because in it Leonardo records several changes of fashion. However, he mentions only two periods of his age, the "puerizia" (childhood) and the "altra età" (manhood). The style of writing corresponds to that of the note on the development of painting from Giotto to Masaccio in Codex Atlanticus 141 r-b, a folio datable *ca.* 1490–1491.[50] As he was then close to forty, Leonardo could certainly refer to that time as that of his manhood.

In the "Treatise on Painting" Leonardo mentions only two of his contemporaries, Botticelli and Della Robbia, but he often directed his criticism to unspecified works of contemporary artists. Chapter 186 (273), from *Libro* A, is directly related to chapter 108 (86), which comes from another lost manuscript. In both these chapters Leonardo alludes to the bad habit of painters of unconsciously reproducing their own features in their works. A reference to Ghirlandaio's frescoes is most probable. In the Sforza period Leonardo had already considered this habit of painters, as one can see in chapter 105 (85), from MS A 23.

Chapter 499 (437), from *Libro* A, is much more useful for the chronology. Here Leonardo considers once again that habit of painters, this time in connection with "judgment, one of the powers of our soul." In this definition Leonardo still follows Alberti's point of view: "But when you judge about beauty, that does not depend on mere opinion but on a certain judgment innate in our mind." [51] In the "Treatise on Painting" Leonardo has many notes concerning "judgment." They may be related to the note in Codex Atlanticus 29 v-a, datable *ca.* 1510: "Our judgment does not reckon in their exact and proper order things which have come to pass at different periods of time; for many things which happened many years ago will seem nearly related to the present, and many things that are recent will seem ancient, reaching back to the far-off period of our youth."

A reference to "judgment" is also found at the end of the long chapter 750 (686) on light and shadow: "Here the opposition says that it does not want so much science, that it is enough to practice drawing from nature. The reply is that there is nothing more deceptive than to rely on our own opinion, without any other proof, as experience always proves to be the enemy of alchemists, necromancers, and other ingenuous simpletons." This chapter was undoubtedly written around 1506–1508 because its paragraphs are drafted in Codex Atlanticus 207 r-a (plate 28),

---

50. Cf. Pedretti (1957a), pl. 8; J. P. Richter (1883), I, 660.
51. Alberti, *De Re Aedificatoria*, ix, 5. Cf. Blunt (1959), pp. 16–17.

a folio dating from the time of Leonardo's activity as an architect in the service of Charles d'Amboise in Milan (cf. detail of the recto of this folio; plate 29, *a*). The concluding sentence of the chapter also evokes a late period, being related to the pages condemning the alchemists in the *Fogli B dell'Anatomia* at Windsor, *ca.* 1503–1505.

To a late period we can attribute some texts on the ethics of painting, in which Leonardo exhorts painters to reach virtue instead of riches; for example, chapter 65 (78), and chapter 834 (982) from MS G 33r. We should not forget, however, that this subject also stems from Alberti's book, so that it can be found in Leonardo's notes from the Sforza period, for example in chapter 76 (256), which was copied from MS Ashburnham 2038, folio 26. Chapter 81 (77), copied from *Libro A* 13, states that the painter should never "imitate another's manner, because as far as art is concerned, he will be called a grandson rather than a son of Nature." In the concluding sentence Leonardo repeats a concept that is often found in the "Paragone": "I say this not for those who wish to become wealthy through the art, but for those who desire fame and honor from it."

Some of the Leonardo notes on "Decorum" are to be dated after 1500 in accordance with those contained in the *Libro A*. In chapter 58 (92) Leonardo recalls having seen an "Annunciation" in which the painter paid no attention to decorum: "As I saw, some days since, in the picture of an angel who, while he was making The Annunciation, appeared to be chasing Our Lady out of the room, with movements which displayed such offensiveness as one might show to a most vile enemy, and Our Lady seemed as if she, in despair, would throw herself from a window." Unfortunately this amusing description is chronologically of no help to us. Since the name of the painter of the "Annunciation" is not specified, a possible *terminus a quo* for the date of the chapter is missing. Sir Kenneth Clark suggests that Leonardo was addressing Botticelli, but many examples of Annunciations of the Quattrocento and Cinquecento, especially the one by Signorelli in Philadelphia,[52] may also be considered candidates for Leonardo's criticism.

In other chapters Leonardo seems to be evoking his own not yet too distant youth, as in chapter 23 (42), when he describes meadows in bloom "where you have had pleasures beside some spring." Leonardo's use of comparisons such as that of a "merchant who collects goods produced by various artisans" is typical of his Sforza period. In the well-known "Proemio" in Codex Atlanticus 119 v-a, *ca.* 1490, Leonardo uses the image of the "last one who arrives at the fair."

Chapter 39 (48) is a criticism of the use of the "prospettografo." This device for drawing perspective had been known in Florence since Alberti. Leonardo describes it in MS A 24, in a note copied by Melzi in chapter 90 (118). In an early folio of the Codex Atlanticus, 1 bis *olim* 386 v-b, Leonardo made a drawing of such a device. He used the "prospettografo" only as an instrument for experiments, and strongly recommends avoiding it in the practice of art. In 1525 Dürer published some models of "prospettografi" as instruments useful in painting portraits. They

---

52. *Johnson Collection*, Philadelphia (no. 136). Cf. Salmi (1955), pl. 65.

must have been widely used in Italy for this purpose condemned by Leonardo. Chapter 39 (48) might be dated soon after 1500, the time when Dürer presumably saw "prospettografi" in Italy.

CHRONOLOGICAL STRUCTURE OF THE
Trattato della Pittura

A chronology of Leonardo's "Treatise on Painting" has always been considered to be limited to the notes that can be retraced in the original manuscripts. Those notes, which occupy roughly one-fourth of the material gathered by Francesco Melzi in the Codex Urbinas, can be dated in accordance with the date of the manuscripts from which they were copied. An attempt to date also the notes that were copied from lost manuscripts might at first sight appear impossible. In reading some of those notes, however, one can perceive certain characteristics of expression which reflect the style of a certain phase of Leonardo's writings. In a similar, although less illusory, manner, copies of lost drawings of Leonardo's may be evaluated. In this case the copy is considered as reflecting a certain phase of Leonardo's style.[53] The stylistic analysis of a copy of a lost note on painting is much more difficult, of course, than a similar analysis of a drawing, and must be supported by convincing comparisons with analogous extant texts.

The material of the Codex Urbinas can be subdivided into two main periods of time: 1487–1492 and 1505–1513, the first and second periods of Leonardo's activity as a theorist of art.

The first period is represented by the notes copied from the Codex Trivulzianus, MS A & Ashburnham 2038, and from other folios of the early 1490's. The second period is represented by the notes in MSS E, F, and G.

During the Sforza period Leonardo had already treated the subject of light and shade, especially in MS C (*ca.* 1490), but only after 1505 did he develop it into the complete book that was used by Melzi in the fifth part of the Codex Urbinas. That book is lost. Many preparatory notes for it are found in folios of the Codex Atlanticus, in the Codex Arundel and in folios at Windsor. Manuscript D, written about 1508, contains a study of the eye and the phenomena of vision and also refers to problems on light and shade. Other notes on this subject are scattered in the notebooks written after 1505, in MSS K, F, G, the lost *Libro* A, and MS E (*Libro* B). The last-named manuscript, written *ca.* 1513–1514, proves that Leonardo continued to write on art during his Roman period. In the Codex Atlanticus and elsewhere there are notes on clouds, wind, rainbow, and horizon datable in the last French period, after 1517.

A period of transition between the first and the second Milanese periods is represented in the "Treatise on Painting" by two notes on the movement of the human body and on landscape copied from MS L, *ca.* 1498–1502. Many chapters of the third part of the Codex Urbinas can be chronologically related to these two notes.

---

53. Cf. Popham (1958), pp. 275–276. See also pp. 145–146 below.

This is roughly the basic chronological structure of Leonardo's *Trattato della Pittura*. The material gathered in the Codex Urbinas is perhaps the best known of Leonardo's production, but it is actually the least explored. Since it is not Leonardo's own compilation, it is usually accepted somewhat reluctantly because it has no value for chronology.[54]

The Florentine tradition of the Quattrocento and especially the pioneering work of Leon Battista Alberti is a basic source of Leonardo's notes on painting. Although Leonardo does not specifically mention the works of his predecessors, he uses them, as Sir Kenneth Clark and others have already pointed out.[55] During his first Milanese period Leonardo's work is still closely dependent upon that of his predecessors. Even when his personal observations caused him to proceed on a line of research far in advance of theirs, Leonardo's ideas were still rooted in tradition. In many notes on painting dated after 1500 he continues to approve theories that he had already accepted in his Sforza period.

Typical of Leonardo in his attitude toward tradition is his insistence on proclaiming painting as a liberal art. In chapter 34 (25) he gives a reason why painting was not accepted among sciences:

If painters have not written about it and reduced it to a science, this is not the fault of painting, and it is not therefore the less noble, since few painters make a profession of letters [allusion to Alberti and Piero della Francesca]; *for their life is not long enough to encompass that. Should we say that the properties of herbs, stones, and trees are not in them for the reason that men have not known them? Certainly not, and we say that those herbs remain noble in themselves, without help of human tongues or letters.*

This chapter is in the style of Leonardo's early writings, and yet it contains a reference to scientific studies that were to become Leonardo's specialty about 1510. It would be reasonable, therefore, to date this chapter in the period of transition, *ca.* 1500, especially on comparing it with the notes on painting in Codex Atlanticus 199 v-a (plate 24), *ca.* 1506–1508. These notes are so close in character to those of the Sforza period that if it were not for the style of the handwriting and the sketches, one would be convinced they were written before 1500.

In chapter 848 (910), which might be as late as those on plants in MS G, Leonardo discusses the transparency of leaves. Emphasizing the importance of such a subject, he affirms: "This has not been employed by anyone before me insofar as I am aware." This statement is an indirect reference to the work of his predecessors. He was conscious of the novelty of his research. Of his work as an art theorist, Leonardo could have said, as he said of his studies on water, "opera e materia nuova, non più detta." [56]

---

54. Cf. Marinoni (1952), p. 28; an exception is Bolelli (1955), pp. 99–105.

55. Clark (1944), pp. 16 ff.; Zoubov (1960), pp. 1–14; Heydenreich (1956), pp. xxiv ff.

56. Windsor 12,663. No section on plants was ever included in the Quattrocento treatises on painting. Only Filarete, p. 660, refers to his own project of a book "de

LEONARDO'S PLANS OF DISCUSSION

Leonardo's plans for a discussion of anatomy during the Sforza period are different from those of the period after 1500. Any time after that, when he was tempted to deviate from the main line of research toward peripheral channels of investigations, he reminded himself that he must stay within his established program: ". . . but this has no relation to our purpose, because we have a program to treat only the movement of limbs." [57]

There are several hints for supporting the assumption that something similar happened to him in his writings on painting. After 1500 he seems to have worked intensely on the preparation of a treatise on painting. His new approach reveals the same method of research he had adopted in his new studies on anatomy. Chapter 838 (898), belonging to the period of his notes on branches of plants copied from MS G, is left practically broken off: ". . . but this will not be discussed in full here, because it is reserved for elsewhere, and it is not related to painting." In a similar chapter, 829 (900), Leonardo once again deviates from his line of research, so that he feels compelled to justify himself: "Although these things do not serve painting, yet I will note them, so as to leave out as little about trees as is possible."

In three notes from a late period, in folios at Windsor and in the Codex Atlanticus, Leonardo expresses his intention of compiling a "libro di pittura." Two of these notes (Windsor 19,076 and Codex Atlanticus 181 r-a) were quoted by Heydenreich in his introduction to McMahon's edition of the Codex Urbinas.[58] The third is in Codex Atlanticus 79 r-c (plate 11), a description of a deluge connected with the famous series of Windsor drawings: ". . . and the rest of this subject will be treated fully in the book on painting." This is proof that about 1515 Leonardo was still concerned in compiling a treatise on painting.

References to the purpose of compiling such a book are also found in the Codex Urbinas. They generally belong to the period 1505–1510. In chapter 213 (178), on the mixing of pigments, a subject closely related to the late note in Codex Atlanticus 181 r-a, Leonardo wrote: "But because here I lack paper, I shall leave the details to be discussed at length in my work on this subject, which will be of great use, as well as very necessary. This description will be placed between the theory and the practice of painting." Leonardo indicates here a basic scheme of arrangement of his "Treatise on Painting," a scheme that was actually followed by Melzi in the compilation of the Codex Urbinas.

In MS Ashburnham 22v, *ca.* 1492, we find the original text of chapter 511 (427): "Painting includes all the ten functions of the eye; that is, light, shade, body, color, form, location, remoteness, nearness, motion, and rest. My little work is woven together of these functions, reminding the painter according to what rules and in

---

agricoltura" ("io uoglio in prima fornire quello de agricoltura, che sapete, che è già fatto il principio, e fattone due libri e più"), but he does not specify whether such a book was in connection with painting or architecture.

57. Windsor 19,045 (An. B 28v); cf. Brizio (1952), p. 495.
58. Heydenreich (1956), p. xx.

what fashion he should reproduce with his art all of these things, the works of nature and the beauties of the world." [59]

In this early phase of his project Leonardo was thinking of a "little work," as if he had envisaged emulating Alberti's *della Pittura*. This early note is obviously related in content to chapter 438 (426), the original of which is lost. In this lost chapter Leonardo no longer considers his program in terms of a "little work." His plan is now more complex. This might be a result of Leonardo's reëlaboration after 1500 of subjects pertaining to the Sforza period. He develops ideas already expressed in that period, modifying them according to the development of his studies on light and shade. The treatment of the subject of light and shade increases to such an extent as to form a separate book:

Light, shade, color, body, form, location, remoteness, nearness, motion, and rest. Of these ten parts of the function of the eye, painting has seven: light, shade, color, form, location, remoteness, and nearness. Light and shade mean shadow and light, or brightness and obscurity, and color. I do not include body, for painting is on a surface, and a surface does not have body as this is defined in geometry. To put it better, that which is visible is included in the science of painting. Therefore, the ten predicates of the eye mentioned above are, according to reason, the subject of the ten books into which I divide my discussion of painting. But light and shade make one single book, which treats of light and shadow and comprises one book only, since shadow is surrounded by or in contact with light, and the same is true of light and shadow, while on the borders light and shadow are always mixed.

The text continues with the notes that Ludwig distinguishes as chapters 438a (636) and 438b (741). In this latter note Leonardo quotes the ninth proposition of his book on light and shade: "The surface of every body takes on the color of the object opposite it." Such a proposition is found frequently in notes on optics and color in MSS E and F, as well as in other manuscripts of his late period.

References to the ten predicates of the eye are also found in the first part of the Codex Urbinas, that is, in the "Paragone," as Heydenreich has already pointed out.[60] These references are in chapters 20 (29) and 36 (51), which are both on painting compared to poetry, and which must have been written before 1500. They are useful as material for comparisons. An outline of a discussion on painting is found in chapters 132 (100) and 133 (102), based once again on the ten predicates of the eye.

A later plan for a discussion on painting is found in chapter 136 (103), which was copied from MS E 79v. Here Leonardo suggests two basic categories: first, perspective, which considers the diminishing of bodies in their appearance, shape, and color; second, action and varieties of figures.

The notes of the first parts of the Codex Urbinas are often so well related one to another that certain groups must be considered to have been copied from one single manuscript. This appears as an indirect proof that Melzi was following a plan estab-

59. See also Codex Atlanticus 90 r-b; Brizio (1952), p. 158.
60. Heydenreich (1956), p. xxiv and n. 39.

lished by Leonardo himself. Melzi did not select; he copied everything he could find
in Leonardo's notebooks pertaining to painting. Obviously, Leonardo would have
preserved only the final version of certain discussions. Chapters 349–350 (365–366)
and 391 (364) are indicative of Melzi's process. The last chapter is connected with
the subject of the preceding ones, but it obviously precedes them chronologically.
In it Leonardo does not recognize any difference in pushing and pulling, contrary
to what he states in the other chapters. Besides, chapter 349 (365) contains a
quotation from the ninth proposition of Leonardo's *De ponderibus*. The notes containing such quotations from books written by Leonardo himself are usually datable
after 1500.

As a preparatory phase of his work, Melzi marked with little circles all the notes
on painting in Leonardo's manuscripts. As evidence that the transcriptions had been
accomplished, he would slash the circles. However, some of the notes that he
transcribed do not have the circle slashed, which might be taken to suggest that
Melzi lacked a precise method.

Apparently Melzi followed the instinctive process of using one manuscript at a
time, because this would explain the insertion of certain notes not in their proper
place in the "Treatise on Painting." Later, he must have realized the inconvenience
of this system, because he asked the advice of an anonymous scholar (Manus 3),
who suggested the transposition of some chapters and modifications of headings.
This plan of modifying the arrangement of chapters was abandoned at the beginning of the third part. A work of classification would have been extremely long and
difficult, considering that Melzi did not first copy the notes onto individual
leaves but instead transcribed directly into a codex. By failing to adopt a system
that allowed for a preliminary organization of the material, Melzi encountered the
same problems as those encountered by Leonardo in the compilation of the Codex
Leicester and the first part of the Codex Arundel. In the *proemio* of the Codex
Arundel, Leonardo addressed the reader:

*O reader, blame me not, because the subjects are many, and the memory cannot
retain them and say "this I will not write because I have already written it." And if
I wished to avoid falling into this mistake it would be necessary, to prevent repetition, that on every occasion when I wished to write a passage I should always read
over all the preceding portion, and this would cause long periods of time to elapse
between one time of writing and another.*

Leonardo's method in assembling notes on hydraulics in the Codex Leicester
may be compared to his method in assembling notes on painting. "I will not consider the demonstrations here," he writes in Codex Leicester 2r, "because I will
reserve them for the ordered work; my concern now is to find subjects and inven-
tions, gathering them as they occur to me; then I will get them in order, putting
together those of the same kind, so that you will not wonder nor will you laugh at
me, reader, if here we jump from one subject to another."

We do not know whether Melzi did not feel that there was any need to use individual leaves as a first phase of his work of compilation, or even whether such a system was ever used in the sixteenth century. In following what we may call the Leonardo system, Melzi was encouraged by a certain homogeneity of contents in manuscripts used in the first part of the Codex Urbinas. These manuscripts were usually of the first Milanese period, because the notes on painting from the late period are scattered throughout notebooks concerning a variety of subjects.

The third part of the Codex Urbinas was planned as a section on the human figure and human and animal movement. Some of the notes gathered in this part were written not exclusively in reference to painting, and only Leonardo himself could have decided how to select or develop them. Apart from this difficulty, Melzi was suddenly faced with another problem connected with the characteristics of the notebooks used by Leonardo after 1500. Since these notebooks were used during travels, the subject matter of their contents varies greatly. In the third part of the Codex Urbinas we find a group of chapters, from 402 (363) to 508 (525), that have no relation to the title of the section. They should have been placed in the sections regarding light and shade, plants, and clouds, and even in the second section regarding studio practice. Similar inconsistencies of method are found in other parts of the "Treatise on Painting." One would expect to find the pertinent notes on the topic of reflected light, "reflessi," gathered together in a section of the fifth part of the Codex Urbinas, namely in the book on Light and Shade, but the notes are actually gathered in two widely separated groups, one in the second and another in the fifth part of the codex.[61]

In his English edition of the Codex Urbinas, McMahon attempts to reassemble the texts of the "Treatise on Painting" according to subject matter. This arrangement can be useful for our purposes, but it should not be preferred to the arrangement given by Melzi which provides us with clues to the character of Leonardo's lost manuscripts.

THE "PARAGONE"

The first part of the Codex Urbinas is dedicated to the comparison of the arts. In the first edition of the *Trattato*, in 1817, it was given the title "Paragone," which has been retained ever since. A separate edition of the *Paragone* with an English translation was prepared by Irma A. Richter in 1949.

The subject of Leonardo's "Paragone" has been recognized unanimously as being Quattrocento in character, an impression that has the support of Lomazzo's statement about a book on the comparison between painting and sculpture written by Leonardo at the request of Lodovico Sforza.[62] Moreover, the originals of four chapters of the "Paragone" are found in Ashburnham 2038, a manuscript of Leonardo's Sforza period.[63] None of the other chapters is known in the extant original manu-

61. Chapters 158–172 (167, 173) and 780–790 (721, 855).
62. Lomazzo (1584), p. 158. Cf. Steinitz (1958), p. 22. See also pp. 15–17 above.
63. Chapters 12 (6); 19 (30); 31 (44); 38 (47).

scripts, but four of them were copied from the lost *Libro* A dating from Leonardo's second Milanese period.[64]

Anna Maria Brizio suggests that in his compilation of the Codex Urbinas Melzi first used manuscripts that Leonardo wrote during the Sforza period, because these manuscripts were the most homogeneous in content.[65] This assumption would be in keeping with Lomazzo's record and with the character of the notes gathered in the first part of the Codex Urbinas. However, since we have evidence of Leonardo having resumed his project of a book on painting after 1500, it is quite probable that he had also developed his discussions on the "Paragone."

Lomazzo copied from the lost "Codex Sforza" a section on clay modeling which does not appear in any extant manuscript or in the notes copied by Melzi in the Codex Urbinas; [66] one would assume, therefore, that the "Codex Sforza" was not among the manuscripts inherited by Melzi. As a manuscript in fairly final form, as it certainly was, its contents should have been copied entirely in the Codex Urbinas, including the long section on clay modeling. It would be unthinkable, however, that Melzi, although not owning it, had not had the same opportunity of reading it as Lomazzo had. We must presume that as this was a "Paragone" limited to painting and sculpture, Melzi only excerpted it, supplementing it with other Leonardo notes on painting compared to music and poetry.[67]

Evidence of notes on the "Paragone" written by Leonardo before and after 1500 leads to the question whether Melzi compiled the "Paragone" from Leonardo's manuscripts of various periods or whether Leonardo himself had resumed and developed his Sforza "Paragone" about 1508–1510.

As we have seen, the concluding section of chapter 43 (52), "Apologia of the Sculptor," was copied from carta 29 of *Libro* A. Ludwig does not indicate this, and reproduces the text without interruption. Actually, in the original manuscript the section copied from *Libro* A was joined to the text of chapter 41 (57), "Com-

---

64. Chapters 41 (57); 43 (52), last paragraph only; 44 (46); 45 (54).
65. Brizio (1956), pp. 309 ff.   66. Pedretti (1957b), pp. 62–67.
67. In his *Memorie* written about 1631, Ambrogio Mazenta speaks of the "most learned discourses" he had read in Leonardo's manuscripts formerly in the Villa Melzi at Vaprio d'Adda; among other things Leonardo "debates and settles the famous question of the preëminence between painting and sculpture by having a Blind Man and an Idiot give the decision in favour of painting. A panel beautifully painted with men and landscapes having been placed in front of the Blind Man, he, having touched it, found it even and smooth. He so marvelled that he could not believe that there were animals, forests, mountains, valleys and lakes until the Duke Lodovico il Moro swore to it. Instead, when a statue was placed before him, by touching it, he knew immediately that here a man was represented. The Idiot was then called, and brushes and blocks of clay having been placed in front of him, he was unable to paint anything, but in the clay he formed perfect natural shapes, feet, arms, and face, which were adequate for obtaining excellent relief." Cf. Gramatica (1919), p. 41; Steinitz (1958), pp. 22–23. The anecdote quoted by Mazenta is found neither in Leonardo's extant manuscripts nor in the lost discussions copied by Melzi in the Codex Urbinas. The reference to Lodovico Sforza as the judge of the dispute suggests that Mazenta had read either the lost Codex Sforza or missing pages of the extant MS A.

parison of Painting and Sculpture," which is also marked "L° A 29." Ludwig does not reproduce this mark, either.

The long chapter 31 (44, 45, 26, 16) is even more revealing. Only its first section was copied from MS Ashburnham 2038, folio 23. The section 31c (16), the original of which is lost, bears no relation to the subject, not even chronologically. (We shall consider this section further in connection with the first chapters of the "Treatise on Painting.") The section 31b (26) must have been unfinished in the lost original, according to the note of the transcriber: "A piece is missing here, as I can see it." All this indicates that Melzi did not use a "Paragone" in its final form, or at least that he supplemented it with notes from other manuscripts.

This alteration of texts in a part of the treatise which is usually considered homogeneous in contents and therefore early in date would strengthen the impression that Melzi arbitrarily mixed notes of different periods, but it is possible that Leonardo himself had rearranged his notes on the "Paragone" in his late period as they appear in the Melzi compilation. Sir Kenneth Clark states that Leonardo's descriptions of the sculptor are an unmistakable reference to Michelangelo.[68] If this is so, Leonardo must have written the "Paragone" after 1500, because before that time he had no occasion to encounter his great rival.

In the list of Leonardo's manuscripts used in the compilation of the Codex Urbinas (plates 2 and 3) the first book is indicated as "libro intero segnato .i." This was probably the manuscript containing a "Paragone" compiled by Leonardo after 1500. Unfortunately this "libro intero" is lost and we have no way to establish to what extent Melzi used it. There is reason to believe, however, that the material on the "Paragone" (considered as an introduction to a book on painting) was, if not arranged by Leonardo himself, at least gathered from two main sources, namely from MS Ashburnham 2038 and from one of the lost manuscripts listed by Melzi. As Melzi left only two blank folios after the first part of the Codex Urbinas, we may infer that he did not expect to find much more material on this subject in Leonardo's manuscripts. The folios left blank increase in each of the successive parts.[69] When the entire book was completed Melzi found another chapter on painting compared to poetry, so he added it to the end of the first part. A note of comment by Melzi himself explains this and indicates where the chapter should be inserted (plate 10, *b*). Brizio suggests that Melzi had found this chapter only later in one of Leonardo's latest notebooks, because in such notebooks the notes on painting, being mixed with notes on other subjects, are more difficult to find.

The existence of a "Paragone" compiled by Leonardo himself after 1500 does not mean that Melzi could not have supplemented it with notes copied from Leonardo's manuscripts of both early and late periods. Such a procedure could ac-

---

68. Clark (1952), p. 83.
69. Cf. McMahon (1956), Vol. II, p. iii. McMahon lists a total of 100 blank folios, but he obviously means "pages." (A folio—recto and verso—represents two pages.) See in this volume Appendix II.

count for some of the repetitious statements in the first part of the Codex Urbinas.

In Leonardo's extant manuscripts there are notes on the "Paragone" that were not copied in the Codex Urbinas. Usually these notes date from a late period. Since they are in a draft form, their omission is justified. Moreover, it would be difficult to find them without a systematic search, particularly the one in an anatomical folio at Windsor,[70] and the other in a discussion on light and shade in Codex Atlanticus 277 v-a, a folio of the characteristic blue paper used by Leonardo after 1508.[71] As we have seen, in Codex Atlanticus 305 r-a, a folio that dates from 1506–1508 because of the topography of the "Neron da Sancto Andrea," there is a note that can be considered to be the draft of chapter 41 (57), that is, *Libro A 48*.

A chapter of the second part of the Codex Urbinas, 59 (89), which has the characteristics of the notes of Leonardo's late period, can be considered as pertaining to discussions on painting compared to sculpture. The note in Windsor 19,071, *ca.* 1513, beginning, "writer, with what letters will you be able to describe the entire human figure, as drawing does," could be transferred from anatomy to the "Paragone," among the notes on painting and poetry. These omissions seem to suggest Melzi's preference for less fragmentary sources. The consistent neatness of the early parts of Melzi's compilation suggests that he was probably copying from well-defined and ordered sources. He must have known which manuscripts Leonardo himself considered as being fairly complete.

We have already seen how often after 1500 Leonardo returned to subjects treated in the first period of his activity,[72] so that it is not surprising to find certain subjects treated in a similar way in two different periods. These subjects are anatomy, hydraulics, mechanics, and painting; to some extent this return to an earlier approach is true also of the style of Leonardo's drawings.[73] Whereas the chronology of the

---

70. Windsor 19,101 (An. C III 7); Brizio (1952), p. 463. See also the note on a fragment at Bayonne, *ca.* 1493: "Il disegno mette le cose in noi per la via dell'occhio, le parole per la via delli orecchi" (Drawing comes to us through the eye, the words through the ears). Cf. Pedretti (1960b), pp. 53–63. A note on music in Codex Atlanticus 382 v-a can also be considered as related to the "Paragone": "La musica ha due malattie, delle quali l'una è mortale e l'altra è decrepitudinale. La mortale è congiunta all'istante seguente a quel della sua creazione. La decrepitudinale la fa odiosa e vile nella sua replicazione" (Music has two ills, the one mortal the other wasting; the mortal is ever allied with the instant which follows that of the music's utterance, the wasting lies in its repetition, making it seem contemptible and mean [MacCurdy: II.437]). In my "Saggio di una cronologia dei fogli del 'Codice Atlantico'" (1957b, pp. 264 ff.) I dated this folio 1497–1500, but I am now convinced that it dates from a later period, *ca.* 1510–1515. The paper and the handwriting, as well as the contents (mechanics and architecture), have characteristics that are found in folios of the Codex Atlanticus used by Leonardo during his Roman period, *ca.* 1515. It also contains a note on ethics that can be related to the notes on the "Deluge." Cf. Gantner (1958), p. 194.

71. Quoted above, p. 16.

72. An example of this is found in chapter 436 (498), similar in subject to chapter 437 (497). The first chapter was copied from MS A 38v, *ca.* 1492, whereas the second was copied from *Libro A*, carta 42, *ca.* 1508–1510.

73. Cf. Brizio (1952), pp. 16 ff.; Clark (1935), p. xlix; Pedretti (1959b), pp. 42–57.

original notes and drawings is based on several elements that help us to define Leonardo's style during various periods, the chronology of the chapters of the *Trattato della Pittura* is based mainly on stylistic comparisons. Let us now take the first chapters of the "Paragone" as an example of how the date of Leonardo's lost notes on painting can be established on the grounds of their style.

The first chapters of the "Paragone" are not on the comparison of the arts but on painting as a science and on the principles of such a science. These chapters form a group of notes chronologically consistent, and at least chapters 1 to 10 are copied in the sequence they must have had in the original. Even chapter 2, although a comparison between painting and poetry, belongs to the series, because it is the continuation of the last paragraph of chapter 1. The comparison with poetry is introduced to prove that painting is a science. The original of chapter 2 had simply the title "Essempio" (Example), which obviously refers to the preceding paragraph. The compiler did copy this title, but later he completed it with his own words "et differenza tra Pittura e Poesia" (and difference between Painting and Poetry). In all the editions of the "Paragone" other than Ludwig's, chapter 2 is removed from its place and no longer explains what Leonardo had said in chapter 1, being put among the notes on the comparison between painting and poetry.

At the bottom of folio lv of the Codex Urbinas, Manus 3 writes a comment to chapter 3 (3): "This chapter on the first principles of the science of painting and the three that follow would have a more suitable place in the second part of this book after the chapter, 'How the first picture originated,' which is on folio 49v." Thus, as early as the time of the work of editing by Manus 3 the significance of the first chapters of the "Paragone" was already lost. There was already a preoccupation with giving order to what Leonardo had written, with little or no concern about Leonardo's way of developing his discussions. However, thanks to Manus 1, that is, Melzi's, we can still recognize how Leonardo intended to organize the first book on painting. The outline is still basically traditional, considering that both Alberti and Piero della Francesca began their treatises with similar definitions of line and point, but the type of reasoning is comparable to Leonardo's definitions of line and point as found in several drafts of his "First Book on Water," drafts written in 1505–1508 in the Codex Arundel and Codex Atlanticus.[74]

The First Book on Water was planned as an introduction containing the definitions of the basic principles of the science of hydraulics, and the first book on painting was most likely planned in a similar way. And one may well wonder whether Melzi's record of a Leonardo manuscript called "Libro intero segnato .i.," that is, the first manuscript listed in the "Memoria et Notta" (plates 2 and 3), was intended as a reference to what Leonardo himself had marked "libro .i.," that is, the "first book on painting," as an ideal counterpart of the "First Book on Water." It was probably this type of approach to his planned treatises that

---

74. Cf. Brizio (1951); Pedretti (1960c), pp. 172–177. See also Codex Atlanticus 253 v-d, a folio of the Sforza period: "Point is that which cannot be divided in any part."

prompted Leonardo's famous remark in one of his late anatomical folios at Windsor: "Let no one read my principles who is not a mathematician." [75]

Irma A. Richter states that Greek geometry served as a model for the first chapters of the "Paragone." [76] It is perhaps not only a coincidence that about 1505 Leonardo intensified his studies of Euclid's *Elements*, as proved by his notes in MS K and by the fact that he assisted Pacioli in preparing the 1509 edition of the *Elements*.[77] The first chapters of the "Paragone," as well as the sixth paragraph of chapter 694f (680), are undoubtedly related in style to the notes for the "First Book on Water" in the Codex Arundel, *ca.* 1505–1508.

In the definition of the basic principles of painting Leonardo adheres to tradition. This attitude is not limited to the writings of his first Milanese period. In folios of the codices Arundel and Atlanticus written after 1500 Leonardo discusses Alberti's *Ludi Matematici* at length.[78] It is possible, therefore, that after 1500 Leonardo developed from Alberti's *della Pittura* his basic definition of the science of painting.

The first notes of the "Paragone" can be compared to many original notes dating after 1500, such as those in Codex Atlanticus 132 r-b. A sentence in a note in Codex Atlanticus 68 v-a, "Like zero in arithmetic, which is actually equal to one

---

75. Windsor 19,118r (An. C IV 14v).
Leonardo's sentence seems to be echoing Aristotle's sentence: "A man investigating principles cannot argue with one who denies their existence" (*Physica*, I. 2). Aristotle's sentence is quoted by Dante, *Convivio*, XV, which Leonardo might have known in the 1490 edition. In MS A 112v Leonardo quotes from the *Convivio*, IV, iii, the famous verses 52–53:

> *chi pinge figura*
> *se non po' esser lei non la po' porre.*

In his late period Leonardo approaches the subject of painting in the way Aristotle approaches science, and therefore he looks for mathematical principles even in the mechanism of the human smile. In fact, in Windsor 19,046 (*Fogli B dell'Anatomia* 29r) he considers the great number of facial muscles and concludes: ". . . and so always there are found as many muscles as correspond to the various attitudes of these lips and as many others as serve to reverse these attitudes; and these it is my purpose to describe and represent in full, proving these movements by means of my mathematical principles." This note dates from the time of the "Mona Lisa," *ca.* 1506.

Around 1510 Leonardo developed the study of facial muscles in relation to the expression of emotions. Cf. Windsor 19,012v (*Fogli A dell'Anatomia* 13v). The Windsor series of heads in profile nos. 12,553, 12,554, 12,556, and 12,557 can be considered as an instance of Leonardo's studies of emotions as expressed by facial muscles. Clark (1935) notes a connection between 19,012v and 12,556, and concludes that this series might date from about 1510.

In chapter 819 (872), *ca.* 1510, on the representation of colors at any distance, Leonardo recommends a practice which is based on the "certainty that belongs to mathematical demonstration." See also note 80 on the next page.

76. Irma A. Richter (1949), p. 20.

77. Cf. Calvi (1925), p. 208. Pacioli (1509b), "Dedicatory Letter," mentions the friends who exhorted him to prepare the edition of *Euclidis*: "quorum mihi carissimus Leonardus Vincius accessit, ut ederem." Cf. Solmi (1908), pp. 147–152.

78. Cf. Pedretti (1960c), p. 173; for the latest edition of Alberti's *Ludi Matematici* see Timpanaro (1926), pp. 3–36.

thousand or to an infinite number of them," can be compared to that of the first chapter of the "Paragone": "If you were to conceive of a whole composed of a thousand points, on dividing any part of that quantity of a thousand, that part, it might well be said, would be equal to its whole. This is shown by zero or nought, the tenth figure of arithmetic, in which nought is represented by o."

The Aristotelian concept of geometry as a "continuous quantity," with which the first chapter of the "Paragone" begins, is enunciated in MS M 18, *ca.* 1500: "Geometry is infinite, because every continuous quantity is infinitely divisible from one direction to another." References to "continuous quantity" are also found in two notes of *Libro* A and in Codex Atlanticus 199 v-b (plate 24), *ca.* 1506–1508. In a very late period Leonardo planned to write a "Treatise on Continuous Quantity." [79]

The concluding section of the first chapter of the "Paragone" seems to indicate with greater clarity the character of Leonardo's notes of his late period: "No human investigation can be termed true science if it is not capable of mathematical demonstration. If you say that the sciences which begin and end in the mind are true, I do not agree, but deny it for many reasons, and foremost among these the fact that the test of experiment is absent from these exercises of the mind, and without these there is no assurance of certainty." Similar concepts are found in notes that proclaim the value of experiment and the necessity for mathematics. These notes are usually from his late period, as that in MS G 94v, *ca.* 1510: "Nothing is proved certain where there is no possibility to apply one of the mathematical sciences." [80]

---

79. Codex Atlanticus 167 r a, *ca.* 1515.
80. See also the notes in Codex Atlanticus 154 r-c and Windsor 19,070. Cf. Brizio (1952), pp. 605–608; MacCurdy:I.627 ff.
"Certainty," "truth," "true information," "true knowledge," and "true science"— again and again these expressions occur in Leonardo's writings dating from after 1510. A number of these are found in *Libro* A; for example, 18: "la seconda cosa è che il pittore con gran discorso bisogna che con sottile investigazione ponga le *vere* qualità e quantità dell'ombre e lumi"; 27: "non si mostra mai integralmente del suo *vero* colore"; 29: "*vero* colore"; 82: "le linee AF e BF dov'è la *verità*"; 86: "volendolo fare con *certa e vera scienza.*" The expression *vera scienza* occurs again in MS E (*Libro* B) 54r (Mac-Curdy:I.488) in a note on the flight of birds: "Per dare la *vera scienza* del moto delli uccelli infra l'aria . . . ," and in a passage on water in Codex Arundel 162r, *ca.* 1508–1510: "E la *vera scienza* di tal retroso si vedrai nell'acqua caduta in iscalini interchiusa infra due piastre di vetro bianco e sottile. . . ." In his early writings Leonardo does not aim so much at achieving "certainty," but approaches the subjects of his studies in a more empirical way. Cf. MS A 38r, *ca.* 1492: "Modo semplice e naturale." In his early period he may refer to "teorica" and "pratica," but in his late period it is always "scienza," namely knowledge, that he opposes to practice. Cf. Lu 750 (McM 686), 1508–1510: "Here the opposition says that it does not want so much science, that it is enough to practice drawing from nature. . . ." This is linked to his observations in MS G 8r (Lu 80; McM 70), "On the Error of Those Who Practice without Science." It is revealing that a marginal note to this passage refers to Horace's *De Ars Poetica:* "Vedi primo la poetrica di Orazio"—probably to the well-known verses 408 ff. Leonardo may have referred to the 1509 edition of Horace (Venice, Aldus), which has a Preface by his patron and friend Iafredo Caroli. The last part of the Codex Urbinas, which can be dated in Leo-

Chapters at the beginning of the "Treatise on Painting" may date from the same period as the first one, 1500–1505, or perhaps later. The discussions on the supremacy of painting are not in contrast with the character of Leonardo's writings of a late period. It should be enough to mention the long attack on the alchemists and necromancers, as well as the pages against the abridgers of books, in folios at Windsor datable from 1505 to 1513.[81]

Other notes in the "Paragone" are undoubtedly related to the four chapters copied from MS Ashburnham 2038; and yet it is always possible that Leonardo had copied or developed, after 1500, notes on painting written during his Sforza period.

NOTES ON STUDIO PRACTICE

The second part of the Codex Urbinas is a collection of precepts for the painter, on studio practice. In the compilation of this part, Melzi used manuscripts from the first and second Milanese periods, in particular MS Ashburnham 2038 and MSS G and E, as well as the lost *Libro* A. One chapter was copied from the Codex Trivulzianus, *ca.* 1487–1490. The chapters of which the originals are lost must have come from early as well as late periods. Chapter 258a (186) was copied from MS A 79, a lost folio which G. B. Venturi transcribed in Paris in 1796.[82]

The second part [83] of the Codex Urbinas represents an autonomous section which can be considered in itself an abridged "Treatise on Painting." Almost every subject developed in other parts of the Codex Urbinas is already present in this part. The part has no title, but in the table of contents, folio 303, it is listed as "Precetti del Pittore," Rules for the Painter. The chronology of this part may appear to be the most difficult in the whole *Trattato*, because it includes writings from every period of Leonardo's activity. The first chapters are copied from the Codex Ashburnham, *ca.* 1492, and MS G, *ca.* 1510–1515. Almost the entire Codex Ashburnham has been copied in this part, along with several passages from MS G, *Libro* A, *Libro* B (MS E), MS F, MS L, and the Codex Trivulzianus. Several of the chapters included in this part could have been placed more appro-

nardo's last years, *ca.* 1515–1518, deals with the "true site of the horizon," and perhaps it is not a coincidence that in his will he has a remark on the "certainty of death, and the uncertainty of its time."

81. Windsor 19,045 (An. B 28v); 19,048 (An. B 31v-r); 19,047 (An. B 30v); 19,-084 (An. C II 14). Cf. Brizio (1952), pp. 494–501, 614–617.

82. Cf. De Toni (1924), pp. 84–85; *Commissione Vinciana* (1938), pp. 1–11.

83. The abridged compilation of the "Treatise on Painting," as it was published in 1651, began with this part. Some of the earlier manuscript copies of the abridged compilation still preserve the title "Parte Seconda." Cf. Steinitz (1958), pp. 49, 53. Other manuscript copies have annotations bearing witness to the existence of an unabridged compilation. These are at the end of the Apograph Nani at Venice: "There is another part of this book; they say that he [Leonardo] left it in Milan"; and at the end of the new apograph in the Raccolta Vinciana, Milan: "There is another part which somebody says was left in Milan." *Ibid.*, pp. 60–62; Pedretti (1959*b*), pp. 446–450.

priately in other parts of the *Trattato*. A section on "Reflections," for example, could have been placed next to a section on the same subject in the fifth part, and the chapters on the human figure should have been placed in the third part. But, as we have already pointed out, this lack of method in the compilation of the Codex Urbinas has the advantage for us of reflecting the nature of the manuscripts from which the compiler was copying. One can sense how several passages must have retained the sequence of the originals, and so their dating becomes easier in that the structure of the original manuscripts can be envisaged in the characteristics of contents and style.

Leonardo's rules for the painter have a certain consistency throughout the whole period of his activity. His recommendations (or, more accurately, his admonitions) in his early period are still basically the same in his late period. In his late period, however, his "precetti" become more concise, moving away from the Quattrocento flavor of a certain idealized image of the "life of the painter." The passage in Codex Ashburnham 27 v-r, "Of the Life of the Painter in His Studio" (chapter 50 [74] of the "Treatise on Painting"), containing the famous sentence "If you are alone you belong entirely to yourself" also recognizes the advantages of companionship as a means of approaching and selecting different methods of study.

In a passage dating from a much later period, Codex Atlanticus 184 v-c (*ca.* 1513–1514), which is not found in the "Treatise on Painting," Leonardo speaks again of the "Life of the Painter." He considers the painter no longer in his studio, but "in the country," and this immediately reveals a new approach to the subject, in accordance with the development of Leonardo's own researches. In his late period as a painter little time is left for activity in the studio. Natural phenomena call for direct observation, and even the study of light and shade is now carried out in the open air. Leonardo repeats the advice of being alone, but he has changed his opinion about the advantage of companionship. He accepts companions only if they "resemble him in a taste for these studies." Independently of the evidence of handwriting one can sense that it is an old man who is writing: ". . . . and if he fails to find any such he should accustom himself to be alone in his investigations, for in the end he will find no more profitable companionship."

Several of the "rules" in the *Trattato*, especially those in the second part, may cause perplexity in the reader who overlooks their chronology. K. R. Eissler, approaching the *Trattato* from the viewpoint of the "psychological interpretation of some statements," stresses Ludwig's opinion that Leonardo's *Trattato* shares with other Renaissance treatises a certain limitedness that "can best be summarized as an almost exclusive concern with craft rather than art." [84] Chapter 114 (90) contains a statement that, according to Eissler, is "a veritable slap to all and everything Leonardo stood for." In that chapter Leonardo states that the painter should aim at practicing art in accordance with a variety of ways so that he will be in agreement, in some part at least, with each of the current opinions held about art.

The text of this advice and of the subsequent explanations is in the style of

---

84. Eissler (1961), p. 228.

Leonardo's writings dating from *ca.* 1492, when the memory of his own training in the studio of Verrocchio at Florence was still fresh. In his early rules for the painter Leonardo must have included many of the lessons he learned there—among others that of listening to the criticism of his fellow painters in the studio. Leonardo's basic concern was always to master painting and draftmanship by means of a rigorous self-discipline. At a later date, in MS K 110 (30)v, *ca.* 1505–1507, he writes: "Men and words are actual, and you, painter, if you do not know how to execute your figures will be like an orator who does not know how to use his words." In *Libro* A 95 Leonardo says that two different judges of like intelligence do not agree with one another in selecting a model of beauty, and therefore the painter should make his selection in accordance with the opinions of both judges. This is basically a Classical attitude, and is typical for a Renaissance man.

In MS G 25r, *ca.* 1510, we find a note that has been copied in the second part of the Codex Urbinas, that is, chapter 52 (91): "The painter is not worthy of praise who does only one thing well, as the nude, or a head, or draperies, or animal life, or landscapes, or such special subjects; for there is no one so dull of understanding that after devoting himself to one subject only and continually practising at this, he will fail to do it well."

The versatility that characterizes the "pittore universale" is again a way to please "different judges of like intelligence." For Leonardo this does not imply a sacrifice of individuality. The painter must make his technical training the tool for achieving "reason," that is, the knowledge of everything he is dealing with. In Codex Atlanticus 76 r-a, which is dated 23 April 1490, Leonardo writes: "The painter who draws by practice and judgment of the eye without the use of reason, is like the mirror that reproduces within itself all the objects which are set opposite to it without knowledge of the same."

For Leonardo the "artist" is always the "painter," or the *operatore della pittura*. The word "artist" implying "creator" is not an invention of the Renaissance. And yet painting is no longer a craft, but has become a science. It is true that many of Leonardo's rules for the painter are still related to a Florentine tradition of craftsmanship, but as soon as Leonardo starts to write on painting, that is, about 1490, he tells the reader how his rules should be taken. In Codex Atlanticus 221 v-d, *ca.* 1490 (MacCurdy:II.279), we read:

These rules are to be used solely in testing figures; for every man in his first compositions makes certain mistakes, and if he does not become conscious of them he does not correct them; therefore in order to discover mistakes you should test your work and where you find there mistakes correct them, and remember never to fall into them again. But if you were to attempt to apply all these rules in composition you would never make a beginning and would cause confusion in your work.

These rules are intended to help you to a free and good judgment; for good judgment proceeds from good understanding, and good understanding comes from reason trained by good rules, and good rules are the children of sound experience, which is the common mother of all the sciences, and arts. If therefore you bear in

mind the precepts of my rules you will be able merely by the accuracy of your judg-
ment to criticize and discern every error in proportion in any work, whether it is
in the perspective or in the figures or other things.

These "children of sound experience"—the rules for the painter as found in
Leonardo's "Treatise on Painting"—reflect all the experiences of Leonardo's career
as a painter. If properly dated and understood they can become basic material for
the historian, and also for the psychoanalyst.

The last section of the second part of the Codex Urbinas, which occupies folios 62
to 78, is on the theory of color, perspective of color, and aerial perspective. Melzi
interrupted a series of precepts on the composition of *istorie* to introduce this concluding section. In fact he had already started to write the title of one more of those
precepts when he suddenly changed his plan. He crossed out the interrupted sentence "Regole da far che le figure" and wrote instead: "Fine—Comincia de Colori."
The chapter Melzi had first thought of copying is nowhere to be found in the
Trattato della Pittura.

The chapters of this section on color come from Leonardo's manuscripts of various
periods: MS A, *ca.* 1492; MS L, *ca.* 1502; MS F, 1508; MS E (*Libro B*), 1513–1514;
MS Trivulzianus, *ca.* 1487–1490; and *Libro* A. A considerable number of the chapters copied from lost manuscripts can be dated in a late period, after 1500, and
especially 1510–1515, by comparison with existing texts and with the several notes
on color in the lost *Libro* A. Chapters related to Lu 193 (McM 235), "Of the Differences in Colors According to their Distance or Nearness," can be compared to
notes in Codex Atlanticus 249 r-c (MacCurdy:II.368), a folio that can be dated
ca. 1513 because of a sketch of anatomy and a note on clouds and wind:

Many things of great bulk lose their visibility in the far distance by reason of
their colour, and many small things in the far distance retain their visibility by reason
of the said colour.

An object of a colour similar to that of the air retains its visibility at a moderate
distance, and an object that is paler than the air retains it in the far distance, and
an object which is darker than the air ceases to be visible at a short distance.

But of these three kinds of objects that will be visible at the greatest distance of
which the colour presents the strongest contrast to itself.

Observations on color and aerial perspective are found in several chapters in
other parts of the *Trattato della Pittura* (for example, at the end of Parts Three
and Five), also dating from Leonardo's late period. Although Leonardo's interest
in this problem is manifested fairly soon in his writings (for example, in MS A,
ca. 1492, and in Codex Atlanticus 160 r-a, *ca.* 1490), it is only in his late period
that it is intensified to such a degree as one would hardly expect from any of the
Florentine painters and theorists of the Quattrocento. The effort to find a mathematical formula for every natural phenomena is typical of Leonardo's late studies,
and is also evident in the way he approaches the problem of the alteration of shape
and color of objects viewed at various degrees of distance.

NOTES ON THE HUMAN FIGURE

The third part of the Codex Urbinas was planned as a book on the human figure, its proportions, and its movements. Melzi must have experienced great difficulty in organizing Leonardo's notes on this subject, for such notes are scattered in manuscripts from every period of Leonardo's activity. Many of them are on anatomical folios, and one can hardly decide whether they were intended to refer to anatomy or to painting. One of the notes on muscles in an anatomical folio at Windsor, 19,014, is marked with Melzi's slashed circle, but this note, similar in character to those of the third part of the Codex Urbinas, was not transcribed in the "Treatise on Painting." Another marked note in a folio at Windsor, 12,614, deals with the movement of the arm, and is related to the notes from *Libro* A; this note also was not transcribed in the Codex Urbinas.

The chronological analysis of the third part of the "Treatise on Painting" must be based on what is known of Leonardo's studies on the human figure. A group of notes in the Codex Urbinas can be dated before 1498, because at that time Luca Pacioli stated that Leonardo had already finished a "book on painting and human motion." In his early period Leonardo was particularly concerned with the problem of proportions. His drawing of the Vitruvian canon can be dated *ca.* 1490, because of the style and the characteristics of the handwriting.[85] The folios at Windsor containing notes on the proportions of the human figure are of similar date.[86] These notes are all marked by Melzi's slashed circle, but they were not transcribed in the Codex Urbinas. As Panofsky pointed out, they were transcribed in the Codex Huygens, together with those on the proportions of the horse.[87] Such studies of proportions must have been common practice in Florentine studios, as witness Verrocchio's drawings of proportions of the horse.[88]

Curiously enough, in his late period Leonardo had practically abandoned studies of proportion, although he continued to recommend them in his precepts for the painter. He became greatly concerned with the study of human motion. Notes on this subject are primarily in the early MS A, and Melzi used them in the Codex Urbinas, together with others which he found in lost manuscripts of the time of the "Battle of Anghiari," and in MS E (*Libro B*) and *Libro A*.

A few chapters of the third part of the Codex Urbinas can be taken as reference material for the chronology of Leonardo's studies on the human figure. In the well-known chapter 368 (396) on how to represent orators, Leonardo's concern

85. This drawing is usually dated 1485–1490. Cf. Popham (1947), pl. 215, and Heydenreich (1949), pl. XVIII. Heydenreich considers this drawing to be an illustration for a projected treatise on painting. Valentiner (1950), pp. 144–145, dates it 1476–1480. My date is based on characteristics of handwriting as compared to those of MS C, *ca.* 1490.

86. They are gathered in the sixth volume of the *Quaderni d'Anatomia*. Cf. Clark (1935), pp. 186–189.

87. Panofsky (1940), pp. 50 ff.   88. Cf. Valentiner (1950), p. 102.

with the study of expression is thus exemplified: "Good orators, when they wish to persuade their hearers of something, always accompany their words with gestures of their hands and arms, although some fools do not so ornament their speeches and on the tribunal seem to be statues of wood through whose mouths the voice of a man, concealed in the tribunal, is conducted by a speaking tube."

With such a note Leonardo intended to begin a series of descriptions of *moti mentali*. A program of discussion on this topic is outlined in various chapters, for instance in those from 357 (385) to 359 (411), and from 370 (408) to 376 (403). Chapter 376 was copied from carta 24 of *Libro A*, and may represent the latest term in the chronological sequence of the notes on this subject. Chapter 368 (396) appears in an intermediate position, being referred to the period 1505–1508. This chapter concludes: "But to return to our intent, here below will be represented and discussed many emotions; that is: anger, pain, sudden fright, weeping, desire, command, negligence, solicitude and the like." The transcriber added: "But note, reader, that although Messer Leonardo promises to treat all the emotions mentioned above, he does not speak of them, I believe, through forgetfulness or some other accident, as can be seen in the original, for after this chapter he writes the heading of another, without writing the chapter, and it is the following: On Representing an Angry Man and into How Many Parts that Emotion is Divided."

Chapter 381 (422), "How the Figure of an Angry Man is Depicted," copied from MS Ashburnham 29v, *ca.* 1492, does not contradict the hypothesis that chapter 368 (396) was of a late period. On the contrary, it may explain why at the end of chapter 368 Leonardo had written only the title of the chapter on the "angry man." Perhaps he recollected having already considered this subject in an earlier notebook and he wished to check that notebook before going any further.

The programmatic line of discussion, "Si figurerà et dirà" (It will be represented in drawing and discussed), as established in chapter 368 is exactly the method of Leonardo's anatomical studies of about 1510. Thus, many short notes in the third part of the Codex Urbinas can be recognized as having been copied from notebooks of Leonardo's late period. In the lost originals these notes must have been illustrated with large drawings representing the movement of man and expressions of *moti mentali*. A fragment in Codex Atlanticus 271 v-c belongs to this category of notes, which are frequently found in folios at Windsor. This fragment, which results from the mutilation of a large drawing, contains a note of the type of those of the third part of the Codex Urbinas. Characteristic of such notes is their title, which is often longer than the chapter itself. The fragment in the Codex Atlanticus reads as follows: [89]

> *On the changes in the muscles of the animals*
> *caused by the bending or stretching of*
> *their limbs.*
> *The thickness of limbs varies by means of the action of their muscles.*

---

89. In my "Saggio di una cronologia dei fogli del 'Codice Atlantico'" (1957*b*, p. 278) I suggested dating this fragment *ca.* 1505–1508.

This note can be placed chronologically between chapters 332 (312) and 333 (321), the latter being copied from *Libro* A. In the former, which indicates the change in muscles during the movement of limbs, Leonardo states: "On this subject a special book will be written." Chapter 271 (296), from *Libro* A, and those from 272 (286) to 277 (310) may relate to this subject.

Leonardo's concern with the mechanics of muscles stems from his study of the surface of the human body. His studies on anatomy cover a period of about twenty years, from *ca.* 1490 to *ca.* 1510. The Codex Urbinas notes on anatomy for the painter should be arranged in correct chronological sequence within this span of time. Such a chronological rearrangement can be compared to that of Leonardo's studies on flight.[90] During the Sforza period Leonardo was concerned with an attempt to construct a machine capable of reproducing the flight of birds. After 1500 he became engrossed in the study of the flight of birds as a science in itself, related to the study of wind.

In his study of the human figure Leonardo was first concerned with surface modeling. In the first phase of his activity he was still rooted in the Quattrocento tradition, studying the proportions, postures, and gestures of the human body. At the beginning of the Cinquecento, Leonardo proclaims to himself the need of a deeper anatomical knowledge. In chapter 340 (329), from MS L, *ca.* 1502, he establishes a new program of research: "How it is necessary for the painter to know anatomy." Such a program is echoed by many notes in the *Fogli B dell'Anatomia* at Windsor. In one of them, Windsor 19,044 (B 27), Leonardo states: "You will make the rule and the measurement of each muscle and give the reason of all their uses, in what manner they work and what moves them. . . ." The drawings in this folio represent the muscles of the back and upper arm; they are stylistically close to the Turin drawing for the "Battle of Anghiari," containing figures of a standing warrior seen from the back, which Raphael reproduces in his "Judgment of Solomon." [91]

Windsor 19,037 (B 20) is a revealing example of the chronological problems in the third part of the "Treatise on Painting." At two different times, namely in 1489–1490 and in 1502–1503, Leonardo wrote in this folio his plans for a discussion on the human figure and movement. In the early program we find titles in which anatomy and painting are still combined, and these are related to the notes in the Codex Urbinas copied from MS A and from other manuscripts of an early date. The program of 1502–1503 is related to chapter 340 (329), copied from MS L 79. Leonardo is now concerned with anatomy as a science in itself, and not only as an auxiliary to the practice of painting and sculpture: "Several muscles come in evidence in the various movements of animals, and several of them are reduced in thickness; on this subject it is necessary to make a long treatise, with the purpose of knowing the places injured by wounds, and also for the purpose of sculptors and painters. . . ."

---

90. Giacomelli (1936).
91. Cf. Popham (1946), pl. 197; Gould (1954), pp. 126–127.

Leonardo's program of research on the mechanics of muscles, as dictated by the need of representing gestures properly, is clearly defined in the above-mentioned chapter 340 (329) from MS L 79:

It is a necessary thing for the painter, in order to be good at arranging parts of the body in attitudes and gestures which can be represented in the nude, to know the anatomy of the sinews, bones, muscles, and tendons. He should know their various movements and force, and which sinew or muscle occasions each movement, and paint those only distinct and thick, and not the others, as do many who, in order to appear to be great draughtsmen, make their nudes wooden and without grace, so that they seem a sack full of nuts rather than the surface of a human being, or indeed, a bundle of radishes rather than muscular nudes.

When Leonardo wrote this program, in 1502, he had already returned to Florence. The concluding sentence reveals to us the prevailing trend among the Florentine artists at that time, and is perhaps an allusion to the young Michelangelo and his followers. In fact, Giovan Paolo Lomazzo, in his *Trattato della pittura* (1584), p. 291, has a similar criticism with a specific reference to Michelangelo: "Beware the painter not to do as Michelangelo did, who, wishing to show how to be a master at anatomy, gave all his figures those muscles that the anatomist alone is able to see through dissection."

The rendering of muscles so as to convey the impression of a "sack of nuts" is criticized again in chapter 334 (309), which must therefore be dated after 1500. After this chapter the compiler transcribes a text from MS G 26r, in which Leonardo explains that "the hollow spaces interposed between the muscles must not be of such a character as that the skin should seem to cover two sticks laid side by side like *c*, nor should they seem like two sticks somewhat remote from such contact so that the skin hangs in an empty loose curve as at *f*; but it should be like *i*, laid over the spongy fat that lies in the angles as the angle *n m o*." "Nuts" and "sticks" are one and the same in Leonardo's terminology, but whereas he uses "nut" to give color to his criticism, he uses "stick" as more suitable to his scientific demonstration.

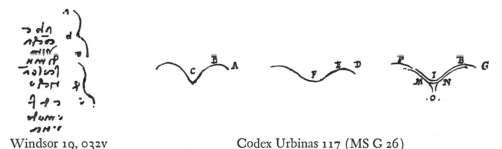

Windsor 19, 032v   Codex Urbinas 117 (MS G 26)

The chapter copied from MS G is illustrated with three diagrams. Two similar diagrams are in Windsor 19,032v (*Fogli B dell'Anatomia* 15v) with the explanation: "*a b c*, hollow of ancient muscle; *c d f* is modern." No doubt Leonardo is here referring to muscles rendered according to ancient and modern usages, and the passage copied from MS G is our only evidence that he did not approve of the antique system which had become in his day the system of rendering muscles as a sack of nuts.

In the period of his studies for the "Battle of Anghiari" Leonardo must have seen several examples of antique statuary, especially if he visited Rome, as it seems he did, at the beginning of the sixteenth century. Cesariano, in his commentary to Vitruvius (Como, 1521), p. xlvit, ranks Leonardo with Mantegna and Bramante as one who achieved "not only excellence, but also nobility" through the study of Roman antiquities. And it was around 1500 that the anonymous Prospectivo Milanese Dipintore dedicated his poem "Antiquarie prospettiche romane" to Leonardo. Leonardo must have known of the antique theory of sculpture as vulgarized by Gauricus in his *De sculptura* published in Florence in 1504, when Leonardo was at work on the "Battle of Anghiari." Gauricus not only mentioned and praised Leonardo but, in common with Leonardo, promoted the grand style of the Cinquecento as opposed to the naturalism of the older generation; and so he criticized Verrocchio for the excessive anatomical detailing of his horse for the Colleoni statue, and Cristoforo Solari for his exaggeration in rendering muscles. These ideas reflect the conflict between naturalism and classicism at the beginning of the sixteenth century, and Leonardo aims at resolving such a conflict by means of a closer examination of antique models and a deeper study of anatomy. As a result, he adopts a more sculptural style and moves toward anatomy as a science in itself.

Chapter 340 (329) from MS L 79 is one of the keys for the chronology of the third part of the Codex Urbinas. After a period of new programs at the beginning of 1500, Leonardo wrote notes on movement, which are illustrated by tiny sketches, as we see in folios of the time of the "Battle of Anghiari," and finally he wrote notes on limbs concerning the structure of bones, as in MS K, *ca.* 1504–1505.[92] This

---

92. The notes and drawings on comparative anatomy in MS K 102 (22)r and 109 (29–30)v are most likely to be dated in Leonardo's second Milanese period, from 1506 to 1508. They are in the third part of MS K, that is, in a section that was written in Milan. Cf. Calvi (1925), pp. 201 ff. One of the notes on folio 109v refers to the name of a Milanese family (Aliprandi). Therefore the notes on painting and hydraulics in the third part of MS K are also to be dated in Leonardo's second Milanese period at the time of *Libro A*. On folio 108 (28)r is a sketch in red chalk of a leg in profile accompanied by a note that establishes a program of study: "Give the anatomy of the leg up to the hip from all its sides, in every action, so as to show everything; veins, arteries, nerves, tendons, and muscles, skin and bones; then with the bones in section in order to show the thickness of the bones." The anatomical notes in MS K are developed in Windsor 12,625, which should therefore be dated from after 1506 (Clark dates it *ca.* 1504 because of the Anghiari type of the figures, but he refers it stylistically to Windsor 12,424, which he dates *ca.* 1506). Moreover, the Windsor drawing contains a word (Cordusio) written in red chalk (top center) which refers to a place in Milan still known today as Piazza Cordusio. See also the drawing in the British Museum (Popham 235) which is similar in technique to the Windsor drawing (red chalk on red prepared paper), and a drawing in the Ambrosiana Library, again in the same technique and also showing legs in profile and front view. The Ambrosiana drawing, which is reproduced in Pedretti (1957b), pl. XVII, contains a note in red chalk referring to Lombard names and localities (Bernardo da Ponte . . . Val di Lugan). Apparently Leonardo developed his studies on comparative anatomy only after the

latter category covers a period from *ca.* 1505 to 1510, and is represented in the Codex Urbinas by notes from chapters 271 to 274 (296, 286, 300, 301), which are close in time to the notes on the anatomical folios at Windsor dated about 1510.

After that time, Leonardo resumed his study of human motion, and established new programs of research, as we can see in *Libro B* (MS E) 20, in a note probably written in Rome in 1513–1514: "Describe which muscles and tendons, through various movements of each limb, become exaggerated, or hidden, or do neither one nor the other. Remember that such a study is most important and necessary for painters and sculptors who would become masters." Sir Kenneth Clark quotes another note from MS E ("O anatomical painter beware, lest in the attempt to make your nudes display all their emotions by a too strong indication of bones, sinews, and muscles, you become a wooden painter") as an unmistakable reference to Michelangelo's painting in the Sistine Ceiling.[93] According to Clark, Leonardo understood that the true purpose of Michelangelo's anatomical display was the expression of emotion, but saw in it the seed of mannerism. Clark's assumption has historical support. In 1586 Giovan Battista Armenini reported what he had heard from a Milanese pupil of Leonardo (perhaps Melzi?): "Leonardo da Vinci, as one of his Milanese pupils has told me, when he once saw such a painting by Michelangelo [i.e., "The Last Judgment"] and probably realized what method had been employed, had the audacity to say that this was the only thing that displeased him in this picture because too few figures were used in too many positions, so that the figure of a youth and the figure of an old man had the same muscles and the same outlines." [94]

The mistake of relating Leonardo's criticism to a painting that he could not have seen does not deprive his pupil's anecdote of its documentary value. Obviously, Leonardo referred not to the figures of the "Last Judgment" but to those of the Sistine Ceiling. Leonardo's opinion reported by Armenini echoes several passages in MS E which were all copied in the Codex Urbinas, as well as certain passages from the lost *Libro A*. As we have pointed out, the latter are basically related to Alberti's theory of *decorum*.

The drawings illustrating the chapters on the human figure in the third part of the Codex Urbinas deserve special attention because they reflect definite phases of Leonardo's style. But before considering them it is necessary to examine in some detail the material that occupies the second half of Part Three, from chapter 402 (363) on. As we have already mentioned, this material deals with a variety of subjects, such as light and shade, color, linear and aerial perspective, landscape, reflection in water, outlines and background of figures, and the effect of relief in painting. It might appear strange that a section of the *Trattato della Pittura* which was intended for the human figure should include this material, but we can see

---

period of the "Battle of Anghiari." The type of human figure in the anatomical drawings of his second Milanese period is still closely related to the Anghiari type of a standing warrior; cf. the Turin drawing in Popham 197.

93. Clark (1952), pp. 130–131.   94. Armenini (1586), pp. 98–99.

that the same thing happens with Leonardo's original manuscripts on anatomy, dating from after 1506, in which notes on these subjects appear frequently. In this section of the *Trattato* the compiler made great use of *Libro* A and *Libro* B, which he had at hand during the compilation of the chapters on the human figure. Of course he used also manuscripts of an earlier period, such as MS Ashburnham and Codex Trivulzianus. And yet one can still perceive which of the notes that are no longer preserved in the originals come from an early manuscript and which come from a late one. In the case of chapter 405 (441) we have the evidence of a date around 1510 given by a draft in the Windsor anatomical folio 19,121r (plate 26). If we look in the original manuscripts for notes on clouds and effects of atmosphere to be compared to analogous chapters in this section, we see that such notes are found in manuscripts dating from about 1508, such as MS F, Codex Leicester, Codex Arundel, Codex Atlanticus, and anatomical folios at Windsor, in which Leonardo was also recording extensive observations on the reflection of the sun in water. These observations were related to his belief that the moon had water, and he intended them to be developed in a section of his projected book on perspective. Chapters on the reflection of water in the third part of the Codex Urbinas (503–508) belong to this category of studies and are another hint of the extent of the original material that has not come down to us. To sum up, the whole Part Three of Codex Urbinas well reflects the activity of Leonardo in the years around 1506 to 1513, including the resuming of subjects already treated in his earlier Sforza period. The subject of the effect of relief in a painting, which is considered in chapters 491 to 497, must have been a common preoccupation of painters in his day. In a chapter that was copied in the second part of the Codex Urbinas, 118 (220), from MS Ashburnham 10, Leonardo states that "many times painters despair of their ability to imitate natural appearance, seeing that their paintings do not have that relief and vividness that things seen in a mirror have," and the explanation he gives of the impossibility of reproducing the effect of relief seen in a mirror is the same as that given in MS Ashburnham 19, in a note copied in the third part of the Codex Urbinas as chapter 493 (489): "Why, of two objects of equal size, will the painted one seem larger than the one in relief." Leonardo attached special importance to this problem throughout his career as a painter, and it is only natural that he should have insisted on it also in his later period when the style of his paintings and drawings aims at conveying a greater effect of plasticity. He takes it up in chapter 432 (*Libro* A 39) and in his studies on binocular vision in MS D, *ca.* 1508. In *Libro* A 38 Leonardo advises the painter how to arrange light and background in order to achieve the best conditions for enhancing the roundness of a figure. And it is again in *Libro* A, 18, that the effect of relief is considered as the "first marvel of painting," and therefore as the main reason for considering painting superior to sculpture, because such an effect can be achieved only through knowledge of the nature of light and shade—a knowledge that the sculptor does not need. Leonardo investigates the optical effect of painted relief and actual relief as early as 1487–1490, in Codex Trivulzianus 38v, a note copied in the Codex Urbinas as chapter 496 (486), and again in the preceding chapters 494 and 495. The originals of these two chapters are lost, but their date could be *ca.* 1492 in common with chapter 493, which was copied from MS Ashburnham 19. But a later date is also possible. In chapter 494 Leonardo refers to the diagram as being placed in the margin, as would be the case with a manuscript dating from after 1500. Moreover,

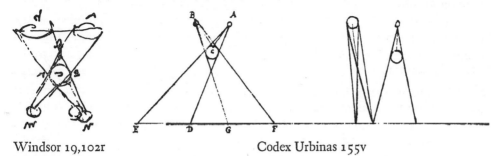

Windsor 19,102r   Codex Urbinas 155v

this diagram is identical to that which illustrates a note in Windsor 19,102r (Richter [1883], I, 29), a folio of anatomy dating from about 1513: "Why will not the picture seen by both eyes produce the effect of relief, as [real] relief does when seen by both eyes, and why should a picture seen with one eye give the same effect of relief as real relief under the same conditions of light and shade."

This preoccupation with achieving the effect of relief in painting has a direct bearing on his anatomical studies. His anatomical drawings, which date from after 1506, are rendered with a technique of shading that conveys the effect of roundness, and establish a type of scientific illustration that reappears only later in the figures of Vesalius' *De humani corporis fabrica* (1543) and in Ruini's *Anatomia del cavallo* (1598).

THE DRAWINGS FOR THE BOOK ON THE VARIOUS STATES AND MOVEMENTS OF THE HUMAN BODY

In his anatomical studies of 1508–1510 Leonardo emphasizes the importance of perspective. In Windsor 19,070 he wrote a famous passage on his own practice of dissection. Among the difficulties in such a work, he includes the proper representation of the human figure: ". . . and even if you have such ability to draw, it might be that your drawing will not be correct in perspective." In another note of that time, concerning perspective in the representation of the human figure, Leonardo writes: "Explain these words, because they are confused." [95] His preoccupation is the three-dimensional representation of objects: "The true comprehension of every figure is obtained by the knowledge of its width, height, and length; then the same thing I use in representing the human figure to every sound intellect." [96] These words evoke Cellini's description of Leonardo's lost book on perspective: ". . . the most beautiful a man ever made, showing how objects foreshorten not only in depth but also in breadth and height." [97]

---

95. Windsor 19,003v (An. A 4v).   96. *Ibid.*
97. Cf. Steinitz (1958), pp. 25–27. See also p. 98 above.

It is hard to say which notes on the human body in Leonardo's manuscripts from about 1510 were intended for the book on painting, and which for the book on anatomy. In the notes on painting of that period the references to the books on anatomy became more frequent. For the first time, Leonardo seems concerned with publishing his studies on anatomy. The format he adopted in his studies indicates that he was concerned with their reproduction. The anatomical studies are presented in large detailed drawings with just a few notes of commentary. In Windsor 19,007 (*Fogli A dell'Anatomia* 8v) Leonardo envisages how his studies should be published: ". . . and as regards this benefit which I give to posterity I teach the method of printing it in order, and I beseech you who come after me, not to let avarice constrain you to make the prints in . . . [*sic*]." Unfortunately, the last word is missing, together with a small piece of the margin. We do not know the type of reproduction Leonardo was referring to. Perhaps he was referring to woodcut, a process widespread in his time. With such a process, his anatomical drawings would not have been reproduced accurately.

From another source we have confirmation that Leonardo intended to publish his anatomical studies, and we are told that his drawings were meant to be reproduced from copper plates. Paolo Giovio, who knew Leonardo personally, writes of Leonardo's anatomical studies as follows:

Secare quoque noxiorum hominum cadavera in ipsis medicorum scholis inhumano foedoque labore didicerat, ut varii membrorum flexus et conatus ex vi nervorum vertebrarumque naturali ordine pingerentur. Propterea particularum omnium formam in tabellis, usque ad exiles venulas, interioraque ossium, mira solertia figuravit, ut ex eo tot annorum opere (infinita exempla) ad artis utilitatem typis aeneis excunderentur. [In order that he might be able to paint the various joints and muscles as they bend and stretch according to the laws of nature he dissected the corpses of criminals in the medical schools, indifferent to this inhuman and disgusting work. He then tabulated all the different parts down to the smallest veins and the composition of the bones with extreme accuracy in order that this work on which he had spent so many years should be published from copper engravings for the benefit of art (Richter [1939], I, 3).]

The Leonardo drawings Giovio is referring to are most likely the *Fogli A dell'Anatomia* at Windsor. This would explain their "unusually dull and lifeless style" (Clark). A calligraphic precision of line and a shading rendered by a minute, uniform hatching are characteristics that Leonardo was expecting from copper engravings. The only other medium available to him—woodcut—was inadequate to render "the smallest veins and the composition of the bones with extreme accuracy."

When he planned a book on painting, he must have kept in mind the same problem. Perhaps for this reason his notes on painting are always illustrated with simple, tiny figures and diagrams, easy to reproduce in woodcut. This can be considered an indirect proof that Leonardo intended to publish a treatise on painting.

The tiny sketches, which are frequent in the notes of the third part of the Codex Urbinas, reflect the style of Leonardo's late period. In Melzi's original codex these

sketches show more evidence of their stylistic relationship with the originals from
which they were copied. They are very close in style to those in Windsor 19,038v
(plate 23) and 19,149, which Sir Kenneth Clark dates from the period of the
"Battle of Anghiari," *ca.* 1503–1504. Some of them are on folios with notes for
the treatise on light and shade, and can thus be dated about 1505–1508. Similar
sketches of a slightly later date are in Codex Leicester, folio 8, and on the cover
of MS F.

Windsor 19,038r (plate 22) contains a plan for a Book on the Human Figure
and Anatomy which appears to be in the handwriting of *ca.* 1489. Notes and
sketches on the movement of the torso, on the upper part of this folio, date from
ca. 1503–1505 because they are related to those on Windsor 12,640, a folio containing studies for the "Battle of Anghiari." (The subject of the movements of
the shoulder is developed in *Libro A* 39.) In the sketches of human figures in
movement dating from the period of the "Battle of Anghiari," *ca.* 1503–1505,
Leonardo adopts the new technique of rendering form by means of lines of shadow
that follow the curves. An example of this type of drawing is to be seen in the
figures on the verso of Windsor 19,038 (plate 23). This characteristic of Leonardo's
drawings after 1503 is reflected in Melzi's copies in the Codex Urbinas; for example, in the figures on folio 120.

Codex Urbinas 120

The Windsor drawing 19,038 is one of the *Fogli B dell'Anatomia* series, namely
the folios in which after 1500 Leonardo resumed his anatomical studies begun
around 1489. The drawings and notes on human movement become more frequent
in Leonardo's manuscripts after 1503. One of them is also found among the notes
on hydraulics in Codex Leicester 8r. A note on a man using up the impetus of his
running in Windsor 19,038v (plate 23) is related to that in Codex Atlanticus
181 r-a, a folio that dates after the period of the "Battle of Anghiari" because of
a note on the problem of Alhazen.[98] Leonardo became concerned with this problem
on optics and geometry at the time of MS F, 1508. This folio of the Codex Atlanticus also contains a note on color with a reference to the book on painting.

Windsor 12,707 represents, as Clark suggested, the type of sketches Leonardo
used about 1505 as illustrations for notes on painting. The parent sheet in the
Codex Atlanticus confirms Clark's dating of this fragment.[99]

---

98. Leonardo's attempts to solve the problem of Alhazen date from after 1506–
1508. Cf. Marcolongo (1937), pp. 71–84.
99. Pedretti (1957a), pl. 25.

Codex Atlanticus 199 v-a (plate 24), which can be dated *ca.* 1506, contains an example of notes on painting illustrated by small diagrams and sketches of human figures in movement. The text contains instructions on how to draw such figures:

On study and order of study. I say that first you ought to learn limbs and their mechanism, and having this knowledge, their actions should come next, according to the circumstances in which they occur in man. And thirdly to compose subjects, studies for which should be taken from natural actions and made from time to time, as circumstances allow; and pay attention to people in the streets and piazze and fields, and note them down with a brief indication of the forms; thus for a head make an O, and for an arm a straight or a bent line, and the same for the legs and the body, and when you return home work out these notes in complete form.

The folio containing this note is of the same kind of paper and ink, as well as handwriting, as the well-known folio containing the estimated cost of every detail of the Trivulzio monument, Codex Atlanticus 179 r-a, *ca.* 1506–1507. It may also be compared to Codex Atlanticus 352 v-c, a folio containing a note and sketch on human movement; the *recto* of this folio carries architectural studies pertaining to the period of Leonardo's activity in the service of Charles d'Amboise, *ca.* 1506–1507.

The above rule on how to draw sketches of human movement can be compared to chapter 64 (257), from MS Ashburnham, folio 8v, *ca.* 1492. In the original manuscript this chapter is illustrated by a sketch of a standing man, not copied by Melzi. This sketch can be compared to Windsor 12,718, a fragment taken from Codex Atlanticus 20 v-b, *ca.* 1502–1503.[100] Such a comparison stresses the difficulty of recognizing a definite difference between sketches of the early period and sketches of the late period. Windsor 19,070 (An. C I 13), which illustrates a note related to chapter 388 (378), that is, *Libro A* 36, is likewise very similar to a sketch in MS A 28v. However, in the early sketches the human figure is usually shown with indications of facial features, whereas in sketches from the late period the human figure is reduced to schematic lines with the head indicated by a simple circle, as Leonardo suggests in the note in Codex Atlanticus 199 v-a (plate 24).

Since the drawings in the Codex Urbinas reflect the style of Leonardo's drawings of definite periods, we can attempt to classify them chronologically. This attempt is limited to the sketches of human figure (see table opposite).

Lomazzo speaks of Melzi as a "great miniaturist," [101] and the drawings in the Codex Urbinas undoubtedly have a miniature-like quality. Some of the diagrams on light and shade copied from MS A are very close to the quality of Leonardo's originals. The profile of a woman in folio 135v of the Codex Urbinas best exemplifies the copyist's ability in rendering the character of Leonardo's sketches.

---

100. Pedretti (1957*a*), pl. 2. See also Reti (1959), pl. 26.

101. Lomazzo (1584), p. 106: ". . . secondo che mi ha raccontato il Signor Francesco Melzi, suo discepolo, grandissimo miniatore. . . ." We must note, incidentally, that suggestions to miniaturists are found in Leonardo's "Treatise on Painting" in chapters 797 (809) and 152 (219).

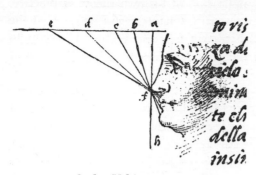

Codex Urbinas 135v

In McMahon's facsimile this sketch appears quite coarse, but Manzi's and Ludwig's editions give an even worse reproduction. Chapter 422 (452), to which this figure belongs, may be dated after 1500, both for its contents and for the reflected style of its illustration. This profile of a woman recalls the type of Isabella d'Este or Mona Lisa. Curiously enough, the first French edition of the "Treatise on Painting" (Paris, 1651) has this chapter illustrated not only by the profile in the diagram but also by what can be considered as the first engraving after the "Mona Lisa." The Italian edition of the *Trattato*, also published in Paris in 1651, does not have such an engraving. A drawing of the "Mona Lisa" is in an apograph of the "Treatise on Painting" in the Bibliothèque National at Paris. (MS Fr. 9154). It might be that the addition of a reproduction of the "Mona Lisa" was suggested by Cassiano dal Pozzo who saw the painting in 1625.

As we have seen, the drawings in the Codex Urbinas are made by the same hand that wrote the text, namely Melzi's. The diagrams were usually made at the same time as the text, because they are in the same pen and ink as that used for the text. The sketches of human figure, on the contrary, were added later in spaces left blank in the text. Melzi used a different pen and ink to draw these figures, tracing a light sketch in pencil or silverpoint.

Chapter 280 (384) seems to allude to the type of sketches Leonardo made for the studies of the "Battle of Anghiari." This may indicate a complementary element in dating Leonardo's lost chapters of the *Trattato della Pittura*. In fact,

---

SKETCHES OF THE HUMAN FIGURE IN THE CODEX URBINAS

Date	Leonardo's Original Drawings	Codex Urbinas, folio
ca. 1492	MS A & Ashburnham 2038	139v, 160v, 219
1503–1508	Codex Atlanticus 199 v-a and 352 v-c; Windsor 19,038v and 19,149	105v, 106, 119v, 120–120v 128, 129v,* 135v
1508–1515	Windsor 12,707, *Libro A*, *Libro B* (i.e., MS E), MS G	104v,† 105,‡ 108–108v, 112–112v, 113–113v, 137,§ 139

* See the sketches of horses in the drawing 15,577 at Turin (Popham 197).
† Copied from *Libro A*, carta 64; cf. Windsor 19,004 (An. A 5r).
‡ Cf. Windsor 19,001 (An. A 2r).
§ Copied from *Libro A*, carta 34; cf. Windsor 12,708, *ca.* 1500–1505, reproduced in Pedretti (1957a), pl. 18.

when Leonardo gives an example of an application of his own theory or practice, he usually refers to his latest experiences as an artist. Chapter 336 (328), "That the Nude Represented with Muscles in Full Evidence Is without Motion," seems to evoke Leonardo's drawings of nudes for the "Battle of Anghiari," of the type of those at Turin and at Windsor.

Even the references to the media of painting and drawing may be useful for establishing the chronology. In chapter 179 (249) Leonardo speaks of the use of silverpoint on paper prepared with bone meal, that is, the use of "carte inossate," which had been the practice in Florentine studios since the time of Cennini. Leonardo used this medium only during the Sforza period. Chapter 219 (144) may also refer to the same period as chapter 179, because Leonardo speaks of the medium of "carte tinte," but this medium is not necessarily related to the Sforza period, because there is no specification of color. About 1483–1490 Leonardo used to prepare the paper with blue ground on which silverpoint produced a blue-gray tone almost like the surface of the paper. These drawings do not have sharp contrasts. After 1500 Leonardo adopted an analogous technique of drawing, that of red chalk on red prepared paper. He used this medium especially from 1504 to 1511, to convey both the vigorous vitality of nudes and the atmospherical effects of distant mountains.[102]

NOTES ON DRAPERY

The studies of draperies are characteristic of the early years of Leonardo's activity, because they were a common practice in the studios of Verrocchio and Ghirlandaio. Leonardo's concern with this subject is not limited to his early period. Thus several notes on drapery in the fourth part of the Codex Urbinas certainly date from the Sforza period, but some of them may date from after 1500.

Windsor 19,121r (plate 26), which can be dated after 1505 because of its relation with the contents of *Libro A*, contains the following drafts of notes on painting:

Variety in the istorie: *Thin cloths, thick, new, and old ones, with broken and entire plaits; sweet ruffles, shaded ones, and less shaded, reflected and not reflected, expeditious and confused ones, according to the distance and various colors; and garments according to rank, long and short, flying and stiff according to the movements; such as fit to the figures, or fly and with the seams flutter upward or downward according to the plaits, and such as cling to the feet and keep off from them, according to the posture or bending or turning or thrusting of the legs within them; such as fit to the joints or keep off from them, according to the tread, or the movement, or the wind which is feigned; and that the plaits be accommodated to the quality of the cloths, transparent or opaque*

The greatest fault of the painter is to repeat the same postures and the same countenances . . . in one. . . .

---

102. Cf. Popham (1946), pls. 233, 235, 236, 238, and 285 *a–b*.

On the thin cloths of the women in walking, running and jumping, and their variety. . .

And in the [book on] painting make a discourse on the cloths and other vestments.

Discourse on the herbs, some of which have the first blossom placed in the upper end of the stem, others have it in the lowest part.

And you, painter, who desires great practice, know that if you [do not] procure it first well yourself, with good foundation, you will make a work with very little honor and less gain, and if you make it good, it will work great honor and utility.

These notes are all crossed out in accordance with Leonardo's system of copying or developing preparatory notes. The last note in this folio is found, with little alteration, in chapter 405 (441) of the "Treatise on Painting." Similar crossed-out notes are found in folios of the Codex Atlanticus, for instance in folio 345 v-b (plate 25), which certainly dates from 1508–1510 because of the sketches on the canalization of the Adda.[103]

In chapter 533 (573) Leonardo recommends the imitation of the Greeks and Romans, "in the manner of revealing limbs when the wind presses draperies against them." In his youth Leonardo studied the collection of antique sculptures gathered in the Medici garden at Florence.[104] Chapter 533 may belong to the first Milanese period, at the time of the following note in Codex Atlanticus 147 r-b: "The imitation of antiquities is more praiseworthy than that of modern works." A date around 1508, however, might also be possible, because during that time Leonardo worked in sculpture, assisting Giovan Francesco Rustici. In Codex Atlanticus 286 v-c, *ca.* 1505–1508, Leonardo wrote "Orto de' Medici, fatiche d'Ercole a Pier Francesco Cinori."

Among Leonardo's drawings of draperies are some from a period after 1500. The famous figure of a "Lady Pointing into Distance" (frontispiece) on Windsor 12,581 and the drawing of "Dancing Maidens" at Venice [105] provide appropriate illustrations of some of the precepts of the above quoted passage from Windsor 19,121.

The Windsor fragment 12,705 (plate 27, *b*) is also a study of drapery. Clark dates it *ca.* 1502 on the basis of a comparison with the sketch in MS L 80v. Richter, on the contrary, uses it as an illustration for Leonardo's note on painting in MS Ashburnham, folio 18, that is chapter 539 (569) of the "Treatise on Painting." [106] The identification in the Codex Atlanticus of the parent sheet of that fragment confirms Clark's suggested date.[107] Recently, Popham has compared Windsor 12,705 to a drawing that Ambrogio Figino had copied from a lost manuscript of Leonardo.[108] Figino's figure represents a man seen from the back in three-quarter view, with a cloak held on the right shoulder (plate 27, *a*). A note of an ancient

---

103. Cf. Codex Atlanticus 141 v-b; Calvi (1925), pp. 295 ff.
104. Cf. Beltrami (1919), document 161.
105. Popham (1946), pl. 126.   106. Richter (1883), I, 391, note.
107. Pedretti (1957*a*), p. 39.   108. Popham (1958), pp. 275–276.

collector, probably Padre Resta, suggests that the figure represents Lodovico Sforza, but such an identification is not reliable. The drawing is rather in the style of the drapery studies in MS L and Windsor 12,705. The profile of the rider, as Popham points out, reflects Leonardo's typical way of representing the eye, the mouth, and the line of the neck. It can be compared to the profiles of kneeling figures in the first folios of MS L.

Ambrogio Figino may have copied this drawing from a Leonardo manuscript similar to MS L. This assumption is supported by the fact that Ambrogio Mazenta presented him with one of Leonardo's notebooks from the Melzi collection, most probably one of those listed at the end of the Codex Urbinas.

THE BOOKS ON LIGHT AND SHADE

In the fifth part of the Codex Urbinas, which is concerned with light and shade, Melzi must have copied a lost manuscript of Leonardo, *De Ombra e Lume*, that is, the one listed in Melzi's "Memoria et Notta" as *Libro* W. This book was composed shortly before 1508, at a time when many notes on this subject were written in the Codex Atlanticus and elsewhere; if not composed, it was at least already outlined when Leonardo in 1508 wrote in MS F 77v: "Sun and Moon—This will come after the treatise on light and shade."

Paolo Giovio, who must have met Leonardo in Milan after 1500 (Giovio was born in Como in 1483), wrote a short but well-informed biography of Leonardo which opens with a reference to Leonardo's writings on painting. We have already considered the passage concerning Leonardo's intention of publishing his anatomical studies, and we know that this must refer to a time close to 1510. The same is true for the other Leonardo studies reported by Giovio: "He laid down that all proper practice of this art should be preceded by a training in the sciences and the liberal arts which he regarded as indispensable and subservient to painting [cf. the *Paragone*]. He placed modeling as a means of rendering figures in relief on a flat surface before other processes done with the brush [cf. Lomazzo's excerpts from a lost *Paragone*]. The science of Optics was to him of paramount importance and on it he founded the principles of the distribution of light and shade down to the most minute details."

This last statement concerning Leonardo's studies on light and shade as being based on optics finds confirmation in Leonardo's own writings of about 1506–1508. MS D, a short treatise on the eye, can be dated, from internal and external evidence, *ca.* 1508. In the last folio of this manuscript Leonardo's observations on the physiology of the eye are linked to the mechanism of the *camera obscura*, and this link represents the meeting-point of his studies on optics and on light and shade. In MS K, written shortly before MS D, the two subjects are still little related one to the other. But diagrams of the eye and diagrams of the play of light transmitted into a dark room become more persistently interrelated in his studies around 1508, as we can see in Codex Atlanticus 190 and 345. Leonardo now uses the *camera obscura* as a tool for the analysis of colors and colored shadows, and accounts of his studies in this field are what we would expect to find in his lost *Libro* W. The newly established foundation on which he bases his studies on light and shade is revealed again in a program laid down in MS E (*Libro B*) 17v, which is headed "Painting" but was not copied in the Codex Urbinas. Again it is the physiology of the eye that leads Leonardo to the study of light and shade and color.

Leonardo had already written a manuscript on this subject in 1490–1491, that is, MS C in the Bibliothèque de l'Institut de France. Melzi listed MS C as "Libro De Ombra e Lume segnato .G." The mark "G." is still visible on one page of the manuscript. Curiously enough, none of the notes from that manuscript was copied by Melzi into the Codex Urbinas. Marinoni points out that none of the passages in MS C is marked with the slashed circle and he therefore suggests that Melzi had used the manuscript in its entirety.[109] But Melzi did not use MS C. It was Leonardo himself who copied from it many entries on the subject of light and shade. We can trace these copies in MS E and in other Leonardo manuscripts of his late period. Melzi was certainly aware of this, since the manuscripts he used contained the latest and probably final version of Leonardo's studies on light and shade. In McMahon's concordance some chapters of the Codex Urbinas are indicated as copied from MS C, whereas they were actually copied from MS E (*Libro B*), since they are marked *L° B*.

If Leonardo copied notes from MS C in MS E, it is not unlikely that he had them included in the other book on light and shade, the one listed by Melzi as "un altro del medesimo segnato .W." [110] This lost book was most probably the main source

109. Marinoni (1952), pp. 235–236.

110. During my recent examination of the Leonardo manuscripts in the Bibliothèque de l'Institut de France, in June, 1963, I noticed that the binding of MS C has a spine considerably larger than the thickness of the manuscript itself, and that the manuscript is not firmly attached to the binding as it should be. This binding, therefore, has room for another manuscript of an even greater thickness than MS C. Moreover, the second flyleaf has been torn along the edge inside the spine. This binding was made when Guido Mazenta, brother of Ambrogio, gave MS C to Cardinal Federico Borromeo, in 1603. (In his *Memorie* Ambrogio refers to this manuscript as having a red velvet binding: "coperto di velluto rosso"; the present binding is in brown leather. The inscription on the present binding reads as follows: VIDI MAZENTAE / .PATRITII. MEDIOLA-NENSIS. / LIBERALITATE / AN. M.D.C.III.) Did Cardinal Borromeo receive only MS C, that is, *Libro G*, or was *Libro W* also attached to it so as to form a single book? Around 1585 the two manuscripts were probably still together in the Villa Melzi at Vaprio as they appear in the Melzi list at the end of the Codex Urbinas:

Libro de Ombra e Lume segnato ,G,
Un altro del medesimo segnato ,W,

Cardinal Borromeo gave MS C to the Ambrosian Library in 1609, but *Libro W* was already missing at that time. However, a few years ago I was informed that a Leonardo manuscript on light and shade similar in format to MS C was seen by a reliable person in one of the libraries of the Princes Borromeo at Milan, in 1958. My attempts to locate the unknown manuscript have so far been unsuccessful.

I may add, for what it is worth, the information that appeared in a Milanese newspaper, the *Gazzetta di Milano*, on March 30, 1866: a certain Dr. Ortori of Milan discovered

for the compilation of the fifth part of the Codex Urbinas. This, of course, did not prevent Melzi from using other manuscripts as well, usually those of a late period, such as *Libro A* and *Libro B* (MS E). In Pierantoni's concordance an attempt is made to indicate many comparisons with preparatory or analogous notes in the Codex Atlanticus, but it is impossible to develop a chronological analysis on the simple ground of such comparisons, since Leonardo himself copied or developed notes on light and shade written in every period of his activity.

The handwriting of the fifth part of the Codex Urbinas suggests that this part was written without frequent interruptions. It has the uniformity of *ductus* that one can expect to find in a copy from a homogeneous source. Therefore we may assume that, with the exception of some notes which were copied from MS A and Ashburnham 2038 and from Windsor 12,604, almost the entire fifth part of the Codex Urbinas was copied from a manuscript of late date.

The extant notes that can be considered as comparative material for dating the chapters of the fifth part of the Codex Urbinas are in particular those of Codex Atlanticus 207 r-a (plate 28), which may be dated *ca.* 1506–1508, being related to Codex Atlanticus 305 r-a, a folio dating from the period of Leonardo's activity in the service of Charles d'Amboise.[111] The notes on light and shade in folio 207 are all crossed out, indicating that they were copied by Leonardo himself elsewhere. Those on the upper part of the folio are very similar to those at the beginning of the fifth part of the Codex Urbinas; those at the bottom are actually a draft of the several paragraphs of the long chapter 750 (686), which is related to the preceding chapters 736 (687), 737 (688), 748 (690), and 749 (679).

The diagrams illustrating these notes and chapters deserve special attention. They show that Leonardo, around 1505, changed his approach to the study of light and shade and color; he moved his experiments from indoors to the open air, and considered light sources in movement.[112] The diagrams that we see in folio 207 of the Codex Atlanticus reappear again and again in the fifth part of the Codex Urbinas. They represent the heavenly vault arching over a geometrical object,

---

a manuscript of Leonardo "composto di 112 pagine in pergamena, trattante dei fenomeni della luce rispetto alla pittura." It seems unlikely that a Leonardo manuscript was written on parchment, unless the specification "in pergamena" was meant for its vellum binding. It is, however, surprising that the content of the manuscript was described as referring to the "phenomena of light in relation to painting." Unfortunately, nothing else is known of this manuscript.

111. Cf. Pedretti (1960*a*), fig. 5.

112. This has been discussed recently by Maria Rzepinska (1962*b*) in an admirable study of the development of Leonardo's theories of color and light and shade.

The diagrams illustrating the notes in Codex Atlanticus 207 r-a are related to that in MS G 3v. The latter illustrates the second paragraph of a passage "On Light," and therefore it pertains to painting and not to astronomy as it appears in Richter (1883), II, 872. Only the first paragraph was copied in the Codex Urbinas (Ludwig 663; Richter [1883], I, 118); in its concluding sentence Leonardo states that "of these things we shall speak in detail in our discourse." Perhaps the long chapter 750 (686) represents the "discourse" Leonardo had planned in MS G 3v, and should therefore be dated around 1510.

usually a sphere, and the light source is represented as moving along the curved line of the sky. The shadow of the object partakes of the reverberation from the sky and of the reflection from the ground. Leonardo's geometrical analyses show how these reverberations and reflections change in value as the light source moves. And when he analyses the light effects on a tree (chapter 869 [914], from MS G 12) he again uses this type of diagram.

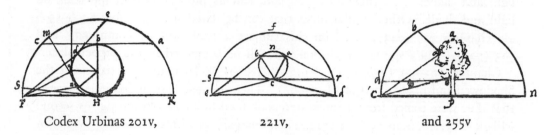

Codex Urbinas 201v,   221v,   and 255v

Other folios of the Codex Atlanticus related to the subject of the fifth part of the Codex Urbinas are 195 r-a, 230 r-b, 238 r-b, 238 v-b, and 258 v-a, all from the period 1506–1508. Folio 241 r-v, which belongs to the same period, is a large sheet of the type of blue-gray paper used by Leonardo after 1508. Many notes on light and shade were written on this type of paper: Codex Atlanticus 236 r-v and 277 v-a are folios of large size which Leonardo kept together, indicating their sequence with capital letters, E, F, G, and so forth.[113]

One of these folios, 277 v-a, contains an outline of the planned book on light and shade. Similar plans are found in Windsor 19,076 (An. C II 6), a folio of the characteristic type of blue-gray paper, which can be dated 1513; a folio of the same series at Windsor, no. 19,077, is dated 3 January 1513 and proves that Leonardo was at Vaprio, probably as a guest of the Melzi family. The list of entries in Windsor 19,076 includes the one already quoted, in which Leonardo reminds himself to reserve for the last section of his book on light and shade, "the figures which appeared in the *scriptoio* of Gherardo Miniatore in San Marco at Florence." This indirect reference to Fra Angelico's frescoes proves that Leonardo, later in his life, was still concerned with problems of art related to the Florentine tradition of the Quattrocento.

Manuscripts belonging to the period of transition, 1495–1497 to 1505, also contain notes on light and shade. The notes in MSS H, I, and M, in the Codices Forster II and III, and in some of the folios of the Codex Arundel (e.g., fol. 232 r-v) can be dated in that period. Notes in MS K, *ca.* 1505, can be considered as a prelude to the resumed project of the book *De Ombra e Lume.* Codex Atlanticus 150 r-a belongs to this preparatory phase of the project.

---

113. About 1640 a copyist in the service of Galeazzo Arconati transcribed almost all the notes on light and shade contained in these folios of the Codex Atlanticus. These copies, requested by Cassiano dal Pozzo for the library of Cardinal Barberini in Rome, are now preserved in the MSS H 227 inf. and H 229 inf. of the Ambrosian Library in Milan. Cf. Pedretti (1962*a*), pp. 61–94.

The folios from the Sforza period in the Codex Atlanticus contain mostly notes on the theory of shadow and notes on optics and perspective. Anna Maria Brizio pointed out that they had been transcribed by Leonardo in MSS A and C.[114]

Some of the notes of the fifth part of the Codex Urbinas can easily relate to a period preceding the compilation of the lost *Libro W*. Chapter 757 (752) is one of these. Here Leonardo states that he will develop the subject in his book on light and shade: ". . . this will be explained in its proper place in the book on light and shade." Other similar notes that can be dated shortly before 1506–1508 are chapters 739 (843), ". . . on this subject a book will be composed," and 783 (723), "But a special treatise on this will be composed in the proper place."

Chapters 791–821 (810, 804) were gathered by Melzi under the title "On the Shadowed and Bright Parts of Mountains." Their homogeneity of contents suggests that they were copied from a single notebook used by Leonardo during his second Milanese period, from 1508 to 1513. Their comparison with the notes on Windsor 12,412 and 12,414, dated *ca.* 1511, is quite convincing. In this section on mountains Melzi also copied notes from *Libro* A and *Libro* B (MS E).

This section on mountains begins with a *pentimento* of the copyist. Melzi intended to begin this section with the chapter 794 (826); he wrote the title of that chapter (*Perchè li monti distanti mostrano più oscure le somita che le loro base*), and then he crossed it out and started with a chapter on perspective. This *pentimento* may give us a hint of the type of manuscript from which Melzi was copying. Chapter 794 (826), with which he intended to begin the section on mountains, must have been on the first page of a Leonardo notebook. Since several pages of that notebook were dedicated to mountains, Melzi must have decided to transcribe them in their original sequence. But he soon realized that the chapter on the first page was not the first chapter written by Leonardo. In fact that chapter begins with the sentence: "Prouasi quel che già detto sull'altra faccia . . ." (With regard to that which has already been said on the preceding page). The "altra faccia" (preceding page) that Leonardo is referring to was presumably the *verso* of the folio that Melzi had initially considered as first to be copied. That folio was actually the last of the notebook he had in his hands, since Leonardo usually filled his manuscripts beginning from the end. Thus Melzi turned to the *verso* of the folio and copied what preceded chapter 794 (826). Hence, chapters 791–793 most likely represent the amount of writing on a page of the lost manuscript from which Melzi was copying. Such an amount of writing could well fit on a page of a size similar to Codex Arundel 113, a folio measuring 20.4 × 14.4 cm. which contains notes on landscapes dating from *ca.* 1508–1510.

The first chapter of the section on mountains in the "Treatise on Painting" is on perspective (*Prospettiva Comune*), and is apparently without bearing on the subject of the section. However, since it was probably copied from the page containing the chapters on mountains, 792–793 (824–825), it can reasonably be dated

114. Brizio (1954), pp. 81–89.

in the same period as the others, that is, from 1508 to 1513. This chapter is on the "perspective of movement." On this subject Leonardo had already written a note in Codex Trivulzianus 38v as early as 1487–1490, but the chapter in the "Treatise on Painting" is more closely related to the notes in Codex Arundel 134v, *ca.* 1508, and MS K 124 (44)r, *ca.* 1505–1507.

Folios 238–241 of the Codex Urbinas are written in a different type of ink, this difference being also perceptible in the facsimile of McMahon's edition. The subjects of the notes gathered here are in various ways related to light and shade; thus this last part can be considered an example of additional notes written on folios that were left blank at the end of the section.

THE NOTES ON TREES AND VERDURE

The last three parts of the "Treatise on Painting" are occupied with notes on plants, clouds, and the horizon. These notes do not present particular problems of chronology, because they are easily recognizable as pertaining to Leonardo's late period, from *ca.* 1508 to 1518; they reflect Leonardo's concern with the vast and elemental workings of nature, in favor of which he had gradually abandoned his interest in the human figure.

The notes on plants in the sixth part of the Codex Urbinas were copied principally from MSS G and E, two notebooks dating from 1510 to 1515. Melzi must also have copied other notes from some notebook of around 1500, of the type of MS M, since Leonardo's notes on botany in MS M [115] appear as a prelude to the more extensive discussions in MS G.

Notes on plant and landscape appear most frequently in Leonardo's manuscripts after 1500. Manuscript L, *ca.* 1502, is probably the starting point of his notes on his new interest. This notebook must be identified as one of the three *librettini* recorded by Melzi at the end of his list of Leonardo's manuscripts. Unfortunately the cover of this notebook was torn off and the original mark has disappeared. Despite this mutilation, we may assume that MS L was the *librettino* marked Y. Such a mark is found on MS L 79r, the page containing a note on painting copied by Melzi in chapter 340 (329) of the "Treatise on Painting." Melzi transcribed only one other note from MS L, the one on folio 75v regarding an atmospheric effect in a landscape (chapter 244 [242]). Although folio 87r contains a note on plants and landscape, Melzi did not copy it. On the verso of this folio is a list of various types of trees which might be one of the first indications of Leonardo's intention of adding a discussion on plants to his book on painting. The sketch in red chalk on folio 81v represents a group of trees which Clark relates to Windsor 12,431 r-v. The notes on plants in Codex Arundel 113 and 114 are already close to the period in which notes on plants were written in MS G. Thus after 1500

---

115. MS M 78v and 79; Brizio (1952), p. 245.

Leonardo decided to include in his book on painting a discussion on plants, a subject he knew had not been treated by anyone before him.[116]

As we have seen, in chapters 829 (900) and 838 (898) Leonardo alludes to one of his own manuscripts in which he had gathered notes on botany. For that manuscript he reserved the notes that were specifically of a scientific character, separating them from those reserved for the book on painting. About the same time, *ca.* 1505, he used a similar method for his anatomical studies. A list of entries in Codex Atlanticus 305 v-a is the proof of the existence of such a manuscript on botany. These items are all crossed out according to Leonardo's customary practice when he was developing a program of discussion elsewhere. In fact, the items on folio 305 v-a were developed, together with a note in Codex Arundel 180r, in the entries of chapter 823 (874); [117] thus Melzi must have used Leonardo's final version in a lost manuscript on botany.

Codex Atlanticus 305 r-a and v-a is related to Codex Atlanticus 207, the folio containing on its recto (plate 28) drafts of chapters on light and shade which are developed in the fifth part of the Codex Urbinas. The verso of folio 207 (plate 29, *a*) contains a topographical sketch of the same area in Milan as that represented on folio 305 v-a, and next to this sketch Leonardo represents the three types of distribution of branches of plants that form the subject of chapter 845 (890). The figure illustrating this chapter on folio 251 of the Codex Urbinas gives the names of the plants.

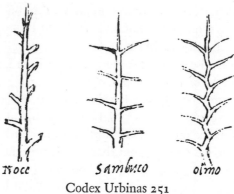

noce   sambuco   olmo

Codex Urbinas 251

It is perhaps of some significance that the years in which Leonardo intensifies his study of plants and verdure are those of his activity as an architect in the service of Charles d'Amboise. The drafts of chapter 823 (874), which is the first chapter in the sixth part of the Codex Urbinas, are on folios containing topographical sketches of the area in Milan where the French governor intended to build a palace designed by Leonardo. In Leonardo's projects for such a palace, in Codex Atlanticus 271 v-a, great emphasis is given to the planning of a garden, and Leonardo carefully gives

116. Chapter 848 (910). See above, note 56.
117. Cf. Pedretti (1960a), pp. 94–95.

instructions for the care of groves of lemons and citrons during the winter. Such is the importance he attaches to the garden that the palace itself seems to be a mere extension of the vegetal world, as in the Shrine of Venus at Cyprus described in Windsor 12,591. One of his plans in Codex Atlanticus 231 r-b has the word "prato" (meadow) inscribed in what seems to be a vast area of ground attached to the palace and subdivided in three sections by rows of columns. Perhaps he had thought of columns in the form of tree trunks, as in Windsor 12,592, which I have already related to his project for the palace of Charles d'Amboise; and columns in the form of trees are to be seen in the sketch of a gate in Codex Atlanticus 260 v-b, which is undoubtedly related to the systematization of the "Neron da Sancto Andrea," the canal running along the south side of the projected palace. The column in the form of a tree trunk, which Alberti already mentioned as suitable for garden architecture and which Bramante employed in the cloister of Sant'Ambrogio in Milan, is now charged with the concept of upward spiral motion which underlies Leonardo's discovery of the law of phyllotaxis in plants, and Leonardo is to employ it again in his later project of a new Medici palace in Florence. The spiral motif in the representation of natural forces becomes more and more frequent in Leonardo's *oeuvre* after 1506. The vegetal growth for the "Leda" (Windsor 12,424), almost resembling a surge of water, has caused recent critics to attach to this painting the symbolism of creative forces of Nature. The body of the goddess seems to stress this symbolism with its upward twist.

Classical subjects related to the vegetal world must have been a predilection of Francesco Melzi. It was during the period of Leonardo's studies on plants and verdure that Melzi painted his "Flora," or "Colombina," which is known to us in several studio replicas. Leonardo might even have lent a hand in his pupil's work. A Melzi drawing for the head of Flora is on the *verso* of Windsor 12,663, one of the folios containing Leonardo's studies on water datable *ca.* 1508. The painting was probably intended as an illustration of a passage in the fifth of Ovid's *Fasti.* The goddess is represented in the moment of raising her left hand with the miraculous flower that will give fertility to Juno, the future mother of Mars:

> *Protinus haerentem decerpsi pollice florem;*
> *tangitur, et tacto concipit illa sinu.*
>
> (255 256)

Ovid says that Flora has colorful draperies because of the golden hue of wheat fields, and because of the beauty and various colors of the flowers (355–358). Flora appears to him in a glowing light of torches against a dark background, and this either because the brightness of the flame attracts attention as the colors of flowers do, or because the dark of night is an appropriate invitation to pleasure:

> *vel qui deliciis nocturna licentia nostris*
> *convenit* . . .   (360–368)

Melzi's "Flora" seems to have been derived from the figure of the Virgin in the London cartoon of St. Anne. This connection is proved by the Berlin painting of "Vertunno e Pomona," which is also attributable to Melzi, and which shows Pomona, the goddess of fruit and gardens, with the lower part of her body in the same pose as the Virgin in the London cartoon, and the head as a replica of that of Flora. This Pomona is again a classical subject which has the vegetal world as a central theme (cf. Ovid, *Metamorpohses*, XIV, 622 ff.), and it gives us a glimpse into the activity of Leonardo's studio around 1510. A Melzi drawing of a foot, which is identifiable as the right foot of the Berlin Pomona, is on the *recto* of the Foglio Resta in the Ambrosiana. This drawing is in red chalk on red prepared paper, as is the series of Leonardo's landscapes at Windsor (nos. 12,410–'416) datable 1511. Moreover, on this very drawing there is a sketch of a landscape undoubtedly by Leonardo; and on its *verso* are notes by Leonardo on smoke, mist, clouds, and landscape comparable to those in MS G—the notebook that is the main source of the sixth part of the Codex Urbinas.

Notes with references to plants and landscape that are scattered in other parts of the "Treatise on Painting" should more logically have been inserted in the sixth part of the Codex Urbinas.[118] Notes on carta 15 of *Libro* A relating to plants were transcribed in chapters 500 and 501 (549, 548). These should also have been placed in the sixth part, whereas a note from *Libro* A copied in this part, chapter 912 (967), should have found its proper place between chapters 803 (830) and 808 (835), which are devoted to the light and shade on mountains.

As we have seen, folios 266–268 of the Codex Urbinas were written with a different kind of ink. They therefore contain notes presumably added at a later time. In this added section are notes on the effect of wind on branches, a subject that is found in notes of Leonardo's Roman period, *ca.* 1515, in folios of the Codex Atlanticus, such as folio 160 r-b.

THE NOTES ON CLOUDS

All the chapters of the last two parts of the Codex Urbinas were copied from manuscripts now lost. The seventh part contains ten chapters on the formation of clouds, their redness at sunset, and their shadows under various conditions of light, including moonlight. These chapters are not arranged systematically as they appear in MacMahon's translation, but they must have been copied in the sequence they had in the lost original. In the notebooks of his late period Leonardo shows his constant preoccupation with combining art and science as in this case—that is, a feeling for pictorial effects coupled with a scientific inquiry into natural phenomena. This type of studies on clouds begins to appear in Leonardo's manuscripts after 1505, at the time of his studies on wind currents related to studies on the flight of birds. In MS F 35r, 1508, he sets a program for the study of clouds: "Write

---

118. Chapters 221–224 (245, 209); 234–235 (237, 241); 260 (244); 261 (236), *ca.* 1492; 420 (550), *ca.* 1492; 642 (737); 738 (735); and 808 (835).

how the clouds are formed and how they dissolve, and what it is that causes vapor to rise from the water of the earth into the air, and the cause of mists of the air becoming thickened, and why it appears more blue or less blue at one time than at another." A hint of such a program is also found in Codex Atlanticus 42 r-a, which is related to Windsor 12,666r and therefore datable 1508 in common with MS F: "Of clouds that increase or diminish in the air and what causes this." But Leonardo does not develop this program until a few years later, being concerned in the meantime with the effects of mist and "thick" air in aerial perspective. He must have considered the study of these effects as a logical introduction to that of clouds and storms. A note on the effect of distortion of towers in air or vapor of decreasing degrees of "thickness" is in Codex Atlanticus 130 v-b, a folio dating from 1511 to 1513 at the time of Leonardo's sojourn in Vaprio d'Adda. This folio is identical, as regards type of paper and contents (military architecture), with folio 134 v-b of the same codex, and the latter has the *verso* (which is not visible because it is laid down) prepared with red ground as the Windsor drawings 12,410–12,416 of 1511. Hints of such studies of military architecture are to be found on the anatomical folio at Windsor 19,109r, which contains also a note on the effect of the density of smoke at the horizon (MacCurdy:II.298), and we know from Windsor 19,077, which is dated January 9, 1513, that certain of Leonardo's studies on military architecture at that time were related to the siege of the Castle of Trezzo near Vaprio.[119] A number of chapters in the last section of the third part of the Codex Urbinas, from folio 143 onward, deal with smoke and mist and their effect on the shape of buildings viewed from a distance. (These chapters develop from the observations on color and aerial perspective gathered in the second part of the Codex Urbinas, and, as we have seen, a folio of the Codex Atlanticus, 249 r-c, *ca.* 1515, related to these observations, also contains a note on clouds.) These chapters on mist could well have been placed in the seventh part among the observations on clouds. One of them, chapter 447 (476), is actually on the subject of clouds: "On the Sun's Rays Coming through Openings in the Clouds," and can be dated about 1515 because of similar notes in Codex Atlanticus 297 v-a.[120] The comparison that follows shows that there might have been another draft in between:

---

119. Cf. Pedretti (1962d), pp. 75–76.
120. This folio is usually ascribed to Leonardo's Sforza period, *ca.* 1495, because of the draft of a letter to a "Magnifica Cecilia," a name that has always been associated with that of the mistress of Lodovico Sforza, Cecilia Gallerani. The paleographic reasons for dating this folio around 1515 are given in my "Spigolature nel Codice Atlantico" (1960), pp. 531–533, 548. The handwriting of the draft of the letter and the drawing of a standing lady, profile to right, are probably by Melzi, although the handwriting somewhat resembles that of Raphael. The draft of the letter refers to the beauty of Campania and Rome (". . . Solo Roma, in che modo potrà esser narrata . . ."), and might be tentatively associated with Raphael's task of surveying Roman ruins. As I pointed out, folio 297 v-a contains notes and diagrams on light and shade belonging to Leonardo's late studies destined to his *Libro* W and comparable to those in Codex Urbinas folios 177v and 209v.

C.A. 297 v-a

Li raçci solari penetratori dellj spira-
cholj interposstj infralle varie globbosita
de nuvolj (fu) *fan disscorso retto e dila-*
tabile / insino alla terra doue si tagliano
(tignjdo dj se tutto col s) *allumjnando*
(colla lor re) coll (a) *lor splendore tuc /*
ta la penetrata aria.

[*This text is preceded by a draft with*
a few variations, e.g.: "*ettinghano di se*
tutti li sito dove si tagliano" (*cf. the simi-*
lar sentence in the chapter in the Co-
dex Urbinas: "*et tingano di se tutti li*
lochi . . .").]

C.U. 143v, Lu 447 (McM 476)

Li razzi solari penetratori delli spira-
coli interposti infra le varie densità e
globosità de nuvoli, aluminano tutti li
siti dove si tagliano, et aluminano etiam

le tenebre, et tingano di se tutti li lochi
oscuri che sono dopo loro le quali oscu-
rità si dimostrano infra li intervalli d'essi
razzi solari.

Another note in this folio of the Codex Atlanticus refers to cloud formations: "le molte e varie figure de nuvoli son fatte da diversi chorsi de venti," and is related to a sentence in chapter 928 (987), in the seventh part of the Codex Urbinas: "e tali nuvoli generano venti nella lor creazione si come nella loro destruzione." Chapter 928 (987) has the title "Della creatione de nuvoli" and appears to be an elaboration of the notes in Codex Atlanticus 279 r-b, a folio consisting of rough paper of a type that Leonardo used around 1513–1515. In both cases Leonardo states that the course of wind is straight, and not circular as Aristotle maintains. He refers specifically to Aristotle in the folio of the Codex Atlanticus ("il vento si muove per retta linea e non circulare, come vuole Aristotele"), but in the chapter of the *Trattato* he refers to Aristotle indirectly, as his imaginary opponent ("e 'l moto loro è recto e non curvo, come uole l'avversario").

A small fragment contained in the Codex Atlanticus, folio 165 v-d (plate 27, *c*), appears to be a section of a page from a notebook of *ca.* 1508–1515. It seems to be a fragment of a marginal note, and is perhaps the only surviving portion of a sheet that contained drawings and notes on clouds. This fragmentary note, being on the redness of the clouds, might be related to the seventh part of the "Treatise": ". . . this came about by reason of the clouds interposed between the earth and the sun, wherefore being in the west it grew red and with its ruddy glow lit as with a haze all the things visible to it, but so much more or less in proportion as these things were nearer or more remote."

References to clouds in other parts of the Codex Urbinas are to be found in chapters dating from Leonardo's late period, as for example chapters 447 (476), 474 (480), 478 (481), 479a (495), 480 (494), and the one copied from *Libro A*, that is, chapter 654 (793). Related to these chapters as well as to the chapters in the seventh part are the notes in MS G 91v and 92v, in Codex Arundel 114–114v and 172, as well as in Codex Atlanticus 38 r-b, 97 v-a, 270 r-a, and in other folios of a late period which are on the same characteristic type of rough paper as the folio 279 r-b mentioned before and folio 162 r-a. The Windsor drawing 12,388, which is related to the studies on the deluge, is also on this type of paper and contains notes on clouds, smoke, and dust. Thus, around 1515, Leonardo's study of clouds and wind currents led him to deal with the idea of energy in nature and with the pictorial effect of storms and natural cataclysms.

To date the Windsor drawings of "The Deluge" after 1515, Sir Kenneth Clark compared them to folio 79 r-c of the Codex Atlanticus (plate 11). This folio is of the same type of rough paper as several of the "Deluge" drawings. In its upper part are notes on wind and water in Melzi's handwriting. Leonardo probably dictated this note to his pupil, since he corrected it with his own hand.[121] One of his notes at the bottom of the folio which deal with the representation of cataclysms refers to his intention of including a special discussion on the effect of storms in the book on painting:

A mountain falling on a town will fling up dust in the form of clouds; but the color of this dust will differ from that of the clouds. Where the rain is thickest let the color of the dust be less conspicuous and where the dust is thickest let the rain be less conspicuous. And where the rain is mingled with wind and dust the clouds created by the rain must be more transparent than those of dust alone. And when flames of fire are mingled with clouds of smoke and water, very opaque and dark clouds will be formed. And the rest of this subject will be treated fully in the book on painting.

We have here the evidence that as late as 1515 Leonardo was planning a discussion on the representation of cataclysms for his book on painting, but only a few hints of such a program are found in the chapters on clouds gathered by Melzi in the seventh part of the Codex Urbinas. The study of clouds must have fascinated Leonardo until the last years of his life, and we know that one of his notes on this subject was written in 1518. On the top center of Windsor 12,391 Leonardo writes with a broad pen and yellowish ink: "The shadows in clouds are lighter in proportion as they are nearer to the horizon." This note is just as short as the last chapter of the seventh part of the Codex Urbinas, which is also on the shadows of clouds. The Windsor drawing 12,391, which represents cloud formations and mountains, is in black chalk or charcoal on paper entirely rubbed over with chalk. Sir Kenneth Clark dates it *ca.* 1512, but we have the evidence that it is one of Leonardo's latest drawings, dating from 1518. Codex Atlanticus 249 r-b, which is joined to folio 249 r-a, is in the same technique and format as the Windsor drawing, and is dated at Amboise the 24th of June 1518. Folios of the same type are Codex Atlanticus 221 v-a and v-b, as well as 256 r-a and r-b, and so are Codex Arundel 245–246, which contain the same problems of geometry as those in Codex Atlanticus 249 r-b. The

---

121. Line 9: the word "vnjta" (joined) is entered by Leonardo.

facsimiles of all these folios are not correct, and only the originals give us the evidence of their chalk preparation. We have no way to explain why Leonardo, in 1518, adopted this curious medium in his manuscripts. The Windsor drawing is our only evidence that he intended this medium as a preparation for black-chalk drawings, and yet this folio was used also for writing a note on painting. Shortly before his death Leonardo's handwriting is surprisingly steady and energetic, whereas his black-chalk drawings have an indeterminateness and softness that seem to convey the effect of wall-stains or stormy clouds.

THE NOTES ON THE HORIZON

The last part of the "Treatise on Painting" is connected with the two preceding ones, in subject matter as well as chronologically. Its subject, the horizon, is complementary to that of plants and clouds, because it defines the boundaries of landscape. Horizon is considered as such in chapters 857 (950) and 862 (953), and also in chapter 241 (234) on color perspective. References to the horizon are found in other parts of the "Treatise," especially in the sixth part.[122]

The subject of the horizon is also found in Leonardo's notes from the early Sforza period. The notes on optics in Windsor 19,148 r-v, which Clark dates *ca.* 1486, contain references to the horizon, but only *ca.* 1515 did Leonardo become greatly concerned with the problem of the horizon.

A note on perspective in MS G 53v sets the problems that are developed in the last part of the Codex Urbinas. This note was obviously destined to be included in the planned book on painting because of the heading "Discourse on Painting," but Melzi copied only the first paragraph into the Codex Urbinas, that is, chapter 489 (484). In the second paragraph Leonardo refers to a visual pyramid which is "concerned with the universe, embracing all the mass of the objects that pass before the eye, as though a vast landscape was seen through a small hole, the number of the objects seen through such a hole being so much the greater in proportion as the objects are more remote from the eye; and thus the base [of the visual pyramid] is formed on the horizon and the apex in the eye." Leonardo considers two types of perspective depending on how their visual pyramids are employed. Thus one type of perspective has the apex of the pyramid in the eye and the base as far away as the horizon; and the other has the base toward the eye and the apex on the horizon. While the first pyramid is "concerned with the universe" the second "has to do with a peculiarity of landscape."

Another note dealing with this subject is in *Libro B* (MS E) 80v: "If the eye is immovable the perspective terminates its distance in a point; but if the eye moves in a straight line the perspective ends in a line, because it is proved that the line is produced by the movement of the point, and our sight is fixed upon the point, and consequently it follows that as the sight moves the point moves, and as the point

---

122. Cf. chapter 643 (681), which is related to the preceding one, 642 (737), on shadows in the verdure of meadows.

moves the line is produced." Melzi did not copy this note either, although it would have linked the observations on landscape in the sixth and seventh parts of the Codex Urbinas to the geometry of the "true site of the horizon" in the eighth part.

In the last part of the Codex Urbinas, Leonardo demonstrates that the "true horizon" is not at eye level as is the horizon of artificial perspective. And since the vanishing point is located on the horizon line, that is, lower than the eye level, the distance of this point is measurable on account of the curvature of the earth. In chapter 936 (988) Leonardo specifies that such a point is seven miles away from a standing observer: "If the eye is placed at the level of the surface of the sea, it sees the horizon near, at a distance of about a mile, but if a man rises to his full height,

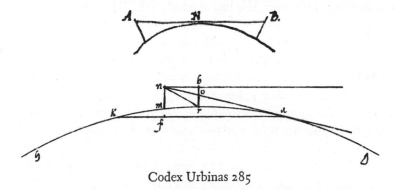

Codex Urbinas 285

then he sees the horizon seven miles away from him." And again, in the same chapter: ". . . but this pyramid is not the one that perspective requires; therefore, it is not found in practice, because it has infinite space from its base to its point, and the one above has seven miles to the base from that point."

In *Libro B* (MS E) 29v there is a note and a diagram referring to a system of measuring the curvature of the surface of the sea. Thus the chapters on the horizon in the last part of the Codex Urbinas can be dated from after 1515. A note directly related to these chapters is in Codex Atlanticus 76 r-b (plate 29, *b*), a folio probably dating from Leonardo's French period, after 1517:

[*Figure*] a n b o c m.

In seven miles of the sphere of the world a man sees the horizon at the feet of another man, and in 14 miles one man sees the said horizon at the height of the eyes of the other man, these men being equal in height.

This can be proved: and be n o m *a 14 mile section of still sea;* a n *and* c m *be the two men mentioned above, each one being able to see as far as the horizon* o, *where the man* b o *is standing. I say therefore that the eye* a *of the man* a n *will see the horizon* o *at the feet of the man* o b, *and the same will do the eye of the man* c m.[123]

---

123. This folio is of the same type of rough paper as folio 76 v-b, which undoubtedly dates from Leonardo's French period because of its projects for a royal palace at Romorantin. Folio 76 r-b is not the recto of folio 76 v-b as I suggested in my chronology of the folios of the Codex Atlanticus (Pedretti [1957*b*], p. 268). The folios are independent of each other; one is simply mounted against the other. How-

Chapter 939 a–b (1004, 1002), which is illustrated with a diagram similar to that of the note in the Codex Atlanticus, synthesizes Leonardo's geometrical concepts of the horizon. Two men placed at a certain distance from each other (14 miles, according to the note in the Codex Atlanticus) are joined by an imaginary straight line which is carried from the head of one to that of the other, the midpoint of this line being tangential to the surface of the earth. Leonardo meditates on the nature of the straight line and concludes that if a straight line is continued for a large distance parallel to the surface of the earth, such a line becomes a curve. This observation, which is already found in MS K 79r-78r (*ca.* 1505), can be linked to a statement in *Libro B* (MS E) 80v: ". . . as the sight moves the point moves, and as the point moves the line is produced." The line thus produced can only be a curve, and so must be the lines in that type of perspective which is "concerned with the universe," that is, a curvilinear perspective which shows objects foreshortened in breadth and height. It is not a coincidence, therefore, that again in *Libro B* (MS E), folio 4r, Leonardo discusses what he calls a "*caso di prospettiva,*" a case of perspective: "Whether a long-extended rectangular wall composed of four sides and four corners appears with the upper and lower sides straight or curvilinear" when the eye of the observer is focused on the center of the wall. The problem is considered again in MS G 32r, which unfortunately contains only the concluding part of a discussion that was written on the missing folio 31. In both notes Leonardo recognizes that the upper and lower edges of a rectangular wall do not appear to be parallel, but appear to converge at their extremities, to the right and to the left. In

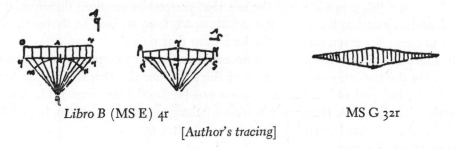

Libro B (MS E) 4r   MS G 32r
[*Author's tracing*]

this note in MS G Leonardo states that the wall appears as a "*corpo bisangolo di lati curvi,*" that is, as a two-angle figure with curvilinear sides, but then he retracts and says: ". . . actually, such a figure will have four angles, two of which are in

---

ever, both folios certainly date from the same period, *ca.* 1517–1518. Baratta (1903), p. 50, had already related this note in the Codex Atlanticus to the chapters on the horizon in the last part of the "Treatise on Painting." He also explains how to determine the distance of the horizon from the eye of a standing man, and proves that Leonardo was mistaken in giving such a distance as seven miles. (A mile in Leonardo's time corresponded roughly to the mile in use today.) A standing man can hardly see more than three miles of the earth's surface measured at sea. The mistake in measurement, however, does not affect Leonardo's geometric principle of the "true site of the horizon." For Leonardo's theory of perspective and its bearing on his observations on the horizon see Rzepinska (1962b) and Pedretti (1963).

the middle, that is one above the other, and the other two opposite each other at the extremities of the wall."

Both solutions, however, are correct. The four-angle figure is the rectangular wall as seen according to artificial perspective: the wall is foreshortened concurrently to the right and to the left as if one foreshortened half were the reflection of the other. The two-angle figure with curvilinear sides is the same wall also represented as foreshortened to the right and to the left, but rendered according to optics, that is, as seen by the eye in movement. Leonardo expresses a preference for artificial perspective, which requires that the eye be fixed in observing an object, but he is aware of the phenomena of optical distortions occurring when the eye has to move to survey an object of large size. In his late observations on landscape he refers to the eye as moving along the horizon line. Artificial perspective cannot be applied in such a case. But this he had already realized in 1502 when he wrote in MS L 21r a note on painting which Melzi did not copy into the Codex Urbinas: "Foreshorten, on the summits and sides of the hills, the outlines of the estates and their divisions; and, as regards the things turned toward you, make them in their true shape."

The notes on the rainbow should also have been placed in the last part of the "Treatise on Painting." In Windsor 19,076, one of the anatomical blue-gray folios of 1513, Leonardo writes: "Reserve the rainbow for the last book on painting, but first you must have the book on colors, in order to show with the colors of the painter the origin of the colors of the rainbow." Leonardo's notes on "mixing of colors" belong to a period after 1508, as can be proved by comparison with the notes in MSS F, G, and in *Libro A* and *Libro B* (MS E). Notes on rainbows begin to appear in Leonardo's manuscripts around 1506–1508, for example in Windsor 19,150 (notes on the colors of the rainbow, illustrated by an eye looking through a spectrum [Richter (1883), I, 288]), but only after 1513 did Leonardo intensify his studies on the rainbow. Thus on the inside of the cover of *Libro B* (MS E) we read: "The colors in the middle of the band of the rainbow blend with one another. The rainbow in itself is not in the rain nor in the eye that observes it, although it is generated from the rain, the sun, and the eye. The rainbow is always seen by the eye that is placed between the rain and the sun; therefore, if the sun is on the east and the rain on the west, the rainbow generates from the rain on the west."

Leonardo's studies on the rainbow carried out after 1513 are developed according to the scheme outlined in Windsor 19,076, that is, as the subject of the last section of his projected book on painting, the penultimate section of that book being on the analysis of the painter's colors. Traces of a development of this program are preserved in two folios of the Codex Atlanticus, 45 r-a, v-a, and 97 r-a, v-a, both dating from *ca.* 1514–1515. These two folios were probably joined together, because they were originally numbered 129 (fol. 97) and 130 (fol. 45). Both contain geometrical studies on the *lunulae*. On folio 45 v-a Leonardo states that he has gathered the rules for the quadrature of the circle and that he is about to begin his treatise "de ludo geometrico" (on geometrical games). Unfortunately this note is not dated, but since another folio in the Codex Atlanticus, 90 v-a, written in the Vatican on July 7, 1514, contains several studies on the quadrature of the circle, Leonardo must have begun his "De ludo geometrico" shortly after that date. One of the first folios of the new treatise is Codex Atlanticus 99 v-b, because it explains what the "ludo geometrico" will deal with. Finally, Codex Atlanticus 184 v-c, which contains an architectural sketch as well as notes on painting (landscape and color) and on the flight of birds, again shows geometrical studies and has the note "De ludo geometrico." All the subjects treated in this folio reappear on folios 45 and 97 (geometry, flight of birds, and color), with the exception of architecture. But a folio similar to folios 45 and 95, that is, folio 114 r-b and v-b, which contains studies on *lunulae*, shows two architectural studies related to those on folio 184 v-c, as well as a sketch of scaffolding for vault which represents a further element for dating this group of folios *ca.* 1514–1515. In fact, this typical system of scaffolding is found again in folios of the Codex Atlanticus dating from Leonardo's Roman period.[124] We can be sure, therefore, that the notes on color and rainbow on Codex Atlanticus 45 and 97 date from after 1514. Moreover, folio 97 r-a contains an isolated note, "nudo del peruzzo" (nude of Peruzzi), which refers to Baldassare Peruzzi. It is well known that Peruzzi was in Rome between 1511 and 1522.

In Codex Atlanticus 45 and 97, which can be considered as a single sheet, Leonardo studies the effects of mixing colors (fol. 45 v-a [Richter (1883), I, 272]) and the phenomenon of the "arco celeste" (fol. 97 v-a, not translated by Richter). What Leonardo calls "arco celeste" has always been translated "rainbow," but in the notes on folio 97 v-a he is undoubtedly referring to halos:

On the Halo

The lower the sun is, the greater the circle of the halo will be, and vice versa.

When the sun is on the west, behind some small and thick clouds, then such clouds will be encircled by a red splendor.

Halos are of 4 kinds, of which one originates directly from the sun. Another kind is that which originates from the sun and from the illuminated edges of an aperture in the clouds that are placed in front of the sun. The rays of the sun, passing through that aperture, produce two concentric halos, one bigger than the other. The bigger one has paler colors; the smaller one has colors of greater intensity.

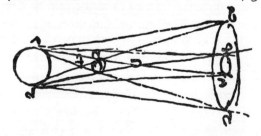

The smaller halo originates from the lines a b c d e, *because of their intersection in* c *due to the aperture* n; *and the bigger halo originates from the rays intersecting*

124. Cf. Pedretti (1962c), p. 90, n. 24.

before the aperture n, *in the point* f, *which also produces the brightness around the edges of such aperture; and the reason for all this will be given in its proper place.*

Again Leonardo refers to the last section of his book on painting ("the proper place"). It is possible that Leonardo did not differentiate between halo and rainbow, since both produce the same range of colors, but he must have been aware of their difference, if not of their causes, because Aristotle describes the halo and the rainbow as two different phenomena. At the head of folio 97 v-a Leonardo writes: "See Aristotle's *De Cielo e Mundo.*" [125]

A note on the "arco celeste" (again the halo and not the rainbow) occurs in Codex Arundel 188v, which can be dated in Leonardo's French period, after 1517. The problem of geometry on the recto of this folio is one of those that Leonardo wrote down in Codex Atlanticus 249 r-b, the folio dated at Amboise, 24 June 1518. In a note to the edition of the Codex Arundel, Enrico Carusi had already pointed out that the handwriting of the note on aerial perspective at the head of this folio is very similar to that of the Codex Urbinas, and suggested identifying this note as Melzi's.

Late in his life Leonardo attached special importance to the study of rainbows and halos because of their bearing on his theory of color. As optical phenomena and as a means of showing the painter the primary colors and their blending and mixtures, they symbolize Leonardo's concept of art as a science. Melzi must have been well aware of Leonardo's plan for the book on painting, since he used a note on the rainbow as a concluding chapter of the Codex Urbinas.

A MISSING BOOK ON PERSPECTIVE

One of Leonardo's well-known precepts for young painters advises the early study of perspective and anatomy.[126] The "Treatise" includes a book on human postures and gestures, but it has no specific book on perspective. Only occasional references to perspective are scattered in various parts of the Codex Urbinas.

A note in Codex Atlanticus 120 r-d can be considered as a fragment of a discussion with Botticelli concerning the laws of diminishing perspective:

Sandro! You do not say why these second things seem lower than the third.
[Diagram] The eye between two parallel lines will never see them at so great a distance that they meet in a point.

---

125. Aristotle discusses the halo and the rainbow in the third book of his *Meteorogica*, the treatise known to Leonardo as the "metaura." See MS F, verso of cover. Curiously enough, a note and diagram on the rainbow with reference to Aristotle is found on a page of a notebook attributed to Antonio da Sangallo the Younger (1485–1546), in the Uffizi, Florence (Dis. Arch. 835).
A scientific illustration of the rainbow and halo phenomena is given by Minnaert (1954), pp. 167 ff.
126. Chapter 47 (59), from MS Ashburnham 2038, fol. 17v.

The folio containing this note can be dated *ca.* 1500 on internal and external evidence. Leonardo's criticism was probably directed to a painting of Botticelli's, most likely the London "Nativity," which is dated 1500, the very year in which Leonardo returned to Florence. Giulio Carlo Argan surmises that the controversy between the two men now flared up again, intensified by the deeply rooted religious convictions of the one and the proud scientific achievements of the other.[127] As Argan points out, the unusual composition, with its hierarchical order of images, unfolds like a ritual in defiance of the laws of perspective.

The problem posed to Botticelli is related to that which Leonardo had already considered in his Codex Ashburnham 19r (Lu 493; McM 489), "Why, of Two Objects of Equal Size, Will the Painted one Seem Larger than the One in Relief"; in *Libro* A 82, "Why, when Measuring a Face and then Painting It Life Size, It Will Appear Larger than Nature"; and in MS D 3r, *ca.* 1508: "Why objects, which are diminished according to artificial perspective (*col punto della prospettiva*), appear considerably smaller than the real ones, even though the latter, when measured, result as being of the same size as those diminished."

These passages of different periods are linked and clarified by two notes in MS K 120 (40)v and 121 (41)r, dating from about 1505–1507, which are illustrated with diagrams similar to those in the folio of the Codex Atlanticus containing the reference to Botticelli:

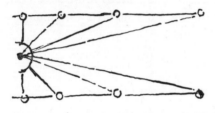

If the eye be in the middle of a course with two horses running to their goal along parallel tracks, it will seem to it that they are running to meet one another. This that has been stated occurs because the images of the horses which impress themselves upon the eye are moving toward the center of the surface of the pupil of the eye.

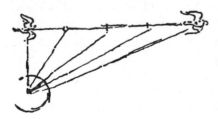

And if a bird flies along a level line separating itself from the eye it will seem to be descending stage by stage with the stages of its movement.

The "level line" along which the bird flies is that which Leonardo has defined as having its extremities unequally distant from the center of the world. This definition of the line, which is developed in the eighth part of the Codex Urbinas, is the subject of a note and diagram in MS K 79r-78v. In the folio of the Codex Atlanticus containing the note addressed to Botticelli we find diagrams that seem to indicate that Leonardo was already meditating on this definition of the line.

---

127. Argan (1957), pp. 127–128.

The problem of perspective posed to Botticelli is found again in the "Treatise on Painting." It is the first paragraph of chapter 476 (493), and can be dated at a late period, *ca.* 1510–1515, because of other references to landscape related to those in *Libro B* and MS G. The first paragraph reads as follows: "Among objects of equal height which are higher than the eye, that which is farthest from the eye will seem the lowest. And if the object is below the eye, that nearest to the eye will seem lowest. Lateral parallels will come together in a point."

We have here a synthesis of what has been discussed in MS K: the objects placed above the eye correspond to the different positions of a bird flying away from the observer along a level line; the two parallel lines which seem to converge to a point in the distance are the tracks of the two horses. Leonardo adds the observation concerning objects seen from above, and this is the case of the bird's-eye perspective that he had discussed with Botticelli in 1500: ". . . the second things seem lower than the third."

Maria Rzepinska, in her invaluable dissertation on Leonardo's "Treatise on Painting," surmises that Leonardo might be referring here to a type of perspective similar to the bird's-eye views of Persian miniatures. In my opinion, Leonardo is simply referring to the position of objects in relation to the horizon line: nothing in his wording authorizes us to believe he had recognized the existence of an "inverted perspective." He does not say that the figures in the foreground appear smaller than those in the background (as in the case of Botticelli's "Nativity"), but he says that the figures in the foreground are to be placed lower than those in the background. He proves geometrically that in bird's-eye perspective the objects in the foreground are to be painted at the bottom of the panel, that is, in the lowest position; whereas in the worm's-eye perspective the lowest position is taken by those objects (e.g., clouds; cf. chapter 480 [494]) that are farthest from the eye, and consequently the objects closest to the eye are to be painted at the top of the panel.

In chapter 481 (488) Leonardo says that an object represented in a painting as being one mile away is seen by the eye through the same angle as that through which the real object is seen. And yet, although both the real and the painted objects appear to one eye as being of equal size and on the same plane, "to two eyes they will not seem to be at an equal distance."

Leonardo was certainly aware of an optical effect of binocular vision, that is, the effect that is made evident to us by the telephoto lens of the camera: when we watch football players on a television screen we see people in the foreground considerably smaller than those in the background, and the lines subdividing the field as diverging instead of converging to a point in the distance. Was the similar effect in Botticelli's "Nativity" intentional or was the painter following a devotional device of Flemish origin in order to emphasize the scene in the grotto? One cannot discard completely the hypothesis that Botticelli was trying to reproduce an optical effect of bird's-eye perspective. This, however, is not confirmed by Leonardo's question, because Leonardo refers to the position of the figures, not to the size. And yet the problem was there, as it was in Ugo van der Goes' altarpiece in Santa Maria Nuova.

Leonardo's studies on binocular vision are found in manuscripts dating from *ca*. 1508, such as MS D and Windsor 19,117r (C. IV. 12v). In MS D 3v we read: "If both eyes see a spherical object, the diameter of which is smaller than the distance between the pupils of the eyes, they will see beyond the diameter of that object, and the more so as that object is placed closer to them. And therefore the central visual lines will see that object as being smaller than it really is." This note is developed in the last chapter of the fifth part of the Codex Urbinas, that is, chapter 821 (804): "*Of Perspective*. When with both eyes you see two equal objects which are each in themselves smaller than the space between your eyes, then the second object will seem larger than the first." The demonstration that follows is illustrated by a diagram.

In his studies on binocular vision Leonardo deals with objects that are not larger than the width between the eyes, and he recognizes that only under this condition does the object closest to the eye appear to be the smallest. This is the principle of the telephoto lens of the camera in approaching distant objects.

Ghiberti's *Third Commentary* is evidence of the Quattrocento concern with optics as a means of investigating the appearance of objects in space—a means that deviates from the laws of artificial perspective. The conflict between the two systems as implied in Ghiberti's complicated analysis of the opinions of Classical and Medieval authors about the nature and the function of the eye has a simple explanation: the mathematical system of perspective requires that a limited field of vision be observed with only one eye; the optical system takes into consideration both eyes, their movements, and the angles of their vision. The optical theories of antiquity were known to the artists of the early Renaissance through the works of Medieval commentators. In fact, Ghiberti's *Third Commentary* is nothing but a paraphrase and often a mere translation of the section on optics in Roger Bacon's *Opus Majus*. Beginning with the sixteenth century, the conflict between the two systems of perspective is sharpened by a new sensory approach in architecture, as exemplified by Bramante's adoption of the principles of Vitruvius. This also coincides with the radical change of Leonardo's style, when his figures are no longer rendered in atmospheric terms but as volumetric entities. His more sculptural style after 1500 is sometimes defined as more classical, and this would be in accordance with his new approach to perspective as a return to the optics of antiquity.

In his studies on geometry in the first years of the Cinquecento Leonardo moves definitely toward stereometry. His studies on stereometry in the Codex Forster date from 1505. His studies on the flight of birds date from the same period. (The diagrams of the spiral movement of birds ascending in the sky suggest a space that can be sensed as an architectural element—a spiral staircase—or as a sculptural one—the *figura serpentinata* of the "Leda.") And concurrently Leonardo undertakes studies on optics as a part of a treatise on perspective. The notes on the eye and the phenomena of vision in MS D which date from about 1508 were envisaged as part of a book on perspective. This is proved by a reference in the "Treatise on Painting." In chapter 741 (806) Leonardo refers to the third rule of his fifth book on perspective, and he mentions that rule again in MS D 10v as "the third rule of the present treatise." But Leonardo's treatise on perspective was not copied into the Codex Urbinas.

Anna Maria Brizio states that Melzi omitted to copy certain notes on perspective contained in MSS G and E because he was not able to understand them.[128] When these notes were written, however, Melzi was so close to Leonardo as a pupil and assistant that he could certainly have received any necessary explanation from his master. According to White, these late notes formulate a theory of curvilinear perspective as opposed to the traditional theory accepted in Leonardo's early writings.[129]

We know that Leonardo wrote a book on perspective. It was a *Discorso* included in a treatise on the three great arts, sculpture, painting, and architecture. In 1542 Cellini acquired a copy of this treatise from an impoverished nobleman at the Court of Francis I.[130] Unfortunately both the original and the copy are lost. According to Cellini, Leonardo's *Discorso* on perspective "was the most beautiful a man ever made, showing how objects foreshorten not only in depth but also in breadth and height." "Leonardo worked out the rules," Cellini continues, "and explained them in such orderly fashion that they were easily comprehended by every one who saw them." Cellini, however, says that he had shown this book to Sebastiano Serlio, "who wished to take out these books on perspective," and "he brought to light as much of them as his intellect was able to understand." Cellini's record is therefore somewhat ambivalent as regards the clarity or otherwise of Leonardo's rules of perspective. Lomazzo also refers to Leonardo's works on perspective as "written very obscurely." [131]

That Leonardo's book on perspective did exist is proved not only by the records of Cellini and Lomazzo but also by Leonardo's own statements in the "Treatise on Painting." In chapter 202 (195) he states: ". . . as is proved in my second book on perspective." And in chapter 910 (966): "The reason is set down in the thirty-second proposition of my book on perspective." Other chapters mentioned by Ludwig and Heydenreich [132] contain references to the book on perspective. All these chapters are of a late period, as chapter 507 (524), which has this concluding note: "This figure should be put with the 42nd section of the book on perspective; without it the explanation of transparent water is of no value." It must be noted that in Codex Arundel 220r Leonardo began his observation on the visual power of the pupil of the eye with a note on the visual rays penetrating the surface of water.

That Leonardo had planned a separate book on perspective explains Melzi's omission of notes on perspective in the Codex Urbinas. Melzi omitted not only

128. Brizio (1956), p. 315.   129. White (1957), pp. 207–218.
130. Cf. Steinitz (1958), pp. 25–27.   131. Lomazzo (1584), p. 264.
132. Ludwig (1882), II, 403–404; Heydenreich (1956), p. xxiv, n. 40.

the notes contained in the late MSS G and E but also those contained in the early MS A. The last-named are on Alberti's "costruzione legittima" and on anamorphical effects. From MS A, Melzi copied only a note on perspective relating to an anamorphical distortion in representing a figure on a curved surface. As we have seen, a similar note was copied from the lost *Libro* A. A note in Codex Arundel 62v proves that after 1500 Leonardo was still concerned with these anamorphical subjects.

The notes on perspective in Leonardo's extant manuscripts represent only a small part of what he wrote. However, they give us some idea of the development of Leonardo's studies on this subject. In the early MS A and in folios of the Codex Atlanticus of about the same date, Leonardo investigates at length the Albertian system of perspective, as if he intended to write a commentary on Alberti's discussion on perspective in *della Pittura*. It seems that in the first years of the 1490's Leonardo exhausted his interest in the problem. In manuscripts dating after 1500 we find no further diagrams of the Albertian system. But from that time on, Leonardo increasingly concerned himself with the phenomena of vision. He developed further Alberti's ideas on aerial perspective, pointing out that an object does not diminish in distance exactly according to the mathematical rules of linear perspective, and that various colors and densities of atmosphere between the object and the eye change our perception of the object in a manner that cannot be codified. There is a famous sentence by Leonardo often quoted to show his presumed attitude toward methaphysical concepts: "Nature is full of infinite reasons which never were in experience." [133] But this sentence is simply the title of the following note on painting: "A dark object seen against a light background appears smaller than it is, and a light object will appear larger against a background of a darker color." Perspective, freed from its rigid geometric scheme, becomes for Leonardo, one of the "infinite reasons which never were in experience."

About 1508 Leonardo discovered that the entire surface of the pupil of the eye has visual power. In MS D 4v he writes: "This is to prove that the whole of the pupil has visual power and that this power is not limited to one point as those who deal with perspective will have it, namely, that all images of objects converge to the eye like a pyramid meeting in one angle where judgment of the things seen is made. Experience here shows the contrary. . . ." Manuscript D, which can be dated *ca.* 1508, is entirely devoted to the study of the eye. Similar studies are found in MS F, which is dated 1508.

It has been assumed by Brizio that Leonardo started to question the Alberti system only *ca.* 1508, and that about 1513–1514 he formulated the new theory that objects recede not only in length but also in breadth and height. Cellini indeed refers to some similar approach as being contained in the lost *Discorso sulla prospettiva*, but this is not necessarily a reference to a theory of curvilinear perspective. As Sampaolesi suggests, Leonardo must have codified the system employed by Donatello in the *tondi* of the Sacrestia Vecchia, in which the foreshortenings in breadth

---

133. MS I 18, *ca.* 1497–1500.

and height occur along straight lines.[134] As I have shown elsewhere, the rule mentioned by Cellini is still preserved in Leonardo's manuscripts.[135]

Leonardo's late notes on perspective do not contradict the early ones. To prove this we have only to mention the note in MS A 41r.[136] This is what we may call a "paradosso di prospettiva," which clearly refers to the presumed theory of curvilinear perspective. The concluding remark, "questa cosa è più disputativa che da usarla" (this is more for the sake of discussion than for practical use), proves that such theoretical discussions on perspective can be traced back as early as 1492. It seems quite possible that at such an early date Leonardo actually discussed problems on perspective with artists of the Milanese circle. Lomazzo gives us some information about the kind of perspective practiced in North Italy and particularly in Milan at the turn of the century.[137] He speaks of Mantegna, Foppa, Bramante, and Bramantino as artists who practiced foreshortening of the kind suggested by the anonymous author of the Codex Huygens; that is, figures represented according to a curved line of intersection parallel to the surface of the eye. Leonardo's *paradosso* of 1492, as well as his diagram of the optical principle of Euclid's,[138] proves his interest in a system of perspective which was already practiced empirically. Leonardo opposed to it the Alberti system, with the paradoxical result that neither system appears correct. The Alberti system, however, was still satisfactory to him, providing that a narrow angle of vision was adopted. That is why, in the page containing the *paradosso*, he advises that the painter should stand at a distance twenty times the size of the object he has to represent. This advice is also expressed, although in different terms, in his late notes in MS E. Thus as early as 1492 Leonardo recognizes the inconsistencies of the Alberti system.

In 1513–1514 Leonardo resumes his early studies on perspective. In MS E he

---

134. Sampaolesi (1960), p. 201. 135. Pedretti (1963), pp. 69–87.

136. Richter (1883), I, 545: "If the point of sight is at T you would make the figures on the circle D B E all of one size, as each of them bears the same relation to the point T. But consider the diagram given below and you will see that this is wrong, and why I shall make B smaller than D E [fig. *a, b*].

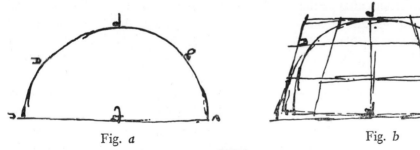

Fig. *a* Fig. *b*

MS A 41r

"It is easy to understand that, in placing two objects equal to each other, the one at three braccia distance looks smaller than that placed at two braccia. This, however, is theoretical rather than practical, because if you stand close by . . . [*sic*]."

137. Lomazzo (1584), pp. 245–277. 138. MS A 38; cf. White (1957), p. 209.

states that the result of a close view employing a wide angle of vision is a combination of the artificial perspective in the painting and the natural perspective of the panel. This is what he calls complex perspective (*prospettiva composta*), that is, anamorphosis. Since anamorphosis can be observed only from one point, Leonardo thinks of how to represent objects as they appear to the eye without lateral distortions. Such distortions occur when the angle of vision is large, namely, when the eye is too close to the object; thus Leonardo recommends that "practice of perspective" that "shows all these objects just as the eye sees them diminished, without obliging a man to stand in one place rather than another so long as the wall does not produce a second foreshortening." White interpreted this passage, and Leonardo's further explanation, as a proof that Leonardo had eventually recognized the necessity of representing objects foreshortened laterally. This is not true: Gioseffi has already given the right interpretation of Leonardo's passage.[139] In addition to Gioseffi's explanation one should consider the note that explains the

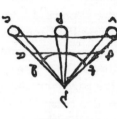

Libro B
(MS E) 16v

diagram in MS E 16v: "Let the plane be D E, above which are represented three equal circles that are placed behind it, that is circles A, B, and C; you now see that the eye, H, will perceive the images of the distant object on the plane as being larger than those that are nearer." (This passage, omitted by White, is written in the margin of the folio and should be inserted in the passage referring to complex perspective, at the point indicated by Leonardo with the sign //.) Thus the diagram clarifies what Leonardo meant in speaking of simple and complex perspective: simple perspective is that which is produced by the intersecting plane farthest from the eye; and complex perspective is that which is produced by the intersecting plane closest to the eye. We can see, therefore, that complex perspective is actually composed, as Leonardo explains, of natural and artificial perspective. That is why in his diagram Leonardo added a curved line parallel to the curvature of the eye *only* in the case of the intersecting plane closest to the eye. This curved line represents the lateral foreshortening of the panel. Leonardo never states that the size of the objects, as they appear on this curved line of intersection, should be transferred onto the intersecting plane of artificial perspective, but he says that the painter should avoid complex perspective (i.e., anamorphosis) and "hold to simple perspective, which does not regard intersecting planes as foreshortened but as much as possible in their proper form." Since the intersecting plane should appear "as much as possible" in its proper form, it should be placed as far as possible from the eye. Leonardo's concluding sentence only apparently supports White's interpretation: "And of this simple perspective in which the intersection cuts the pyramids by which the images are conveyed to the eye at an equal distance from the eye, we are given constant experience thanks to the curved form of the light of the eye on which

139. Gioseffi (1957), pp. 106–120.

the visual pyramids are intersected at an equal distance from the visual faculty." Leonardo is still referring to what happens to the panel picture; he repeats that the panel foreshortens laterally because the visual pyramid is intersected by the curved surface of the eye. In other passages overlooked by White, Leonardo gives even the ratio of lateral foreshortening, establishing the rule mentioned by Cellini.[140]

In *Libro* A Leonardo pays tribute to Alberti's system, speaking of perspective as "a most subtle discovery in mathematical studies." [141] We cannot really say that Leonardo's various statements on the subject are so difficult to reconcile.[142] His statements are never contradictory. He clearly distinguishes natural perspective as optics from artificial perspective as a "subtle discovery in mathematical studies." He recognizes immediately, as early as 1492, that the Alberti system could not be completely satisfactory because of optical laws; but he does not reject it. He only recommends reducing its inconsistencies by employing a narrow angle of vision.

The representation of a human figure foreshortened according to a curved line of intersection indicates not a method but a practice. Lomazzo even specifies that painters should fix a charcoal to a long reed in order to draw figures on a high wall from a convenient distance, implying the use of natural perspective.[143] A well-trained eye does not need the laborious process proposed by the author of the Codex Huygens. Giulio Romano's bold foreshortenings were obtained by drawing from a reticulated mirror reflecting models of small size.[144] And Lomazzo tells us that Michelangelo could well say that he "learned how to behold things so that he may be able to express them by hand, adding moreover that the eye may be so practised in these matters, that by mere sight, without more angles, lines and distances, it may be able so to guide the hand, that it shall represent whatsoever it lifts, but not otherwise than that which it sees beholding it perspectively." [145]

Ambrogio Figino, a Milanese painter active in the second half of the sixteenth century and acquainted with Leonardo's and Michelangelo's traditions, explains a system of proportion identical to that illustrated by the anonymous author of the Codex Huygens,[146] and states that no geometric system is more practical to foreshorten figures so measured than the painter's own eye:

---

140. MS E 4; MS G 32; Cf. Pedretti (1963), pp. 69 ff.
141. *Libro* A 18.   142. Chastel (1961), p. 100.
143. Lomazzo (1584), p. 284.
144. The device is described by Cristoforo Sorte in his *Osservazioni nella pittura* published in 1580; cf. Barocchi (1960), I, 298–299.
145. Lomazzo (1584), p. 262.
146. Cf. Gregorio Comanini, *Il Figino* (1590; reprinted in Barocchi [1962], III, 361): "e 'l pittore, se vuol figurare un eroe, farà l'imagine di dieci faccie, con l'ordine che io dirò. . . ." In the figures on folio 3 of the Codex Huygens, Panofsky (1940), p. 21, counts nine face units according to the Italo–Byzantine canon, whereas, as Figino has explained, application of the Vitruvian canon gives ten face units, as illustrated in folio 1 of the Codex Huygens. Figino's explanation is undoubtedly related to the figures on folio 3 of the Codex Huygens: "The first face is from the roots of the hair to the bottom of the chin; the second is from the pit of the throat to the bottom of the nipple and breast; the third is from the breast to the navel; the fourth is from

It is true that for the practicing painter it is necessary to have (as Michelangelo said) the compasses in the eye, because it is impossible to proceed easily in fore-shortening a human figure whose proportions have been established first with the compass. Although Alberto Durero had taught the system of foreshortening by means of lines, his system, besides being scarcely used, seems to me of little or no profit at all. I do not think that one could make that great figure of Giona in Michelangelo's Sistine Chapel by first measuring it with the compass according to a system of proportion, and then foreshortening the entire body with the exception of the legs. It is true, however, that from the proportion of the legs one could obtain the proportion of the entire foreshortened body.[147]

Late in the sixteenth century the Brunelleschi *perspectiva artificialis* was still considered the only correct system of perspective. In his commentary to Vignola's *Practica della Prospettiva* (1583) Egnazio Danti goes into a long discussion to prove how false perspective can be when obtained with a certain instrument invented by Baldassare Lanci, an engineer of Urbino.[148] This instrument is based on the principle of recording data on a sheet of paper fixed on a curved surface equidistant from the eye. According to Danti, perspective so obtained would be false as soon as the sheet of paper is detached from its support. And this is exactly what happens to Leonardo's perspective when the diagrams of MS E are interpreted—as White interprets them—as illustrations of the principle of curvilinear perspective. Curiously enough, the diagram given by Danti is remarkably similar to that given by Leonardo.

Leonardo's missing book on perspective contained no more than what we know from his extant manuscripts, with the possible exception of the rules concerning the two-point perspective. From Caporali's commentary to Vitruvius' *De Architectura* published in 1536 we learn that Leonardo practiced such a system.[149] Caporali, an architect, had probably met Leonardo in Rome between 1513 and 1516, and in his commentary he refers to Leonardo, who had been dead seventeen years: ". . . and in our time Leonardo Vinci of Florence, with whom we have spoken about this perspective, and he affirms that he does it, more than anyone else, with two centers, or, rather, vanishing points." This quotation is significant because it includes a statement made by Leonardo himself. In his late period Leo-

---

the navel to the beginning of the genitals; the fifth is from the beginning of the genitals to the middle of the thigh; the sixth is from the middle of the said thigh to the knee, providing that half a face be left below the knee; the seventh is from the bottom of the knee to the middle of the leg; the eighth is from the middle of the leg to the malleolus; the ninth results from the height of the foot plus the half-face of the knee; the tenth and last one results from the section between the roots of the hair and the top of the head plus the section between the chin and the pit of the throat."

147. Barocchi (1962), III, p. 361.
148. *Practica della Prospettiva* (2d ed.; 1644), pp. 61–62.

149. Vitruvius (1536), p. 16: ". . . et āchor' al tēpo nr̄o Leonardo vīce da Firēze co'l qu*a*le hab / biam' p*a*rlato seco di essa prospettiva, & esso ne affirma farla piu degli altri con doi cētri o vederi ch' dir / vogliamo. . . ."

nardo was still following a system of perspective that antedated Alberti. As Robert
Klein has recently proved, the two-point perspective had been a studio practice since
the time of Giotto.[150] In Leonardo's "Annunciation" in the Uffizi the perspective
of the pavement is based on that system.[151] This practice is never mentioned in the
Quattrocento treatises on perspective, and even Leonardo has no specific reference
to it. Viator (1505) is believed to have been the first to codify the two-point perspective.[152] That the system was known to the artists of the Quattrocento is implicit
in Caporali's statement that Leonardo used it "more than any one else."

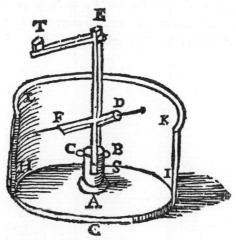

Baldassare Lanci's device for representing objects according to curvilinear perspective
(Vignola, *Practica della Prospettiva*. Rome, 1583).

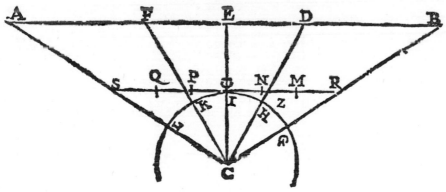

Egnazio Danti, Commentary to Vignola's *Prospettiva* (Rome, 1583), p. 61. Danti
demonstrates that perspective obtained with such an instrument is false. Data are recorded on a sheet of paper fixed on the curved surface LG, which represents the
intersection of the visual cone according to curvilinear perspective. When the paper is
removed from its support, the data LKIHG take the place of the points QPONM in
the intersection of artificial perspective SR.

150. Klein (1961), pp. 211–230.   151. Cf. Sampaolesi (1954), pp. 33–39.
152. Cf. Ivins (1938).

Caporali's statement, which refers to the late period of Leonardo's activity, may well serve as a conclusion to our interpretation of the development of Leonardo da Vinci's theory of art. It proves historically what we have suggested through the chronology of Leonardo's writings in general and of his lost *Libro* A in particular: Leonardo's advanced views in the study of natural phenomena in his late period are never separated from ideas that can be traced back to the early Renaissance. Leonardo thus links two great periods in the history of Italian art. That his ideas became widespread in the Cinquecento is documented by Caporali, Serlio, Cellini, and Lomazzo. Pietro Accolti's *Treatise on Perspective* published in 1625 contains a "Discorso sul Disegno" which may be considered to be the first publication of the abridged version of Leonardo's "Treatise on Painting." [153]

---

153. Pedretti (1962*b*), pp. 292–294.

1. Leonardo da Vinci. Old man seated on the bank of a river; and studies of swirling water. Pen and ink; *ca.* 1513. Windsor, Royal Library, 12,579r.

*Memoria, et Notta di tutti i pezzi
de Libri di'mano di Leonardo, quali
compongono in sieme Lo presente libro
del Trattato di Pittura.*
et Prima.
Il Libro Intiero, segnato . i —
Libro segnato — A . et . Z . —
Libro segnato . ——— . ✚ .
Libro d'ombra e'lume
segnato —— . G .
Un'altro del medesimo
segnato —— . W . —
Libro segnato . —— . ♋ .
Libro segnato . — . ♋ .
Libro segnato . — . ⊠ .
Libro segnato . — — ✳ — A .
Libro segnato . — — . ♉ . —
Libro segnato . — . B .

2–3. Francesco Melzi. List of Leonardo's manuscripts used in the compilation of the *Trattato della Pittura*. Codex Urbinas 1270, folios 230v–231.

libro segnato. ———— . ✳ . —
libro segnato. ———— . φ . —
Libro segnato. ———— . A . —
libro segnato ——— . @ . —
Et tre altri libretini ————
Uno segnato ———— . Δ . —
l'altro segnato ———— . Y
Et l'altro segnato ———— . Λ . —
Che sono tutti .n°. XVIII.

3

4. Leonardo da Vinci. Notes on hydraulics copied from *Libro* A. Codex Leicester, folio 21r.

Capitoli ne quali si trouua difficultà y intellig.a d'legga di Leonardo da vinci dua pittura
li titoli de quali sono li seguenti, secondo la copia che si troua in Roma dalla quale
cauaua quella che si remandaua al P.e Ant.o dello guilielmo il fauore del disegno

Cap. 16. Modo d'augumentare e destra l'ingeg.o o uare fraens folio

cap. 2. Dell esser vniuersale fol. 2

cap. 7. Del modo di studiar fol. 2

cap. 14. Del corregger gl'errori che si scopri fol. 3

cap. 34. Del ritrarre al lume di candela fol. 7 at.o

Cap. 65. Come si deue figurar una Notte fol. 13

Cap. 66. Come si deue figurar una fortuna fol. 13 at.o

Cap. 67. Come si deue figurar una battaglia fol. 14

Cap. 74. Se il lume deue esser tolto in faccia o da parte equale o a più gratia fol. 17

Cap. 88. De termini de riflessi nel suo campo fol. 20 at.o

cap. 99. Dell accompagnar li colori l'un con l'altro e che l'uno dia gra all'altro fol. 23

Cap. 117. qual parte del Colore ragioneuolm.te deue esser i più bella fol. 28 at.o

Cap. 123. Quale e la superficie cuoderina de più colore fol. 30

Cap. 137. De campi che si conuengono all'ombra e ai lumi fol. 32 at.o

Cap. 157. De Colori de lumi incidenti e riflessi fol. 36

Cap. 161. De Colori fol. 37 at.o

Cap. 164. De Colori fol. 38 at.o

cap. 165. Del uero Colore fol. 39

Cap. 160. Delle misure d'le misure dell huomo dal suo nascim.to al suo ult.o crescim.to fol. 40 at.o

Cap. 160. Come li puttini hanno le giunture contraie agli huoi.ni nelle loro giun. de fol. 41

Cap. 197. quando e maggior differenza d'altezza di spalle nelle attitudini dell huomo e in che conto fol. 47 at.o

cap. 211. Come li Muscoli sincoti e grossi fol. 54

Cap. 231. Delli moti appropriati agli effetti degli huoi. 58

cap. 265. Ponderatione de corpi che non si muouono fol. 62 at.o

cap. 290. Della finestra doue si mette la figura fol. 70 at.o

Cap. 307. Pittura di fig.a e corpo fol. 74 at.o

Cap. 309. Perche una med.ma Campagna si dimostra alcuna uolta magg.re o minore tendo fol. 74

Cap. 311. De raggi solari che penetrano li Giraioli de nuuoli fol. 76 at.o

Cap. 314. Della prospettiua lineale fol. 79 at.o

Cap. 333. Del fumo fol. 82

cap. 362. Del far una Pittura d'eterna uernice fol. 91

cap. 372. Delle pieghe de panni in reto fol. 94

li capitoli segnati non confrontati ☧ Et altri non li trouano in questi libri

5. Cassiano dal Pozzo. List of chapters of the abridged version of Leonardo's *Trattato della Pittura* to be checked against the original manuscripts. Milan, Ambrosian Library, Codex H 228 inf.

no de membri piegabili, mai diminuiscano, o'crescano di
loro lunghezza. —

di _____ to,

I.ª A. cav. 14

[7]

'da occidente sara un'altro obbietto del medesimo lume alluminato il quale sara d'altro colore chel primo obbietto on
de con suoi   razzi re
flessi rissalta   in uer
leuante e per   cote con
suoi razzi nel   le parte
del primo obbietto a lui uolta e li si tagliano e'suoi razzi
e'rimangano fermi in sieme cõ loro colore e'splendore —

[24]

oncauo e'di sotto vetto, ss.ᵗ o'di sopra concano, o'conuesso ss.
o'uero di sopra connesso e'di sotto vetto ss, o'di sopra cõ
esso e'di sotto concano —   P.A. ca. 22
ricatura del naso col ciglio e'di due
raggioni cioe, o'che le'concaua o che le'

[29]

non ue altro che quatro uarieta cioe, lungo, corto, alto
con la punta e'basso, i nasi concaui sono di tre sorti

direto · concauo · sopra · e'sopra · e'in mezo · e'disotto · disotto · in mezo · disotto

de li quali alcuni hanno la concauità nella parte
superiore alcuni nel mezo et altri nella parte inferiore
li nasi conuessi, ancora si uariano in tre modi cioe'alcu
ni hanno il gobbo nella parte di sopra, alcuni in mezo
e d'altri nella parte disoto, li sporti che mettono in mezo
il gobbo del naso si uariano in tre modi cioe o'sono diui-
ti o'sono concaui, o'ueramente sono conuessi,

il gobbo in mezo fra vette, il Gobbo in mezo fra curate, il Gobbo in mezo fra
lineti,   lineti conuesse,   lineti concaue
·LT·

[30]

si uaria dal campo, e'la parte d'esso cãpo alluminato
non termina mai in eso campo alluminato cõ la sua pri
ma

corpo luminoso   razzo luminoso   corpo ombroso   chia

rezza,   anzi
infra'l   razzo uisuale,   campo
e'l primo   lume
del corpo,   s'inter
pone un,   occhio   termi
ne, del corpo ch'io' piu oscuro chel campo, o'chel lume del
corpo, — respemine, — —

[35]

pra altri corpi d'egual colore, il termine e'l conaesso
parra piu oscuro che col connesso termine terminera
il termine   de laste equi
giacente pai   ra in campo
bianco di gra   de oscuria
e'in campo   scuro parra
piu che altra sua parte chiarissimo ancora che il
lume che sopra l'aste discende sia sopra essa aste

[54]

per dicerne cause delle quali la pi e'che l'aria in
terposta infra l'occhio el p; e minor soma che

quella che s'interpone infra l'occhio e'l, a, e percou
seguente e'piu chiara, la seconda e'che l'aria e'piu

[66]

con debita disposicione sopra il centro del suo sosten
taculo _____

delle finestre doue si uitrae le figure L.ª A.
sia la finestra delle stanze de pittori fatte dinpanate

[67]

6–7. Francesco Melzi. Copies of drawings and diagrams of Leonardo's *Libro* A. The numbers refer
to the chapter-numbers of the present reconstruction.

[81]

si rimoue dal precetto suo ririato,
    Del bilicho delle figure,
la figura possa sopra un de suoi piedi la spalla di
quello lato che possa fia sempre
piu bassa che l'altra, e la fontanella della gola sara sopra il mezo
della gamba che possa, el medesimo
                                    acha=

L.A. cr. 39

parte orientali o uero quella parte che s'interpone
nfra'l sole et l'occhio, sara tanto piu oscura quanti elle

il'occhio piu uicina. tale accidente acadera in
uella parte che fia piu uicina al sole cioe che para

[88]

[82]

l.b. e'la larghezza del uiso ede'posta nella distantia
della cauta. c.f. doue son le guancie et essa liauelo
a'stare in   dietro tutto
.a.c. et allo   ua le tempia
sarebbono o   portate nella
distantia: .o.v. dalle linee. a.f. et   b.f. si che a
la differentia. c.o. et. v.d. si che si conclude che la
linea. c.f. et la linea. d.f. per essere piu corte aa

[85]

npossibil e'ch'alcuna memoria possa riseruare tutti gli aspetti o'mutattione d'alcuno membro di qualungn'animale
si sia, questo   caso, esemplifi-
caremo co'la   dimostratione
d'una mano   et perch'ogni
quantita cō-   tinua e'di ni-
sibile in m,   finito il moto
del occhio   che riguarda
la mano, e'si moue da, a, al, b, si moue per uno spattio, a, b,
il quale, e' ancora lui quantita continua et per conseguenn

tale pittura a'uederla da una finestra od altro

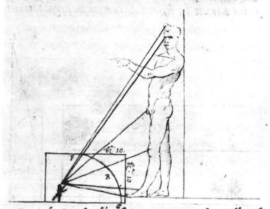

spiraculo perche l'occhio non a'attendere alla pla

[90]

[86]

ro, d azuro luminoso e'metti con esso la piu oscura
ombra. fato questo uede se l'obbietto e'sperico o'co
lunnale o'qua   duato o'come c'si
sia e's'egli e'spe   uico tira le linee
dalli stremi della   pariete oscura
al centro d'esso obbietto sperico e'doue esse linee si

egamenti, per la qual cosa la misura del braccio disteso
n confa con la misura del braccio pieghato, c,
    Cresce il braccio e'diminuisce in sia la
auietu de l'ultima sua astensione, e'pie-
iamento la ottaua parte della sua lun-
iezza   L'A cao. 64.
    l'acrescimento e'raccurtamento del brac-
o del osso che auanza fuora de la giontu
t del braccio il quale come uedi nella figura
l, fa lungo tratto della spalla al gomito
endo l'angholo d'esso gomito minore che retto
anto piu cresce quanto tal'angholo dimi-
uisce e'tanto piu diminuisce quanto el pre'
mo angholo si fa maggiore,
anto piu cresce lo spacio della spalla al c.
                                    gomito,

[108]

7

[107]

[110]

[116]

[130]

8. Leonardo da Vinci. Drawings illustrating notes on hydraulics copied from *Libro A*. Codex Leicester, folios 24v, 15, 13, 21. The numbers refer to the chapter-numbers of the present reconstruction.

perde tanto di grandezza, e de colore quanto l'aquista,
de remottione. Adonque la pittura, e filosofia perche la
filosofia tratta de moto anmentatiuo, e diminutiuo ilqua-
le si troua, nella sopra detta propositione della quale fare-
mo la conuersa, e dire, la cosa ueduta dal occhio aguis-
ta tanto de grandezza, e notitia, e colore quanto quanto
ella diminuisce lo spattio interposto infra essa, e l'occhio
che la uede. *porchè seguitare il 2 tometto di segna ch dice Si prouala Pittura* **78**

Chi biasima la pittura biasima la natura perche
l'opere del pittore rapresentano l'opere d'essa natura, e per
questo il detto biassimatore ha carestia de sentimento **58**

Si proua la pittura essere filosofia perche essa tratta del
moto de corpi nella prontitudine delle loro attioni, e la
filosofia anchora lei s'astende nel moto, **87**

Tutte le scientie che finiscono in parolle hà, si presto
morte come uista eccetto la sua parte manuale cioe lo
scriuere ch'è parte mecchanicha, **9**

Come la pittura abbraccia le
superfitie figure, e colori de
corpi naturali e la filosofia
sol s'astende nelle loro
uirtu naturali,

questo cap⁰ è sta unito ci quello di sopra e fatto uno

La pittura s'astende nelle superfitie, colori, e figure de qualon=
que cosa creata dalla natura, e la filosofia penetra den=
tro alli medesimi corpi considerando in quelli le lor proprie,
uirtu ma non rimane satisfatta con quella uerità che fa
il pittore che abbraccia in se la prima uerita di tali corpi,
perche l'occhio meno se inganna, **10**

9. Codex Urbinas, folio 4.

chi piacceuoli suaui et diletteuoli di fioriti prati con uarij
colori, piegati da suaue onde dalli suaui moti di uenti,
riguardando dietro al uento che da lovo si fugie, fiumi,
discendenti co'li empitti de gran diluuij dalli alti monti che si cacciano in anti le deradicate piante miste co'sassi,
radici, terra e'schiuma, cacciandossi, in anzi cio che si
contrapone alla sua ruina, et il mare con le sue proccelle,

qua mi ricordo
della mirabile
discritione del
diluuio dello
Autore!

10.　*a.* Codex Urbinas, folio 36 (detail).

PARTE.

delle quali māca la scoltura.

ornata d'infinite speculazioni che la scultura nō la dopra,

20

De Pittura e Poesia

Per fingere parole La poesia supera la Pittura et per fingere
fatti la Pittura supera la poesia et quella proportione che'
da' fatti alle parole tal'e' dalla Pittura alla essa poesia
perche i fatti sono subbietto dell'occhio et le parole subbietto
dell'orecchio, et cosi li sensi hanno la medesima proportione
in fra lovo quale hanno li lovo obbietti infra se medesimi et
per questo giudico la pittura essere superiore alla poesia
ma per non sapere li'suoi'operatori dire la sua ragione
e'vestata l'ongho tempo sanza aduocati. Perche ella no
por la ma per se si dimostra e'termina ne fatti et la poesia
finisce in parole co'le quali come briosa se stessa lauda

✱ Questo capitolo de Pittura et poesia, e ritrouato. doppe
s'auer scritto tutto l'libro però mi pare stare ble.
bene s'ei seguissi dietro il cap. quale sieria e'
meccanica et quale nō e' meccanica. a car. 19. f. 1.
piu tosto dietro al cap. arguitione dl poeta contra'l pittore
a car. 14. f. 2 . ouero dietro al seguente,

10.　*b.* Codex Urbinas, folio 28v.

11. Leonardo da Vinci. Notes on hydraulics and on the representation of a Deluge. The notes on the upper part of the folio were written by Francesco Melzi at Leonardo's dictation. Pen and ink and black chalk; *ca.* 1515. Codex Atlanticus, folio 79 r-c.

12. Leonardo da Vinci. Drawing of fires. Red chalk on red prepared paper. Leonardo's notes in red chalk, dated December, 1511, are transcribed in pen and ink by Francesco Melzi. Windsor, Royal Library, 12,416.

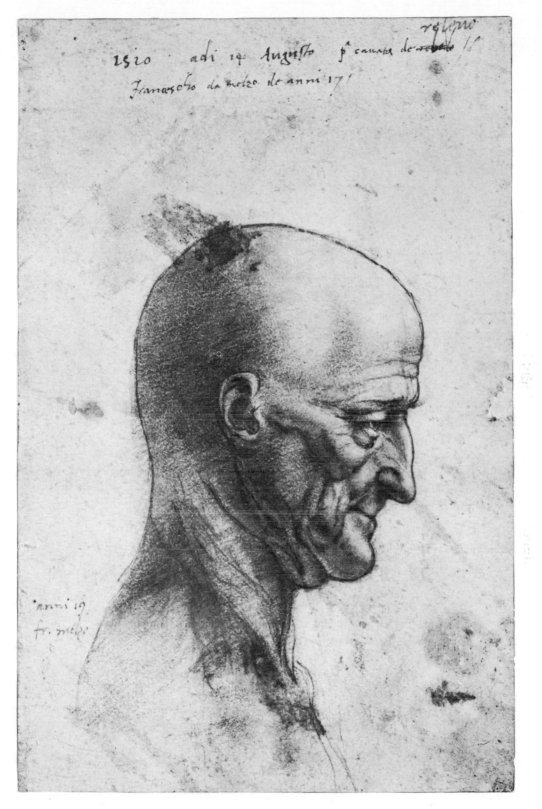

13.   Francesco Melzi. Drawing of an old man. Red chalk. Signed and dated 1510, August 14. Milan, Ambrosian Library.

, 28,

Notta come il seguente mezo capitolo
ua posto dietro al'altro suo mezo qual comincia a'carte,
.27. del presente libro et resta diuiso a'car, 23, fac, 2, al-
segno, W, et finise, cosi; L'OPERA da quello guasta, errore
occorso per la lettera che mancina et perche era trameg-
giato su n'altra carta al contrario, ───────

. SECVNDA .

. 85,

qui finisse il capitolo, Come si debbe figurare una bataglia
il quale comincia a'carte, 83. errore acaduto et scritto dal
autore, in due diuerse maniere, et tinti d'inchiostro, però segue, al segno, L.T,

378

· Del rizzarsi l'huomo da sedere
di sito piano,   I°. A. car. 25.

Stando l'huomo a'sedere nel pauimento la prima cosa
che fa, nel suo leuarsi, e' che tra da se il piede e'possa la
mano in terra da quel lato chesi uol leuare e'gitta la
persona sopra il braccio che possa, et mette il gionocchio
in terra da quel lato chesi uol leuare ───────

I°. A. car. 26. Trouo scritto apresso al capitolo di sopra il suggetto
del suo contrario ma poi nò ne parla niete, et e'questo.✶

. ✶. · Del cadere l'huomo a'sedere in,
───────   sito piano, ───────

519

· De Pittura   I°. A. car i.

L'azuro dell'aria c'di color composto di luce et di
tenebre, la luce diro per causa di l'aria aluminata
nelle particule della humidità, infra essa aria infusa per le tenebre diro l'aria pura la qual non e' di-
uisa in attimi cioe particule d'humidità nella qual
s'habbi apercottere li razi solari et di questo siuede
l'essempio nell'aria che s'interpone infra l'occhio et le
montagne ombrose per l'ombre della gran' copia delli
alberi che sopra essa si trouano o'uero ombrosa in quella
parte che non e'percossa dalli razi solari la qual aria
si fa azura c'non si fa azuia nella parte sua luminosa e'peggio nella parte coperta di nene, ───────

14. a, b, c, d. Details from the Codex Urbinas: folios
28, 85, 127v, and 154v respectively.

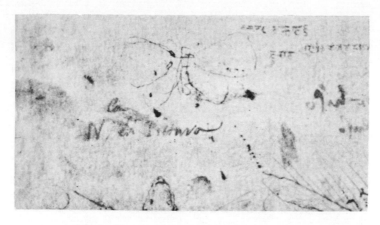

15. *a*. Leonardo da Vinci. MS B (Ashburnham 2037), folio 98v; note by Melzi: "N.ᴵᵃ di Pittura."

15. *b*. Leonardo da Vinci. Codex Arundel, folio 93v; note by Melzi: "Nᴵᵃ· di Pitᵗᵃ."

15. *c*. Leonardo da Vinci. Codex Atlanticus, folio 88 v-a; note by Melzi: "Schizzi d'ogni sorte."

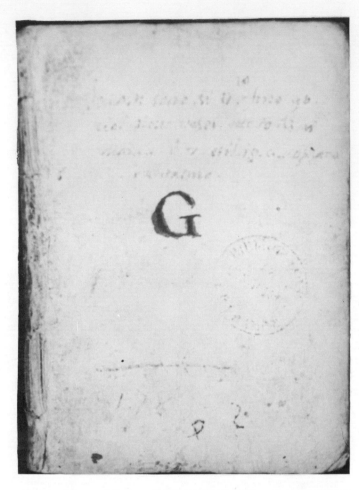

16. *a.* Cover of Leonardo's MS G. Collation note by Melzi.

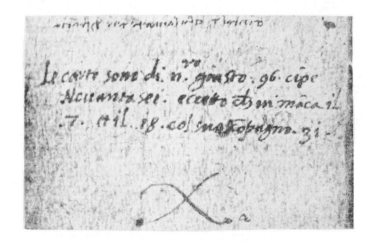

16. *b.* Detail of the verso of the cover of Leonardo's MS G.

MELTIVS.

17. *a*. Codex Urbinas, folio 78v; Melzi's signature (enlarged).

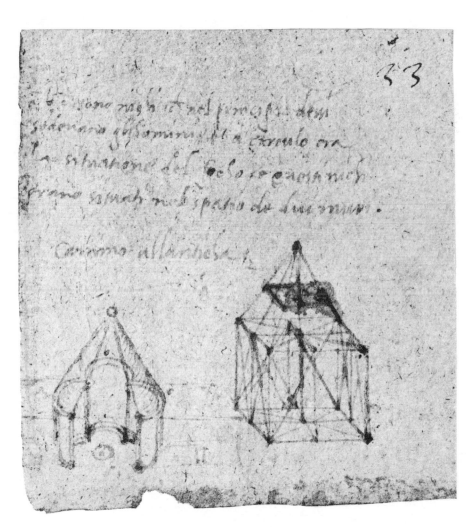

17. *b*. Francesco Melzi. Notes and sketches on a "camino all'anticha." Pen and ink; *ca.* 1515. Codex Atlanticus, folio 335 v-e (detail).

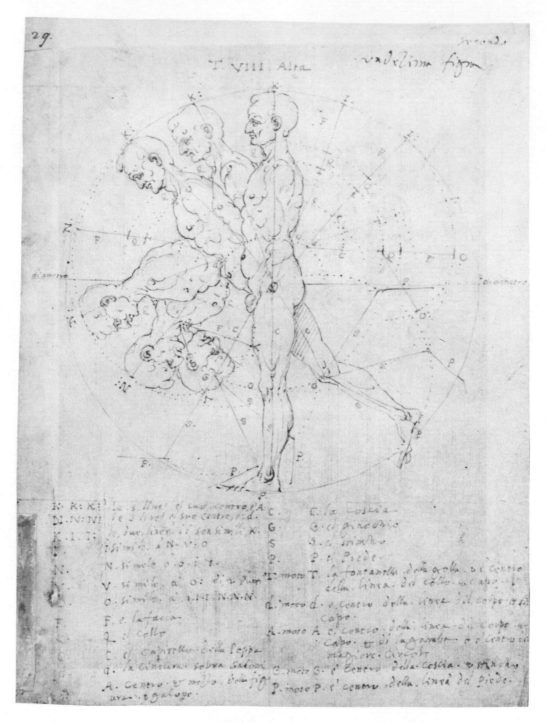

18. Codex Huygens, folio 29. New York, Pierpoint Morgan Library, Codex M. A. 1139.

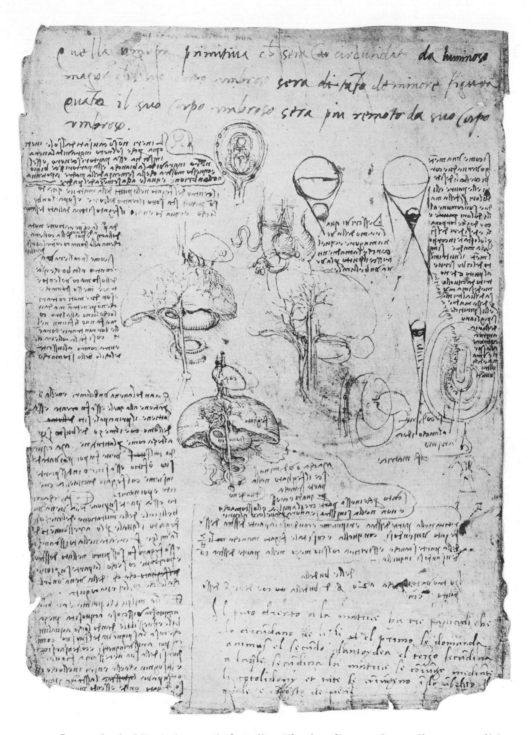

19. Leonardo da Vinci. Anatomical studies. The four lines and two diagrams on light and shade (top) are by Francesco Melzi. The note on anatomy in the lower right corner is by an anonymous assistant of Leonardo's. Pen and ink; *ca.* 1510–1512. Windsor, Royal Library, 19,102v.

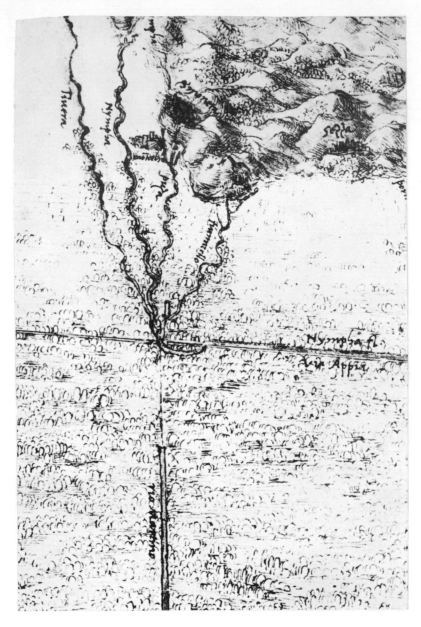

20. Leonardo da Vinci and Francesco Melzi. Map of the Gulf of Gaeta (detail). Pen and ink and wash; *ca.* 1514. Windsor, Royal Library, 12,684.

21. Leonardo da Vinci. Notes on hydraulics and drawings of human figures. The sketches of landscape and the note "Mag^ce pr. hon." are by Francesco Melzi. Pen and ink; *ca.* 1506. Windsor, Royal Library, 12,641r.

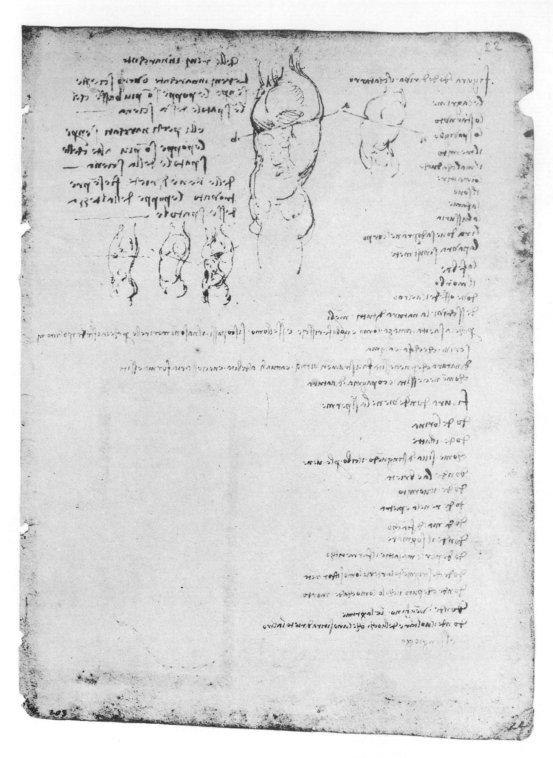

22.   Leonardo da Vinci. Plan for a Book on the Human Figure and Anatomy, *ca.* 1489 (right column); notes and sketches on the movement of the torso, *ca.* 1503–1505. Pen and ink. Windsor, Royal Library, 19,038r.

23. Leonardo da Vinci. Notes and sketches on human movement. Black chalk and pen and ink; *ca.* 1503–1505. The first two lines at the head of the folio date from *ca.* 1489. Windsor, Royal Library, 19,038v.

24.   Leonardo da Vinci. Notes on painting. Pen and ink; *ca.* 1505–1508. Codex Atlanticus, folio 199 v-a.

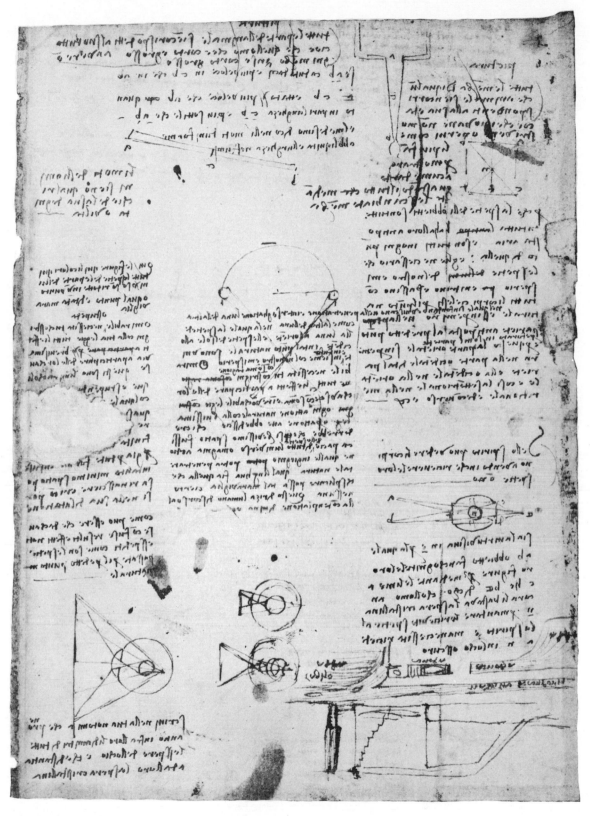

25. Leonardo da Vinci. Notes on painting (crossed out), on optics, and on the canalization of the Adda River. Pen and ink; *ca.* 1508. Codex Atlanticus, folio 345 v-b.

26.   Leonardo da Vinci. Sketches on anatomy and crossed-out notes on painting. Pen and
ink; *ca.* 1506–1508. Windsor, Royal Library, 19,121r.

27. *a.* Ambrogio Figino. Copy of a lost drawing by Leonardo da Vinci. Red chalk. London, British Museum, King's MS 323.

 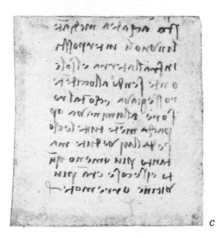

b   *c*

27. *b.* Leonardo da Vinci. Studies of draperies. Pen and ink; *ca.* 1502. Windsor 12,705; formerly in Codex Atlanticus, folio 366 r-b.

27. *c.* Leonardo da Vinci. Fragment of a note on painting; *ca.* 1508–1510. Codex Atlanticus, folio 165 v-d.

28. Leonardo da Vinci. Crossed-out notes on light and shade (developed in the fifth part of the Codex Urbinas). Pen and ink; *ca.* 1506–1508. Codex Atlanticus, folio 207 r-a (detail).

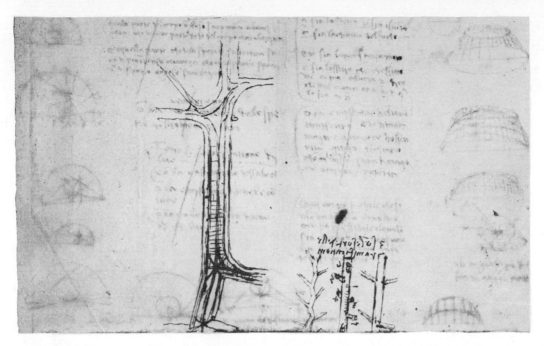

29. *a*. Leonardo da Vinci. Topographical sketch of the area of the "Neron da Sancto Andrea" in Milan, and sketches of the phyllotaxy of plants. Pen and ink; *ca.* 1506–1508. Codex Atlanticus, folio 207 v-a (detail).

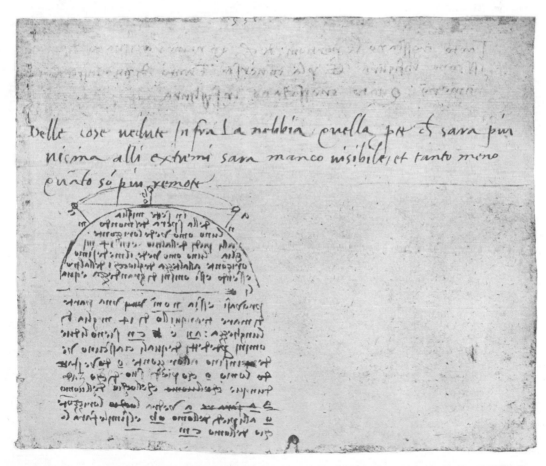

29. *b*. Leonardo da Vinci. Note and diagram on the horizon, and a note on aerial perspective (Melzi's handwriting). Black chalk and pen and ink; *ca.* 1517–1518. Codex Atlanticus, folio 76 r-b.

30.   Cover of Leonardo's MS F, showing Melzi's mark. Paris, Bibliothèque
de l'Institut de France.

31. Cover of Leonardo's MS E (*Libro* *B*), showing Melzi's mark. Paris, Bibliothèque de l'Institut de France.

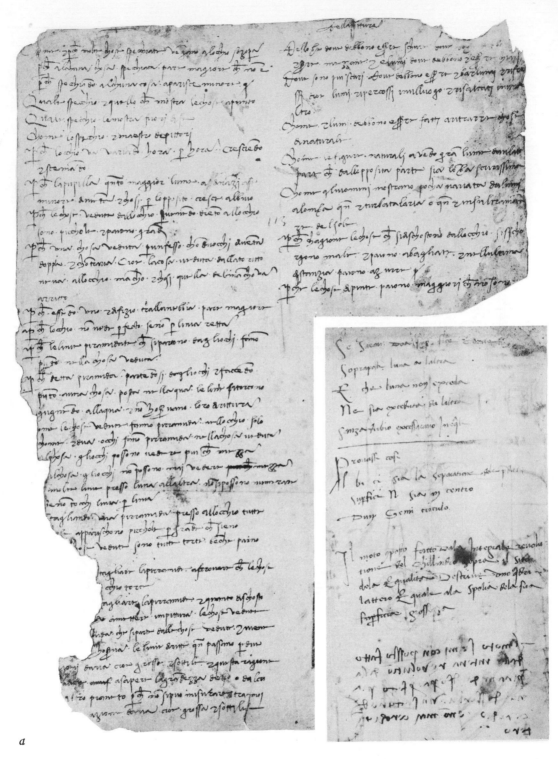

32. *a*. Ambrogio de Predis (?). A list of headings of Leonardo's notes on painting. Codex Atlanticus, folio 360 r-c; *ca.* 1508.

32. *b*. Ambrogio de Predis (?) and Leonardo. Notes on geometry. Codex Atlanticus, folio 207 v-a (detail); *ca.* 1508.

PART THREE
CONCORDANCES

THE CHAPTERS of the "Treatise on Painting" are indicated by their number in the Ludwig edition. Their titles are taken from McMahon's translation with some changes. The subsequent numbers indicate the folios of the Codex Urbinas and, in parentheses, the chapter-numbers of McMahon's rearrangement. When a chapter, or part of it, is found in one of Leonardo's extant manuscripts, the indication of its source is given according to the following standard abbreviations:

MS A	MS A in the Bibliothèque de l'Institut de France, Paris.
MS Ash.	MS Ashburnham 2038 in the Bibliothèque de l'Institut de France, Paris (the complement of MS A).
MSS C, E (*Libro B*), F, G	Other manuscripts in the Bibliothèque de l'Institut de France, Paris.
MS Tr.	Codex Trivulzianus, Castello Sforzesco, Milan.
W.	Folios in the Royal Library at Windsor Castle (*Catalogue* by Sir Kenneth Clark, 1935).

When the date of a chapter is not certain a note is added suggesting other possibilities of dating. Similar notes are also added when a comparison with notes in the Codex Atlanticus (indicated by C.A.) or elsewhere may help to suggest the dating of a chapter of the "Treatise on Painting." (The references to *Libro A* give the number of the carta, not the chapter.)

Comparisons with chapters of the "Treatise on Painting" are given according to the chapter-numbers in the Ludwig edition (indicated by Lu).

If one needs to find the date of a certain chapter and knows only McMahon's (McM) number, one must first find Ludwig's number in McMahon's concordance. Sometimes authors (Clark, Venturi, and others) use the numbers of Borzelli's edition in their references to the "Treatise on Painting." A concordance Ludwig–Borzelli is given by Marinoni (1954), p. 274.

A "Concordance: Leonardo's MSS–Codex Urbinas 1270" is given on pages 222–226 and a "Concordance: Codex Urbinas 1270–'Editio Princeps'" in Appendix IV (pp. 241–251).

A List of the Chapters of Leonardo da Vinci's Trattato della Pittura *with Their Suggested Dates and Their Concordance with the Extant Manuscripts*

PART ONE

1. *Whether or Not Painting Is a Science.*
   1–1v (1)   1500–05
   Cf. Lu 443.
2. *Exposition of Difference between Painting and Poetry.*
   1v (21)   1500–05
3. *On the First Principle of the Science of Painting.*
   1v–2 (3)   1500–05
4. *Basis of the Science of Painting.*
   2 (2)   1500–05
5. *On the Second Principle of Painting.*
   2 (4)   1500–05
6. *What Does the Science of Painting Include.*
   2–2v (5)   1500–05
7. *What Science Is Most Useful and of What Does Its Utility Consist?*
   2v–3 (17)   1500–05
8. *On Imitable Sciences.*
   3–3v (18)   1500–05
9. *How Painting Embraces All the Surfaces of Bodies and Includes Them.*
   3v–4 (14, 78, 58, 87, 9)   1500–05
10. *How Painting Encompasses the Surfaces, Forms, and Colors of Natural Bodies, but Philosophy Only Their Natural Properties.*
    4 (10)   1500–05
    A note by Melzi states that the chapter was joined to the preceding one.
11. *How Sight Is Less Deceived than Any Other Sense, in the Perception of Lu-* minosity, Transparency, and Uniform Media.
    4v (11)   ca. 1492
    Cf. W. 19,019 (An. B 2), notes concerning the senses and their connection with the central nervous system (early period, 1489).
12. *How He Who Disparages Painting Loves neither Philosophy nor Nature.*
    4v–5 (6); MS Ash. 20   ca. 1492
13. *How the Painter Is Master of All Sorts of People and of All Things.*
    5 (35)   ca. 1492
14. *On the Poet and the Painter.*
    5–5v (31)   1500–05
15. *Comparison between Poetry and Painting.*
    5v–7 (23, 36, 38, 24, 27)   1500–05
    Lu 15a corresponds to McM 27. "Essempio tra la poesia e la pittura." Thus, in the original this chapter came after the preceding one. Cf. Lu 2.
16. *Which Is the More Damaging to a Man, to Lose His Sight or His Hearing?*
    7–7v (13)   1500–05
    Connected with the preceding one (cf. Lu 15a). The concept may belong to the first period, ca. 1492, but the reasoning appears later.
17. *How the Science of Astronomy Is Born of the Eye, because It Was Created by the Eye.*
    7v (15)   1500–05

Concepts of geometry and arithmetic typical of the early 1500's. Cf. Lu 1.

18. *The Painter Argues with the Poet.*
7v–8 (22)   ca. 1492
Possibly 1500–05. Cf. Lu 15.

19. *How Painting Exceeds All the Works of Man because of the Subtle Reflections That Pertain to It.*
8–8v–9 (30);
MS Ash. 19–19v   ca. 1492

20. *Difference between Painting and Poetry.*
9–9v–10 (29)   ca. 1492
"Ten ornaments of nature." Cf. Lu 511 (*ca.* 1492) and 438 (after 1500).

21. *What Difference There Is between Painting and Poetry.*
10–10v (40)   ca. 1492
Mention of the *Calumny* of Apelles. Cf. Lu 19.

22. *Difference between Poetry and Painting.*
10v–11 (37)   ca. 1492
Probable reference to Dantes' commentators.

23. *On the Difference and Similarity of Painting and Poetry.*
11–11v–12–12v (42)   ca. 1492
Perhaps reëlaborated after 1500.

24. *On the Eye.*
12v–13 (12)   ca. 1492
Cf. Lu 15 and 16.

25. *Dispute between the Poet and the Painter and What Difference There Is between Poetry and Painting.*
13–13v–14 (33)   ca. 1500
Considerations on mathematical astronomy; cf. Lu 17. Leonardo mentions one of his own paintings of religious subjects, probably a Madonna, "bought by a man who fell in love with her." Concepts and reasoning still basically of the Sforza period.

26. *Argument of the Poet against the Painter.*
14–14v (32)   ca. 1492

27. *Reply of King Mathias to a Poet Who Competed with a Painter.*
14v–15–15v (28)   ca. 1492

28. *Conclusion of the Dispute between the Poet and the Painter.*
15v–16 (34)   ca. 1500
Concepts of the Sforza period; type of reasoning closer to 1500.

29. *How Music Must Be Called a Sister, a Younger Sister, of Painting.*
16–16v (39)   ca. 1492

30. *The Musician Speaks with the Painter.*
16v–17 (43)   ca. 1492

31. *The Painter Gives the Degrees of Things Presented to the Eye as the Musician Gives the Degrees of the Voices Presented to the Ear.*
17–17v–18 (44, 45, 26, 16);
MS Ash. 23   ca. 1492
Only the first section concords with MS Ash. 23: "Although things placed . . . from degree to degree." The other texts, however, must be of the same period. After 31b the transcriber notes: "A piece is missing here, as I see it." Chapters Lu 31a, 31b, and 31c are respectively McM 45, 26, and 16. Probably these notes do not come from an ordered compilation but from a codex like MS A & Ash.

32. *Conclusion of the Dispute between Poet, Painter, and Musician.*
18–18v–19 (41)   ca. 1492
It might be closer to 1500, but still in the Sforza period.

33. *Which Science Is Mechanical and Which Is Not?*
19–19v (19)   ca. 1500
Cf. Lu 25.

34. *Why Painting Is Not Numbered among the Sciences.*
19v–20 (25)   ca. 1500
Like the preceding one, to which it is related, it might be earlier, although later than 1492.

35. *Beginning Discussion on Sculpture and whether or Not It Is a Science.*
20 (49)   ca. 1500
Probably late in the Sforza period.

36. *Difference between Painting and Sculpture.*
20–20v–21–21v (51)   ca. 1492

Reference to the "ten different subjects" of the painter.

37. *The Painter and the Sculptor.*
  21v–22–22v (56)   ca. 1492
Reference to Della Robbia.

38. *How Sculpture Requires Less Intelligence than Painting and How Many Aspects of Nature Are Lacking in It.*
  23–23v (47);
  MS Ash. 25–24v   ca. 1492
The text continues on folio 28 in McM 53. The chapter has two added notes, probably of similar date.

39. *On the Sculptor and the Painter.*
  13v–14–14v (48)   1500–05
Reprobation of the use of the "prospettografo."

40. *Comparison of Painting and Sculpture.*
  24v–25 (55)   1500–05
Perhaps later. See the following chapter.

41. *Comparison of Painting and Sculpture.*
  25–25v (57); *Libro A* 29   1508–10

42. *Comparison of Painting and Sculpture.*
  25v–26 (50)   1505–10

43. *Apologia of the Sculptor.*
  26v–27 (52)   1505–10
The last section, "The sculptor will say . . . more durable than sculpture," is marked L° A 29.

44. *How Sculpture Is Indebted to Light but Painting Is Not.*
  27 (46); *Libro A* 29   1508–10

45. *The Difference between Painting and Sculpture.*
  27–27v (54); *Libro A* 17   1508–10

Addition to 38. *We know that he who is experienced . . . that sculpture does not employ.*
  28–28v (53); MS Ash. 25   ca. 1492
Continuation of chapter 38.

46. *On Painting and Poetry.*
  28v (20)   1505–10
Chapter added after the compilation of the book proper.
Folios 29–29v and 30–30v are blank.

PART TWO

47. *What the Student Should Learn First.*
  31 (59); MS Ash. 17v   ca. 1492

48. *What Study the Young Should Follow.*
  31 (62)   ca. 1510
Cf. Lu 51 and 52 (MS G 25), and also Lu 55 (*Libro A* 55). However, it could be possibly of the Sforza period.

49. *What Rules Should Be Given to Boys Who Paint?*
  31–31v (60); MS Ash. 28   ca. 1492

50. *On the Life of the Painter in His Study.*
  31v (74); MS Ash. 27v   ca. 1492

51. *Characteristics of the Youth Disposed toward Painting.*
  31v (64); MS G 25   ca. 1510

52. *Rule for the Painter.*
  31v (91); MS G 25   ca. 1510

53. *How Should a Young Man Proceed in His Study?*
  32 (69)   ca. 1510
Cf. Lu 48.

54. *How to Study.*
  32 (67)   ca. 1510

55. *Study of the Young Painter.*
  32 (68); *Libro A* 24   1508–10

56. *What Should the Mind of the Painter Be Like?*
  32–32v (71); MS Ash. 2   ca. 1492

57. *On the Painter's Judgment.*
  32v (81)   1505–10
Cf. Lu 141 (*Libro A* 44) and Lu 406 (*Libro A* 41). See also Lu 483 (MS G 19); Brizio (1952), p. 434. An analogous subject is in Lu 75 (MS Ash. 26), Brizio (1952), p. 220; and in MS Ash. 33v.

58. *Statement of Rules for the Painter.*
  32v–33–33v (92, 72)   1500–05
Lu 58a corresponds to McM 72; for this cf. MS Ash. 27.

59. *Rules for the Painter.*

           33v (89)   1500–05

Perhaps earlier. For the reference to the "Paragone" cf. Lu 41 (*Libro A 29*) and C.A. 305 r-a.

60. *Precepts of the Painter.*

           33–33v (93)   *ca.* 1492

Botticelli is mentioned here for his opinion on landscapes.

61. *On Being Universal.*

           34 (94)   1505–10

Cf. Lu 57. However, it could be of the Sforza period.

62. *Rules for the Painter.*

           34 (82)   1505–10

Same subject as the preceding chapter. Perhaps they both come from the same manuscript.

63. *Rules for the Painter.*

        34 (61); MS Ash. 10   *ca.* 1492

64. *Rules for the Painter.*

        34 (257); MS Ash. 8v   *ca.* 1492

65. *On the Painter and His Rules.*

        34–34v–35 (78, 84)   1505–10

Reflections on riches and virtues; cf. Lu 81 (*Libro A 13*). The subject, however, is of the Sforza period: see, e.g., Lu 76 (MS Ash. 26). Lu 65a corresponds to McM 84. Both paragraphs probably come from the same manuscript.

66. *Way to Augment and Stimulate the Mind toward Various Discoveries.*

        35v (76); MS Ash. 22v   *ca.* 1492

Only the first section comes from MS Ash. 22v. The second, although almost identical, could be later than 1500.

67. *On Studying When You Awake or before You Go to Sleep in Bed in the Dark.*

        36 (65); MS Ash. 26   *ca.* 1492

68. *Pleasure of the Painter.*

        36–36v (280)   *ca.* 1492

Although it may seem late on account of reference to the description of deluge, it is more closely comparable to Lu 147 (MS Ash. 21).

69. *On Games That Draftsmen Should Play.*

        36v–37 (75); MS Ash. 26v   *ca.* 1492

70. *That Diligence Should Be Learned before Quick Execution.*

        37 (63); MS Ash. 27v   *ca.* 1492

71. *Whether or Not It Is Better to Draw in the Company of Others.*

        37–37v (73); MS Ash. 26v   *ca.* 1492

72. *How to Memorize Well.*

        37v (66); MS Ash. 24   *ca.* 1492

73. *That a Painter Is Not Praiseworthy unless He Is Versatile.*

        37v–38 (95); MS Ash. 25v   *ca.* 1492

74. *On the Sad Illusion of Those Who Falsely Call Themselves Painters.*

        38 (79); MS Ash. 25   *ca.* 1492

75. *How the Painter Should Be Disposed to Listen to Everybody's Judgment While He Is at Work.*

        38–38v (83); MS Ash. 26   *ca.* 1492

76. *How a Man Engaged on an Important Work Should Never Trust His Memory So Much that He Will Not Deign to Draw from Nature.*

        38v (256); MS Ash. 26   *ca.* 1492

77. *Of Those Who Censure Drawing on Feast Day and Investigating the Works of God.*

        38v–39 (80)   *ca.* 1492

It might also be of the late Roman period, 1513–1515, as a reflection of contrasts at the court of Leo X. Cf. C.A. 226 v-a, *ca.* 1515: ". . . because nothing can be loved or detested if you first do not know it."

78. *On Variety in Figures.*

        39 (97); MS G 5v   *ca.* 1510

79. *On Being Versatile.*

        39–39v (96); MS G 5v   *ca.* 1510

80. *On the Error of Those Who Practice without Science.*

        39v (70); MS G 8   *ca.* 1510

81. *On Imitating Other Painters.*

        39v (77); *Libro A 13*   1508–10

82. *Program of Representation.*

        39v (112); MS Ash. 33   *ca.* 1492

83. *On Representation.*

        39v (117); MS Ash. 31v   *ca.* 1492

84. *On Representing an Object.*

        40 (114); MS Ash. 29   *ca.* 1492

84a. *Note in your drawing. . . .*

        40 (109);

        Libro B 17 (MS E 17)   1513–14

85. *How the Light Should Be High in Drawing from Nature.*
    40 (129); MS Ash. 33   *ca.* 1492
86. *What Lights Should Be Selected for Drawing the Shapes of Objects?*
    40–40v (140)   1508–10
Cf. Lu 87 and 93.
87. *On the Quality of Light in Which to Represent Relief, Natural or Simulated.*
    40v–41 (136); *Libro A* 37   1508–10
88. *On Drawing the Nude.*
    41 (121); MS A 28v   *ca.* 1492
89. *On the Representation of the Relief.*
    41 (116); MS Ash. 10   *ca.* 1492
90. *How to Draw a Site Correctly.*
    41–41v (118); MS Ash. 24   *ca.* 1492
91. *How to Represent Landscapes.*
    41v (139); MS G 19v   *ca.* 1510
92. *On Representing the Shadow of Bodies by the Light of a Candle or Lamp.*
    41v (132); *Libro A* 38   1508–10
93. *Under What Conditions a Face Is to Be Represented to Give It Grace through Shadow and Light.*
    41v–42 (137)   1508–10
Cf. Lu 86.
94. *How to Represent Shadow, Both Simple and Compound.*
    42 (141)   1508–10
Cf. Lu 110 and 709. See also the following chapter, which was copied from *Libro A.* On universal and particular light in Leonardo, see Brizio (1952), p. 457, n. 1.
95. *On the Light in Which to Represent the Flesh Tones of Faces or Nudes.*
    42 (143); *Libro A* 30   1508–10
Cf. Lu 709 and 816.
96. *On Representing Figures in Narrative Paintings.*
    42–42v (264); MS Ash. 10   *ca.* 1492
97. *Learning to Draw from a Well-Posed Figure.*
    42v (119); MS Ash. 24   *ca.* 1492
98. *When One Should Consider the Selection of Material.*
    42v–43 (122); MS Ash. 27   *ca.* 1492
99. *On Gestures.*
    43 (123); MS Ash. 27   *ca.* 1492

Continuation of the preceding chapter.
100. *To Represent a Nude or Other Object from Nature.*
    43 (113); MS A 1   *ca.* 1492
101. *Proportion and Division of the Figure.*
    43 (120); MS A 1   *ca.* 1492
102. *Way to Represent Relief at Night.*
    43 (131); MS A 1v   *ca.* 1492
Similar to the later text Lu 92 (*Libro A* 38).
103. *How the Painter Should Place Himself with Respect to the Light and Relief.*
    43–43v (133); MS A 23   *ca.* 1492
104. *On the Kind of Light.*
    43v (128); MS A 23   *ca.* 1492
105. *On the Self-Deception Experienced in Judging Parts of the Body.*
    43v (85); MS A 23   *ca.* 1492
106. *How It Is Necessary for the Painter to Know the Inner Structure of Man.*
    43v–44 (124); MS Ash. 27   *ca.* 1492
107. *On the Defect Which Those Masters Have Who Repeat the Same Expressions in Faces.*
    44 (274)   1505–10
Cf. Lu 109.
108. *On the Greatest Defect of Painters.*
    44–44v (86)   1505–10
Cf. Lu 109.
109. *Precepts: The Painter Should Not Make a Mistake in Selecting the Figure of Which He Makes a Specialty.*
    44v–45 (87); *Libro A* 28   1508–10
110. *Defect of Painters Who Depict an Object in Relief Indoors in One Light and Then Place It in the Country or Elsewhere Where There Is Another Light.*
    45–45v (142)   1505–10
Cf. Lu 94 and 709.
111. *On Painting and Its Division.*
    45v (101)   1505–10
112. *Form and Its Division.*
    45v (105)   1505–10
113. *Proportion of Parts of the Body.*
    45v (104)   1505–10
Chapters 111–113 seem to preserve the sequence they might have had in the original manuscript. For the reference

to the quality of limbs cf. Lu 376 (*Libro A* 24). However, these chapters might have been written in the Sforza period, *ca.* 1490–1495; cf. C.A. 349 r-b, a note on the difference of movements in young and old men.

114. *On Shunning the Calumnies and Varying Judgments of Those Who Practice Painting.*

46 (90)   *ca.* 1492

The chapter ends: "Of this mention will be made below." Therefore, the following chapter is connected with it.

115. *On Movements and Various Opinions about Them.*

46 (250)   *ca.* 1492

Cf. C.A. 139 r-d, *ca.* 1490. See also Lu 180. Subject developed later: cf. Lu 376 (*Libro A* 24).

116. *Shun Profiles, That Is, Sharp Edges for Objects.*

46–46v (156)   *ca.* 1492

Background of figures. Cf. Lu 151 and 251–252 (*Libro A* 25, 27). See also Lu 418 (MS Ash. 31v). Subject developed later.

117. *How Errors Are Not Noticed in Small Objects as Much as They Are in Large.*

46v (88); MS Ash. 14v   *ca.* 1492

118. *Why a Painting Can Never Appear to Have as Much Relief as Do Objects in Nature.*

46v–47 (220); MS Ash. 10   *ca.* 1492

119. *Why Depicting Rows of Figures One Above the Other Is a Method to Be Avoided.*

47–47v (265); MS Ash. 16   *ca.* 1492

120. *What Method of Painting It Is Best to Employ to Make Objects Stand Out.*

47v (135)   1510–15

Cf. MS E 32v; Brizio (1952), p. 457, n. 1. See also Lu 790.

121. *Which Requires Greater Consideration and Is More Useful: the Lights and Shadows of Bodies or Their Contours?*

47v–48 (106)   1505–10

122. *Which Is of Greater Importance: Movement Originating from the Men-*

tal Conditions of Living Creatures, or Their Shadows and Light?

48 (111)   1505–10

Cf. Lu 357–359 and 370–376, all on "moti mentali."

123. *Which Is of Greater Importance: That the Form Should Abound in Beautiful Colors, or Display High Relief?*

48 (108)   1505–10

Chapters 121–123 seems to preserve the sequence they must have had in the original manuscript. Perhaps chapter 120 also comes from the same manuscript.

124. *Which Is More Difficult: Light and Shade, or Good Drawing?*

48–48v (107); MS Ash. 1   *ca.* 1492

125. *Precepts for the Painter.*

48v (126);

Libro B 19 (MS E 19v)   1513–14

126. *Memorandum by the Author to Himself.*

49 (127);

Libro B 20 (MS E 20)   1513–14

127. *Rules of Painting.*

49 (251)   1500–05

Suggestions on sketching. Cf. C.A. 199 v-a; Brizio (1952), p. 460. Topic basically of the Sforza period. Cf. Lu 64 (MS Ash. 8v).

128. *Rules of Painting.*

49–49v (218)   1500–05

Placement of the figures at various distances. Cf. Lu 487 (*Libro A* 27); see also Lu 153. Probably earlier: cf. Lu 149 (MS Ash. 18); Brizio (1952), pp. 200–201.

129. *How the First Picture Originated.*

49v (98); MS Ash. 7v   *ca.* 1492

130. *How a Painting Should Be Seen from Only One Window.*

49v–50 (216); MS Ash. 17v   *ca.* 1492

131. *Of the First Eight Parts into Which Painting Is Divided.*

50 (99)   *ca.* 1492

Cf. Lu 511 (MS Ash. 22v).

132. *How Painting Is Divided into Five Parts.*

50 (100)   *ca.* 1492

133. Painting is divided into two principal parts. . . .

50–50v (102)   *ca.* 1492

Placed in the codex under the title of chapter 132. Lu 131–133 perhaps come from the same folio.

134. On Pictures in Outline.

50v (115); MS Ash. 14v   *ca.* 1492

135. On Painting.

50v (130); MS Ash. 14v   *ca.* 1492

136. On the Parts of Painting.

50v (103); MS E 79v   1513–14

The transcriber does not indicate the source as *Libro B.*

137. On the Selection of Beautiful Faces.

50v–51 (276); MS Ash. 27   *ca.* 1492

138. How to Select an Atmosphere to Make Faces Attractive.

51 (134); MS Ash. 20v   *ca.* 1492

139. On Beauty and Ugliness.

51 (277); *Libro A* 27   1508–10

140. On Beauty.

51v (278); *Libro A* 44   1508–10

141. On Judges of Various Beauties of Equal Excellence in Various Bodies.

51v (279); *Libro A* 44   1508–10

142. How Small Children Should Be Represented.

51v (252); MS Ash. 17v   *ca.* 1492

143. How Old Men Should Be Represented.

51v (254); MS Ash. 17v   *ca.* 1492

144. How Women Should Be Represented.

51v (253); MS Ash. 17v   *ca.* 1492

145. How Old Women Should Be Represented.

52 (255); MS Ash. 17v   *ca.* 1492

146. How One Ought to Represent Night.

52 (284); MS Ash. 18v   *ca.* 1492

147. How to Represent a Storm.

52v–53 (281); MS Ash. 21   *ca.* 1492

148. How One Ought to Represent a Battle.

53–53v (282);

MS Ash. 31–30v   *ca.* 1492

The text follows on folio 85.

149. On the Way to Deal with Distant Objects in Painting.

53v–54 (230); MS Ash. 18   *ca.* 1492

150. How the Air Should Be Lighter the Lower You Depict It.

54 (227); MS Ash. 18v   *ca.* 1492

151. To Cause Forms to Detach Themselves from Their Background.

54 (152)   1505–10

Background of figures. Cf. Lu 116; see also Lu 251, 252, 423, and 497 (*Libro A* 25, 27, 30, 26). The subject, however, is already treated in the Sforza period: cf. Lu 418 (MS Ash. 31v), Brizio (1952), p. 234, in relation with Lu 423 (*Libro A* 30). See also MS Ash. 26; Richter (1883), I, 285.

152. On Representing the Sizes of Painted Objects.

54–54v (219)   1505–10

Cf. Lu 797.

153. On Defined and Indistinct Objects.

55 (217)   1505–10

Cf. Lu 486 and 487 (*Libro A* 16, 27). See also Lu 128, and the next chapter.

154. Figures Separated from One Another Should Not Appear to Be Joined Together.

55 (260)   1505–10

155. Whether the Light Should Be in Front or Come from the Side of the Figure, and Which Lends More Attractiveness.

55–55v (138)   1505–10

It seems to evoke the portrait of "Mona Lisa." But this chapter, like the preceding ones back as far as Lu 151, might be earlier, *ca.* 1500.

156. On Reflection.

55v (157); MS Ash. 14v   *ca.* 1492

157. Where There Cannot Be Any Reflection.

55v (158); MS Ash. 14v   *ca.* 1492

158. On Reflected Lights.

55v–56 (167)   1505–10

159. On the Reflections of Light That Surround Shadow.

56 (163)   1505–10

160. *Where Reflected Lights Are of Greater or Less Brightness.*
                56–56v (166)   1505–10
161. *What Part of a Reflected Light Will Be the Brightest?*
                56v (160)   1505–10
It quotes the sixth proposition of the Book on Light and Shade.
162. *On the Reflected Colors of Flesh.*
                56v–57 (174)   1505–10
It quotes the third proposition of the Book on Light and Shade, and the sixth proposition of the Book on Perspective.
163. *Where Reflected Lights Are Most Readily Perceived.*
                57 (165)   1505–10
164. *On Double and Triple Reflected Lights.*
                57 (161)   1505–10
165. *How No Reflected Light Is Simple but Is Mingled with the Visual Images of the Other Colors.*
                57v (169)   1505–10
Cf. Lu 248 (*Libro A* 18). See also Lu 214.
166. *How Reflected Lights Are Rarely of the Color of the Body at the Point Where They Meet It.*
                57v (168)   1505–10
167. *Where Reflected Light Is Most Seen.*
                57v–58 (164)   1505–10
168. *On Reflected Lights (1st, 2d, 3d, 4th).*
                58 (172)   1505–10
169. *Reflection of Light.*
                58 (170)   1505–10
Chapters 158–169 seem to come from the same codex, preserving the sequence they must have had in the original. The small diagrams (Lu 161, 164, 165, 166) are typical in manuscripts of late period, such as MSS E, F, and G. In Lu 162 we find quoted the third proposition of the second Book on Light and Shade: "The surface of every ⟨opaque⟩ body will take on the color of its opposite object." See also Lu 170–172 from *Libro A*. Another

group of notes on "riflessi" is in chapters 780–790.
170. *On Reflection.*
                58–58v (175); *Libro A* 39   1508–10
171. *On the Color of Reflected Lights.*
                58v (162); *Libro A* 42   1508–10
172. *On the Edges of Reflected Lights against Their Background.*
                58v (173); *Libro A* 49   1508–10
After this chapter the transcriber writes: "End of reflected lights."
173. *On the Method of Learning to Compose Figures in Narrative Paintings.*
                58v–59 (258); MS Ash. 27v   ca. 1492
174. *On Placing a Figure in the First Plane of a Narrative Painting.*
                59 (263); MS Ash. 23   ca. 1492
175. *On Posing Figures.*
                59 (125); MS A 29   ca. 1492
176. *Method of Composing Narrative Paintings.*
                59v (262)   1505–10
Quotation of a proposition from the Book on Perspective.
177. *On Composing Narrative Painting.*
                59v (266)   1505–10
It seems to evoke the "Battle of Anghiari": "pazzia bestialissima" (most brutal madness).
178. *Variety among the People in Narrative Paintings.*
                59v–60 (20)   1505–10
Cf. Lu 183 and 186 (*Libro A* 32, 37). Chapters 176–178 seem to come from the same manuscript, preserving the sequence they must have had in the original.
179. *How to Learn the Movement of Man.*
                60–60v (249)   ca. 1492
Reference to the use of silverpoint and of the "carte inossate" (paper prepared with bone meal), media that Leonardo employed only in the Sforza period.
180. *How a Good Painter Must Depict two Things: Man and His Mind.*
                60v (248)   ca. 1492
Cf. Lu 115.

181. *On the Composition of Narrative Painting.*
60v (259)   ca. 1492
Cf. Lu 127.

182. *On Not Ornamenting the Figures in Narrative Paintings.*
60v–61 (275)   ca. 1492
Cf. Lu 538–539 (MS Ash. 17v–18).

183. *On Variety in Narrative Paintings.*
61 (268); Libro A 32   1508–10

184. *On Narrative Painting.*
61 (272); Libro A 32   1508–10

185. *Conformity in the Parts of Narrative Paintings.*
61 (269); Libro A 32   1508–10

186. *On Diversifying the Expression of Faces in Narrative Paintings.*
61 (273); Libro A 37   1508–10

187. *On Varying the Vigor, Age, and Complexion of Figures in Narrative Paintings.*
61–61v (271); Libro A 50   1508–10

188. *On the Components of Narrative Paintings.*
61v (267)   ca. 1492
Possibly later, although still in the Sforza period. Cf. Lu 25.

189. *Rules for the Composition of Narrative Paintings.*
61v–62 (261)   ca. 1492
Stains on walls. Cf. Lu 66. Together with the preceding chapter, it probably belongs to the same codex from which the second section of Lu 66 was copied. At the end the transcriber notes: "End, beginning of colors."

190. *On Putting Colors Together in Such a Way That Each Makes the Other Attractive.*
62–62v (185, 183)   1505–10
Composition of the colors of the rainbow, with reference to a further discussion on this subject, "as will be set forth in the proper place." A later date is thus possible. Cf. Lu 944.

191. *How to Make the Colors in Your Paintings Vivid and Beautiful.*
62v (191)   1505–10
Cf. Lu 254 (*Libro A* 29–30).

192. *On the Tones of the Shadows of Any Color.*
62v–63 (200)   1505–10

193. *On the Differences in Colors According to Their Distance or Nearness.*
63 (235)   1505–10
Cf. C.A. 249 r–c (MacCurdy:II.368). See also Lu 228 and 234.

194. *At What Distance the Colors of Objects Are Entirely Lost.*
63 (229)   1505–10

195. *At What Distance from the Eye the Colors of Objects Are Lost.*
63v (224)   1505–10

196. *Color of the Shadow of White.*
63v (206)   1505–10
It quotes the ninth proposition of the Book on Light and Shade. Cf. Lu 247 (MS F 75).

197. *What Color Will Create the Blackest Shadow?*
63v (207)   1505–10

198. *On the Color Which Does Not Display Any Difference in Varying Densities of Air.*
64–64v–65 (232)   1505–10
Chapters 197–198 were probably together in the original. They had the same length of line, as proved by mistakes in the transcription. See in this volume, p. 112 and note 47.

199. *On Perspective of Colors.*
65–65v (231)   1505–10

200. *On Color That Does Not Change in Different Densities of Air.*
65v–66 (233)   1505–10

201. *Whether Different Colors Can Appear to Be of Uniform Obscurity because of a Common Shadow.*
66 (194)   1505–10

202. *Why the Colors and Forms of Bodies Are Lost through What Seems to Be Darkness but Is Not.*
66–66v (195)   1505–10
The theme is treated in various periods: cf. Lu 700 (MS Ash. 10), Lu 244 (MS L 41v), Lu 245 (MS E 17v–18). See also Lu 628. Lu 202 is certainly from after 1500, because here

Leonardo alludes to the second proposition of his Book on Perspective.

203. *How Nothing Seems Its True Color if It Does Not Have Light from Another, Similar Color.*

66v (197)   1505–10

Cf. Lu 217.

204. *On Colors Which Vary in Their Nature through Contrast with Their Backgrounds.*

66v (151)   1505–10

Cf. Lu 252 (*Libro A* 27).

205. *On the Mutation of Transparent Colors Placed upon or Superimposed over Divers Colors with the Varying Ways in Which They Veil the First Colors.*

67 (179)   1505–10

Color of smoke. Cf. Lu 515 and 516 (MS G 22v–23). See also Lu 470.

206. *What Part of a Color Looks Most Beautiful in Painting?*

67 (190)   1505–10

207. *How Every Color That Does Not Shine Is More Beautiful in Its Illuminated Parts than in Those Shadowed.*

67–67v (187)   1505–10

Chapters 190–207 seem to come from the same manuscript, probably a Book on Colors like the one mentioned by Vasari. Perhaps these chapters follow the sequence they might have had in the original. The diagrams (198 and 199) are typical of late manuscripts.

208. *On the Visibility of Colors.*

67v (239); MS Ash. 18   ca. 1492

209. *What Part of a Color Ought, According to Reason, to Be the Most Beautiful?*

67v (199); MS Ash. 32v   ca. 1492

210. *How the Beauty of Color Must Be in the Lights.*

67v (188); MS Ash. 33   ca. 1492

211. *On the Green Color Made of Oxidized Copper.*

67v–68 (214)   ca. 1492

212. *Increasing the Beauty of Copper Green.*

68 (215)   ca. 1492

Chapters 211 and 212, which were probably copied from the same folio, appear to be related to the notes on painting in the early MS A.

213. *On the Mixture of Colors, One with Another, Which Extends to Infinity.*

68–68v (178)   1505–10

Concepts related to the principles of continuous quantity, typical of Leonardo's late period. The words "because here I lack paper" seem to indicate a codex completely written. Perhaps it is the same codex from which chapters 190–207 were taken. If we take into account that Leonardo usually started his manuscripts from the end, the following chapters would precede this concluding note on color.

214. *On the Surface of Every ⟨Opaque⟩ Body.*

68v–69 (201)   1505–10

The sentence "The surface of every shadowy body takes on the color of the object opposite" is typical of late notes on light and shade.

215. *What Surface Is Most Receptive to Colors?*

69 (205)   1505–10

216. *Which Side of the Body Will Be Tinged Most with the Color of the Object Opposite?*

69 (171)   1505–10

217. *What Part of the Surface of Bodies Appears Most Beautiful in Color?*

69 (198)   1505–10

Cf. Lu 203.

218. *On the Flesh Tones of Faces.*

69v (240, 144)   1505–10

Effect of light on a clear cloth placed on the head. Cf. Lu 238, 445, 708. See also Lu 492, ca. 1492.

219. To draw objects in relief, painters should stain the surface of the paper with a tint that is medium dark. . . . This is the second part of Lu 218, corresponding to McM 144. During this period, 1505–1510, Leonardo used to tint the paper red, a method similar to the one he adopted about 1490. In the first period he employed silverpoint on paper prepared with blue ground or

bone meal (cf. Lu 179); in the second period he used red chalk on red prepared paper.

220. *On Gradations in the Same Color Seen at Different Distances.*

69v (228)   1505–10

221. *On Foliage Seen in the Country.*

69v–70 (245)   1505–10

222. *What Foliage Will Seem Bluest?*

70 (247)   1505–10

Related to the preceding one. Quotation of the seventh proposition of the Book on Perspective.

223. *Which Is the Surface That Shows Its True Colors Less than Others?*

70 (210)   1505–10

224. *What Body Will Show You Its True Color Most?*

70 (209)   1505–10

Related to the preceding one, of which it constitutes the reversed proposition.

225. *On the Brightness of Landscapes.*

70–70v (192)   1505–10

226. *Common Perspective and the Diminution of Color at a Great Distance.*

70v–71 (226)   1505–10

Blue of the sky. Cf. Brizio (1952), pp. 588–592. See also Lu 490 (*Libro A 1*). Leonardo had already treated this subject during his Sforza period. Cf. MS G 18, Richter (1883), I, 303; and MS H₂ 77v, Richter (1883), I, 304.

227. *On Objects Reflected in the Waters in Landscapes, Beginning with Air.*

71 (212)   1505–10

Angles of incidence and reflection. Cf. MS F.

228. *Diminution of Colors through the Medium Lying between Them and the Eye.*

71 (222)   1505–10

Cf. MS G 53v; Richter (1883), I, 306. See also Lu 235.

229. *On Backgrounds Which Are Suitable for Shadows and Lights.*

71 (148)   1505–10

230. *How to Solve the Problem when White Borders on White or Dark.*

71–71v (150)   1505–10

231. *On the Nature of Colors in the Background behind White.*

71v (154, 155)   1505–10

Lu 231a corresponds to McM 155. Note on the persistence of images. Cf. MS K 120

232. *On the Backgrounds of Figures.*

71v (149)   1505–10

233. *On the Backgrounds of Painted Objects.*

71v–72 (145)   1505–10

234. *On Those Who, Painting in the Country, Represent the Most Distant Object as the Darkest.*

72 (237)   1505–10

It could be of the Sforza period, since it is against Cennini, p. 56: "And the farther away you have to make the mountains look, the darker you make your colors." Cf. Panofsky (1961), p. 105, n. 56. MS G 53v, however, proves that in his late period Leonardo was still concerned with this problem. See also Lu 193, 228 and C.A. 249 r–c (MacCurdy:II.368).

235. *On Colors of Things Distant from the Eye.*

72–72v (241)   1505–10

Continuation of the preceding chapter. Cf. Lu 228.

236. *Qualities of Painting.*

72v (110)   1505–10

237. *On the Reflection and Color of Sea Water Seen from Various Points of View.*

72v (213)   1505–10

238. *On the Nature of Contrasts.*

72v (184)   1505–10

Cf. Lu 218, 248, 445, 708.

239. *On the Color of the Shadows of Any Body.*

72v–73 (202)   1505–10

Cf. Lu 431 and 816.

240. *On the Perspective of Colors in Dark Places.*

73 (223)   1505–10

241. *Perspective of Colors.*

73 (234)   1505–10

242. *On Colors.*

73 (189)   1505–10

243. *Whence Comes the Blue of the Air.*
        73–73v (225)   1505–10
Cf. Lu 226.
244. *On Colors.*
        73v (242); MS L 75v   *ca.* 1502
245. *On Colors.*
    73v–74 (193);
        Libro B 18 (MS E 18)   1513–14
Melzi notes: "Another chapter follows
on this folio 18 in L° B."
246. *On Backgrounds of the Figures of
    Bodies in Painting.*
            74 (146); *Libro B*
                (MS E 4)   1513–14
247. *Why White Is Not a Color.*
            74 (204); MS F 75   *ca.* 1508
248. *On Colors.*
        74–74v (196); *Libro A* 18   1508–10
Cf. Lu 238.
249. *On the Color of Incidental and Re-
    flected Lights.*
        74v–75 (159); *Libro A* 19   1508–10
250. *On the Color of Shadows.*
            75 (203); *Libro A* 20   1508–10
251. *On Objects Placed against a Light
    Background and Why This Practice Is
    Useful in Painting.*
        75–75v (147); *Libro A* 25   1508–10
252. *Backgrounds.*
        75v (153); *Libro A* 27   1508–10
253. *On Colors.*
        75v (182); *Libro A* 27   1508–10
254. *On Colors That Result from the
    Mixture of Other Colors, Which Are
    Called Secondary.*
    75v–76 (176);
        Libro A 29, 29–30, 30   1508–10
255. *On Colors.*
        76–76v (177); *Libro A* 30   1508–10
256. *On Colors Reflected on Lustrous
    Objects of Varied Colors.*
        76v (211); *Libro A* 38   1508–10
257. *On the Color of Bodies.*
            76v (243)   *ca.* 1492

See the following chapter. Cf., however,
C.A. 249 r–c (MacCurdy:II.368), *ca.*
1513.
258. *On Color.*
        76v–77 (180, 186, 221,
                181)   *ca.* 1492
The transcriber states that chapters 258
and 258c (McM 180, 181) are taken
from the same manuscript.
Chapter 258a (McM 186) comes from
the lost folio 79 of MS A (transcribed
by G. B. Venturi). The reference to a
preceding text ("as I say above") could
be applied to chapter 257, which is
actually of similar subject. Cf. Lu 457.
See also MS I 17v–18, C.A. 126 v-b,
and MS F 22; Brizio (1952), pp. 241,
408, and 417. Particularly fitting is a
comparison with C.A. 126 r-b, which
Brizio (1952), p. 408, dates after 1500,
but which is certainly of the Sforza period. Cf. Pedretti (1957b), p. 271.
Chapter 258b (McM 221) comes from
MS Tr. 39.   1487–90
259. *On True Color.*
            77 (208)   *ca.* 1492
260. *On the Color of Mountains.*
        77–77v (244, 246)   *ca.* 1492
Cf. Lu 262. See also MS Ash. 4 (a note
not transcribed by Melzi).
Lu 260a corresponds to McM 246.
261. *How the Painter Ought to Put the
    Color Perspective into Practice.*
    77v–78 (236); MS Ash. 22v   *ca.* 1492
262. *On Aerial Perspective.*
    78–78v (238); MS Ash. 25v   *ca.* 1492

Addition to 148. *And put opposite parts
of the body forward . . . footprints
full of blood.*
            85–85v (283);
        MS Ash. 31–30v   *ca.* 1492
Continuation of chapter 148.
Folios 79–85 and 86–102 are blank.

PART THREE

263. *On the Changes in the Measure-
    ments of Man through Movement of
    His Limbs in Different Directions.*
            103 (292)   1490–95

The title of this chapter must have been
Leonardo's own, since Melzi incorpo-
rates it in the title of the third part of
the "Treatise on Painting": "Here be-

gins the part on the various conditions and movements of man, and proportions of limbs, and first. . . ."

264. *On Changes in the Measurements of Man from His Birth to the End of His Growth.*

103 (285)   1490–95

265. *How Children's Joints Differ in Size from Those of Men.*

103–103v (290);
MS Ash. 28   *ca.* 1492

266. *On the Difference in Measurements of Children and Men.*

103v (289); MS Ash. 28v   *ca.* 1492

267. *On the Joints of the Fingers.*

103v–104 (299)   1490–95

A date after 1500 can be suggested by a comparison with C.A. 99 v-a; Richter (1883), I, 354.

268. *On the Joints of the Shoulders and Their Increase and Decrease.*

104 (298)   1490–95

Connected with the preceding chapter. Reference to the "Treatise on Anatomy."

269. *On Shoulders.*

104 (359); *Libro A* 26   1508–10

Continuous quantity; cf. Lu 300 and 402 (*Libro A* 40). Ludwig's text is altered by a lapsus of transcription.

270. *On General Measurements of Bodies.*

104–104v (291); *Libro A* 36   1508–10

271. *On Measurements of the Human Body and Flexing of the Limbs.*

104v–105 (296); *Libro A* 64   1508–10

Cf. W. 19,141; Richter (1883), I, 365.

272. *On Proportions of the Parts of the Body.*

105 (286)   1510–15

Cf. Lu 375 (MS E 6v).

273. *On the Joint of the Hand with the Arm.*

105 (300)   1508–10

Cf. Lu 271.

274. *On the Joints of the Feet and Their Increase and Decrease.*

105–105v (301)   1508–10

Cf. W. 19,001; *Fogli A dell'Anatomia* 2.

275. *On Limbs That Diminish when They Are Bent, and Increase when They Are Extended.*

105v (302)   1508–10

Cf. Lu 271 and 273.

276. *On Limbs That Become Thicker in Their Joints when They Are Bent.*

105v (303)   1508–10

Related to the preceding one, to which it was perhaps an introduction.

277. *On the Limbs of Nude Men.*

105v (310)   1508–10

Cf. Lu 333, 334, 363.

278. *On Powerful Motions of Man's Limbs.*

105v (369)   1505–10

Cf. Lu 348, 392, 393.

The drawing reflects the style of the sketches in W. 19,038 and 19,149. A comparison with the sketch in C.A. 352 v-c can also suggest a date 1500–1505. Cf. Pedretti (1957*b*), pp. 168–169.

279. *On the Movements of Man.*

105v–106–106v (373)   1500–05

Probably related to the preceding one.

280. *On the Attitudes and Movements of Limbs.*

106v–107 (384)   *ca.* 1505

Probable reference to the studies for the "Battle of Anghiari."

281. *On the Joints of Parts of the Body.*

107 (358); *Libro A* 26–27   1508–10

282. *On the Parts of the Body in Man.*

107 (438); *Libro A* 28   1508–10

283. *On the Parts of the Body.*

107–107v (317); *Libro A* 65   1508–10

Only the second paragraph of the chapter, "On the Foot," is marked as being copied from *Libro A*.

284. *On Composition of Limbs of Creatures.*

107v (288); *Libro A* 50   1508–10

Cf. Lu 375 (MS E 6v).

285. *On the Motions of Features.*

107v–108 (418)   *ca.* 1492

Subject treated also after 1500. The last sentence reveals more clearly the character of notes of the Sforza period. For the reference to perspective cf. Lu 119

(MS Ash. 16); for the comparison of a painting with a "shop with merchandise for sale in rectangular drawers" cf. Lu 23.

286. *On Movements in the Human Face.*
        108 (419)   ca. 1492
Related to the preceding one.

287. *Quality of Expressions of Faces.*
        108 (414); *Libro A* 13   1508–10

288. *On Features and Description of the Face.*
        108–108v (417); *Libro A* 22   1508–10

289. *On Making a Man's Portrait in Profile after Having Seen Him Only Once.*
        108v (416); *Libro A* 23   1508–10

290. *Method of Remembering the Shape of a Face.*
        109 (415); MS Ash. 26v   ca. 1492

291. *On the Beauty of Faces.*
        109 (413)   1500–05
Cf. Lu 669.

292. *On Physiognomy and Chiromancy.*
        109–109v (425)   1500–05
Perhaps earlier. See, however, W. 19,-045, 19,048, 19,047; Brizio (1952), pp. 494–501.

293. *On Locating the Parts of the Body.*
        109v (307); MS Ash. 20   ca. 1492

294. *On the Gestures of Figures.*
        109 (398); MS Ash. 20   ca. 1492

295. *On Attitudes.*
        109v (335); MS Ash. 20v   ca. 1492

296. *On the Movements of the Parts of the Body when Man Is Represented, and that These Should Be Appropriate.*
        110 (402)   ca. 1492
It seems to be related to the subject of "accidenti mentali" treated in Lu 285 and 286. However, it would be later. See the following chapters.

297. *Each Motion of the Figure Should Be Painted in such a Way that It Gives a Lifelike Effect.*
        110 (395)   1505–10
Cf. Lu 367 and 376 (*Libro A* 24), and also Lu 368. A date 1500–1505 is also possible.

298. *On Motions Appropriate to the Emotion of Him Who Moves.*
        110 (401)   1505–10

299. *On Motions Appropriate to Men of Varying Ages.*
        110–110v (388)   1505–10
Cf. Lu 376 (*Libro A* 24).

300. *On the Movements of Man and Other Animals.*
        110v (362)   1505–10
Continuous quantity. Cf. Lu 269 and 402 (*Libro A* 26, 40).

301. *On the Same Action Seen from Varied Points.*
        110v (361)   1505–10
Continuous quantity. Related to the preceding chapter.

302. *On Composition of the Parts of the Bodies of Nudes and Their Function.*
        110v (308)   1505–10
Cf. Lu 333a (*Libro A* 14).

303. *On the Display or Concealment of the Muscles of Each Part in the Attitudes of Living Creatures.*
        110v–111 (313)   1505–10
Related to the preceding chapter. A date 1500–1505 is also possible; cf. Lu 340 (MS L 79).

304. *On the Movements of Man and Other Animals.*
        111–111v (355)   1505–10
A date in the Sforza period is also possible, in reference to Pacioli's report (1498).

305. *On Motion in Man and Other Animals when Running.*
        111v (347)   1505–10
See the following chapter and Lu 374.

306. *When, During a Man's Actions, the Difference in the Height of His Shoulders Is Greatest.*
        111v–112 (351)   1505–10
Quotation of the ninth proposition of the "Book on Local Motion." Figures to be compared to the sketches in W. 12,707 and *Libro A*. Cf. Pedretti (1957b), pp. 185–186.

307. *How the Whole Distribution of a Man's Weight Changes when an Arm Held Against the Side Is Extended.*
        112 (343)   1505–10
A date in the Sforza period is also possible.

308. *On Man and Other Animals Whose Center of Gravity Is Not Too Remote from Their Supports When They Move Slowly.*

112 (349)   1505–10

Cf. Pedretti (1957*b*), p. 183.

309. *On the Man Who Carries a Weight on His Shoulders.*

112–112v (342)   1505–10

Cf. Lu 315 and 324 (*Libro A* 13, 51). Figures similar in style to the sketch W. 12,707. A date in the Sforza period is also possible: cf. C.A. 349 r-b, Richter (1883), I, 382; and the first note in W. 12,555.

310. *On the Distribution of Man's Weight upon His Feet.*

112v (339)   1505–10

Cf. Lu 397.

311. *On Man in Motion.*

112v (348)   1505–10

312. *On the Balance of Weight on Its Legs of Any Motionless Animal.*

112v–113 (345)   1505–10

Cf. Lu 317.

313. *On Man's Bending and Stretching.*

113 (293)   1505–10

"A special treatise will be written on this." Cf. *Fogli A dell'Anatomia* and the following text from *Libro A.* See also Lu 271 (*Libro A* 64).

314. *On Bending.*

113 (304); *Libro A* 14   1508–10

315. *On Equilibrium.*

113–113v (340); *Libro A* 14   1508–10

316. *On Human Motion.*

113v (360);

Libro B 15 (MS E 15)   1513–14

The last two lines are not in MS E.

317. *On Motion Created by the Destruction of Balance.*

113v (346)   1505–10

Cf. Lu 312.

318. *On Balance of Figures.*

113v–114 (336); *Libro A* 39   1508–10

Figure comparable to W. 12,707.

319. *On Grace of Limbs.*

114 (382), MS Ash. 29v   *ca.* 1492

320. *On Freedom of Limbs.*

114–114v (383);

MS Ash. 30   *ca.* 1492

321. *On a Single Figure Not in Narrative Painting.*

114v–115 (386)   1505–10

"Scambiar del moto" (human movement equivalent to ambling). Cf. Lu 388 and 389 (*Libro A* 25, 26). Pedretti (1957*b*), pp. 152 ff.

322. *What Are the Principal Requirements with Regard to the Figures?*

115 (388)   1505–10

323. *On Balancing the Weight about the Center of Gravity in Bodies.*

115 (330); *Libro A* 51   1508–10

324. *On Figures That Have to Handle or Carry Weights.*

115 (341); *Libro A* 51   1508–10

325. *On Postures of Men.*

115–115v (399);

Libro A 32   1508–10

326. *Variety in Attitudes.*

115v (389); *Libro A* 33   1508–10

327. *On the Attitudes of Figures.*

115v (404); *Libro A* 48   1508–10

328. *On the Attention of Bystanders at an Unusual Event.*

115v–116 (391)   1500–05

". . . as will be said in the fourth book on movement." A date in the Sforza period is also possible.

329. *Quality of Nudes.*

116 (318)   1500–05

Cf. Lu 340.

330. *How Muscular Men are Short and Thick.*

116 (325)   1500–05

331. *How Fat Men Do Not Have Thick Muscles.*

116v–117 (326)   1500–05

Cf. Lu 335 for the possibility of a later date.

332. *On the Display or Concealment of the Muscles of Each Part in the Attitudes of Living Creatures.*

116v (312)   1500–05

". . . and on this a special book will be written." Chapters 329–332 are re-

lated to one another and could have been copied from the same manuscript.
333. On Muscles.

116v (321);
Libro A 14 and 20   1508–10

The notes from the second paragraph onward are gathered by Ludwig under chapter 333a.

334. On Not Including All the Muscles of Figures Unless They Are Exerting Great Force.

116v–117 (309)   1500–05

Cf. Lu 340.

335. On the Muscles of Animals.

117 (327); MS G 26   ca. 1510

"Spongy fat." Cf. Lu 331. The transcriber notes: "The end is lacking."

336. That the Nude Represented with Muscles in Full Evidence Is without Motion.

117–117v (328)   1500–05

337. That the Muscles of Nude Figures Should Not Be Exaggerated Too Much.

117v (319)   1505–10

Cf. Lu 333 (Libro A 14).

338. That Those Who Are Inclined to Be Fat, Increase a Good Deal in Strength after Their Early Youth.

117v–118 (372)   1500–05

339. How Nature Tries to Conceal the Bones of Animals, insofar as the Arrangement of Their Parts Permits.

118–118v (324)   1500–05

Related to the preceding chapter.

340. How It is Necessary for the Painter to Know Anatomy.

118v (329), MS L 79   ca. 1502

Brizio (1952), p. 409. Cf. Lu 334.

341. On the Lengthening and Shortening of Muscles.

118v–119 (305)   1500–05

342. Where Tendons without Muscles Are Found in Man.

119 (314)   1500–05

343. On the Eight Bones Which Exist in the Middle of the Tendons in Various Joints of Man.

119 (315)   1500–05

Anatomical considerations on the in-

creasing of age. Cf. W. 19,027 (An. B 10r-v); Brizio (1952), pp. 492–494.

344. On the Muscles between the Chest and Pubis.

119–119v (306)   1500–05

345. On the Farthest Twist That a Man Can Make in Looking Backward.

119v (379)   1505–10

Reference to the "Book on Anatomy."

346. How Near One Arm Can Be Brought to the Other, in Back.

119v–120 (380)   1505–10

347. How Far the Arms Can Be Brought over the Chest with the Elbows over the Center of the Chest.

120 (381)   1505–10

348. On the Use of Force by a Man Who Would Strike a Great Blow.

120 (368)   1505–10

Chapters 345–348 seem to come from the same manuscript, preserving the sequence they must have had in the original. The tiny figures reflect the style of those in W. 19,038v and 19,-149. A date 1500–1505 is also possible; see C.A. 352 v-c, and Lu 278, 279, 392, 393. Cf. Pedretti (1957b), pp. 168–169.

349. On the Compound Force of a Man, and First That of His Arms Will Be Discussed.

120–120v (365)   1500–05

For the figure of the bones of the arm cf. W. 19,026 (An. B 9v). This chapter continues in the following one.

350. Which Is the Greater Power in a Man, That of Pulling or Pushing?

120v–121 (366)   1500–05

Related to the preceding one. Cf. MS E 15; Brizio (1952), p. 452. See also the earlier Lu 391.

351. On Limbs of the Body That Bend and the Flesh That Covers Them where They Bend.

121 (297)   1500–05

Cf. Lu 271.

352. On Turning the Calf without Turning the Thigh.

121–121v (375)   1500–05

Cf. W. 19,035v and 19,037 (An. B 18 and 20).

353. *On Creases in the Flesh.*
121v–122 (316); *Libro A* 14   1508–10

354. *On Man's Simple Movement.*
122 (356)   1500–05

355. *On Man's Compound Movement.*
122 (357)   1500–05
Related to the preceding one.

356. *On Motions Appropriate to Man's Actions.*
122 (367)   1500–05

357. *On the Motions of Figures.*
122–122v (385)   1500–05
A date in the Sforza period is also possible. Cf. Lu 189. See also MS K₃ 110 (30)v; Brizio (1952), p. 420. For the reference to orators see Lu 368. For the advice not to repeat the movements of limbs see W. 19,149v.

358. *On Movements.*
122v (405)   1500–05

359. *On Great and Small Degrees of Emotions.*
122v (411)   1500–05
Continuation of the preceding chapter.

360. *On the Same Emotions in Men of Diverse Ages.*
122v–123 (407)   1500–05
Chapters 354–360 seem to come from the same manuscript, preserving the sequence they must have had in the original.

361. *On Gestures.*
123 (412); *Libro A* 20   1508–10

362. *On the Eighteen Positions of Man.*
123 (374); MS Ash. 29   ca. 1492
The word "otto" in the heading is an obvious error for "diciotto," as shown by the heading in the original.

363. *On the Disposition of Limbs in Relation to Forms.*
123 (311)   ca. 1500

364. *On Parts of the Body according to Age.*
123 (320)   ca. 1500

365. *On the Variety of Faces.*
123–123v (397)   ca. 1500

366. *On the Composition of the Parts of Animals.*
123v (322)   ca. 1500
Chapters 363–366 seem to be related. A date in the Sforza period is also possible. However, cf. Lu 366 and 340. See also C.A. 345 v-b, *ca.* 1508.

367. *How the Figure Is Not Praiseworthy if It Does Not Display the Passion of the Spirit.*
123v (400); MS Ash. 29v   ca. 1492
Cf. Lu 297 and 376.

368. *How the Hands and Arms Must, in All Their Actions, Display the Intention of the Mind That Moves Them.*
123v–124 (396)   1505–08
"Moti mentali" (Emotions). Program of discussion partly developed in *Libro A.* A transcriber's note states that the following chapter, "On Representing an Angry Man," which represents the beginning of the planned discussion, has only the heading. See above, pp. 132–133.

369. *On Representing an Angry Man and into How Many Parts that Emotion Is Divided.*
124 (396, n. 8)   1505–08
Title without text, related to the preceding chapter. A previous discussion on this subject is to be found in Lu 381 (MS Ash. 29v).

370. *On Motions Appropriate to the Mind of One Who Moves.*
124–124v (408)   ca. 1500
A date in the Sforza period is also possible. Cf. Lu 363–366. See also Lu 285 for the sentence "This is to be put in the chapter on madness and on buffoons and their morris-dances." However, see Lu 177 for the reference to the "pazzia bestialissima" (most brutal madness). The following chapters up to Lu 374 seem to be taken from the same manuscript.

371. *How Mental Stimuli Move a Person with the Greatest Facility and Ease.*
124v (409)   1500–05

372. *On the Motions Occasioned in the Mind by Some Object.*
> 124v (410)   1500–05

The sentence "There will be a long discussion concerning such problems" seems to indicate the priority of this chapter to others of similar subject.

373. *On Common Motions.*
> 124v (406)   1500–05

374. *On the Motion of Animals.*
> 124v–125 (294)   1500–05

Bearing of shoulders when walking. Cf. Lu 305; Pedretti (1957b), p. 185. Reference to the walk of birds. Cf. Lu 435 (*Libro A* 51) for another subject related to birds.

375. *That Every Part of the Body Should in Itself Be in Proportion to the Whole Body.*
> 125 (287);
> *Libro B* (MS E 6v)   1513–14

Cf. Lu 284 (*Libro A* 50). See also C.A. 345 v-b, *ca.* 1508.

376. *How Figures Not Expressive of the Mind Are Twice Dead.*
> 125–125v (403); *Libro A* 24   1508–10

Cf. Lu 297 and 367. See also a text of the Sforza period in C.A. 139 r-d; Richter (1883), I, 593.

377. *On the Observation of Decorum.*
> 125v (387)   1505–10

Cf. Lu 184 and 376 (*Libro A* 32, 24).

378. *On the Age of Figures.*
> 125v (393); *Libro A* 40   1508–10

379. *Kinds of Men in Narrative Composition.*
> 125v–126 (391)   1505–10

It seems to contradict Lu 183 and 187 (*Libro A* 32, 50). See, however, Lu 378 (*Libro A* 40).

380. *On Representing the One Who Speaks among a Number of Persons.*
> 126–126v (424);
> MS Ash. 21   *ca.* 1492

381. *How the Figure of an Angry Man Is Depicted.*
> 126v (422); MS Ash. 29v   *ca.* 1492

Cf. Lu 369.

382. *How a Man in Despair Is Depicted.*
> 126v (423); MS Ash. 29v   *ca.* 1492

Concept taken up again in later texts. Cf. Lu 384 (*Libro A* 33).

383. *On Harmony of Limbs.*
> 126v–127 (323);
> MS Ash. 28v   *ca.* 1492

384. *Of Laughing and Weeping and the Difference between Them.*
> 127 (420); *Libro A* 33   1508–10

385. *On the Same.*
> 127 (421); *Libro A* 28   1508–10

386. *On Poses of Infants.*
> 127–127v (390); *Libro A* 13   1508–10

387. *On Poses of Women and Girls.*
> 127v (392); *Libro A* 13   1508–10

388. *On a Man's Rising-Up from Sitting on Level Ground.*
> 127v (378); *Libro A* 25, 26   1508–10

Cf. W. 19,070; Pedretti (1957b), fig. 57. According to a transcriber's note the original text was followed by the title of a chapter on the contrary movement. See Lu 389.

389. *On a Man's Falling into a Seated Position on the Flat Ground.*
> 127v (378); *Libro A* 26   1508–10

Subject of the "scambiar del moto" treated in Lu 321. Cf. Pedretti (1957b), pp. 152 ff.

390. *On Jumping and What Helps the Jump.*
> 127v–128 (377)   1500–02

Cf. MS L 28v and C.A. 164 r-a. Pedretti (1957b), pp. 162–166. See also Lu 401.

391. *On the Motion of Figures in Pushing or Pulling.*
> 128 (364)   1500–05

Cf. Lu 349–350, which are later because they contain the final version of a discussion on this subject.

392. *On the Man Who Would Throw an Object Away from Himself with Great Energy.*
> 128 (371)   1500–05

Cf. Lu 278 and 279. Cf. Pedretti (1957b), pp. 168–169.

393. *Why He Who Drives an Iron into the Ground Raises the Opposite Leg in a Curve.*
> 128v (370)   1500–05

In the Codex Urbinas this chapter does not have a figure. Ludwig uses the one from chapter 348 on folio 120. "Ferro" (Iron) in the title has the meaning of a child's whip-top. On the subject of the "calmone" or whip-top cf. MS E 50v. Pedretti (1957b), pp. 166–170.

394. *Balance of Bodies Not in Motion.*

128v (332)   1500–05

Sketch of Hercules and Anteus reflecting the style of Leonardo's sketches after 1500.

395. *On the Man Who Stands on Two Feet, Resting More Weight on One Foot.*

129 (337)   1500–05

396. *On Poses of Figures.*

129 (334)   1500–05

397. *On the Balance of a Man Standing on His Feet.*

129–129v (331)   1500–05

Chapters 395–397 are related to one another. Lu 397 ends: "A special book will be written about this balance." Cf. Lu 310

398. *On More or Less Rapid Motion from One Place to Another.*

129v (350)   1500–05

"Moto Locale." A date in the Sforza period is also possible, in agreement with Pacioli's record (1498).

399. *On Four-Footed Animals and How They Move.*

129v (344)   1500–05

Sketch of a horse reflecting the style of the first studies for the Trivulzio monument. Cf. Turin drawing no. 15,-577. For the subject of the chapter see Pedretti (1957b), pp. 182–183.

400. *On the Relation in Size of Each Half of a Man to the Other Half.*

129v–130 (295)   1500–05

401. *How There Are Three Movements When a Man Jumps Upward.*

130 (376)   1500–02

Cf. MS L 28v and Lu 390. Pedretti (1957b), pp. 162–166.

402. *That It Is Impossible to Memorize All the Aspects and Changes of the Parts of the Body.*

130–130v (363);

Libro A 40   1508–10

Continuous quantity. Cf. Lu 269 (*Libro A 26*) and Lu 300.

403. *On the First Four Parts That Are Required of the Figure.*

130v (430)   1508–10

It seems to evoke the subject of the "Leda" (Möller's suggestion).

404. *Discourse on Practice.*

130v–131 (442)   *ca.* 1492

Note on costume. Cf. Lu 541, which is close to it also stylistically.

405. *On the Practice Sought with Great Anxiety by the Painter.*

131–131v (441)   *ca.* 1510

Final version of the text drafted in W. 19,121. See above, p. 145. The notes on painting on that folio are all crossed out, indicating the they were subsequently developed or transcribed elsewhere.

406. *On the Painter's Judgment of His Own Work and That of Others.*

131v (439); *Libro A 41*   1508–10

407. *On the Painter's Judgment of His Own Work.*

131v–132 (440);

MS Ash. 28   *ca.* 1492

408. *How the Mirror Is the Master of Painters.*

132–132v (432);

MS Ash. 24v   *ca.* 1492

409. *How a Good Painting Is to Be Recognized and What Qualities It Must Have to Be Good.*

132v (429)   1508–10

Cf. Lu 284 (*Libro A 50*), and 483 (MS G 19).

410. *How the True Picture Exists on the Surface of the Flat Mirror.*

132v–133 (431)   1508–10

Transcriber's note: "This chapter had better come before that above."

411. *Which Painting Is the More Laudable.*

133 (433)   1508–10

Note on proportions. Possibly 1490–1495. Error of the painter who presumes to correct nature. Cf. Lu 706. See also Lu 270 (*Libro A* 36).

412. *What Is the Primary Objective of the Painter.*

133–133v (434)   1508–10
Cf. Lu 45 (*Libro A* 17).

413. *Which Is of More Importance: Shadows or Outlines.*

133v (435)   1508–10
Chapters 409–413 were probably copied from the same manuscript, preserving the sequence they had in the original, as the transcriber's note to Lu 410 seems to suggest. Chapter 413 alludes to the device of the "prospettografo." Cf. Lu 90 (MS Ash. 24). The reference to the Book on Light and Shade could be applied to the lost *Libro W.*

414. *How Figures Should Be Illuminated.*

133v–134 (443);
MS Ash. 33   *ca.* 1492

415. *Where the Spectator Should Stand to Look at a Painting.*

134 (555); MS Ash. 32v   *ca.* 1492

416. *How High the Point of Sight Ought to Be Placed.*

134–134v (500);
MS Ash. 31   *ca.* 1492

417. *How, According to Reason, Small Figures Should Not Be Finished.*

134v (510); MS Ash. 31v   *ca.* 1492
Leonardo treated aerial perspective as early as the Sforza period, developing Alberti's theory.

418. *What Background a Painter Should Use for His Works.*

134v (454); MS Ash. 31v   *ca.* 1492
"Campi" (Background). Subject developed at a later period.

419. *Precept for Painting.*

134–135 (446);
MS Ash. 31v   *ca.* 1492
Light and Shade. Subject developed at a later period.

420. *On Representing a Wooded Place.*

135 (550); MS Ash. 31v   *ca.* 1492
Plants. Subject developed at a later period.

421. *How One Should Make an Imaginary Animal Seem Natural.*

135 (554); MS Ash. 29   *ca.* 1492

422. *On Places Which Should Be Selected in Order to Give Objects Relief and Grace.*

135–135v–136 (452)   1505–10
Cf. Lu 466.

423. *On Separating and Detaching Figures from Their Backgrounds.*

136 (456); *Libro A* 30   1508–10
Cf. Lu 246 (MS E 4).

424. *On the Difference between Forms in Shadow and in Light, in Diverse Situations.*

136 (450)   1505–10

425. *On Avoiding Lacks of Proportion in Settings.*

136–136v (499); *Libro A* 31   1508–10
Lu 425a is actually the title of the preceding chapter: "Bodies Should Correspond in Size as Well as in Function to the Matter Concerned." A transcriber's note informs: "This proposition is set forth rather than explained; therefore, read what precedes it."

426. *On the Boundaries of Bodies Called Outlines or Contours.*

136v (511); *Libro A* 32   1508–10

427. *On the Parts of Surfaces Which First Are Lost through Distance.*

136v (505); *Libro A* 37   1508–10

428. *On Surface Conditions That Are Lost First in Receding from ⟨Opaque⟩ Bodies.*

136v–137 (522); *Libro A* 38   1508–10

429. *On the Nature of Contours of Bodies upon Other Bodies.*

137 (463); *Libro A* 30   1508–10

430. *On the Figure Which Moves against the Wind.*

137 (354); *Libro A* 34   1508–10

431. *On the Windows of Rooms in Which Figures Are Drawn.*

137–137v (451);
Libro A 38   1508–10
Cf. Lu 816.

432. *Why, when Measuring a Face and then Painting It Life Size, It Will Appear Larger than Nature.*

137v (496); *Libro A* 39   1508–10
Cf. MS Arundel 220, *ca.* 1508; Richter (1883), I, 84.

433. *Whether the Surface of Every*

Opaque Body Takes on the Color of the Opposite Object.

    137v–138–138v (469);
           Libro A 40   1508–10

434. *On the Movement and Running of Animals.*

    138v (352); *Libro A* 50   1508–10

435. *On Bodies Which Move by Themselves, Either Quickly or Slowly.*

    138v–139 (353); *Libro A* 51   1508–10

436. *To Make a Figure Which Appears to Be Forty Braccia High in a Space of Twenty Braccia, with Corresponding Members, the Figure to Stand Erect on Its Feet.*

    139–139v (498); *Libro A* 42   1508–10

437. *To Make a Figure on a Wall of Twelve Braccia Appear to Be Twenty-Four Braccia in Height.*

    139v–140 (497); *MS A* 38v   *ca.* 1492

438. *Painting, Its Divisions and Components.*

    140–140v (426, 636, 741)   1505–10
Lu 438a (McM 636) and 438b (McM 741) do not appear in the codex as separate sections. Lu 438b contains elements of Leonardo's late period, e.g., the quotation of the ninth proposition of the Book on Light and Shade. The first section, which is a subject similar to Lu 511 (MS Ash. 22v), could be of the same late period.

439. *Painting and Its Definition.*

    140v (436); *Libro A* 39   1508–10

440. *Painting in a Universal Light.*

    140v–141 (453)   1505–10

441. *On Backgrounds Proportioned to the Bodies Placed against Them, and First of Plane Surfaces of a Uniform Color.*

    141 (455)   1505–10

442. *Painting. On Form and Body.*

    141–141v (461)   1505–10
The transcriber started to copy this chapter before the preceding one. Near its title he put the mark ".F."; if this is a reference to the original manuscript, the chapter would have been copied from a lost folio of the Codex Trivulzianus and thus its date would be 1487–1490. The subject, however, is thor-

oughly treated in manuscripts of a later period. Chapters 442–445 seem to have been taken from one single manuscript.

443. *Painting. That Part of the Body Loses Its Distinctness First Which Is of Least Extension.*

    141v–142 (501)   1505–10
Quotation of the sixth rule of the Book on Perspective. Observation on point and line; cf. Lu 1.

444. *Why the Same Countryside Sometimes Looks Larger or Smaller than It Is.*

    142–142v (529)   1505–10
Cf. Lu 791 ff. For a possible anticipation of date see C.A. 126 r-b, a text that Brizio (1952), p. 408, judges to date after 1500, but which is certainly of 1492–1495 because of the type of handwriting.

445. *Painting.*

    142v (457)   1510–15
Cf. Lu 446, 448, 449, 457, and *passim* in the following texts. See also Lu 218 and 708. For the subject of towers seen in the mist cf. C.A. 130 r-b, *ca.* 1513; Brizio (1952), p. 419.

446. *On Cities and Other Things Seen through Thick Air.*

    143–143v (533)   1510–15
Cf. Lu 465 and 910. See also the Folio Resta in the Ambrosian Library; Pedretti (1957b), pp. 249–253.

447. *On the Sun's Rays Penetrating Openings in the Clouds.*

    143v–144 (476)   1510–15
Sketch of a cloud occupying the sun. It reflects Leonardo's late style. Cf. W. 12,388. A draft of this chapter is in C.A. 279 v–a. See above, p. 156.

448. *On Objects That the Eye Sees below It, Combined with Mist or Thick Air.*

    144 (539)   1510–15
Quotation of the "19th proposition of the 2d." The same subject is already treated in the Sforza period. Cf. MS Ash. 18.

449. *On Buildings Seen in Thick Air.*

    144 (536)   1510–15

450. *Which Object Is Apparent from Afar.*

       144 (539)   1510–15

451. *On the View of a City in Thick Air.*

       144v (535)   1510–15
Related to the preceding one. Cf. Folio Resta; Pedretti (1957*b*), pp. 249–253. There is also a discussion of the Sforza period on this subject. Cf. C.A. 160 r-a, 1490–1492.

452. *On the Lower Contours of Distant Objects.*

       144v–145 (537)   1510–15
Cf. Lu 457.

453. *On Objects Seen from Afar.*

       145 (508)   1505–10

454. *On Blue, Which Distant Landscapes Appear to Be.*

       145 (518)   1505–10

455. *Which Are Those Parts of Bodies Which Lose Distinctness because of Distance.*

       145 (502)   1508–10
Cf. Lu 473.

456. *Why Objects, the More They Are Removed from the Eye, Are the Less Perceived.*

       145v (504)   1508–10
Cf. Lu 427 (*Libro A* 37).

457. *Why Parallel Towers Appear in the Mist to Be Narrower at the Foot than at the Top.*

       145v–146 (540)   1510–15

458. *Why Faces Seem Obscure from a Distance.*

       146 (514); MS Ash. 20v   *ca.* 1492

459. *Why a Man Seen at a Certain Distance Is Not Recognized.*

       146–146v (503);
       MS Ash. 20v   *ca.* 1492

460. *Which Are the Parts Which First Are Lost to Notice in Bodies Which Are Remote from the Eye, and Which Are Preserved the Longest.*

       146v (509)   1508–10
Cf. Lu 456. See also MS E 80v; Brizio (1952), p. 459.

461. *On Linear Perspective.*

    146v–147 (491); MS Ash. 23   *ca.* 1492

462. *On Bodies Seen in the Mist.*

       147 (534)   1508–10

463. *On Heights of Buildings Seen in the Mist.*

       147–147v (541)   1510–15
Cf. Lu 452, 457.

464. *On Cities or Buildings Seen in the Mist in the Morning or Evening.*

       147v (470);
       Libro B 3 (MS E 3v)   1513–14

465. *Why Objects Placed Higher in the Distance Are More Obscure than Those That Are Lower, Even When the Mist Is Uniform in Thickness.*

       147v–148 (538);
       Libro B 3 (MS E 3v)   1513–14
Concordance not given by Carusi and McMahon. Cf. Lu 446 and 910.

466. *On Spots of Shadow That Appear on Distant Bodies.*

       148–148v (523)   1505–10
Cf. Lu 422.

467. *Why the Shadows of Bodies on White Walls Are Blue at Sunset.*

       148v–149 (478)   1508–10
Quotation of the eighth and eleventh propositions of the Book on Light and Shade. A later date, 1510–1515, is also possible.

468. *Where Smoke Is Brighter.*

       149 (472)   1508–10
Cf. Lu 515 and 516 (MS G 22v–23). See also Lu 205 and 470, and MS F 18; Brizio (1952), p. 417. A later date, 1510–1515, is also possible.

469. *On Dust.*

       149 (479)   1508–10
Possibly later, 1510–1515.

470. *On Smoke.*

       149–149v (471)   1508–10
Chapters 468–470 seem connected. At the end of chapter 470 the transcriber writes: "Below this chapter there was a cleft in the mountain, an opening within which played a flaming fire, drawn by pen and shaded with watercolor, an admirable and vital thing to see." This description evokes a drawing like W. 12,404 (Melzi's copy) of 1510–1515.

471. *Painting.*

       149v (465)   1508–10

Propositions of the Book on Light and
Shade. Perhaps later. Cf. Lu 472.

472. *On the Side of the Opaque Body.*
                    149v (448);
     Libro B 17 (MS E 17)   1513–14
Cf. Lu 819.

473. *Precept for Painting.*
                    150 (507)   1508–10
Cf. Lu 455. See also Lu 797.

474. *Precept for Painting.*
                    150–150v (480)   1510–15
Objects in the mist. Redness of the
clouds on the horizon.

475. *On the Outlines of a White Object.*
                    150v–151 (462, 520)   1510–15
Chapter 475a is actually a text sepa-
rated from Lu 475. Its title, in the original manuscript, must have been the
last section of chapter 475, i.e., the
paragraph marked by an asterisk: "That
Object Will Appear Most Detached
and Farthest from Another Which Is
Seen against a Background Most Different from Itself." The subject could
indicate an earlier date, 1508–1510. Cf.
Lu 456 and 460.

476. *Precept.*
                    151 (493, 526, 512)   1510–15
Lu 476 and 476b correspond to McM
526 and 512. They are related to the
preceding ones.

477. *Precept.*
                    151–151v (547, 528, 483)   1510–15
Lu 477a and 477b correspond to McM
528 and 483. Notes on atmosphere related to the preceding and following
chapters. For the reference to the pupil
of eye and to the observation of a star
through a hole in a paper, see Lu 628.
See also MS D 5 (*ca.* 1508).

478. *Precept.*
                    151v (481, 475, 477)   1510–15
Lu 478a and 478b correspond to McM
475 and 477.

479. *Precept.*
                    152 (482, 495)   1510–15
Lu 479a corresponds to McM 495. Related to the preceding one. City illuminated by the sun at sunset. Clouds.

480. *Precept.*
                    152–152v (494)   1510–15

Clouds. Related to the preceding one.

481. *Precept.*
                    152v–153 (488)   1510–15
Perspective. Subject similar to the propositions of the Sforza period. This chapter, however, seems to be related to the
preceding ones. The series of "Precetti"
473–481 seems to have been copied
from the same manuscript.

482. *On Painting.*
                    153 (464); MS G 23v   *ca.* 1510

483. *On the Judgment That You Have
to Make about a Painter's Work.*
                    153–153v (428); MS G 19   *ca.* 1510

484. *On the Relief of Forms Distant
from the Eye.*
                    153v (467)   1510–15
An earlier date, 1508–1510, is also possible.

485. *On the Edges of Illuminated Ob-
jects.*
                    153v (460)   1508–10
Note for the Book on Light and Shade.
See also the quotation in Lu 457.

486. *On Outlines.*
                    153v–154 (506); Libro A 16   1508–10

487. *On Flesh Tones and Figures Distant from the Eye.*
                    154 (468); Libro A 27   1508–10
Connected with the preceding. Cf. Lu
128 and 153.

488. *On Painting.*
                    154–154v (445); MS G 32   *ca.* 1510

489. *Discussion on Painting.*
                    154v (484); MS G 53v   *ca.* 1510
Brizio (1952), pp. 447–448. Only the
first section of the original note is here
transcribed: "Perspective, insofar as it
relates to painting . . . at different distances."

490. *On Painting.*
                    154v (519); Libro A 1   1508–10
McMahon's concordance erroneously
gives MS Ash. 26.

491. *Precept.*
                    154v (459)   *ca.* 1492
Backgrounds. It is related to the following chapter. See also Lu 257.

492. *Precept.*
                    154v–155 (466);
                    MS Ash. 26   *ca.* 1492

Relief of painted figures, in relation to their background and the color of cloths. Cf. Lu 238. Concordance omitted by Carusi and McMahon, but given by Pierantoni. Cf. Brizio (1952), p. 221.

493. *Why, of Two Objects of Equal Size, the Painted One Seems Larger than the One in Relief.*

155–155v (489);
MS Ash. 19   ca. 1492

494. *Why the Object Perfectly Drawn from Nature Does Not Seem to Be in the Same Relief as the Natural Object.*

155v–156 (487)   ca. 1492

All the subjects treated in chapters 491–494 are developed in manuscripts of a later date. Cf. Lu 432 (*Libro A* 39). This chapter, therefore, could possibly date from 1505–1510. See also Windsor 19,102r (Richter [1883], I, 29).

495. *Which Seems in Higher Relief, the Relief Near the Eye or That Far from the Eye.*

156 (485)   ca. 1492

See the preceding chapter, which probably comes from the same manuscript. See also the following chapter.

496. *Precept.*

156v (486); MS Tr. 38v   1487–90

497. *On Making Objects Appear Detached from Their Backgrounds, That Is, from the Walls on Which They Are Depicted.*

156v (458); *Libro A* 26   1508–10

498. *Precept.*

156v–157 (444)   1508–10

Universal light. Cf. Lu 94, 110, and 709. See also Brizio (1952), p. 457, n. 1.

499. *How Figures Often Resemble Their Masters.*

157 (437); *Libro A* 15   1508–10

500. *On Portraying the Parts of the World.*

157 (549); *Libro A* 15   1508–10

501. *On Depicting the Four Seasons of the Year or Things Connected with Them.*

157–157v (548); *Libro A* 15   1508–10

502. *On Painted Wind.*

157v (551);
Libro B 6 (MS E 6v)   1513–14

503. *On the Beginning of a Shower.*

157v–158 (552)   1510–15

At the end of the text the transcriber writes: "In the middle of this chapter there was a foreshortened view of a city, on which rain fell, illuminated here and there by the sun; touched with water-color, a very beautiful thing to see, also by the author's own hand." Cf. Lu 470 for a similar description of drawing. The comparison with W. 12,-409 may suggest an earlier date for this chapter, 1500–1505. The following chapter, which was probably copied from the same manuscript, contains the description of a deluge.

504. *On Composing a Storm of Wind and Rain.*

158–158v (553)   1510–15

Description of a deluge. Cf. MS G 6v, and W. 12,665; Brizio (1952), pp. 422–427

505. *On the Shadows Cast by Bridges upon Water.*

158v (545)   1510–15

506. *On the Likenesses, Bright or Dark, That Are Imprinted upon Places in Light or Shade Found between the Surface and the Bottom of Clear Waters.*

158v–159–159v (546)   1510–15

507. *On Water Clear and Transparent Down to the Bottom.*

159v–160 (524)   1510–15

508. *On the Foam of Water.*

160 (525)   1510–15

Chapters 503–508 seem to come from the same manuscript. A date 1508–1510 is also possible because of the subject of hydraulics. In the original manuscript the illustrations for chapters 507 and 508 were in the margin, as are those of the Codex Leicester.

509. *Precept for Painting.*

160 (490); MS Ash. 13   ca. 1492

510. *Precept.*

160v (333)   1490–5

Perhaps it was taken from one of the lost folios of MS A.

511. *On the Ten Functions of the Eye, All Pertaining to Painting.*

    160v (427); MS Ash. 22v   ca. 1492
Cf. Lu 438.

512. *On Sculpture.*

    160v–161 (556); MS A 43   ca. 1492

513. *To Make a Painting with an Everlasting Varnish.*

    161–161v (557)   1490–5
Perhaps it was taken from one of the lost folios of MS A. Cf. Lu 510 and 514.

514. *How to Use Color on Linen.*

    161v (558)   1490–5
Related to the preceding.

515. *On the Smoke from Cities.*

    161v–162 (473); MS G 22v   ca. 1510

516. *On Smoke and Dust.*

    162 (474); MS G 23   ca. 1510
Cf. Lu 468–471.

517. *Precept for Perspective in Painting.*

    162–162v (521)   1508–10
"The eye, without moving, will never know, by means of linear perspective how much distance there is between the object that lies between it and another object. . . ." Cf. MS E 80v; Brizio (1952), p. 459.

518. *The Eye Situated at a High Level Which Sees Objects High and Low.*

    162v (530)   1508–10

519. *The Eye Situated at a Low Level Which Sees Objects Low and High.*

    162v–163 (531)   1508–10
Chapters 517–519 are interrelated and perhaps come from the same manuscript.

520. *Why the Convergence of All the Visual Images That Come to the Eye Occurs at a Single Point.*

    163 (492)   1508–10

A date in the Sforza period or at the beginning of 1500 is also possible. Cf. C.A. 208 v-b (1508–1510) and 214 v-b (1508–1510), and Lu 481 (MS G 13). See also Lu 473.

521. *On Objects Reflected in the Water.*

    163 (542)   1505–10

522. *On Objects Reflected in Muddy Water.*

    163 (543)   1505–10

523. *On Objects Reflected in Running Water.*

    163–163v (544)   1505–10
For a possible earlier date cf. MS H$_2$ 76v; Richter (1883), I, 206.

524. *On the Nature of the Medium Lying between the Eye and the Object.*

    163v (515)   1505–10

525. *Effects of the Medium Which Is Enclosed by a Common Surface.*

    163v (516)   1505–10
Chapters 521–525 are interrelated. The subject, hydraulics, and the style of the texts are similar to the notes in MSS H and I, possibly suggesting an earlier date, ca. 1500.

526. *On Objects.*

    164 (447); Libro A 18   1508–10
Lu 526a corresponds to McM 513.

527. *On Diminution of Colors and Bodies.*

    164 (525); Libro A 16   1508–10

528. *On Interposing Transparent Bodies between the Eye and the Object.*

    164 (517, 449); Libro A 16   1508–10
Lu 528a corresponds to McM 449.
Folios 164v–167 are blank.

PART FOUR

ON DRAPERIES *

529. *On Draperies That Clothe Figures.*
    167 (559)   1500–05

530. *On Draperies That Clothe Figures in Much-Folded or Stiff Manner.*
    167 (561)   1500–05

* In the Codex Urbinas the title of the Fourth Part is "De Panni et Modo di Vestire le Figure con Grazia et degli Abiti, et Nature de Panni. L. P° [Libro Primo?]" (On Draperies and How to Dress Figures with Grace, and on Garments and Nature of Draperies. L. P° [First Book?]).

531. *On Clothing Figures Gracefully.*
        167 (568)   1500–05
532. *On Draperies That Clothe Figures,*
and Their Folds.
        167–167v (564)   1500–05
533. *On the Way to Clothe Figures.*
        167v–168 (573)   1500–05
Chapters 529–533 seem interrelated. A
date in the Sforza period is also possible.
534. *On Draperies.*
        168 (562); MS A 79   ca. 1492
From a lost folio of MS A (Apograph
G. B. Venturi).
535. *On Draperies in Motion or Static.*
        168–168v (567)   1505–10
Cf. Lu 430.
536. *Opinion Regarding Draperies and*
Their Folds, Which Are of Three Sorts.
        168v (566)   ca. 1492
537. *On the Nature of the Folds in*
Draperies.
        168v–169 (563); MS Ash. 4   ca. 1492
538. *How Folds Should Be Made in*
Draperies.

169–169v (572);
        MS Ash. 17v   ca. 1492
539. *On Making Few Folds in Draperies.*
        169v (569); MS Ash. 18   ca. 1492
Cf. Lu 182.
540. *On Folds of Draperies in Foreshort-*
ening.
        169v–170 (560); MS A 79   ca. 1492
From a lost folio of MS A (Apograph
G. B. Venturi).
541. *On Ways of Clothing Figures and*
of Diverse Garments.
        170–170v (574)   ca. 1492
Cf. Lu 404.
542. *On the Eye Which Sees the Folds*
of Drapery That Surround a Man.
        170v (565)   1505–10
543. *On the Folds of Draperies.*
        170v–171 (570)   1505–10
544. *On Folds.*
        171 (571)   1505–10
Chapters with the suggested date 1505–
1510 are to be compared with the notes
in W. 19,121. See above, pp. 144–145.
Folios 171v–175 are blank.

PART FIVE

ON LIGHT AND SHADE

545. *What Is Shadow?*
        175 (575)   1508–10
Cf. Lu 550 and 665. See also W. 19,-
076 (An. C II 6); Brizio (1952), p.
448: ". . . provasi per la prima di
questo che dice: tenebre essere privazione di luce e ombra è allevazione di
tenebre e di luce." For similar definitions in notes of the Sforza period see
Lu 548–549, and C.A. 116 r-b and
250 r-a.
546. *What Difference There Is between*
Shadow and Darkness.
        175 (581)   1508–10
Cf. Lu 550 and the note to the preceding text.
547. *From What Does Shadow Derive?*
        175 (579); MS A fol.?   ca. 1492
Copied in MS H 227 inf. 47v from an
unspecified folio of the missing section

of MS A (fols. 65–80). Cf. Pedretti
(1962a).
548. *On the Essence of Shadow.*
        175–175v (576); MS A 21v   ca. 1492
549. *What Are Light and Shadow?*
        175v (577); MS Ash. 22   ca. 1492
550. *What Are Shadow and Darkness?*
        175v (580); MS E 32v   1513–14
See the following text.
551. *Into How Many Parts Is Shadow*
Divided?
        175v (583); MS E 32v   1513–14
Cf. Lu 545–547. See also Lu 556.
Chapters 550–551 are not marked Lº B.
552. *On Shadow and Its Division.*
        175v (584); *Libro A* 33   1508–10
553. *On Two Kinds of Shadows and into*
How Many Parts They Are Divided.
        175v–176 (590, 591, 592,
613, 705, 744); *Libro A* 34   1508–10

McMahon's numbers are respectively Lu 553–553e. Carusi indicates the concordance of 553c, 553d, and 553e with MS E 32v. These texts of MS E are marked with the little circle not crossed out. Chapter 553 is marked *Lᵒ A*. It is possible that the texts in MS E were variants or repetitions.

554. *Which Shadow Is Darker, the Primary or the Derivative.*
176 (711)   1508–10

555. *On Shadow.*
176–176v (745); MS A 67   *ca.* 1492
From a lost folio of MS A (Apograph G. B. Venturi). McM 657 corresponds to Lu 555a, for which Carusi suggests a concordance with MS E 32. (Pierantoni and McMahon give the correct concordance, MS Ash. 9v.)
555a (657); MS Ash. 9v   *ca.* 1492

556. *What Differentiation Is There from Shadow to Darkness?*
176v (582)   1508–10
Cf. Lu 551.

557. *What Difference Is There between Simple Shadow and Compound Shadow?*
176v (589)   1508–10
McMahon gives the concordance "B.N. 248v." The MS Ashburnham 2038 does not have such a number of folios. Perhaps McMahon intended to suggest a comparison with the text in Codex Arundel 248v; Richter (1883), I, 124.

558. *What Is the Difference between Compound Light and Compound Shadow?*
176v (593)   1508–10

559. *How Compound Light and Compound Shadow always Border on One Another.*
176v–177 (594)   1508–10

560. *That the Outline of a Simple Shadow Will Be Less Clear than the Outline of a Compound Shadow.*
177 (634)   1508–10

561. *On the Compound Derivative Shadow.*
177–177v (707)   1508–10

Quotation of the ninth proposition of the Book on Light and Shade. Cf. C.A. 37 r-a.

562. *How Primary and Derivative Shadows Are Connected.*
177v (697)   1508–10

563. *How the Simple Shadow Is Connected with the Compound Shadow.*
177v–178 (708)   1508–10
The transcriber adds to the title: "And its figure is the second above." Chapters 561–563, as well as the following one, probably come from the same manuscript.

564. *On Simple and Compound Primary Shadows.*
178 (709)   1508–10

565. *On the Outlines of a Compound Shadow.*
178v (633)   1508–10

566. *On the Termination of the Simple Shadow.*
178v (612)   1508–10
Related to the preceding one. Cf. Lu 553c and 596 (*Libro A 34* and *Libro B 31*).

567. *What Shadow Does the Light Make Which Is Equal to the ⟨Opaque⟩ Body in the Form of Its Shadows?*
178v (614)   1508–10
Cf. MS C 7v; Richter (1883), I, 160.

568. *What Shadow Does an ⟨Opaque⟩ Body Cast Which Is Greater than the Luminous Body?*
178v (638)   1508–10

569. *How Many Sorts of Shadow There Are?*
179 (597)   1508–10
McMahon gives the concordance with MSS E 3v and G 3v, but these are variants. Cf. Brizio (1952), pp. 428, 450.

570. *How Many Kinds of Shadow Are There?*
179 (585)   1505–08
Cf. Lu 574.

571. *How Many Are the Sorts of Primary Shadow?*
179 (587)   1505–08

572. *In How Many Ways Does Primary Shadow Vary?*

179 (588)   1505–08

573. *What Variations Does the Derivative Shadow Possess?*

179–179v (759)   1505–08

574. *How Many Shapes Does the Derivative Shadow Have?*

179v (615)   1505–08

Chapters 570–574 seem to come from the same manuscript. That they are previous to chapters 588–589 seems indicated by the concluding statement of 574: ". . . these three sorts of derivative shadows will be fully discussed." (Not translated by McMahon.)

575. *On the Shadow That Moves with Greater Velocity than the Body Casting the Shadow.*

179v (659)   1508–10

Apparently related to the preceding ones, although it appears subsequent to Lu 582. On the same subject see Lu 593 (MS E 30v). See also MS C 3v; Richter (1883), I, 218.

576. *On the Derivative Shadow Which Is Much Slower than the Primary Shadow.*

179v–180 (660)   1508–10

McMahon indicates the concordance with MS E 30v, which is actually Lu 593. Lu 576 is the continuation of the preceding chapter. Together with the following chapters 577–582, it seems to come from a single manuscript.

577. *On the Derivative Shadow Which Is Equal to the Primary Shadow.*

180 (661)   1508–10

578. *On the Derivative Shadow Distant from the Primary Shadow.*

180–180v (731)   1508–10

579. *Nature or Condition of Shadow.*

179v (714)   1508–10

580. *What an Augmented Shadow Is.*

179v (715)   1508–10

581. *Whether the Primary Shadow Is Stronger than the Derivative Shadow.*

180v (710)   1508–10

Quotation of the fourth proposition of the Book on Light and Shade. Cf. W. 19,149v; Richter (1883), I, 183.

582. *On Movement of Shadows.*

181 (658)   1508–10

It ends with the sentence "This matter will be treated individually in its proper place." Cf. Lu 574 and 793 (MS E 30v).

583. *Impact of the Derivative Shadow and Its Conditions.*

181 (626)   1508–10

584. *On Derivative Shadow and Where It Is Greatest.*

181–181v (616)   1508–10

585. *On the Death of the Derivative Shadow.*

181v (698)   1508–10

586. *On the Maximum Power of the Derivative Shadow.*

181v (700)   1508–10

587. *On Simple Shadow of the First Degree of Obscurity.*

181v–182 (694)   1508–10

588. *On the Three Varying Forms of Derivative Shadows.*

182 (619)   1508–10

589. *Variations in Each of the Three Derivative Shadows Mentioned.*

182 (620)   1508–10

Related to the preceding. Cf. Lu 574.

590. *That Derivative Shadows Are of Three Kinds.*

182–182v (617); MS E 32   1513–14

The original text is marked with the crossed-out circle, but the copy does not have the mark *Lº B*. Quotation from the first proposition of the Book on Light and Shade: "That thing is entirely ended of which no part exceeds its limits." There is also a quotation of the second proposition of the same book. The texts in MS E 32v reproduce propositions already written in the Sforza period. Cf. Brizio (1952), p. 457, n. 1.

591. *That Derivative Shadows Are of Three Kinds.*

182v (625); *Libro A* 24   1508–10

592. *Quality of Shadows.*

183 (734); *Libro B* 30
(MS E 30v)   1513–14

593. *On the Motion of a Shadow.*
183 (662);
Libro B 30 (MS E 30v)   1513–14
Cf. Lu 575–577 and 582.

594. *On the Pyramidal Shadow.*
183–183v (621);
Libro B 31 (MS E 31)   1513–14

595. *On the Simple Derivative Shadow.*
183v (618);
Libro B 31 (MS E 31)   1513–14

596. *On Compound Derivative Shadow.*
183v (611);
Libro B 31 (MS E 31)   1513–14

597. *Whether Shadow Can Be Seen through the Air.*
183v (596)   1508–10

598. *Whether a Derivative Shadow Is Darker in One Place than in Another.*
183v–184 (730)   1508–10
A date at the beginning of 1500 is also possible; cf. MS H₂ 66v (Richter [1883], I, 152) and MS K 31v (Richter [1883], I, 175).

599. *Which Derivative Shadow Will Show the Sharpest Outlines.*
184 (727)   1508–10

600. *In How Many Ways Is the Impact of the Derivative Shadow Transformed?*
184 (623)   1508–10

601. *In How Many Ways Does the Extent of the Impact of the Shadow Vary from the Original Shadow?*
184–184v (624)   1508–10

602. *How the Derivative Shadow, when It Is Surrounded Wholly or in Part by an Illuminated Background, Is Darker than the Primary Shadow.*
184v (712)   1508–10

603. *How the Primary Shadow Which Is Not Attached to a Plane Surface Is Not of Even Darkness.*
184v–185 (713)   1508–10
Reference to the "angolo della contingenzia." Cf. MS F.

604. *Conditions Governing Objects Darkened by Each Shadow.*
185 (716)   1508–10

605. *What Background Makes Shadows Darker.*
185–185v (742)   1508–10

Cf. Lu 670 (MS G 12v). Chapters 597–605 seem to come from the same manuscript.

606. *Where the Derivative Shadow Is Most Obscure.*
185v (699); *Libro A* 33   1508–10

607. *On Shadows.*
185v–186 (632); *Libro A* 35   1508–10

608. *On the Outlines Which Surround Derivative Shadows at Their Impact.*
186 (758)   1508–10
Cf. W. 19,076; Richter (1883), I, 204.

609. *How Every ⟨Opaque⟩ Body Creates as Many Shadows as there Are Luminous Parts That Surround It.*
186 (788)   1508–10

610. *On the Various Degrees of Obscurity of the Shadows Surrounding the Same ⟨Opaque⟩ Body.*
186 (702)   1508–10
A date in the Sforza period for chapters 608–610 is also possible. See the following chapters.

611. *On the Shadow Made by One Body between Two Equal Lights.*
186v (703); MS Ash. 30   ca. 1492

612. *That the Body Which Is Nearer the Light Makes the Larger Shadow and Why.*
186v (631); MS Ash. 30   ca. 1492

613. *Why the Shadow Larger than Its Cause Is Disproportionate.*
186v (629); MS Ash. 30   ca. 1492

614. *Why a Shadow Which Is Larger than Its Cause Has Indistinct Outlines.*
186v–187 (729);
MS Ash. 30   ca. 1492

615. *How the Separate Shadow Is Never Similar in Size to Its Cause.*
187 (628); MS Ash. 29v   ca. 1492

616. *What Difference Is There between a Shadow Attached to a Body and One Which Is Separated from It.*
187–187v (595);
MS Ash. 22   ca. 1492

617. *Nature of the Derivative Shadow.*
187v (635)   1508–10
Cf. Lu 560.

618. *On the Shapes of Shadows.*
187v (627)   1508–10

Connected with the preceding. For a possible earlier date cf. MS H₂ 76v; Richter (1883), I, 163.

619. *On Derivative Shadow Created on Another Derivative Shadow.*

        187v (706)   1508–10

Cf. Lu 553d (*Libro A* 34). Diagram type of MS G and Folio Resta. Cf. Pedretti (1957*b*), pl. XVI.

620. *On the Outlines of the Derivative Shadow.*

        187v (732)   1508–10

621. *On the Extension of the Derivative Shadow.*

        187v–188 (637)   1508–10

622. *Where the Derivative Shadow Is Darkest.*

        188 (704)   1508–10

623. *On the Variations of Shadows when the Sizes of the Lights That Create Them Vary.*

        188 (600)   1508–10

624. *On Variations in the Shadow without Diminution of the Light That Causes It.*

        188 (608)   1508–10

625. *On the Shadow That Is Changed into Light.*

        188 (693)   1508–10

626. *On the Light That Is Changed into Shadow.*

        188 (692)   1508–10

627. *On the Derivative Shadow Created by a Light of Long Shape Which Strikes on an Object Similar to Itself.*

        188–188v (630)   1508–10

Quotation of the fourth proposition of the Book on Light and Shade.

628. *That Shadows Should Always Participate in the Color of the Body Casting the Shadow.*

        188v–189 (753)   1508–10

How the pupil of the eye varies in size during the day and night. Cf. MS L 41v and MS E 17v; Brizio (1952), pp. 407, 453. See also Lu 202. For the stars seen through a hole in the paper cf. Lu 477. For the color of the moon see the notes in MSS F and Leicester.

629. *On White Objects Distant from the Eye.*

        189 (811)   1508–10

Color of the sky; red and blue.

630. *On the Shadows of Distant Objects and Their Colors.*

        189 (814)   1508–10

Related to the preceding. Perhaps all the chapters from 617 to 630, and more, come from the same manuscript.

631. *On Shadows on an Object and Which Primary Shadows Are Darkest.*

        189–189v (754)   1508–10

Quotation of the seventh proposition of the ninth book on Light and Shade.

632. *Which Side of the Surface of a Body Is Most Impregnated with the Color of Its Object.*

        189v (755)   1508–10

633. *Which Part of the Surface of a Body Casting Shadow It Is on Which the Colors of the Objects Are Mingled.*

        189v–190 (796)   1508–10

634. *Which Part Is of Medium Shadow on the Surface of a Body Casting Shadow.*

        190 (767)   1508–10

635. *On ⟨Opaque⟩ Bodies Which Are Polished and Lustrous.*

        190 (670)   1508–10

636. *Which Principal Shadow on the Surface of Bodies Will Have Less and Which More Difference from the Luminous Sides?*

        190–190v (787)   1508–10

637. *On Shadows Depicted on the Shadowed Side of Opaque Bodies.*

        190v (746)   1508–10

638. *Which Body Takes on the Greatest Quantity of Shadow.*

        190v (601)   1508–10

639. *Which Body Takes on the Greatest Quantity of Light.*

        190v (603)   1508–10

640. *What Body Takes on the Deepest Shadow.*

        190v–191 (735)   1508–10

641. *On the Quality of Obscurity in Shadows.*

        191 (689)   1508–10

642. *On the Shadow of the Verdure of Meadows.*

        191 (737)   1508–10

643. *Precept for Painting.*

        191–191v (681)   1508–10

Related to the preceding.

644. *On Shadows Which Are Not Consistent with the Illuminated Side.*

        191v–192 (798)   1508–10

Quotation of the seventh proposition of the fourth (?, or ninth) book on Light and Shade. The same proposition is quoted in 631 and in several other notes of that period. The observation on the sun and the moon is related to the notes in MSS F and Leicester. See also Lu 628.

645. *On the Light of ⟨Opaque⟩ Bodies Which Are Almost Never of the True Color of the Illuminated Body.*

        192 (797)   1508–10

Quotation of the seventh proposition of the fourth book on Light and Shade. See the preceding text. See also Lu 654 (Libro A 21).

646. *How Shadows Appear at Great Distance.*

        192 (816); MS Ash. 20v   *ca.* 1492

647. *On the Breadth of Shadows and of Primary Lights.*

        192–192v (851)   1508–10

Chapters 647–650 are connected with one another. Their being numbered 1st, 2d, 3d, and 4th seems to indicate the sequence they must have had in the original manuscript. Their date in the Sforza period is also possible.

648. *On the Greater or Lesser Density of Shadows.*

        192v (852)   1508–10

649. *Where Shadows Deceive the Judgment Which Determines Their Greater or Lesser Density.*

        192v (853)   1508–10

650. *Where Lights Deceive the Judgment of the Painter.*

        192v (854)   1508–10

651. *On Shadow on Objects.*

        192v (863); MS G 11v   *ca.* 1510

652. *On Quality of Lights and Shadows.*

        192v–193 (763); Libro A 12   1508–10

653. *On Shadows and Lights and Colors.*

        193 (599); Libro A 19   1508–10

654. *On Lights and Shadows and Their Colors.*

        193–193v (793); Libro A 21   1508–10

655. *On Lights and Shadows on Objects.*

        193v (794); Libro A 20   1508–10

656. *On the Imperceptible Outlines of Shadows.*

        193v (685); Libro A 37   1508–10

657. *On the Qualities of Lights and Shadows on ⟨Opaque⟩ Bodies.*

        193v (683); Libro A 42   1508–10

658. *On the Appearance of Lights and Shadows.*

        193v–194 (747); Libro A 42   1508–10

659. *On Lights.*

        194 (748); Libro A 43   1508–10

660. *On Lights and Shadows.*

        194 (604); Libro A 48   1508–10

661. *On Lights and Shadows Which Tinge the Surfaces of the Countryside.*

        194–194v (836)   1508–10

Blue of the sky. Cf. MSS F and Leicester. For a possible earlier date cf. MS H 77v; Brizio (1952), p. 239. Moreover, the style of writing recalls that of passages in the MS A. Thus this chapter, as the following, might have been copied from a lost folio of that manuscript.

662. *On Derivative Light.*

        195 (586); MS A fol.?   *ca.* 1492

Copied in MS H 227 inf. 47v from an unspecified folio of the missing section of MS A (fols. 65–80). See also Lu 547. Cf. Pedretti (1962a).

663. *On Lights.*

        195 (598); MS G 3v   *ca.* 1510

It ends: "Of these things we shall speak separately in our discourse." The transcriber omitted the discussion and figure that are in the original.

664. *On Illumination and Luster.*

        195 (769)   1508–10

665. *On Light and Shadow.*

        195 (578)   1508–10

Cf. Lu 545–547, 550.

666. *On Light and Shadow.*

195–195v (728)   1508–10

Quotation of the eighth proposition of the fifth book on Light and Shade.

667. *On Lights and Shadows.*

195v (847); MS Ash. 16v   *ca.* 1492

668. *On Light and Shadow.*

195v–196 (791);
MS Ash. 33v   *ca.* 1492

669. *On Lights and Shadows.*

196 (848);
Libro B 3 (MS E 3)   1513–14

670. *On Lights between the Shadows.*

196 (743); MS G 12v   *ca.* 1510

Owing to a typographical lapsus Mc-Mahon's concordance has MS C.

671. *On Bright and Dark.*

196 (840)   1508–10

672. *On Brightness and Darkness.*

196–196v (842)   1508–10

Related to the preceding.

673. *On the Four Fundamentals Which Must Be Considered Primarily in Painting Shadows and Lights.*

196v (841)   1490–5

Concepts of the Sforza period: concern with form and disregard for color.

674. *On the Nature of the Light That Illuminates ⟨Opaque⟩ Objects.*

196v–197 (680)   1508–10

675. *On Universal Lights on Polished Bodies.*

197 (771)   1508–10

676. *On ⟨Opaque⟩ Bodies Which Are Polished and Lustrous.*

197 (770)   1508–10

677. *How Objects Surrounded by Universal Light Create Specific Lights on Many of Their Own Sides.*

197 (726)   1508–10

Cf. Lu 931.

678. *On the Lights and Shadows by Means of Which Natural Objects Are Imitated.*

197v (864)   1508–10

679. *On Shadows and in What Bodies They Cannot Be Very Dark and So Also of Light.*

197v–198 (738)   1508–10

Shadows on clothes and plants.

680. *On the Particular Light of the Sun or Other Luminous Body.*

198 (671)   1508–10

681. *On the Universal Light of the Air Where the Sun Does Not Strike.*

198–198v (682)   1508–10

682. *On Universal Light Mixed with the Particular Light of the Sun or Other Light.*

198v (684)   1508–10

683. *On the Medium Shadow Which Falls between the Illuminated and the Shadowed Parts of Bodies.*

198v–199 (718)   1508–10

684. *Whether a Large Light of Little Strength Is as Strong as a Small Light of Great Strength.*

199 (691)   1508–10

685. *On the Medium Shadow Contained between the Principal Lights and Shadows.*

199 (645)   1508–10

The text informs us that the figure will be used also in the following proposition.

686. *On the Position of the Eye That Sees More or Less Shadow Depending on the Movement That It Makes around the ⟨Opaque⟩ Body.*

199–199v (646)   1508–10

Related to the preceding.

687. *In What Position the Shadow of Spherical Bodies Is Never Seen.*

199v (647)   1508–10

688. *That Position or Rather That Distance around the Spherical Body at Which There Is Never Lack of Shadow.*

200 (650)   1508–10

689. *What Light Makes the Shadows of Bodies Most Different from Their Lights?*

200–220v (695)   1508–10

690. *On Various Objects Close Together Seen at a Great Distance.*

200v (817)   1508–10

Similar to the Sforza text Lu 646, but chronologically closer to Lu 786.

691. *On the Position Where the Object Appears Darkest.*

200v (820)   1508–10

Mountains. Pierantoni suggests a comparison with C.A. 126 r, 1492–1495.

692. *Where and in What Color Shadows Lose Most of the Natural Color of the ⟨Opaque⟩ Objects.*

200v–201 (783)   1508–10

Cf. Lu 254 and 654 (*Libro A* 29, 21).

693. *Which Color of Body Will Make a Shadow More Different from Light; That Is, Which Will Be Darker.*

201 (784)   1508–10

Related to the preceding. Pierantoni indicates similar concepts in MS C 8v and C.A. 221 v-c. I previously dated this folio of the Codex Atlanticus *ca.* 1500, but it should be dated earlier because of the type of handwriting and the frequent punctuation. Cf. Pedretti (1957*b*), p. 275.

694. *On That Part of a Body Which Will Be Most Illuminated by a Light of Even Quality.*

201–203v   1508–10

This chapter, complemented by Lu 694a-f, constitutes a unified group of notes arranged according to the sequence they probably had in the original. Many of them, e.g., 694f, are of a pocket-notebook type. An earlier date, 1505–1508, is also possible.

Concordance: 694, 201–201v (675); 694a, 201v (676); 694b, 201v–202 (677); 694c, 202 (678); 694d, 202–202v (760); 694e, 202v (725); 694f, 202v–203–203v (860).

695. *Equality of Shadows on an ⟨Opaque⟩ Object Illuminated by Unequal Light Sources Placed at Various Distances.*

203v (607)   1508–10

696. *What Light Source Is It Which Causes Only Half of a Shaded Sphere to Be Seen.*

203v–204 (605)   1508–10

697. *Whether It Is Possible That at Any Distance a Luminous Body Can Illuminate Only Half of an ⟨Opaque⟩ Body Smaller than Itself.*

204 (606)   1508–10

698. *On Different Degrees of Shadow Portrayed in Painting.*

204–204v–205
(724, 812, 813)   1508–10

Quotation of the ninth proposition of the Book on Light and Shade. McM 812 and 813 correspond to Lu 698a and 698b.

699. *Which Colors Vary Most from Light to Shadow.*

205 (739)   1508–10

Cf. Lu 692 and 693.

700. *All Colors in Distant Shadows Are Unknown and Indistinguishable.*

205–205v (815);
MS Ash. 10   *ca.* 1492

701. *On the Colors of the Visual Images of Objects Which Tinge the Surfaces of Opaque Bodies.*

205v (790)   1508–10

Cf. Lu 692. A date in the Sforza period is also possible. Cf. Lu 668 (MS Ash. 33v).

702. *On the False Color of the Shadows of Opaque Bodies.*

205v–206 (766)   1508–10

703. *What Is Really the True Shadow of the Color of Bodies?*

206 (803)   1508–10

704. *Which Object Most Tinges with Its Likeness the White Surfaces of Opaque Bodies.*

206–206v (785)   1508–10

705. *On Conditions of the Surfaces of Bodies.*

206v (792)   1508–10

The first sentence is similar to the text in MS E 17.

706. *On the Color of Shadows and How Dark They Become.*

206v (765)   1508–10

707. *On the Colors of Lights That Illuminate ⟨Opaque⟩ Bodies.*

206v–207 (789)   1508–10

708. *How Shadows with Lights Appear When They Are in Contrast to One Another.*

207 (801)   1508–10

Effects of lights and shadows on black and white clothes. Quotation of the third proposition of the ninth book on

Light and Shade. Cf. Lu 218, 238, and 445.

709. *What Objects Related to the Flesh Cause Them to Show Shadows in Harmony with the Lights.*

    207–207v (800)   1508–10

Related to the preceding. Cf. Lu 94 and 110. See also Lu 95, 431 (*Libro A* 38), and 816.

710. *On Shadows on Faces Passing along Wet Streets Which Do Not Seem Compatible With Their Flesh Tones.*

    207v (802); *Libro A* 47   1508–10

711. *On the Quality of the Air in Shadows and Lights.*

    207v (764); MS Ash. 33v   *ca.* 1492

712. *On Small Lights.*

    208 (761); MS Ash. 33v   *ca.* 1492

713. *What Surface Shows the Greatest Difference between Brightness and Darkness.*

    208 (740)   1508–10

In the heading, "maggior" (Greatest) is an error, contradicted by the text.

714. *Is the Greatest Difference between Shadows and Lights in Near or in Distant Objects?*

    208 (821)   1508–10

715. *What Body Is It Which, with the Same Color and Distance from the Eye, Has Lights That Least Differ from Its Shadows?*

    208–208v (696)   1508–10

716. *Why the True Shape of a Body That Is Enveloped in Light and Shadow and with Outlined Surfaces Is Recognizable.*

    208v (844)   1508–10

717. *On the Distinctness of the Shadows in Landscapes and the Objects Located Therein.*

    208v (656); MS Ash. 18v   *ca.* 1492

718. *On What Surfaces Is True and Equal Light to Be Found.*

    208v–209 (668)   1508–10

See the following chapter and Lu 755.

719. *On the Brightness of Derivative Light.*

    209–209v (669)   1508–10

720. *On the Remoteness and Nearness, When a Man Leaves and Approaches the Same Light, and of the Variations in His Shadows.*

    210 (663)   1508–10

Cf. C.A. 241v

721. *On the Changes Which a Fixed Light Brings to the Shadows Created on Bodies That, without Moving Their Feet, Bend Over, or Down, or Arise.*

    210 (664)   1508–10

Concept of continuous quantity applied to the movement of shadow.

722. *Which Object, Exposed to Light, Increases Its Shadowed Side.*

    210 (602)   1508–10

Pierantoni suggests a comparison with C.A. 47 v-b, 1510–1515, and with the heading in C.A. 250 v-a, *ca.* 1492.

723. *Which Object, the More It Approaches to the Light, the More Diminishes on Its Shaded Side.*

    210v–211 (609)   1508–10

724. *Which Object Does Not Increase or Diminish Its Shaded or Its Luminous Side whatever the Closeness to the Body That Illuminates It.*

    211 (610)   1508–10

Pierantoni indicates the comparison with C.A. 236 r-a, a folio of blue paper of *ca.* 1510. Chapters 722–724 are interrelated and seem to come from the same manuscript.

725. *Of Objects of Equal Size That Which Is Illuminated by the Greater Light Will Have a Shorter Shadow.*

    211–211v (639);
    MS Ash. 10v   *ca.* 1492

The text of this chapter is the Lu 725a.

725a. *Those Objects Which Are Nearer to the Light Source or More Remote from It Will Have Shorter or Longer Derivative Shadows.*

    211v–212 (639, 640);
    MS Ash. 10v   *ca.* 1492

This heading is actually the text of the preceding chapter.

726. *Objects Scattered about a Room Illuminated by a Single Window Will Have Shorter or Longer Derivative Shadows Depending on whether They*

*Are More or Less in Line with That
Window.*

    212–212v (643, 644);
        MS Ash. 11   *ca.* 1492

727. *See the preceding text* (McM 644).

728. *Every Shadow Produced by an
⟨Opaque⟩ Body Smaller than the Source
of Light Will Cast a Derivative Shadow
Tinted with the Color of Its Origin.*

    212v–213–213v (756);
        MS Ash. 13v   *ca.* 1492

729. *That Part of an ⟨Opaque⟩ Body Is
Least Luminous Which Is Exposed to
the Least Light.*

    213v (757); MS Ash. 13v   *ca.* 1492

730. *Light Which Falls on ⟨Opaque⟩
Bodies between Equal Angles Has the
Greatest Degree of Brightness, and
That Body Is in Greater Darkness
Which Receives Light between Less
Equal Angles; Both Light and Shadow
Function through Pyramids.*

    213v–214–214v (674);
        MS Ash. 14   *ca.* 1492

731. *Each Shadow Cast by Objects in a
Room Is Directed Along Its Center
Line Toward a Single Point Created
by the Intersection of the Rays of Light
in the Center of the Breadth and
Depth of the Window.*

    214v–215 (642);
        MS Ash. 15   *ca.* 1492

732. *Every Shadow, with All Its Differ-
entiations, Which, with Distance, Increases in Width More than Its Source,
Has External Lines Which Converge
between the Light and the ⟨Opaque⟩
Body.*

    215v (641); MS Ash. 15v   *ca.* 1492

733. *Each ⟨Opaque⟩ Body Lies Between
Two Pyramids, One Dark and the
Other Illuminated, the One Seen and
the Other Not, and This Happens only
When the Light Enters through a
Window.*

    215v–216 (622);
        MS Ash. 15v   *ca.* 1492

734. *What That Light Is Whose Shadow
Can Never Be Seen Even When the
Eye Is Farther Away from the ⟨Opaque⟩*

*Sphere than Is the Light and Is be-
hind the Light.*

    216–216v (648)   1508–10
Diagram of small dimension, typical of
late texts. Pierantoni indicates the same
subject in Codex Arundel 170v.

735. *On the Eye Which at a Great Dis-
tance Will Never Have a View of the
Shadow of the ⟨Opaque⟩ Body Which
Is Blocked when the Light Source Is
Smaller than the ⟨Opaque⟩ Body.*

    216v (649)   1508–10
Related to the preceding.

736. *On the Shadow of an Opaque
Sphere Placed in the Air.*

    216v–217 (687)   1508–10
Pierantoni indicates a similar heading
in C.A. 190 r-b, *ca.* 1508. But cf. C.A.
207 r-a (plate 28). See also Lu 750.

737. *On the Shadow of an Opaque
Sphere Which Is Placed on the Ground.*

    217–217v (688)   1508–10
Related to the preceding.

738. *On the Shadows of Somewhat Transparent Bodies.*

    217v (735)   1508–10
Shadows of leaves. Cf. Lu 894 (MS G
10v).

739. *On the Principal Shadow Which
Falls between Direct and Reflected
Light.*

    217v (843)   1508–10
An anticipation of 1505–1508 is also
possible. The text ends: "On this subject a book will be composed."

740. *On the Contours of Objects Which
First Lose Clarity.*

    217v–218 (807)   1508–10
Pierantoni indicates similar concepts in
C.A. 176 v-a, 1492–1493, and in MS
E 80–80v.

741. *On the Outlines of Opaque Bodies.*

    218 (806)   1508–10
Pierantoni suggests a comparison with
MS E 80–80v. Reference to the "3rd of
the 5th of Perspective." Cf. similar quotation in MS D (*ca.* 1508) 10v: "3rd of
the present [treatise]."

742. *How the Contours of ⟨Opaque⟩ Objects Seen by the Pupil of One Eye at*

a Time Are Not in the Same Place on That Object.

218–218v (805)   1508–10

743. *How That Opaque Body Will Have the Most Indistinct Outlines Which Is Nearest the Eye That Sees It.*

218v (808)   1508–10

Because of similarity of subject matter and the style of the figures, chapters 740–743 seem to come from the same manuscript, preserving the sequence they had in the original. Similar subjects, however, are found in notes of various periods: e.g., C.A. 144 v-a–b (*ca.* 1492), MS I 49v, MS G 29v, MS D 10v, MS F 31r, and MS E 15. See also C.A. 174 v-b, 1516–1517.

744. *How One Should Know What Part of the Body Ought to Be More or Less Luminous than the Rest.*

218v–219–219v (672, 673);
MS Ash. 32   *ca.* 1492

The paragraph "Where the angles made by the direct lines are more nearly equal . . ." was taken from W. 12,604, *ca.* 1490. Also the figure on folio 219 comes from the Windsor folio.

745. *How the Contours of Objects in Light and Shade Are always Changed by the Color and Light Value of What Borders the Outline of Their Surfaces.*

219v–220 (750);
MS Ash. 32   *ca.* 1492

746. *On the Highest Points of Light Which Move and Change Shape as the Eye That Sees the Object Changes.*

220 (779); MS Ash. 32   *ca.* 1492

747. *The Manner in Which Shadows Made by Objects Should Terminate.*

220–220v (867);
MS Ash. 32v   *ca.* 1492

748. *Which Part of the Sphere Is Least Illuminated?*

220v (690)   1508–10

Cf. C.A. 37 r-a, 148 v-a, and 207 r-a, all of the same period, *ca.* 1506–1508.

749. *Which Part of the Sphere Is More Illuminated?*

220v–221 (679)   1508–10

750. *What Part of an Opaque Sphere Is Least Illuminated?*

221–221v–222 (686)   1508–10

Chapters 748–750 are interrelated and are probably taken from the same manuscript. They are drafted in C.A. 207 r-a (plate 28). Cf. Lu 736. The conclusion of Lu 750 evokes the invectives against the alchemists. Cf. W. 19,045, 19,047, and 19,048; Brizio (1952), pp. 494 ff. See also MS G 3v (Richter [1883], II, 872).

751. *On the Proportion of Illuminated Parts of Objects to Their Reflected Lights.*

222–222v (717)   1508–10

752. *On the Darkest Area of Shadow on Spherical or Columnar Bodies.*

222v (719)   1508–10

753. *How the Shadows Cast by Specific Lights Are to Be Avoided because Their Ends Are Like Their Beginnings.*

222v (856); MS Ash. 21v   *ca.* 1492

754. *On Giving the Proper Lights to Illuminated Objects According to Their Locations.*

222v–223 (866)   1508–10

Quotation of the fourth proposition of the first book on Light and Shade. The concluding sentence, "And so we shall make appropriate mention of this in the proper place," indicates a priority of this chapter to Lu 789 (MS G 15).

755. *Rule for Giving the Proper Lights and Shadows to a Form or Body with Several Sides.*

223–223v (667)   1508–10

Pierantoni indicates a similar concept in MS C 8v.

756. *Rule for Placing the True Brightness of Light on the Side of the aforesaid Object.*

223v–224 (869)   1508–10

Related to the preceding. For the tiny figure of a spoon indicated as a measure of colors see Lu 433 (*Libro A 40*): "Take a little spoon, hardly larger than an ear-spoon."

757. *Why the Illuminated Area around a Derivative Shadow Seems Brighter*

inside a House than in the Open Country.

224 (752)   1508–10

Probably earlier, perhaps of the Sforza period. The discussion is interrupted: "It happens because . . . [*sic*]. This will be explained in its proper place in the book on light and shade." Pierantoni suggests a comparison with MS E 32v; Richter (1883), I, 240.

758. *On Placing Lights.*

224–224v (868);
MS Ash. 28v   *ca.* 1492

759. *On Giving Aid by Means of Artificial Lights and Shadows to the Simulation of Relief in Painting.*

224v (845); MS Ash. 21v   *ca.* 1492

760. *On Surrounding Bodies with Varying Lines of Shadows.*

224v–225 (846);
MS Ash. 21v   *ca.* 1492

761. *Way of Making the Shadow on Bodies Consistent with the Light and the Body.*

225 (870); MS Ash. 23   *ca.* 1492

762. *On the Location of Lights and Shadows of Objects Seen in the Country.*

225 (666)   1508–10

Quotation of the ninth proposition of the Book on Light and Shade.

763. *When the Sun Is in the East and the Eye Is Toward the North or South.*

225–225v (653)   1508–10

Cf. Lu 150 (MS Ash. 18v). Chapters 763–765 are related to one another and must be of late period.

764. *On the Sun and the Eye in the East.*

225v (652)   1508–10

Quotation of the ninth proposition of the Book on Light and Shade.

765. *On the Sun in the East and the Eye in the West.*

225v (654)   1508–10

Lu 765a is the final sentence of Lu 765. For that reason McMahon does not separate it.

766. *Reminder to the Painter.*

225v (655)   1508–10

Related to the preceding.

767. *On the Consistency of Shadows with Their Lights.*

225v–226 (795)   1508–10

Quotation of the first proposition of the fourth book on Light and Shade.

768. *In What Part of ⟨Opaque⟩ Bodies the Colors Will Appear to Be of Greatest Beauty.*

226 (762)   1508–10

769. *Why the Borders of ⟨Opaque⟩ Bodies Sometimes Look Brighter or Darker than They Are.*

226 (751)   1508–10

A date in the Sforza period is also possible. Cf. Lu 745 (MS Ash. 32) and C.A. 126 r-b. For the late period cf. C.A. 195 r-a, v-a, 1508–1510.

770. *What Difference There Is Between the Illuminated Part of the Surface of ⟨Opaque⟩ Bodies and the Lustrous Part.*

226–226v (773)   1508–10

In the original this text may also have followed the preceding.

ON LUSTER

771. *On the Luster of ⟨Opaque⟩ Bodies.*

226v (777)   1508–10

772. *How Luster Is More Powerful against a Black Background than against Any Other.*

226v–227 (778)   1508–10

Related to the preceding.

773. *How Luster upon a White Field is of Little Strength.*

227 (775)   1508–10

774. *On the Size of Luster on Polished Bodies.*

227 (776)   1508–10

775. *What Difference There Is between Luster and Light.*

227 (774)   1508–10

776. *On Light and Luster.*

227–227v (780); MS E 31v   1513–14

Not marked L° B.

777. *On Those Bodies Which Have Light without Luster.*
        227v (772); MS E 31v   1513–14
Not marked *L° B.*

778. *Which Bodies Those Are That Will Possess Luster but Not an Illuminated Part?*
        227v (781); MS E 31v   1513–14
Not marked *L° B.*

779. *On Luster.*
        227v–228 (782);
        (*Libro A* 23)   1508–10
The chapter is formed by ten paragraphs, arranged by Ludwig in nine notes. The mark *L° A* refers to the seventh paragraph, not to the eighth as Ludwig indicates. An earlier date for the other paragraphs is also possible. Cf. MS H₂ 90v; Richter (1883), I, 134.

ON REFLECTED LIGHTS

780. *On the Shadow Interposed between Incident Light and Reflected Light.*
        228–228v (721)   1508–10

781. *Where the Reflection of Light Must Be Dimmest.*
        228v (720)   1508–10
Quotation of the fourth proposition of the Book on Light and Shade.

782. *Why Reflected Light Is Seen Little or Not at All Under Universal Light.*
        228v–229 (722)   1508–10
Reference to the same proposition quoted in the preceding chapter.

783. *In What Way Reflected Light Is Created under Universal Light.*
        229–229v (723)   1508–10
The text ends: "But a special treatise on this will be composed in the proper place." Chapters 780–782 could be later; see the following chapter.

784. *What Lights Make the Shape of Muscles Appear Clearest and Sharpest.*
        229v (849)   1508–10
The comparison with Lu 669 (MS E 3) may suggest a later date, 1510–1515.

785. *How White Bodies Should Be Represented.*

        229v–230 (786);
        MS Ash. 20   *ca.* 1492
The concluding sentence is related to the "Paragone."

786. *On the Eye That Is in a Bright Light and Looks Toward a Dark Place.*
        230–230v (818)   1508–10
Quotation of the fourth proposition of the Book on Light and Shade.

787. *On the Eye That Sees Objects in a Bright Place.*
        230v (819)   1508–10
Reference to the same proposition quoted in the preceding chapter.

788. *On the Lights and Shadows of Cities.*
        230v (651); MS G 19v   *ca.* 1510

789. *On the Illumination of the Lower Parts of Bodies Crowded Together, as in Picturing Men in Battle.*
        230v–231 (865); MS G 15   *ca.* 1510

790. *On Specific Light.*
        231 (855); MS E 32v   1513–14
Not marked *L° B.* Concordance omitted by Carusi, Pierantoni, and McMahon. Cf. Lu 120, and Brizio (1952), p. 457, n. 1.

ON THE SHADOWED AND BRIGHT PARTS OF MOUNTAINS

791. *Common Perspective.*
        231–231v (810)   1508–10
Cf. Codex Arundel 134v and MS K 124 [44]r. See also Lu 797.

792. *On the Peaks of Mountains as Seen from Above.*
        231v–232 (824)   1510–13

Quotations of the "seventh of the fourth," and of the "third of the ninth" of the Book on Light and Shade.

793. *On Air Which Makes the Bases of Mountains Appear Brighter than Their Peaks.*
        232 (825)   1510–13

It continues in the following text.

794. *Why Distant Mountains Appear Darker at the Summit than at the Base.*

232–232v (826)   1510–13

Continuation of the preceding text: "With regard to that which has already been said on the preceding page."

795. *On the Summits of Mountains That Are Revealed to the Eye, One above the Other, and How Their Relative Distance Does Not Accord with Their Relative Color.*

233–233v (823)   1510–13

796. *On the Summits of Mountains That Do Not Diminish in Color According to the Distances between These Summits.*

233v (833)   1510–13

797. *On the Error of the Painter Regarding the Size of Trees and Other Objects in the Landscape.*

233v–234 (809)   1508–10

Cf. Lu 152, 455, and 473, which, together with this, may belong to the same period as the notes in 792–796 and 798–799, which seem taken from the same notebook on the shadowed and bright parts of mountains.

798. *Why Mountains Seen at a Great Distance Appear Darker at the Summit than at the Base.*

234 234v (827)   1510 13

799. *Why Mountains Appear to Have Summits That Are Darker than Their Bases When Seen at a Great Distance.*

234v–235 (828)   1510–13

800. *How One Should Not Represent Mountains as Blue as in Summer.*

235 (831);
Libro B 19 (MS E 19)   1513–14

801. *How Mountains in the Shadow of Clouds Take on a Blue Color.*

235–235v (832)   1508–10

A date after 1510 is also possible. Quotation of the fifth proposition of the second book on Light and Shade.

802. *On the Air That Is Seen in the Mountains.*

235v (831); *Libro A* 32   1508–10

803. *On Mountains and Their Treatment in Painting.*

235v (830); *Libro A* 33   1508–10

804. *Painting Which Shows the Necessary Shape of the Alpine Mountains and Hills.*

235v–236–236v (837)   1508–10

Connected with the following. It is similar to the notes in the Codex Leicester, but a date after 1510 is also possible in comparison with Lu 806, which appears closer to the texts on the "Deluge." Baratta (1903), pp. 91, 108, relates this chapter to texts in Codex Atlanticus 160 v-a, 185 v-c, and MS G 48v, all dating from 1510–1515.

805. *Painting, and How Mountains Grow.*

236v (838)   1508–10

Connected with the preceding: "Because of that which has been concluded just before this. . . ."

806. *Painting and Portraying the Characteristics and Component Parts of Mountainous Landscapes.*

236v–237–237v (839)   1510–15

Reference to the effect of thunderbolts striking the rocks of high mountains. Cf. MS E (*Libro B*) 1r: ". . . I have found traces of the same power in the rocks of the high Apennines and especially in the rock of La Vernia." Cf. Baratta (1903), pp. 73–75. See also note to Lu 804.

807. *On Mountains.*

237v (829)   1510–15

808. *On Mountains.*

237v (835)   1510–15

Chapters 804–808 were probably taken from the same manuscript.

The following chapters were added later with a different ink. They are not related to mountains, but they are additions to the fifth part, on folios that had been left blank.

809. *Precept.*

238 (859)   1508–10

A date in the Sforza period or after 1500 is also possible.

810. *On the Human Body Which Turns in Space and Receives the Same Light*

on Various Sides Giving Rise to In-
finite Variations.

238–238v (665, 822, 733)   1505–10
Lu 810a and 810b correspond to McM 822 and 733. Quotations of the seventh and eighth books on perspective (810a). Concepts of continuous quantity applied to the movement of Shadows.

The word "humano" in the heading is changed by Ludwig to "allumato."

811. On the Light and Shade of ⟨Opaque⟩ Objects.

239 (850)   1505–10

812. On Bodies Illuminated by the Air without Sunlight.

239–239v (861, 862)   1508–10
McM 862 corresponds to the second paragraph of Ludwig's text. Quotations of propositions of the Book on Light and Shade: 5th of the fourth, and 7th of the ninth.

813. Which Shadow Is Darkest?

239v (701)   1508–10

814. On Light.

239v (857)   1508–10

815. Precept.

239v (768)   1508–10

816. Precept.

239v–240 (799)   1508–10
Walls of the same color as the object placed between them. Cf. Lu 155, 239,

and 709. See also Lu 95 and 431, both from *Libro A* 38.

817. On Outlines of Objects Changed through the Medium of Background.

240 (749)   1508–10
Quotation of the seventh proposition of the Book on Light and Shade.

818. Precept for Depicting Shadows.

240–240v (871)   1508–10
The mark *L.T.* beside the title is repeated at the end of the following chapter. (The meaning of *L.T.* is not clear. However, as Melzi used this mark to designate a passage copied at the end of the second part of the Codex Urbinas as being the omitted section of Lu 148 [cf. plate 14, *b*], it might represent an abbreviation of "lasciato tronco" [left incomplete].)

819. On the Representation of Colors at Any Distance.

240v–241 (872)   1508–10
Reference mark *L.T.* at the end of the text. A date after 1510 is also possible. The method of drawing on paper of the same color as the mountains is also mentioned in Lu 479.

820. On Reflected Light.

241 (858)   1505–10

821. On Perspective.

241–241v (804)   1505–10
Folio 242 is blank.

PART SIX

ON TREES AND VERDURE

822. Discussion of Kinds of Blossoms on the Flowering Branches of Shrubs.

243 (941)   1508–10

823. On Branches of Plants.

243–243v (874)   1508–10
Eleven paragraphs comparable to the notes in MS M 78v–79; Brizio (1952), p. 245. These paragraphs are found in draft form in C.A. 305 r-a, 1506–1508. The third and fourth paragraphs are found in draft form in Codex Arundel 180v, 1506–1508; Brizio (1952), p. 245. Cf. Pedretti (1960a), pp. 65–96.

824. On the Branching of Trees.

243v–244 (896)   1508–10

825. On the Branching of Trees.

244 (897)   1508–10
The figure of a section of forked trunk refers to a young tree. The figure referring to an old tree was erroneously inserted in the following chapter, on fol. 244v.

826. On the Smaller Branching of Trees.

244–244v (904)   1508–10
The error of copying in this chapter the figure belonging to the preceding

one ("Questa va posta in margine presso la pianta giovane") demonstrates the original contiguity of the two notes. One may suspect that the error was due to Leonardo himself, and that Melzi copied the note of correction; in fact, the figure of the preceding chapter is placed in the center, not in the margin of the text. The reference to the "margine" denotes a type of notebook with marginal columns which is characteristic of Leonardo's manuscripts of his late period.

827. *On the Proportion That the Branching of Plants Have to One Another.*

244v–245 (899)   1508–10
Pierantoni indicates the same subject in MS G 25.

828 & 828a–f. *On the Branches of Trees.*
245–245v–246 (878, 880,
895, 877, 879, 894, 881)   1508–10
Cf. Lu 845, 846, and 850. McMahon's texts are respectively Lu 828a–828f. Pierantoni's identification of Lu 828d in MS G 5 is incorrect. See C.A. 305 r-a for a similar text. Cf. Pedretti (1960a), p. 65–96.

829. *On the Branching of Trees.*
246–246v (900)   1508–10
Cf. MS M 78v–79 also for the type of drawing. The date is in accordance with that of the preceding chapter and it is suggested by the comparison with the notes in C.A. 305 r-a. This chapter comes from a manuscript on painting: "Although these things do not serve painting, yet I will note them, so as to leave out as little as possible about trees."

830. *On the Branches of Plants.*
246v–247 (876); *Libro B 6*
(MS E 6v)   1513–14
831. *On Growth of Leaves Upon Their Stems.*
247 (887); MS G 16v   *ca.* 1510
832. *On the Branches of Plants and Their Foliage.*
247–247v–248 (875);
MS G 30v–32v   *ca.* 1510

833. *On Growth of Branches in Plants.*
248 (889); MS G 33   *ca.* 1510
834. *Why Planks Are Many Times Not Straight in Their Grain.*
248v (982, 873); MS G 33   *ca.* 1510
835. *On Trees.*
248v (970)   1510–15
Cf. *passim* in the texts on the shadowed and bright parts of mountains; e.g., Lu 806. See also Lu 851.
836. *On Trees.*
248v–249 (955)   1508–10
Cf. Lu 888 (MS G 26v).
837. *On the Branches of Trees.*
249 (888)   1508–10
838. *On Branching Which, During the Same Year, Is Sent Forth Again on the End of Branches That Have Been Cut.*
249–249v (898)   1500–05
The text concludes: "But this will not be discussed in full here, because it is reserved for elsewhere, and it does not relate to painting." Cf. Lu 829.
839. *On the Proportion of Branches to Their Nourishment.*
249v–250 (883)   1500–05
Perhaps earlier. On the intensity of the flow of lymph into injured parts of plants see C.A. 76 r-a, dated 23 April 1490.
840. *On Growth of Trees and in Which Direction They Grow Most.*
250 (885)   1508–10
Cf. Lu 806.
841. *Which Branches of Trees Are Those Which Grow Most in One Year?*
250–250v (886)   1508–10
See the preceding chapter.
842. *On Bark of Trees.*
250v (893)   1508–10
843. *On the North Side of the Trunks of Trees.*
250v (909)   1508–10
844. *On Bark of Trees.*
250v–251 (908)   1508–10
845. *On Diversity That Branchings of Trees Show.*
251 (890)   1508–10
See C.A. 207 v-a, 1506–1508: "3 sono le sorte delle ramificazioni," with three

sketches which can be compared with those of this chapter and of the following. Cf. Pedretti (1960a), fig. 5.

846. *On Plants That Send Forth Their Branches Opposite One Another.*

251–251v (891)   1508–10

847. *On Accident Which Makes the aforesaid Plants Bend.*

251v (892)   1508–10

Chapters 845–847 appear to be interrelated.

848. *On the States of the Foliage of Trees.*

251v–252 (910)   1508–10

849. *On the Transparency of Leaves.*

252 (928)   1508–10

Cf. Lu 788 and 894 (MS G 10v).

850. *On the Center of the Thickness of Trees.*

252 (882)   1508–10

Cf. Lu 828 f.

851. *Which Tree in the Forest Grows with the Most Consistent Thickness and to the Greatest Height?*

252v (907)   1508–10

Cf. Lu 835 and 840 in reference to Lu 806.

852. *What Tree Is Most Deformed in Regard to Its Thickness and of Least Height and Most Durability?*

252v (906)   1508–10

Connected with the preceding.

853. *On Trees and Sawn Planks Which Never Bend of Themselves.*

252v (984)   1508–10

854. *On the Planks Which Keep Straight Best.*

252v–253 (983)   1508–10

855. *On the Cracking of Planks When They Dry.*

253 (985)   1508–10

856. *On Planks That Do Not Crack Open When They Dry.*

253 (986)   1508–10

857. *Branches and Twigs of Trees at Different Distances.*

253 (950)   1510–15

Cf. Lu 862. Horizon; cf. Part Eight, *passim.* See also Lu 862 and 909.

858. *On the Part of Trees at a Great Distance Which Remains Clear.*

253–253v (957)   1510–15

The continuation is in the following chapter.

859. *On Distances More Remote than Those Aforementioned.*

253v (959)   1510–15

860. *On the Ends of Branches of Leafy Trees.*

253v–254 (911)   *ca.* 1510

Cf. Lu 892–894 (MS G).

861. *Why the Same Trees Seem Brighter near at Hand than at a Distance.*

254 (952)   *ca.* 1510

862. *Why Trees after a Certain Distance Are Brighter the Farther Away They Are.*

254–254v (953)   1510–15

Cf. Lu 857 and 909.

863. *On the Difference in Shadows of Trees in the Same Light in a Landscape Under a Specific Light.*

254v (919)   1510–15

864. *On Light on Branches and Foliage.*

254v–255 (954)   1510–15

Connected with the preceding.

865. *On the Form That Trees Take Where the Trunk Nears the Roots.*

255 (884)   1510–15

Pierantoni indicates the same subject in MS G 1.

866. *On the Sizes of Lights and Shadows on Leaves.*

255 (916)   1510–15

867. *On the Illumination of Trees.*

255–255v (917); *Libro* B 18

(MS E 18v)   1513–14

868. *Reminder to the Painter about Trees.*

255v (969);

Libro B 18 (MS E 18v)   1513–14

869. *On the Universal Light That Illuminates Trees.*

255v–256 (914); MS G 12   *ca.* 1510

870. *On Trees and Their Lights.*

256 (978); MS G 11v   *ca.* 1510

871. *On the Illuminated Side of Foliage and Mountains.*

256 (948); MS G 15   *ca.* 1510

872. *On Lights on Dark Leaves.*
256–256v (938); MS G 28v ca. 1510
873. *On the Light on Foliage of Green Tending Toward Yellow.*
256–256v (938); MS G 28v ca. 1510
874. *On Trees Which Are Illuminated by the Sun and the Air.*
256v (937); MS G 28v ca. 1510
875. *On the Highlight on the Foliage of Trees.*
256v–257 (936) 1508–10
Quotations of rules from the Book on Light and Shade. Pierantoni indicates the same subject in MS G 3v.
876. *On the Green of Leaves.*
257 (930) 1508–10
877. *On the Darkness of a Tree.*
257 (940) 1508–10
878. *On Trees.*
257 (929) 1508–10
879. *On Trees Below the Level of the Eye.*
257–257v (918) 1508–10
Cf. C.A. 184 v c, 1515–1517.
880. *On Sparse Tops of Trees.*
257v (912) 1508–10
881. *On Landscape Fading into the Distance.*
257v (958) 1508–10
882. *On the Azure Color Which Distant Trees Acquire.*
257v–258 (960) 1508–10
883. *On the Sun Which Illuminates the Forest.*
258 (975) 1508–10
884. *On the Luminous Parts of the Foliage of Plants.*
258–258v (951) 1508–10
Chapters 875–884 seem to come from the same manuscript.
885. *On Trees That Are between the Eye and the Light.*
258v (933); MS G 9v ca. 1510
886. *On the Incidental Color of Trees.*
258v (949); MS G 24 ca. 1510
887. *On the Appearance of Chance Conditions.*
258v (965); MS G 24 ca. 1510
888. *What Outlines Distant Trees Dis-*

play against the Air Which Forms Their Background.
258v–259 (956); MS G 26v ca. 1510
889. *On Shadows of Trees.*
259 (922);
Libro B 19 (MS E 19) 1513–14
890. *On Shadows and Transparencies of Leaves.*
259–259v (974) 1508–10
891. *On Shadows of Transparent Leaves.*
259v–260 (973);
MS G 3v–4 ca. 1510
892. *On Never Portraying Foliage Transparent to the Sun.*
260 (977); MS G 4v–5 ca. 1510
893. *On the Shadow of the Leaf.*
260–260v (939);
MS G 10–10v ca. 1510
894. *On Dark Leaves in Front of Transparent Ones.*
260v (927); MS G 10v ca. 1510
Cf. Lu 738.
895. *On Young Trees and Their Leaves.*
260v (976); MS G 8 ca. 1510
896. *On the Color of Leaves.*
260v–261 (926); MS G 8v ca. 1510
897. *On Trees That Send Forth Straight Branches.*
261 (913); MS G 9 ca. 1510
898. *On the Shadows of Trees.*
261–261v (921); MS G 22 ca. 1510
899. *On Trees in the East.*
261v (923); MS G 21v ca. 1510
900. *On Trees in the East.*
261v (924); MS G 22v ca. 1510
901. *On the Shadows of Trees in the East.*
261v–262 (925); MS G 21 ca. 1510
902. *On Plants in the South.*
262 (920); MS G 20v ca. 1510
903. *On Meadows.*
262 (943); MS G 20v ca. 1510
904. *On the Grass of Meadows.*
262 (945); MS G 9v ca. 1510
905. *On the Shadow of Foliage.*
262 (980); MS G 15 ca. 1510
906. *On Landscape in Painting.*
262–262v (968) 1508–10
907. *Why the Shadow of Leafy Branches Does Not Appear as Strong in Their*

Luminous Parts as in the Parts Opposite.

                    262v (962)   1508–10

908. *Which Part of the Branch of the Tree Will Be More Shaded?*

                    262v (915)   1508–10

909. *How Trees Are Seen.*

          262v–263 (971)   1510–15

Horizon. Cf. Lu 857 and 862.

910. *Painting of the Mist Which Covers the Landscape.*

          263–263v (966)   1510–15

Cf. Lu 446, 457, and 465.

911. *On Landscape.*

                    263v (961)   1510–15

Blue of air. A date 1506–1508 is also probable. Cf. Lu 490 (*Libro A 1*). See also MS F 48v.

912. *On Landscapes in the Mist at Sunrise or at Sunset.*

          263v–264 (967);

                    Libro A 41   1508–10

This and the two preceding texts are not related to plants.

913. *On Trees Seen from Below.*

     264–264v (932); MS G 6   *ca.* 1510

914. *Description of the Elm.*

          264v–265 (901);

                    MS G 27–27v   *ca.* 1510

915. *On the Leaves of the Walnut.*

     265 (902); MS G 28   *ca.* 1510

916. *On the Aspects of Landscapes.*

     265v (931); MS G 21   *ca.* 1510

917. *On the Openings through Trees.*

     265v (963); MS G 25v   *ca.* 1510

918. *On Trees Which Cover the Interstices One of Another.*

     265v–266 (964, 934);

                    MS G 25   *ca.* 1510

McM 934, which corresponds to Lu 918a, is not found in MS G. Like the other texts up to the end of Part Six, it is written in different ink. Perhaps it was added later, together with the others, on folios that had been left blank. The title of the following text, "Precepts for Plants and Foliage," is written in the narrow space between the lines, but it should come before Lu 918a because it refers to a group of notes (918a, 919, 919a) that were probably found after a more accurate search.

919. *Precepts for Plants and Foliage.*

          266–266v–267

                    (946, 947)   1508–15

Lu 919a corresponds to McM 947. See the comment on the preceding text. For the texts on the effect of wind on leaves, see C.A. 1610 r-b, 1513–1514.

920. *On Mixing the Color for the Underpainting for Depicting Trees.*

                    267 (979)   1508–10

The trees in the backgrounds of the "Adoration of the Magi" and "St. Anne" appear to be depicted according to the instructions given in this chapter.

921. *Precept.*

          267–267v (903)   1508–10

Subject of the branching of trees.

922. *Precept on Trees.*

                    267v (905)   1508–10

923. *On Grass.*

                    267v (944)   1508–10

Cf. Lu 903 and 904 (MS G).

924. *On Foliage.*

     267v–268 (972, 942)   1508–10

Lu 924a corresponds to McM 942.

925. *Precept, for Imitating the Color of Leaves.*

                    268 (981)   1508–10

Process analogous to that suggested for portraying mountains. Cf. Lu 479 and 819.

Folios 268v–274v are blank.

PART SEVEN

ON CLOUDS

926. *On Clouds.*

     275 (989)   1510–15

927. *On the Redness of Clouds.*

     275–275v (991)   1510–15

928. *On the Creation of Clouds.*
275v–276 (987)   1510–15
Cf. C.A. 279 r-b, *ca.* 1515.

929. *On Clouds and Their Heaviness and Lightness.*
276 (988)   1510–15

930. *Why Clouds Are Made of Mist.*
276 (990)   1510–15

931. *On Air All Cloudy.*
276v (995)   1510–15
Cf. Lu 677.

932. *On the Shadows of Clouds.*
276v (994, 992)   1510–15
Lu 932a corresponds to McM 992.

933. *On Clouds.*
276v (996)   1510–15
Lights and shadows of trees under the universal light of a cloudy sky.

934. *On Clouds beneath the Moon.*
276v–277 (997)   1510–15

935. *On Clouds.*
277 (993)   1510–15
Cf. Lu 932a.
Some of these chapters on clouds might date from Leonardo's French period, *ca.* 1517–1518. Cf. Windsor 12,391, now identified as Leonardo's latest drawing (1518). See above, pp. 157–158.
Folios 277v–282v are blank.

PART EIGHT

ON THE HORIZON

936. *What Is the True Location of the Horizon?*
283–283v–284 (998)   1515–18
Paragraph 936c contains a description of the horizon of the sea shore of Egypt.
All these chapters on the horizon are probably from Leonardo's French period, *ca.* 1517–1518. Cf. C.A. 76 v-a (plate 29) and Codex Arundel 188v, which is related to C.A. 249 r-b, the folio dated 24 June 1518.

937. *On the Horizon.*
284 (999)   1515–18

938. *On the True Horizon.*
284–284v (1000)   1515–18

939. *On the Horizon.*
284v–285
(1005, 1004, 1002)   1515–18
Lu 939a and 939b correspond to McM 1004 and 1002.

940. *On the Horizon.*
285 (1001)   1515–18

941. *A Man Standing with His Feet at the Level of the Sea, Sees the Horizon Lower than Eye-Level.*
285–285v (1003)   1515–18

942. *On the Horizon Reflected in Running Water.*
285v (1006)   1515–18
Quotation of the sixth proposition of the Book on Perspective.

943. *Where the Horizon Is Reflected on the Wave.*
285v–286 (1007)   1515–18

944. *Why the Dense Air Near the Horizon Becomes Red.*
286 (1008)   1515–18
Rainbow. Cf MS E, verso of the first cover; Brizio (1952), p. 591. See also Lu 190.
Folios 286v–300v are blank.

Carusi, Pierantoni, and McMahon have already worked out concordances indicating the sources of the chapters in the Codex Urbinas 1270. Up to now no one has attempted what we may call a "reverse concordance," which will enable one to locate a given passage from one of Leonardo's original notebooks in the Codex Urbinas. The usefulness of such a concordance is evident: it helps us to recognize at a glance the sources not listed in the concordances of Carusi, Pierantoni, and McMahon. As an example, with these passages at hand we were able to identify the originals of ten chapters of the *Trattato della Pittura*. Such a concordance also helps to familiarize us with Melzi's method of gathering Leonardo's notes on painting. Some of the notes marked by Melzi with a small circle, crossed out or not, were not transcribed in the Codex Urbinas, probably from simple forgetfulness.[1] However, it is possible that their exclusion was deliberate, particularly if similar material had already been copied from elsewhere.

---

1. See for instance MS E 18. The text of Lu 245 should have been completed with another which follows it in the original. The transcriber omitted a section of the chapter, as a marginal note by Manus 3 points out: "Another chapter follows this one in folio 18 in *Libro B*."

MS A contains a number of notes that are countersigned with Melzi's circle (slashed or not) but have not been transcribed in the Codex Urbinas. In the following list of the folios of MS A containing such notes Melzi's countersigns are given between brackets: 2r, note on light and shade [o]; 3v, note on light and shade [o]; 62v, note on proportion [o] (another note and two figures on the proportion of the horse's head are copied in Codex Huygens 75r); 63r, eight notes on proportion [ø]; 85r (Ash. 5r), three notes on light and shade [.]; 84r (Ash. 4r), note on light and shade [*nota*]; 89v (Ash. 9v), note on the movement of arm and shoulder [ø], and note on light and shade [o]; 92v (Ash. 12v), note on the eye and vision [o]; 93r (Ash. 13r), note on aerial perspective [o]; 96v (Ash. 16v), note on the effect of relief [*nota*]; 97v (Ash. 17v), note on the *istoria* [ø]; 98r (Ash. 18r), note on *decorum* and perspective [*nota*]; 102v (Ash. 22v), note on the movement and posture of man and animals [ø].

A few notes on painting in MS G, which are not countersigned in any way, might have been omitted on purpose because their subject was developed elsewhere. Curiously enough, Melzi's slashed circle is found next to a well-known allegorical sentence and figure on folio 89r of this manuscript: "One pushes down another: by these bricks [*quadrelli*] are represented the life and conditions of mankind." Melzi might have considered the word "quadrelli" as implying "pictures." (According to Baldinucci [1631], p. 93, "*quadrello*, ouuero mattone, è una tavola ad angolo retto," which indicates an architectural member, the plinth.) Melzi must have realized that the passage has really nothing to do with painting and therefore he did not copy it in the Codex Urbinas.

The Ludwig chapters are listed according to their sequence in the folios of the corresponding Leonardo manuscript. The asterisks distinguish the concordances not given by Carusi, Pierantoni, or McMahon.

MS A, *ca.* 1492

Manuscript A; Bibliothèque de l'Institut de France, Paris. Originally of 114 folios. A section of 50 folios, which was stolen in the last century, constituted the original Codex Ashburnham 2038, sixteen folios of which are lost. A few notes on painting in two of the lost folios, 67 and 79, are known from G. B. Venturi's transcriptions. Two other notes on painting, on unspecified folios of the missing section, are preserved in copies in MS H 227 inf. in the Ambrosian Library, Milan. After folio 80 the folio numbers of MS Ashburnham 2038 are indicated in parentheses. The original mark on the cover has disappeared.

MS A: 21 x 14 cm.; MS Ash.: 23 x 16.5 cm.

MS A *folio*	Ludwig	MS A *folio*	Ludwig
1	100,101	99–99v (19–19v)	19
1v	102	100 (20)	785,12,293,294
23	103,104,105	100v (20v)	138,458,646,459,295
28v	88	101 (21)	147,380
29	175	101v (21v)	759,760,548,753
38v	437	102 (22)	549,616
43	512	102v (22v)	66,511,261
[65–80]	547*,662*	103 (23)	461,174, 31,761
[67]	555*	104 (24)	72, 90, 97
[79]	258a*,534*,540*	104v (24v)	408
81 (1)	124	105 (25)	74
82 (2)	56	105–104v (25–24v)	38
84 (4)	537	105v (25v)	262, 73
88v (8v)	64	106 (26)	67, 75, 76,492*
89v (9v)	555a	106v (26v)	290, 69, 71
90 (10)	700, 63, 89, 96,118	107 (27)	98, 99,106,137
90v (10v)	725a,725	107v (27v)	173, 70
91 (11)	726–727	107v–107 (27v–27)	50
93 (13)	509	108 (28)	407, 49
93v (13v)	728,729	108v (28v)	383,265,266,758
94 (14)	730	109 (29)	362,421, 84
94v (14v)	134,135,156,157,117	109v (29v)	367,381,382,319,615
95 (15)	731	110 (30)	320,611,612,613,614
95v (15v)	732,733	111 (31)	416
96 (16)	119	111–110v (31–30v)	148
96v (16v)	667	111v (31v)	417,418, 83,419,420
97v (17v)	47,129,130,538,143, 144,145,142	112 (32)[2]	744,745,746
		112v (32v)	209,415,747
98 (18)	208,539,149	113 (33)	414, 82, 85,210
98v (18v)	150,717,146	113v (33)v	668,711,712
99 (19)	493		

2. In the edition of the Commissione Vinciana folios 112 and 113 are transposed.

MS E, 1513–1514

Manuscript E; Bibliothèque de l'Institut de France, Paris. Notebook of 80 folios, originally 96. A stolen section of 16 folios is lost. Eleventh on Melzi's list of the Codex Urbinas sources, as *Libro B*.

15.4 x 9.6 cm.

MS E folio	Ludwig	MS E folio	Ludwig
3	669	19v–20	125
3v	464,465*	20	126
4	246	30v	592,593
6v	375,502,830	31	594,595,596
15	316 [3]	31v	776,777,778
17	84a,472	32	590
18	245	32v	550,551,553c–e,
18v	867*,868		790*
19	800,889	79v	136

3. The last two lines were copied from another manuscript.

MS F, 1508

Manuscript F; Bibliothèque de l'Institut de France, Paris. Notebook of 96 folios. Eighth on Melzi's list of the Codex Urbinas sources. Original mark: a square with diagonals, ⊠.

14.5 x 10 cm.

Melzi copied only the note on folio 75 (Lu 247).

MS G, 1510–1515

Manuscript G; Bibliothèque de l'Institut de France, Paris. Notebook of 93 folios, originally 96. Thirteenth on Melzi's list of the Codex Urbinas sources. Original mark: Φ.

14 x 19.5 cm.

MS G folio	Ludwig	MS G folio	Ludwig
3v	663	21	916,901
3v–4	891	21v	899
4v–5	892	22	898
5v	78, 79	22v	900,515
6	913	23	516
8	80,895	23v	482
8v	896	24	886,887
9	897	25	51, 52
9v	904,885	25v	917,918
10–10v	893	26	335

MS G folio	Ludwig	MS G folio	Ludwig
10v	894	26v	888
11v	651,870	27–27v	914
12	869	28	915
12v	670	28v	872,873,874
15	871,905,789	30v–32v	832
16v	831	32	488
19	483	33	833,834
19v	788, 91	53v	489
20v	902,903		

MS L, 1497–1502

Manuscript L; Bibliothèque de l'Institut de France, Paris. Notebook of 94 folios. Probably one of the three "librettini" mentioned at the end of Melzi's list of the Codex Urbinas sources. The original mark has disappeared.

10.1 x 7.5 cm.

Melzi copied only two notes, from folios 75v and 79 (Lu 244 and 340).

CODEX TRIVULZIANUS, 1487–1490

Codex Trivulzianus; Castello Sforzesco, Milan. Manuscript of 51 folios, original number of folios unknown. Ninth on Melzi's list of the Codex Urbinas sources, and the fifth item of the Arconati donation. Original mark on the cover: F.

21 x 14 cm.

Melzi copied only two notes, from folios 38v and 39 (Lu 496 and 258b).

WINDSOR 12,604, 1487–1490

Windsor 12,604; 20.3 x 14.3 cm. Surviving page of a lost manuscript. Texts marked with Melzi circles. Copied in Lu 744.

APPENDIXES

APPENDIX I

The Original Marks of Leonardo's Manuscripts
(PLATES 2 and 3)

AT THE END of the Codex Urbinas, Francesco Melzi listed the Leonardo manuscripts used in his compilation (although nothing was extracted from MS C, the fourth source listed), indicating them with marks that are still found in some of the surviving codices. On the basis of this inventory, from which codices without notes on painting were excluded, we find that twelve manuscripts by Leonardo have been lost.

Manuscript A in the Bibliothèque de l'Institut de France, Paris, was certainly one of the eighteen books listed by Melzi, for it contains many notes transcribed in the Codex Urbinas; but unfortunately no mark or note by Melzi is clearly visible on its vellum binding. However, since this binding is the original, it must have had a collation note, which might have been: "Le carte sono di n⁰ giusto .114. cioè cento quattordici" (The folios are of correct number, 114, that is one hundred and fourteen), followed by the manuscript's code mark. This type of note is found in all the other manuscripts in the Institut de France which were used by Melzi (see plate 16). The collation note of MS A was on the back cover, that is, at the beginning of the manuscript, considering Leonardo's habit of beginning his notebooks at the end. In fact, there is an area in the upper part close to the stamp of the library in which a vague impression of Melzi's note is still visible, but unfortunately the original mark cannot be identified with certainty, although some trace is left of what might have been the mark A et Z. It would be worthwhile to ascertain this in order to prove that MS A was the second on Melzi's list and not the first listed as "libro intero segnato i" (A Complete Book on Painting marked i). This "libro intero" could have been a compilation made by Leonardo himself after 1500, including a final version of the "Paragone."

i

I. *Lost.* Perhaps identifiable with the Codex Sforza, *ca.* 1495–1498, mentioned by Luca Pacioli (1498) and by Lomazzo (1584). Probable contents: comparison of the arts, human motion. Similar to MS A & Ashburnham. It could be also a compilation made by Leonardo after 1500.

II. *Lost.* It might be the present MS A & Ashburnham. The original mark of MS A has disappeared.

III. *Lost.*

IV. *Book on Light and Shade,* that is, MS C in the Bibliothèque de l'Institut de France, Paris. Manuscript of 29 folios; 31 x 22 cm.; *ca.* 1490. Although not used by Melzi, the mark corresponds. The page numbers are written by Melzi. The binding is not original, but Melzi's mark, G, is found on folios 2 and 29. Folio 29 also contains Melzi's note: "Le carte sono di nᵒ 28 cioè Ventiotto."

V. *Lost.* Another *Book on Light and Shade.* Perhaps later than the preceding, 1508–1515. It probably contained the treatise *De Ombra e Lume,* which Melzi used for the fifth part of the Codex Urbinas. Codex Atlanticus folios 236 and 241 are probably drafts for this book.

VI. *Lost.*

VII. *Lost.*

VIII. MS F in the Bibliothèque de l'Institute de France, Paris. Notebook of 96 folios; 14.5 x 10 cm.; 1508. Hydraulics, painting, flight of birds, mechanics. (See plate 30.)

IX. Codex Trivulzianus, Castello Sforzesco, Milan. Manuscript of 51 folios; 21 x 14 cm.; 1487–1490. Studies on grammar and other subjects, such as architecture, light, and caricatures. Melzi's mark, *F,* is on the cover, together with its number 5, in the deeds of the Arconati donation. Melzi transcribed in the Codex Urbinas the notes on painting in folios 38v and 39. In Melzi's list the letter *F* is crossed out and corrected to A. For *Libro* A see no. XIV below.

X. *Lost.*

XI. MS E in the Bibliothèque de l'Institut de France, Paris. Notebook of 80 folios, originally 96; 15.4 x 9.6 cm.; 1513–1514. Hydraulics, painting, mechanics, flight of birds. (See plate 31.)

XII. *Lost.*

XIII. MS G in the Bibliothèque de l'Institut de France, Paris. Notebook of 93 folios, originally 96; 14 x 9.5 cm.; 1510–1515 (notes on painting, *ca.* 1510). Painting, hydraulics, mechanics.

XIV. *Lost. Libro* A reconstructed in part from the notes on painting copied by Melzi in the Codex Urbinas and from notes on hydraulics copied by Leonardo himself in the Codex Leicester. Format, contents, and date similar to those of MSS E, F, and G, 1508–1515.

XV. *Lost.*

XVI–
XVIII. Three *Librettini*, that is, pocket notebooks, one of which is still extant. MS L, in the Bibliothèque de l'Institut de France, was certainly indicated with one of the marks, but its mark has disappeared; it was on the sheathing paper of the cover, which has been torn in part. However, MS L can be tentatively identified with the *librettino* marked Y, because that mark is found on folio 79r, the page containing one of the two notes copied by Melzi. Folio 75v contains the other note on painting transcribed in the Codex Urbinas. MS L is a notebook of 94 folios; 10.1 x 7.5 cm.; 1497–1502. Military architecture, flight of birds, painting. It is the notebook Leonardo used during his activity as a military architect in the service of Cesare Borgia.

THE "O S X Q" MARKS

It is well known that modern studies on Leonardo began with the researches of Baldassarre Oltrocchi (1714–1797), librarian of the Ambrosiana in the second half of the eighteenth century. His researches, which were not published until 1925, were used by his successor Carlo Amoretti for the compilation of the *Memorie storiche* which appeared as an introduction to the 1804 edition of Leonardo's *Treatise on Painting*. Up to that time, references to the Leonardo MSS were given according to so complicated a system that G. B. Venturi found it necessary, in 1797, to introduce the more practical system of marks A to M, and N for the Codex Atlanticus (Oltrocchi was the first to designate the Leoni volume as "Codice Atlantico"; *see* Ritter [1925], pp. 56, 69). The marks used by Oltrocchi and Amoretti were probably intended to classify the Ambrosiana MSS in four groups (O, S, X, Q) according to their format, thus:

O = MSS of *ca.* 30 x 22 cm. MS C [O]

S = MSS of *ca.* 22 x 15 cm. {
MS D [S]
MS B [Sa]
MS A [Sb]
}

X = MSS of *ca.* 15 x 10 cm. {
MS G [Xa]
MS F [Xb]
MS E [Xc]
}

Q = MSS of *ca.* 10 x 7 cm. {
MS M [Q]
MS H [Qa]
MS I [Qb]
MS L [Qc]
}

Ravaisson-Mollien and others attribute these marks to Oltrocchi himself. But they must date from an earlier period, soon after the MSS entered the Ambrosian Library, and certainly before Arconati's death in 1648. In fact the mark S is found also in the Codex Trivulzianus, the MS that Arconati gave to the Ambrosiana in 1637 and which he later exchanged for MS D. In 1674, when MS K entered the Ambrosian Library as a gift of Count Archinti, the "O S X Q" marks were already on the other MSS. In fact, MS K does not have the Q mark. And since the Arconati deeds of donation indicate only the Melzi marks and notes of collation, the "O S X Q" marks must have been added between 1637 and 1648, probably by the authors of the Leonardo treatises compiled at the request of Cardinal Barberini, that is, the *Del moto e misura dell'acqua* and the MSS H 227 inf. and H 229 inf.

Neither Oltrocchi nor Amoretti use the "O S X Q" marks consistently in their citations. Sometimes they might refer to MS E as the codex marked B (the Melzi *Libro B*), and not as codex Xc. Moreover, they might refer to MS F as codex X or Xb, and to MS B as codex S instead of Sa. (In the MSS the letter of classification appears first on the flyleaf and then on the first folio with the sub-letter designating the MS proper—obviously Oltrocchi and Amoretti were referring only to the letter of classification.) Because of a mistaken reading of the *c* in the mark Qc, Oltrocchi and Amoretti refer to MS L as codex Qr or QR. Similarly, they misread the mark on MS I (Qb) as Q_s.

The Ambrosiana MSS, now at Paris, also bear earlier marks and indications of the number of folios of each of their parts, usually a double letter followed by a number; for example, NN 48 (MS H 142v), SS 32 (MS K 80v), LL 48 (MS K 128v). We cannot determine whether or not these marks were made while the MSS were still in Melzi's possession. Marks by the same hand appear also in the similar notebooks known today as Codices Forster; for example, BB 14 (Forster I, 54v), and KK 62 (Forster II, 1r).

APPENDIX II

Signatures and Foliations of the Codex Urbinas 1270 *

B denotes Blank; *r*, recto; *v*, verso; *Br*, only *the recto is blank*;
Bv, only the verso is blank; *a, b, c*, etc., folios not numbered

No. of signature	Folios	Diagrams and Notes
1st	1– 8	1r, PARTE PRIMA
2d	9–16	
3d	17–24	
4th	25–30	

27 ⎯⎯⎯⎯⎯⎯⎯⎯⎯⎯⎯ 28
26 ⎯⎯⎯⎯⎯⎯⎯⎯⎯⎯⎯ 29B
25 ⎯⎯⎯⎯⎯⎯⎯⎯⎯⎯⎯ 30B

30v, catchword: *Quello*

31r, PARTE SECONDA

5th	31–38	
6th	39–46	
7th	47–54	
8th	55–62	
9th	63–70	
10th	71–78	
11th	79–86	

78v, catchword: *Meltivs*

82B ⎯⎯⎯⎯⎯⎯⎯⎯⎯⎯⎯ 83B
81B ⎯⎯⎯⎯⎯⎯⎯⎯⎯⎯⎯ 84B
80B ⎯⎯⎯⎯⎯⎯⎯⎯⎯⎯⎯ 85
79B ⎯⎯⎯⎯⎯⎯⎯⎯⎯⎯⎯ 86B

79r, catchword: *Meltivs*
86v, catchword: *Mel*

[12th	87–102]	*Missing*
13th	103–110	103r, PARTE TERZA
14th	111–118	
15th	119–126	
16th	127–134	
17th	135–142	
18th	143–150	
19th	151–158	
20th	159–166	

162 ⎯⎯⎯⎯⎯⎯⎯⎯⎯⎯⎯ 163
161 ⎯⎯⎯⎯⎯⎯⎯⎯⎯⎯⎯ 164Bv
160 ⎯⎯⎯⎯⎯⎯⎯⎯⎯⎯⎯ 165B
159 ⎯⎯⎯⎯⎯⎯⎯⎯⎯⎯⎯ 166B

* The composition of each signature has been checked against the original manuscript.

No. of signature	Folios	Diagrams and Notes
21st	167–174	167r, PARTE QUARTA

170 ───────────────── 171^{Bv}
169 ───────────────── 172^{B}
168 ───────────────── 173^{B}
167 ───────────────── 174^{B}

22d	175–182	175r, PARTE QUINTA
23d	183–190	
24th	191–198	
25th	199–206	
26th	207–214	
27th	215–222	
28th	223–230	
29th	231–238	
30th	239–242-d	

242^{B} ───────────────── 242-a^{B}
241 ───────────────── 242-b^{B}
240 ───────────────── 242-c^{B}
239 ───────────────── 242-d^{B}

31st	243–250	243r, PARTE SESTA
32d	251–258	
33d	259–266	
34th	267–274	

270^{B} ───────────────── 271^{B}
269^{B} ───────────────── 272^{B}
268^{Bv} ───────────────── 273^{B}
267 ───────────────── 274^{B}

| 35th | 275–282 | 275r, PARTE SETTIMA |

278^{B} ───────────────── 279^{B}
277^{Bv} ───────────────── 280^{B}
276 ───────────────── 281^{B}
275 ───────────────── 282^{B}

| 36th | 283–290 | 283r, PARTE OTTAVA |

286^{Bv} ───────────────── 287^{B}
285 ───────────────── 288^{B}
284 ───────────────── 289^{B}
283 ───────────────── 290^{B}

| 37th | 291–298 | |

294^{B} ───────────────── 295^{B}
293^{B} ───────────────── 296^{B}
292^{B} ───────────────── 297^{B}
291^{B} ───────────────── 298^{B}

| 38th | 299–306 | 301r, TABLE OF CONTENTS |

302^{Bv} ───────────────── 303
301 ───────────────── 304
300^{B} ───────────────── 305
299^{B} ───────────────── 306

No. of signature	Folios	Diagrams and Notes
39th	307–314	Folio 308v, blank
40th	315–322	Folios 315v, 316v, blank

41st 323–329-a

326		327*Bv*
325		328*Bv*
324		329*Bv*
323		329-a*B*

42d 331–[333]

331 *Bv*		[332]
330*Br*		[333]

330v–331: *Memoria et Notta di tutti i pezzi
de libri di mano di Leonardo.* . . . .

Folio 330 misnumbered 230
Folio 331 misnumbered 231
Folios 332–333 blank and not numbered

APPENDIX III

A List of Headings of Notes on Painting
on Folio 360 r-c of the Codex Atlanticus

(PLATE 32)

CODEX ATLANTICUS 360 r-c (plate 32, *a*) contains two columns of headings of notes on painting. The right column is headed "Della Pittura" (On Painting). Pierantoni (1921), page 90, refers to this page as a possible Index of a "Book on Painting" planned by Leonardo. The handwriting, however, is not Leonardo's, although many of the entries are related to problems in manuscripts of Leonardo's late period, including *Libro* A. This list, therefore, can be dated within the second Milanese period of Leonardo's activity, 1506–1513. Its date can be focused around 1508 because the same handwriting appears in Codex Atlanticus 207 v-a, the folio containing a topographical sketch of the area of the "Neron da Sancto Andrea" in Milan, *ca.* 1508, as well as a sketch of the phyllotaxy of plants (see plate 29, *a*) which is related to the notes on painting in MS G.

The notes on folio 207 v-a (plate 32, *b*) concern a problem of geometry which Leonardo develops in the same folio. Whereas the lists of folio 360 r-c are transcribed in the edition of the Codex Atlanticus as being in Leonardo's handwriting, the notes on folio 207 v-b are not transcribed, thus implying they are not Leonardo's.*

There is no way to identify the author of these notes. It was certainly someone close to Leonardo, but this handwriting is not Melzi's. It has none of the early sixteenth-century characteristics of Melzi's handwriting, being noticeably fifteenth

---

* The Italian text reads as follows: "Se sarono doa super*fice* curue / sopraposta luna a laltra / E che luna non exceda / Ne sia exceduta da laltra / sanza dubio excessarano Jneq^{a}le / Prouassi cosi / A bi ci sia la separatione della pr*edetta* / super*fice* N sia in centro / Dun semi circulo." "Il moto composto fatto Dala Integrale reuolu/tione del Chillindro sopra il sito / dela Equalita Deskriue vno q^{a}dri-/lattero Equale ala spolia dela sua / (*superficia*) grossezza." Owing to the missing diagram the first note cannot be explained. However, the notes can be rendered in English as follows: "If two surfaces with curved sides are placed one above the other and one does not exceed the other nor be it exceeded by the other, no doubt they will not be equal [?]. Let us prove it: A B C be the line separating one surface from the other; N be the center of a semicircle." "A cylinder that makes a complete turn over a plane describes a quadrangle equal to the area around that cylinder."

century in style. The author was probably a Milanese who was in contact with Leonardo in the years after 1506. In the first note on folio 207 v-a the word "exceda" is Lombard in spelling. The style of handwriting suggests that the author was probably an aged person in 1506. Giovan Ambrogio de Predis is the only Milanese painter who was closely associated with Leonardo both before and after 1500: the first time in 1483 working on the altarpiece of the "Virgin of the Rocks" for the Confraternity of St. Francesco Grande in Milan, and again after 1506 assisting Leonardo in the replica of that painting. Ambrogio's brother, Evangelista, who was also an assistant of Leonardo's in 1483, died in the 1490's. Ambrogio de Predis must have had an intimate knowledge of Leonardo's theory of art, since he was able to follow the Master's profound change of style in the London replica of the "Virgin of the Rocks." †

A comparison of the handwriting of Codex Atlanticus 360 r-c with that of the signature "Johanes Ambrosius de predis" in the contract of 1483 for the "Virgin

The signature of Ambrogio de Predis (*traced by author*) in the contract for the "Virgin of the Rocks," 1483. Archivo di Stato, Milan.

of the Rocks" appears quite convincing. Unfortunately no facsimile of later writings of Ambrogio is available.‡

---

† After the discussion by G. Castelfranco (*Raccolta Vinciana*, XVIII, 185–187) there is no reason to believe, as a few scholars still do, that Leonardo painted the London replica for the contract of 1483, and that the Louvre version was done during Leonardo's first Florentine period, before 1482. As Castelfranco points out, the London replica is in the style of Leonardo's works dating from his second Milanese period. And we may add that the theories on light and shadow and on color in *Libro* A seem to find their application in the London painting.

‡ In Codex Arundel 100–105 there are notes on light and shade written by a hand which varies in style and speed. There are instances in which this hand shows a remarkable similarity with that of the list in Codex Atlanticus 360 r-c (cf. especially folios 101r and 103r), although these notes are obviously drafts. They must have been copied elsewhere because almost all of them are crossed out. Folio 103v shows that Leonardo himself crossed them out, including his own remark which he had inserted after the second note: "di dello spiracholo tondo e lume lungo [come] la percussione fia lunga" (tell about the round hole and the long upright light, and how the cast of the shadow will be long extended). This and other notes by Leonardo in this group of folios serve to date the notes of his unknown pupil and assistant as *ca.* 1490–1495. This pupil must be a Lombard as he uses Lombard spelling (*vnbroxo* and *luminoxi* for *ombroso* and *luminosi*). These notes as well as those in Codex Atlanticus 360 r-c might have been written by Ambrogio de Predis or by G. A. Boltraffio (1467–1516). Boltraffio entered Leonardo's studio in the early 1490's and was again with Leonardo in 1510 (cf. MS G *cover*: "addj 26 di settembre Antonio si ruppe la gamba à a stare 40 di," and Windsor 19,092: "vedi il tornio del Beltraffio e falli trarre una pietra"). However, no positive identification is possible because no example of Boltraffio's handwriting is known to us.

The following transcription of Codex Atlanticus 360 r-c is complemented with an interpretation of the fragmentary lines. Comparisons with notes in Leonardo's extant manuscripts and in the Codex Urbinas are suggested, along with an English translation of the text.

CODEX ATLANTICUS 360 R-C ʃ

ʃ I have numbered the entries for convenience of reference.

[FIRST COLUMN, RIGHT]
dellappittura

[1] Dello[m]bre doue debbono essere schure doue lo[m]bre debbon / essere mezzane e elumji doue debbono (e) essere chiari

[2] Doue sono piu scurj. doue debbono essere e barlumj e rifre/ssi cioe lumj.ripercossj inulluogo.e risaltatj inuna/ltro.

[3] Chome.elumj.debbono esser fattj aritrarre chose / djnaturale

[4] Chome le figure.naturalj avēdo grā lume daunlato / pare che dallopposita parte sia lōbra scurissima

[5] Chome gliuominj mostrano pocha uariata da lumj / alombra q̄n e turbata laria o q̄n e insultramōt[a]/re del sole.

[6] Per che chagione lechose che sidischostono dallocchio . sisscho/rgono male . e paiono . abagliate . e enellultima / distanzia .paiono.azurre (p)

[7] Perche le chose dipinte.paiono.maggiorj che nōsono

[SECOND COLUMN, LEFT]

[8] Chome.eperche molte chose specchiate . vegono alocchio sozopra

[9] perche alchuna chosa . specchiata . pare magiore che nō e.

[10] perche specchīado.alchuna cosa.aparisce minore. (q)

On Painting

[1] Of the shadows, where they should be darker and less dark; and of lights, where they should be bright.

[2] Where [lights] should be less bright. Where to find glimmerings and reflections, that is, lights which fall on one place and reflect to another.

[3] How light should be arranged in portraying from Nature.

[4] How figures which are lighted strongly on one side appear to have a very dark shadow on the opposite side.

[5] How men do not appear with sharp lights and shadows when the sky is cloudy or at sunset.

[6] For what reason things which are removed from the eye become blurred and at the greatest distance become azure.

[7] Why painted things appear bigger than they actually are.

[8] How and why many things reflected [from water] come into the eye upside down.

[9] Why some of the things which are reflected [from water] appear greater than they actually are.

[10] Why some of the things which are reflected [from water] appear smaller than they actually are.

1. Cf. Lu 631–635, 648, 657 (Libro A 42), 658 (Libro A 42), 659 (Libro A 43), 685–686, 813–814.
2. Cf. Lu 170 (Libro A 39), 171 (Libro A 42), 172 (Libro A 49).
3. Cf. Lu 85–86, 87 (Libro A 37), 93, 95 (Libro A 38). See also Lu 414 (MS Ash. 33).

4. Cf. Lu 652 (Libro A 12).
5. Cf. Lu 487 (Libro A 27).
6. Cf. Lu 427 (Libro A 37), 428 (Libro A 38), 455, 473–474.
7. Cf. Lu 432 (Libro A 39).
8–12. Cf. Lu 506–507. See also Codex Arundel 93v (Richter [1883], I, 207).

[11] Quale specchio.equello che mostra lechose apunto

[12] Quale.specchio.lemostra fuorj de se

[13] Chome lo specchio.emaestro de pittorj

[14] Perche locchio.va variādo.hora.per hora. .cresciēdo / escemādo.

[15] Perche lapupilla.qūto [= quanto] maggior lume.a dinazi asse / minore. diueta .echosi. per lopposito . cresce . albuio

[16] Perche lcchose. vedute dallocchio . peruenēdo.drēto allocchio / sono. picchole. epaiono.grādj.

[17] Perche vna.chosa veduta.perunfesso. chō duocchj diuēta / doppia. echōtraria.cioe. lacosa.ueduta.dallato ritto / ne ua.allocchio. mācho.echosj.quella.delmācho va / arritto

[18] Perche.essēdo.vno.edifizio.trallanebbia.pare maggiore

[19] Perche locchio. ̄no uede perfecto. senō per linea retta

[20] Perche le linie piramidate . che sipartono . dagliocchj . fāno / pūto nella chosa vcduta.

[21] Perche detta piramida . partēdosj. dagliocchj efaccēdo./ pūto.auna chosa.posta nellaquu. le linie sitorcono / gugnēdo . alla qua enō hosseruano , loro dirittura

[11] What mirror is that which shows things as they are.

[12] What mirror shows them outside itself.

[13] How the mirror is the painter's teacher.

[14] Why the eye changes from one hour to the other, that is, enlarges and diminishes in size.

[15] Why the pupil [of the eye] decreases in size as the light to which it is exposed increases, and why, conversely, it increases in the dark.

[16] Why things seen by the eye, when transmitted into the eye are small and yet they appear large.

[17] Why a thing seen through a hole by two eyes becomes double and reversed, that is, the right side goes to the left eye and the left side goes to the right eye.

[18] Why an edifice in the mist appears greater than it is.

[19] Why the eye sees things in their proper form only along a central straight line.

[20] Why visual pyramids have their bases in the eyes and their apexes in the things observed.

[21] Why, when the said pyramid is carried from the eyes to a thing submerged in water, its lines bend in entering the surface of the water and change their course.

13. Cf. Lu 408 (MS Ash. 24v), and 410.
14. Cf. MS E (*Libro B*) 17v (Richter [1883], I, 24). See also MS I, 41v, Codex Forster II₂ 158v, and MS I₁ 20r (Richter [1883], I, 35–38).
15. Cf. MS D 5r and *passim*. In Lu 202 Leonardo refers to his explanation of this phenomenon as being given in his "second book on perspective."
16. MS D, *passim*.
17. MS D 9r.
18. Cf. Codex Atlanticus 126 r-b (Brizio [1952], p. 408) and 130 v-b (MacCurdy:I. 304). See also Lu 449, 462–463.
19. "Linea retta" has been translated "central straight line" in accordance with the explanation given by Leonardo in Windsor 19,148v (Richter [1883], I, 130): "I say that the eye projects an infinite number of lines which mingle or join those reaching it

which come to it from the object looked at. And it is only the central line from this sense-organ that can discern and discriminate colours and objects; all the others are free and illusory. . . . Light acts in the same manner, for in the effects of its lines (= rays), and particularly in perspective, it much resembles the eye." Cf. Codex Atlanticus 204v (Richter [1883], I, 72): "In the practice of perspective the same rules apply to light and to the eye." See also MS D 8v (Richter, I, 79A): "At the centre terminates the median line which is constantly being turned on those objects where a distinct and true perception of shapes is required. This line is straight and without intersection."
20–23. Cf. MS G 53v (Richter [1883], I, 89). See also MS D 5 v-r (Brizio [1952], p. 399).

[22] [Ch]ome le chose vedute fanno pira-mida . nellocchio . solo

[23] [E ch]ome . e dua . occhj faño pir-ramida . nellachosa ueduta

[24] [Qu]alchosa . gliocchj possono uedere piu che mezza

[25] [Qu]alchosa . gliocchj ño possono. maj vedere (*piuch*) mezza

[26] [Perche] molte linie presso luna al-laltra . ño sipossono numerare / seño tocchj linia.per linia

[27] [Perche] tagliando. vna pirramida presso allocchio tutte / [le cho]se appa-rischono picchole per grade che sieno

[28] [Perche le ch]ose vedute sono tutte torte . beche . paino / [diritte]

[29] [Come si debbe] tagliare lapirramide . atrrouare che lechose / [paiono allo]cchio torte

[30] [Come si debbe] tagliare lapirramide . equanto dischosto / [dallocchio] amettere . inpittura . lechose vedute

[31] [Quella pira]mida.che siparte dalle chose vedute.euiene / [allocchio ño] hoserua . le linie dritte qn passano per.due / [reg]ionj daria cioe grossa . esottile . e questa ragione / [contr]adicie.(*amis*) asapere lagradezza del so o dalcu/[n]altro pianeto perche ño si puo misurare trannoj / [el so per] azione daria. cioe.grossa esottile

[22] How the visual pyramid has its apex in the eye when things are seen by one eye.

[23] And how the visual pyramids have their apexes in the eye when things are seen by both eyes.

[24] What is that object of which the eyes can see more than half.

[25] What is that object of which the eyes can never see the complete half.

[26] Why several lines one close to the other cannot be counted if one does not touch one line after the other.

[27] Why, when cutting a visual pyramid close to the eye, all the things appear small regardless of how big they are.

[28] Why things seen are all curved al-though they appear straight.

[29] How the visual pyramid should be cut in order to explain why the eye sees things curved.

[30] How the visual pyramid should be cut, and how far from the eye, in order to paint the things seen.

[31] That pyramid which has the base in the things and the apex in the eye does not follow straight lines when passing through two qualities of air, that is, thick and thin air; and this is why one cannot establish the actual size of the sun or any other planet—because of the intervening atmosphere.

24–25. Cf. MS D 4r.

27. Cf. MS A 8v (Richter [1883], I, 93).

28–29. Reference to "curvilinear perspec-tive." Cf. MS E (*Libro B*) 4r (Pedretti [1963], pp. 85–86). The word "atrrouare" in item 29 can be read as well "aprouare" with no change of meaning.

30. Cf. MS E (*Libro B*) 16r (Richter [1883], I, 108). See also Pedretti (1963), pp. 77–78.

31. Cf. Lu 462 ff. See also Windsor 19,148v (Richter [1883], I, 130): ". . . be-cause the lines from the eye and the solar and other luminous rays passing through the atmosphere are obliged to travel in straight lines unless they are deflected by a denser or rarer air, when they will be bent at some point."

APPENDIX IV

Concordance: Codex Urbinas 1270–"Editio Princeps"

AN ABRIDGED VERSION of Leonardo's *Trattato della Pittura* originated from the Codex Urbinas as early as the second half of the sixteenth century. A copy of the abridged version was made by Cassiano dal Pozzo between 1630 and 1640, and was illustrated with figures by Nicola Poussin. A copy of this copy was given to Raphael Du Fresne, who published it in Paris in 1651.[1]

Sixteenth-century copies of the abridged version still exist; for example, the one owned by the painter Lanino Lanini (1512–1583), which is preserved in the Biblioteca Marciana at Venice.[2] But we do not know who made the first selection from the Codex Urbinas nor do we know why this abridgment was made. Probably the editor wished to reduce the bulk of Leonardo's chapters into a convenient handbook for painters. The criteria of selection do not provide any clues to the identity of the editor, for every painter active in that period would have made such a selection, omitting the material that had no direct bearing on the current practice of painting. Federico Zuccaro, referring to Leonardo's writings on painting, could well say that "we teachers of design do not need such rules, except those which Nature herself gives us in order to imitate her."[3] This attitude against Renaissance principles culminates in Poussin's drastic statement that "whatever might be worthy in Leonardo's *Trattato* can be written on one sheet of paper using a very large script."[4] And Abraham Bosse went even further by saying that "in order to become a real painter one should do the contrary of what Leonardo suggests in his rules."[5] Michelangelo would not have bothered to have Leonardo's writings selected; he wrote to Varchi: "As for him who wrote that painting is nobler than sculpture, if he understood the other subjects on which he wrote no better than this, my servant could have done better."[6] On the other hand, Galileo showed an

---

1. For the story and description of these apographs up to the "editio princeps" see Steinitz (1958), pp. 45 ff. (Group B).

2. *Ibid.*, B-17.   3. Zuccaro (1607), p. 134.

4. "Tout ce qu'il y a de bon en ce Livre se peut écrire sur une feuille de papier en grosse lettre." Steinitz (1958), p. 148.

5. ". . . estant certain que pour arriver à la perfection de vray Peintre, il se faut servir de regles toutes contraires à celles de ce pretendu L. de Vinci." Quoted from Steinitz (1963), p. 253.

6. I. A. Richter (1949), p. 91.

appreciation for Leonardo's *Trattato* when he said that "others have all the precepts of Leonardo da Vinci and yet they do not know how to paint a stool." [7] Guido Reni had a copy of the *Trattato* and Annibale Carracci said that if he had known of it earlier he would have been spared twenty years of labor.

The prototype of the abridged version of the *Trattato* is still unidentified, and probably is lost. However, several manuscript copies, or "apographs," still exist which date from the period prior to the "editio princeps" of 1651. One of them might be the prototype of the abridged version. An attempt to identify this prototype would require an enormous work of comparison and concordance of texts and figures, with no other result, perhaps, than that of establishing the chronological sequence of the known copies.[8] Such a result would be valuable in itself, since it would lead us to the identification of the earliest and latest copies in existence, namely, the one closest to the Codex Urbinas and the one closest to the "editio princeps." [9] It would be premature to undertake such a project at this stage, when

---

7. "Altri posseggono tutti i precetti del Vinci sulla pittura e non saprebbero poi dipingere uno sgabello" (Pedretti [1957*b*], p. 149, n. 2).

8. The sequence given by K. T. Steinitz in Group B of her 1958 Bibliography requires certain revisions. Manuscript B-1, the famous Codex Barberinus 4304, is given the first place in order of time, whereas B-2 and B-3, respectively the Ottobonianus 2984 and the Casanatense 968, have a better chance of being identified as closer to the Codex Urbinas 1270. (According to K. T. Steinitz, the Ottobianus 2984 comes from the Urbino Library, but this is an error originating from Uzielli [1884], p. 335.) Manuscripts B-6 (Codex Pinellianus D 467) and B-17 (Codex Lanino) can be decisively dated in the sixteenth century, because Pinelli died in 1601 and Lanino in 1583. Even the last of the series, B-23 (Belt 35), can claim an earlier position in the chronological sequence of these apographs. In fact, Belt 35 can be identified as the source of B-21, that is, the Codex Furini in Modena. A note in Belt 35, folio 4r, gives the ownership of the codex: "Questo Libro è di Giovanni di Simone di Francesco Berti Fiorentino et de' suoi Amici" (This Book belongs to Giovanni di Simone di Francesco Berti of Florence and to his Friends). A note dated August 2, 1632, on the first leaf of the Modena MS informs us that the painter F. Furini made his copy from that which was in the possession of Simone Berti, that is, from our Belt 35. This gives us the evidence that Belt 35 dates before 1632. Nothing is known about the Berti family, but Furini says that he had the MS (Belt 35) from Simone, who was a pupil of his, and that it was Simone's father, Giovanni, who had made the compilation that was lent to him. It is likely, therefore, that Belt 35 was made in the sixteenth century. At the end of Belt 35 is a note in which the compiler explains that some of the chapters are misnumbered because he did not want to deviate from the source he was using. Because of these errors the total number of chapters is 368. The only copies of the B-Group to have 368 chapters are B-21 (Furini), which was copied from Belt 35, and B-10 (Magliabechiano–Gaddi 373), which could be the source of Belt 35. A newly reported manuscript, the Riccardianus 2136 in the Riccardiana Library, Florence, also has 368 chapters (*see* Steinitz [1963], pp. 224–225). On folio 49–49v of Belt 35 the numbers of the chapters have special marks, including a Φ, somewhat like the so-called Melzi mark (a slashed circle).

9. The identification of the apograph used by the printer of the "editio princeps" is a problem still unsolved, in spite of the efforts of a number of scholars. K. T. Steinitz (1963), pp. 245–254, has stated the problem clearly and her identification of the original drawings by Poussin in MS H 228 inf. is convincing. But we do not know whether Cassiano dal Pozzo gave Raphael Du Fresne the copy containing the original drawings by Poussin, although it seems unlikely that he did. And if he did, it seems

so much about the original material is still unknown, but I hope to be able to carry it out at a later date. As a preparation for this work I have made a concordance of the chapters in the *Trattato* with those in the basic sources available in print. Thus the 1882 Ludwig and 1817 Manzi editions of the Codex Urbinas are compared with the two basic editions of the abridged versions: the 1792 Fontani and the 1651 Du Fresne. The reason for doing so is evident. The Ludwig edition gives the chapters of the *Trattato* in the sequence of the Codex Urbinas and must therefore be taken as the basis for the comparison with the pages of the Manzi edition (which has no chapter-numbers) and with the editions of the abridged version. Of the latter, the Fontani edition comes first in our concordance because it was based on an abridged version (Codex Riccardianus 2275) [10] that is earlier than the abridged version used for the Du Fresne edition (Dal Pozzo's apograph).

Independently of the purpose for which it was compiled, the concordance can be of assistance to readers who wish to locate in the Codex Urbinas a passage quoted from one of these basic editions of the *Trattato*.

Numbers in italic identify the chapters that are abbreviated in the Fontani and Du Fresne editions. Some of these chapters are abbreviated also in the Manzi edition, e.g., Ludwig 81.

The numbers I, II, III, etc., are placed in front of the Ludwig chapters that correspond to the first chapters of each of the eight parts of the Codex Urbinas.

	LUDWIG 1882 no.	MANZI 1817 page	FONTANI 1792 no.	DU FRESNE 1651 no.	LUDWIG 1882 no.	MANZI 1817 page	FONTANI 1792 no.	DU FRESNE 1651 no.
I.	1	1–2	—	—	10	5	—	—
	2	2	—	—	11	5–6	—	—
	3–5	49	—	—	12	6	—	—
	6	50	—	—	13	6–7	—	—
	7	47	—	—	14	7–8	—	—
	8	3–4	—	—	15–15a	8–10	—	—
	9	4–5	—	—	16	10–11	—	—

unlikely that Du Fresne gave the printer so precious a manuscript. Only a painstaking comparison of the text of the existing copies with the text of the "editio princeps" may lead us to the identification of the copy used by the printer. As one of the "test-chapters" for such a comparison we may suggest chapter 157 in the Du Fresne edition (which happens to be our *Libro A* 22) because it contains a mistake of line-repetition. In the same manner as a similar mistake by Melzi enabled us to identify the length of a line in the original *Libro A*, we are able now to identify one line of the copy used by the printer of the "editio princeps." The line is: "equali in colore, & in splendore può essere alluminato da essi lumi." I have looked for this line in all the manuscripts that have been claimed to be the sources of the "editio princeps" (Leningrad, Ganay, H. 228 inf., Belt 36), but none of them has this type of line. Therefore the manuscript is lost or is one of the several copies listed by K. T. Steinitz in her Group E. This group includes apographs identified as copies from the "editio princeps," but it is possible that one of them had the spaces for the figures left blank when the printer used it, and that the figures were added later by copying those of the printed edition.

10. Steinitz (1958), B-8.

LUDWIG 1882 no.	MANZI 1817 page	FONTANI 1792 no.	DU FRESNE 1651 no.
17	11	—	—
18	12	—	—
19	12–14	—	—
20	14–15	—	—
21	15–16	—	—
22	17	—	—
23	17–20	—	—
24	20–21	—	—
25	21–23	—	—
26	23	—	—
27	23–25	—	—
28	25–26	—	—
29	27	—	—
30	27–28	—	—
31–31c	28–29	—	—
32	29–31	—	—
33	31–33[1]	—	—
34	33	—	—
35	34	—	—
36	34–36	—	—
37	36–38	—	—
38	38–40	—	—
39	41–42	—	—
40–42	42–45	—	—
43	45–46	—	—
44	46	—	—
45	46–47	—	—
46	—	—	—
II. 47	50	1	1
48	50–51	2	2
49	51	3	3
50	51–52	—	—
51	52	4	4
52	52	5	5
53	53	6	6
54–55	53	7	7
56	53–54	—	—
57	54	—	—
58	54–56	—	—
58a	56	8	8
59	56	—	—
60	56–57	9	9
61	57	10	10
62	57	11	11
63	57–58	12	12
64	58	13	13
65	58–60	14	14
65a	60	15	15
66	60–61	16	16

LUDWIG 1882 no.	MANZI 1817 page	FONTANI 1792 no.	DU FRESNE 1651 no.
67	61	17	17
68	61–62	—	—
69	62–63	—	—
70	63–64	18	18
71	64	—	—
72	64–65	—	—
73	65	—	—
74	65–66	—	—
75	66	19	19
76	66–67	20	20
77	67–68	—	—
78	68	21	21
79	68–69	22	22
80	69	23	23
81	69	24	24
82	—	—	—
83–84	69	25	25
84a	70	26	26
85	70	27	27
86	70–71	28	28
87	71	29	29
88	72	30	30
89	72	31	31
90	72–73	32	32
91	73	33	33
92	73	34	34
93	73–74	35	35
94	74	—	—
95	74	36	36
96	74	37	37
97–99	—	—	—
100	75	38	38
101	75	39	39
102	75	—	—
103	75	40	40
104	75	41	41
105	76	42	42
106	76	43	43
107	76–77	—	—
108	77–78	44	44
109	78	45	45
110	79	46	46
111	79	47	47
112	79	48	48
113	79–80	49	49
114	80	—	—
115	80–81	50	50
116	81	51	51
117	81–82	52	52
118	82–83	53	53

[1] At the end of this chapter the paragraph corresponding to Ludwig 31a is added.

LUDWIG 1882 no.	MANZI 1817 page	FONTANI 1792 no.	DU FRESNE 1651 no.	LUDWIG 1882 no.	MANZI 1817 page	FONTANI 1792 no.	DU FRESNE 1651 no.
119	83	54	54	174	107	90	91
120	83–84	55	55	175	107–108	91 [4]	89
121	84	56	56	176	108	92	92
122	84	—	—	177	108–109	93	93
123–124	85	—	—	178	109	94	94
125	85–86	—	—	179–180	109–110	95	95
126	86	57	57	181	110	96	96
127	87	58	58	182	111	—	—
128	87	—	—	183–185	111	97	97
129	88	—	—	186–187	111–112 [5]	98	98
130	88	59	59	188	112	—	—
131–132	88	—	—	189	113	98	98
133–134	89	—	—	190–190a	114	99	99
135	89	60	60	191	114–115	100	100
136–137	90	—	—	192	115	101	101
138	90–91	—	—	193	115	102	102
139–141	91	—	—	194	115–116	103	103
142	92	61	61	195	116	—	—
143	92	62	62	196	116	104	104
144	92	64	64	197	116–117	105	105
145	92	63	63	198	117–119	106 [6]	106
146	92–93	65	65	199	119	107	107
147	93–94	66	66	200	120	108	108
148	94–97	67 [2]	67	201	120–121	109	109
149	97	68	68	202	121	110	110
150	98	69	69	203	121–122	111	111
151	98	70	70	204	122	112	112
152	98–99	71	71	205	122	113	113
153	99	72	72	206	123	114	114
154	99–100	73	73	207	123	115	115
155	100	74	74	208	123	116	116
156	100–101	75	75	209	123–124	117	117
157	101	76	76	210	124	118	118
158	101	77	77	211	124	119	119
159	101–102	78	78	212	124–125	120	120
160	102	79	79	213	125–126	121	121
161	102–103	80	80	214	126	122	122
162	103	81	81	215	126–127	123	123
163	104	82	82	216	127	124	124
164	104	83 [3]	83	217	127	125	125
165	104–105	84 [3]	84	218	127–128	126	126
166	105	85 [3]	85	219	128	127	127
167–170	105–106	86	86	220	128	128	128
171	106	87	87	221	128	129	129
172	106	88	88	222	129	130	130
173	107	89	90	223	129	131	131

---

[2] Erroneously printed 68 (LXVIII).   [3] The diagram is omitted.

[4] Fontani has figure and diagram combined; Du Fresne has only the figure.

[5] Manzi follows the altered and abbreviated version of Fontani and Du Fresne.

[6] The words in the diagram are omitted.

LUDWIG 1882 no.	MANZI 1817 page	FONTANI 1792 no.	DU FRESNE 1651 no.
224	129	132	132
225	129–130	133	133
226	130–131	134	134
227	131	135	135
228	131	136	136
229	131	137	137
230	131–132	138	138
231–231a	132	139	139
232	132	140	140
233	133	141	141
234	133	142	142
235	133–134	143	143
236	134	144	144
237	134	145	145
238	135	146	146
239	135	147	147
240	135	148	148
241	135–136	149	149
242	136	150	150
243	136	151	151
244	136–137	152	152
245	137	153	153
246	137	154	154
247	137–138	155	155
248	138	156	156
249	139	157	157
250	139–140	158	158[7]
251	140	159	159[8]
252	140	160	160
253	141	—	—
254	141–142	161	161
255–257	142	162	
258–258b	143[9]	163	162
258c–259	143	164	
260–260a	143–144	165	163
261	144–145	166	164
262	145	167	165
ad. 148	[See Ludwig 148]		
III. 263	147	168	166
264	147	169	167
265	148	170	168
266	148	171	169

LUDWIG 1882 no.	MANZI 1817 page	FONTANI 1792 no.	DU FRESNE 1651 no.
267	149	172	170
268	149	173	171
269	149	174	172
270	150	175	173
271	150–151	176	174
272	151	177	175
273	151	178	176
274	152	179	177[10]
275	152	180	178
276	152	181	179
277	152	182	180
278	153	183	181
279	153–154	184	182
280	154–155	185	183
281	155	186	184
282	155	187	185
283	156	188	186
284	156	—	—
285	156–157	189	187
286–287	157	—	—
288[11]	157–158	190	188
289	158	191	189
290	159	192	190[12]
291	159	193	191
292	159–160	—	—
293	160	—	—
294	160	—	—
295	161	194	192
296	164	195	193
297–298	161		
299	161–162	—	—
300–301	162	—	—
302	162	196	194
303	163		
304	163–164	—	—
305	164	197	195
306	164–165	198–199	196–197
307	165	200	198
308	166	201	199
309	166	202	200
310	167	203	201[13]
311	167	204	202[14]
312	167	205	203[15]

[7] The letters are omitted from the diagram.   [8] The words are omitted from the diagram.
[9] Manzi follows the altered version of Du Fresne.
[10] Du Fresne alters the figure, by representing only the bones of the foot.
[11] Figures only in the Codex Urbinas.   [12] The last sentence is omitted from the abbreviated version.
[13] Only Du Fresne has the figure.
[14] Only Du Fresne has the figure, which is an elaboration of the second figure of Ludwig 309.
[15] Only Du Fresne has the figure.

LUDWIG 1882 no.	MANZI 1817 page	FONTANI 1792 no.	DU FRESNE 1651 no.	LUDWIG 1882 no.	MANZI 1817 page	FONTANI 1792 no.	DU FRESNE 1651 no.
313	167	206	204 [16]	357	185–186	244	242
314 [17]	167	207	205	358–359	186	—	—
315	168	208	206	360	186–187	—	—
316	168	209	207	361	187	245	243
317	169	210	208	362–364	187	—	—
318	169	211	209	365	188	246	244
319 [18]	169–170	212	210	366–367	188	—	—
320	170–171	213	211	368	188–189	—	—
321	171	214	212	370	189–190	247	245
322	171	215	213	371	190	248	246
323	171–172	216	214	372	190	249	247
324	172	217	215	373	190–191	250	248
325	172	218	216	374	191	251	249
326	172	219	217	375	191	252	250
327	172–173	220	218	376	191–192	—	—
328	173	221	219	377	192–193	253	251
329	173	222	220	378	193	254	252
330	174	223	221	379	193	255	253
331	174	224	222	380	193–194	256	254
332	174	225	223	381	194	257	255
333–333a	175	226	224	382	194	258	256
334	175	—	—	383	195	—	—
335	175–176	—	—	384–385	195–196	259 [20]	257
336	176	227	225	386	196	260	258
337	176–177	228	226	387	196	261	260
338	177	—	—	388–389	196	—	—
339	177–178	—	—	390	197	262	259
340	178	—	—	391	197	—	—
341	179	229	227	392	198	263	261
342	179	230	228	393	198	264	262
343	179	231	229	394 [21]	198–199	265	263
344	180	232	230	395	199	266	264
345	180	233	231	396	199–200	267	265
346–347	181	234 [16]	232	397	200	268	266
348	181	235 [19]	233	398	200–201	269	267
349	181–182	236 [19]	234	399	201	270	268
350	182–183	237 [19]	235	400	201	271	269
351	183	238	236	401	201–202	272	270
352	183–184	239	237	402	202	273 [22]	271
353	184	240	238	403	202–203	—	—
354	184–185	241	239	404	203–204	—	—
355	185	242	240	405	204	274	272
356	185	243	241	406	204	275	273

---

[16] The figure is omitted.   [17] Only the Codex Urbinas has a figure and the word "dito." See *Libro* A 7.

[18] The last sentence in the Codex Urbinas has "e di unir co'lle menti" instead of "e diuincolamenti" as in the original MS Ash. 29. Manzi follows the abbreviated version, deleting these words.

[19] The figure is omitted.   [20] Erroneously printed 269 (CCLXIX).

[21] The Codex Urbinas has three figures in one. Fontani has three figures separated. Du Fresne has only one figure.

[22] The diagram is omitted.

LUDWIG 1882 no.	MANZI 1817 page	FONTANI 1792 no.	DU FRESNE 1651 no.	LUDWIG 1882 no.	MANZI 1817 page	FONTANI 1792 no.	DU FRESNE 1651 no.
407	205	276	274	454	227	319	317
408, 410	205–206 [23]	277	275	455	227	320	318
409	—	—	—	456	228	321	319
411	206	278	276	457	228	—	—
412	207	279	277	458	229	322	320
413	207	280	278	459	229–230	—	—
414	207–208	281	279	460	230	323	321
415	208	282	280	461	230–231	324	322
416	209	283	281	462	231	325	323
417	209	284	282	463	231–232	326	324
418	209	285	283	464	232	327	325
419	210	286	284	465	232	328	326
420	210	287	285	466	233	329	327
421	210	288	286	467	234	330	328
422	211	289	287	468	234	331	329
423	212	290	288	469	234	332	330
424	212	291	289	470	235	333	331
425–425a	212	292	290	471–481 [26]	235–240	334–339	332
426	213	293	291	481	240–241	340	333
427	213	294	292 [24]	482	241	341	334
428	213	295	293 [24]	483	241–242	342	335
429	214	296	294	484	242	343	336
430	214	297	295	485	242	344	337
431	214	298	296	486	243	345	338
432	214–215	299	297	487	243	346	339
433	215–216	300	298	488–492	243–244	347	340
434–435	216–217	301	299	493	245	—	—
436	217	302	300	494	245–246	348	341
437	217–218	303	301	495	246–247	—	—
438	218	—	—	496	247	—	—
438a–b	219	304	302	497	247	349	342
439	219	—	—	498	247–248	350	343
440	219–220	305	303	499	248	—	—
441	220	306	304	500	248	351	344
442	220–221	307	305	501	248–249	352	345
443	221–222	308	306	502	249	353	346
444	222	309	307	503	249–250	354	347
445	223	310	308	504	250–251	—	—
446	223–224	311	309	505	251	355 [27]	348 [27]
447	224–225	312	310 [25]	506	251–253	—	—
448	225	313	311	507	253	—	—
449	225	314	312	508	254	—	—
450	225	315	313	509	254	356	349
451	226	316	314	510	254	357	350
452	226–227	317	315	511	254–255	—	—
453	227	318	316	512	255	358	351

[23] Manzi follows the abbreviated version, and omits chapter 409.   [24] The titles are interchanged.
[25] The figure is omitted.
[26] Ludwig 478 is omitted from the abbreviated version. In Du Fresne 333 the title is the first sentence of Ludwig 481; in Fontani it is the last sentence of Fontani 339.   [27] The diagram is omitted.

LUDWIG 1882 no.	MANZI 1817 page	FONTANI 1792 no.	DU FRESNE 1651 no.	LUDWIG 1882 no.	MANZI 1817 page	FONTANI 1792 no.	DU FRESNE 1651 no.
513	255–256	359	352	590	288	—	—
514	256–257	360	353	591–592	289	—	—
515–516	257	—	—	593	289–290	—	—
517	257–258	361	354	594–597	290	—	—
518	258	—	—	598–600	291	—	—
519–521	259	—	—	601	291–292	—	—
522–524	260	—	—	602	292	—	—
525	260–261	—	—	603	292–293	—	—
526–526a	261	362	355	604–605	293	—	—
527	261	363	356	606	293–294	—	—
528–528a	261	364	357	607	294	—	—
				608	294–295	—	—
IV. 529–531	263	—	—	609–611	295	—	—
532	264–265	365	358	612–614	296	—	—
533–534	265	—	—	615	296–297	—	—
535	265–266	—	—	616–617	297	—	—
536	266–267	366	359	618	297–298	—	—
537	267	367	360 [28]	619–622	298	—	—
538	267–268	368	361	623–626	299	—	—
539	267	—	—	627	299–300	—	—
540	268	369	362	628	300	—	—
541	269–270	—	—	629–630	301	—	—
542	270	370	363	631	301–302	—	—
543	270–271	} 371	364	632–633	302	—	—
544	271			634	302–303	—	—
				635–637	303	—	—
V. 545–547	273	—	—	638–640	304	—	—
548	273–274	—	—	641–642	305	—	—
549–551	274	—	—	643	305–306	—	—
552–553d	275	—	—	644	306	—	—
554–556	276	—	—	645	306–307	—	—
557	276–277	—	—	646–648	307	—	—
558–559	277	—	—	649–652	308	—	—
560	277–278	—	—	653	309	—	—
561	278	—	—	654	309–310	—	—
562	278–279	—	—	655–658	310	—	—
563	279–280	—	—	659–660	311	—	—
564–565	280	—	—	661	311–312	—	—
566	280–281	—	—	662	312	—	—
567–569	281	—	—	663	312–313	—	—
570	281–282	—	—	664–665	313	—	—
571–573	282	—	—	666	313–314	—	—
574	282–283	—	—	667–668	314	—	—
575–576	283	—	—	669–672	315	—	—
577	283–284	—	—	673–674	316	—	—
578–580	284	—	—	675–677	317	—	—
581–582	285	—	—	678	318	—	—
583–585	286	—	—	679	318–319	—	—
586–588	287	—	—	680–681	319	—	—
589	287–288	—	—	682–684	320	—	—

[28] Erroneously printed 350 (CCCL).

LUDWIG 1882 no.	MANZI 1817 page	FONTANI 1792 no.	DU FRESNE 1651 no.	LUDWIG 1882 no.	MANZI 1817 page	FONTANI 1792 no.	DU FRESNE 1651 no.
685	321	—	—	751–753	357	—	—
686	321–322	—	—	754	358	—	—
687	322	—	—	755	358–359	—	—
688	322–323	—	—	756	359–360	—	—
689–690	323	—	—	757–758	360	—	—
691	323–324	—	—	759	360–361	—	—
692–693	324	—	—	760–761	361	—	—
694–694f	325–328	—	—	762–764	362	—	—
695	328	—	—	765–765a	362–363	—	—
696	328–329	—	—	766–767	363	—	—
697	329	—	—	768–770	364	—	—
698–698b	329–330	—	—	771–773	365	—	—
699–700	331	—	—	774	365–366	—	—
701	331–332	—	—	775–777	366	—	—
702	332–333	—	—	778	366–367	—	—
703–704	333	—	—	779	367–368 [29]	—	—
705	333–334	—	—	780	368	—	—
706–707	334	—	—	781	368–369	—	—
708	334–335	—	—	782	369–370	—	—
709–710	335	—	—	783–784	370	—	—
711–713	336	—	—	785	370–371	—	—
714–716	337	—	—	786	371–372	—	—
717–718	338	—	—	787–788	372	—	—
719	339	—	—	789	372–373	—	—
720	339–340	—	—	790	373	—	—
721	340	—	—	791	373–374	—	—
722	340–341	—	—	792	374	—	—
723	341	—	—	793	374–375	—	—
724	341–342	—	—	794	375–376	—	—
725–725a	342	—	—	795	376	—	—
726	342–343	—	—	796	376–377	—	—
727	343	—	—	797	377	—	—
728	343–344	—	—	798	378	—	—
729	344	—	—	799	378–379	—	—
730	344–345	—	—	800	379	—	—
731	345–346	—	—	801–803	380	—	—
732	346	—	—	804	380–381	—	—
733	346–347	—	—	805	382	—	—
734	347	—	—	806	382–383	—	—
735	347–348	—	—	807	383–384	—	—
736	348	—	—	808–809	384	—	—
737–738	349	—	—	810–810b	384–385	—	—
739	349–350	—	—	811	386	—	—
740–741	350	—	—	812	386–387	—	—
742–743	351	—	—	813–815	387	—	—
744	351–352	—	—	816	381–388	—	—
745–746	353	—	—	817	388	—	—
747–748	354	—	—	818	388–389	—	—
749	354–355	—	—	819	389–390	—	—
750	355–357	—	—	820–821	390	—	—

[29] The seventh paragraph (*Libro A* 23) is used as a heading by Manzi.

	LUDWIG 1882 no.	MANZI 1817 page	FONTANI 1792 no.	DU FRESNE 1651 no.		LUDWIG 1882 no.	MANZI 1817 page	FONTANI 1792 no.	DU FRESNE 1651 no.
VI.	822	391	—	—		883	419	—	—
	823	391–392	—	—		884	419–420	—	—
	824	392	—	—		885–887	420	—	—
	825	393	—	—		888	420–421	—	—
	826	393–394	—	—		889	421	—	—
	827	394	—	—		890	421–422	—	—
	828a–f	394–395	—	—		891	422–423	—	—
	829	395–397	—	—		892	423	—	—
	830–831	397	—	—		893	423–424	—	—
	832	398–399	—	—		894–896	424	—	—
	833	399	—	—		897–898	425	—	—
	834–834a	399–400	—	—		899–902	426	—	—
	835–836	400	—	—		903–906	427	—	—
	837	400–401	—	—		907–908	428	—	—
	838	401–402	—	—		909	428–429	—	—
	839	402	—	—		910	429–430	—	—
	840	402–403	—	—		911–912	430	—	—
	841	403	—	—		913	430–431	—	—
	842	403–404	—	—		914	431–432	—	—
	843–845	404	—	—		915	432	—	—
	846	404–405	—	—		916	432–433	—	—
	847	405	—	—		917–918	433	—	—
	848	405–406	—	—		919–919a	434–435	—	—
	849	406	—	—		920	435–436	—	—
	850	406–407	—	—		921–922	436	—	—
	851–853	407	—	—		923–924a	437	—	—
	854	407–408	—	—		925	437–438	—	—
	855–856	408	—	—					
	857	408–409	—	—	VII.	926	439	—	—
	858–859	409	—	—		927	439–440	—	—
	860	409–410	—	—		928	440–441	—	—
	861	410–411	—	—		929	441	—	—
	862	411	—	—		930–932a	442	—	—
	863	411–412	—	—		933	442–443	—	—
	864	412	—	—		934–935	443	—	—
	865	412–413	—	—					
	866–867	413	—	—	VIII.	936	445–447	—	—
	868–870	414	—	—		937	447	—	—
	871–873	415	—	—		938	447–448	—	—
	874	415–416	—	—		939–939b	448	—	—
	875	416	—	—		940–941	448–449	—	—
	876–878	417	—	—		942	449	—	—
	879	417–418	—	—		943	450	372	365
	880–882	418	—	—		944	450	—	—

APPENDIX V

General History of the Leonardo Manuscripts

THE *Memorie* OF Giovan Ambrogio Mazenta (1635) contain a detailed account of the dispersion of the Leonardo MSS from 1585 to 1630. His story is well known, but the excerpts of his *Memorie* included in recent publications[1] concern the vicissitudes of the manuscripts and not the scraps of information that Mazenta gives about the contents of those manuscripts. A reconsideration of his story is therefore appropriate at this point.

Mazenta describes how a tutor in the service of the Melzi family, Gavardi d'Asola, stole 13 Leonardo MSS from the Villa Melzi, taking them to Florence to sell them to the Grand Duke of Tuscany; and how, upon the failure of this project because of the Grand Duke's death in 1587, Gavardi went to Pisa and met Mazenta who convinced him to return the MSS to their owner, offering to do so himself. Ultimately Mazenta became the legitimate owner of those 13 MSS because Dr. Orazio Melzi (Francesco Melzi's heir), unaware of their value, did not care to take them back, stating that much more Leonardo material was still in his villa at Vaprio. The news spread immediately. Many went to Vaprio hunting for papers of Leonardo. Pompeo Leoni, a sculptor in the service of the King of Spain, promised special favors and offices in the Milanese Senate to Melzi in exchange for Leonardo MSS. Melzi, probably having exhausted the Leonardo material, ran to Mazenta and begged him to return the MSS he had allowed him to keep. But Mazenta and his brother Guido returned only seven MSS, which went to Leoni. Six MSS remained with the Mazentas. Of these, one went to Cardinal Borromeo (MS C), one to the painter Ambrogio Figino (lost), and one to the Duke of Savoy (lost). The three MSS that remained in the hands of Guido also went to Leoni after Guido's death; and Leoni took them apart in order to mount their pages onto the leaves of a huge scrapbook (the Codex Atlanticus) in which he was gathering much of the Leonardo material obtained from Melzi.

But at this point Mazenta's story is unclear, and it contains at least one anomaly. His brother Guido died in 1613, and therefore Pompeo Leoni could not have received the three MSS after Guido's death, because Pompeo died in Spain in 1610. The crucial sentence "E questo [i.e., Pompeo Leoni] accogliendone altri li sfogliò,

---

1. Cf. Richter (1939), II, 393 ff.; Belt (1948), pp. 3–14. For a critical edition of Mazenta's *Memorie* see Gramatica (1919).

e ne fece un gran libro" does not necessarily imply that Leoni took apart the three Mazenta MSS as well as others in order to compose the Codex Atlanticus. It might mean that only the other MSS were taken apart. Moreover, if the pages of three MSS were included in the Codex Atlanticus, it would not be difficult to recognize them as such, and even to attempt the reconstruction of the three books. But this is not the case, and one is left with the impression that Leoni, in assembling the Codex Atlanticus, used only unbound files left loose by Leonardo himself. The only MS he might have taken apart (to compose the Windsor volume, not the Codex Atlanticus) is the anatomical book at Windsor known today as *Fogli B dell'Anatomia*. The folios of this book show the indentations of the stitches that originally kept them together [2] (but only a few stitch-indentations appear in the folios gathered in the Codex Atlanticus.) In addition to the Codex Atlanticus, Leoni took other Leonardo MSS to Spain, among them, no doubt, the present MS B in the Institut de France. In fact, this MS has annotations in Spanish in his handwriting. If he had taken apart three Mazenta MSS, why should he not have taken apart MS B also? Presumably he would not have taken apart MSS of the type of MS B, and the Mazenta MSS were most likely of this type.

In a few passages of his *Memorie* Mazenta speaks of the type and contents of the MSS stolen by Gavardi:

About fifty years ago, thirteen MSS of Leonardo da Vinci came into my possession. Some of them were in-folio, and others in-quarto, written from right to left. . . .

How long Leonardo had studied this great project [i.e., the canalization of Lombardy] one can see in his above-mentioned books, which contain beautiful observations, illustrated with drawings, on the nature, weight, motion, and swirls of water, and on various machines for the control of water and for many other usages as well.[3] One enjoys reading these books because of the intelligence and erudition of the Author in Arithmetic, Geometry, Optics, Painting, and Architecture.[4] He also shows a good acquaintance with history, explaining how locks were used by the Egyptians in order to profit from the waters and wealth of the Nile, and how Pliny and Trajan had discussed in their letters the project of making a navigable course of water from Nicomedia to the sea by means of rivers and lakes—if it was not, perhaps, that they were thinking of a similar project for joining Milan to Nuovocomo, which was Pliny's birthplace. . . .[5]

---

2. The anatomical folio at Weimar was originally part of this series, as shown by identical stitch-indentations. See the forthcoming article by K. Steinitz in *Raccolta Vinciana*, XX.

3. Mazenta could not have seen the Codex Leicester. The notes on water he is referring to might be the ones in MS F; but also MSS on painting, such as MSS A and C, have sections on water, as has the lost *Libro* A. Drawings of hydraulic machines are found in MS B.

4. This description can be applied to the MSS that are now in the Institut de France. Arithmetic and geometry are found in MSS A and B, optics in MSS A and C, and architecture in MSS B and Trivulzianus. It appears certain that Mazenta had no MSS on anatomy.

5. These discussions on the canalization of the Nile and of the Bitinia region are not

Seven of the above-mentioned books were returned [to Orazio Melzi] and six remained with the Mazentas. One of these six, which is in-folio, with a red velvet cover,[6] *was given as a present to the late Cardinal Federico [Borromeo], and it is now preserved in the Ambrosian Library. It treats of light and shade very philosophically, and it is very useful for painters and for those who are interested in perspective and optics. . . .*

I have read in these books the most learned discourses and rules to find the central line [axis] in statues and paintings,[7] *with drawings and examples most ingeniously and beautifully set before the eyes. He teaches how to make studios for the painters with the light adjusted to the sun, maintaining that square windows with angles make [the light] false and discordant to nature. . . .*[8]

Here he debates and decides the famous question of the preëminence between painting and sculpture. . . .[9] *[Author's translations]*

In these excerpts Mazenta always speaks of "libri," that is, books, some of which were in-folio and others in-4to. Mazenta specifically refers to MS C as being in-folio. By the category in-4to he might have intended to designate books such as MSS A, B, and Trivulzianus; he might have included in this category also MSS of an in-8vo format, such as MSS E, F, G, and perhaps *Libro A*, but doubtfully pocket-size notebooks (those which Melzi calls "librettini") such as MSS H, I, L, and M. We have no way of knowing the format of the lost MSS—the ones given to Figino and to the Duke of Savoy—[10] in which Mazenta might have read the passages that have not come down to us.

---

found in the existing Leonardo MSS. Mazenta must have read them in MSS now lost or in missing pages of still existing MSS (e.g., MSS B and Trivulzianus). The letters of Pliny the Younger, governor of the Bitinia, on a canalization project involving the Sabangia lake and the Kirassou river can therefore be considered as another source of Leonardo's writings. Cf. C. Plinii Caecilii Secundi, *Epistolarum libri novem* (Lipsiae, 1908), Epist. XLI, XLII, LXI, pp. 283–284, 292. These letters were known in the fifteenth century, and Alberti refers to them in his *De Re Aedificatoria*, Book X. They are mentioned also by Guido Mazenta, *Discorso intorno al far navigabile il fiume Adda* (1599), p. 10.

6. The present binding of MS C is not in red velvet but in brown leather. Since the inscription referring to the presentation to Cardinal Federico is dated 1603, the MS presumably had a different binding when Mazenta saw it. See in this volume p. 147.

7. Cf. MS A 28r.

8. Cf. MS A 4v and MS B 20v (Richter [1883], I, 511–512).

9. In this paragraph, which is reproduced in its entirety in this volume, p. 122, Mazenta quotes an anecdote which is no longer preserved in the existing MSS. Perhaps he had read it in the missing folios of MS A, or in a book on the *Paragone* (*Libro .i.?*) which has not come down to us.

10. The MS that Mazenta gave to Ambrogio Figino cannot be identified with the one Lomazzo refers to as a book on mills which Figino owned before 1590.

The Duke of Savoy MS was probably lost during one of the fires that destroyed the greater part of the Royal Library at Turin in 1667 and 1672. It has passed unnoticed, as far as I know, that in the Codex Resta, folio 2, there is a note by Padre Resta concerning MSS and drawings acquired by a Prince of Savoy: "Veramente sono state celebratissime in Milano le anatomie de' cavalli, e tutti i moti d'un cavaliere combattente a cavallo che fece per il signor Gentil Borri, parte delle quali furono vendute in un libro ad uno de' Sig. Prencipi di Savoia in tre milla scudi ed altri passarono in casa dei Signori

Each of the MSS in his hands must have had a binding. It would seem unlikely that Gavardi had taken away any unbound volumes from the Villa Melzi. He had planned to sell them to the Grand Duke of Tuscany, and therefore he must have chosen those books which appeared as units in themselves, not unbound files.

Mazenta himself informs us that Leoni obtained Leonardo material directly from Orazio Melzi. This material most likely consisted of unbound files and MSS of the type of MS D, which is actually one single signature with a simple hard cover. In the Villa Melzi there must have been a considerable number of such signatures, and so Leoni might have been responsible also for the composition of the Codex Arundel, which is in fact a volume composed of signatures of different dates, similar in format to MS D.

This early phase of the dispersion of the MSS shows that there must have been a tremendous loss of Leonardo material within the period of a few years. Ten MSS and two pocket-notebooks of the Melzi list in the Codex Urbinas are still unaccounted for. From the way the material in the Codex Atlanticus and in the Windsor volume is mutilated, we have the evidence that there must have been enough additional material to form another volume of the same bulk as the Codex Atlanticus. We do not know how many MSS Leoni brought to Spain, and how many came back.[11] The "infinite number of volumes" seen by De Beatis in France in 1517 is reduced to a little more than a dozen items in the reports from the end of the sixteenth century.

The general history of the Leonardo MSS, which I offer here in the form of a chart, contains two newly reported entries: under the date 1566 is the mention of a MS that was listed in the property of the Duke of Amalfi, a relative of Cardinal Luigi d'Aragona. Professor D'Arrigo, who has published this document recently,[12]

Magenta, e per mezzo d'un pedante passarono al Cav. Leone Leoni. . . ." (In truth, Leonardo's anatomies of the horse have been much celebrated in Milan, and so the drawings representing the actions of a horseman fighting on horseback, which Leonardo did as illustrations of a book by Signor Gentile Borri; part of which were gathered in a volume and sold to one of the Princes of Savoy for three thousand *scudi*, and part went into the house of Signori Mazenta. These, through the handling of a tutor [*pedante*], went to Cav. Leone Leoni.) This passage contains a number of inaccuracies, as is usual with the writings of Padre Resta (there is, for instance, a confusion about a tutor [Gavardi?] giving the Mazenta MSS to Leone Leoni, father of Pompeo, who died in 1590), but at least it contains, inaccurate as it might be, the only other reference, besides Lomazzo's to Leonardo's illustrations for the book of Gentile de' Borri.

11. Up to the beginning of the last century there were two Leonardo MSS in the Biblioteca Nacional at Madrid which may have come from Leoni. Cf. Bartolomeo José Gallardo, *Ensayo de una Biblioteca Española* . . . (Madrid, 1866), p. 174: Vinci (Leonardo da). Tratados de fortificacion, estatica, mecanica y geometria, escritos al reves, y en los años 1491 y 1493 (Aa, 19, 20).

12. A. d'Arrigo (1958). The inventory of books in the possession of the "*quondam* Duca di Amalfi" is dated 30 September 1566 and is in the Archivio di Stato, Naples, Vol. 3208 *bis*, fol. 35 ff. Alfonso Piccolomini II, Duke of Amalfi and Count of Celano, died in Pozzuoli, February 17, 1559. Cf. G. M. Monti, "I Piccolomini d'Aragona Duchi di Amalfi, un quadro di Raffaello e la biblioteca di Papa Pio II," *Studi sulla Repubblica Marinara di Amalfi a cura del Comitato per la celebrazione di Amalfi Imperiale* (1935).

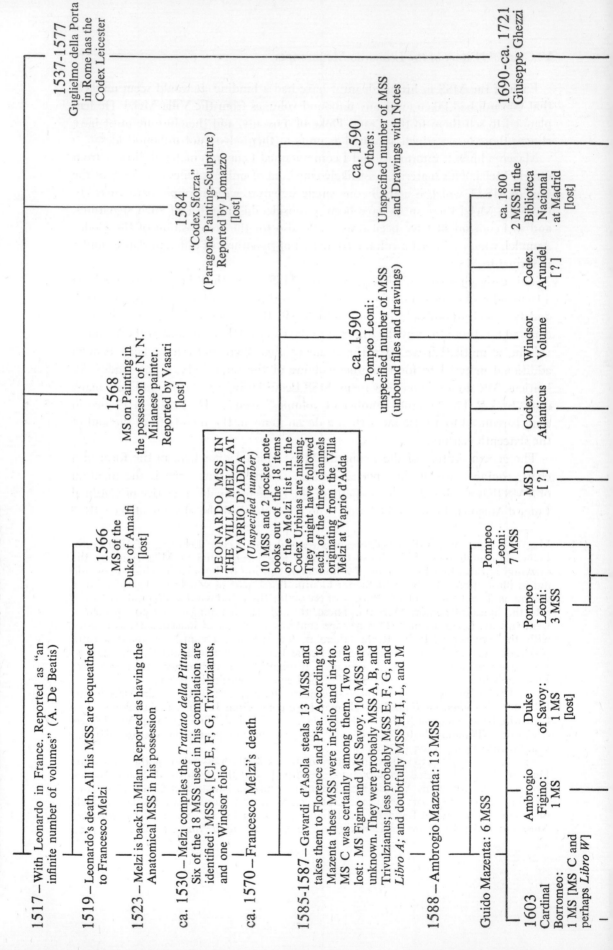

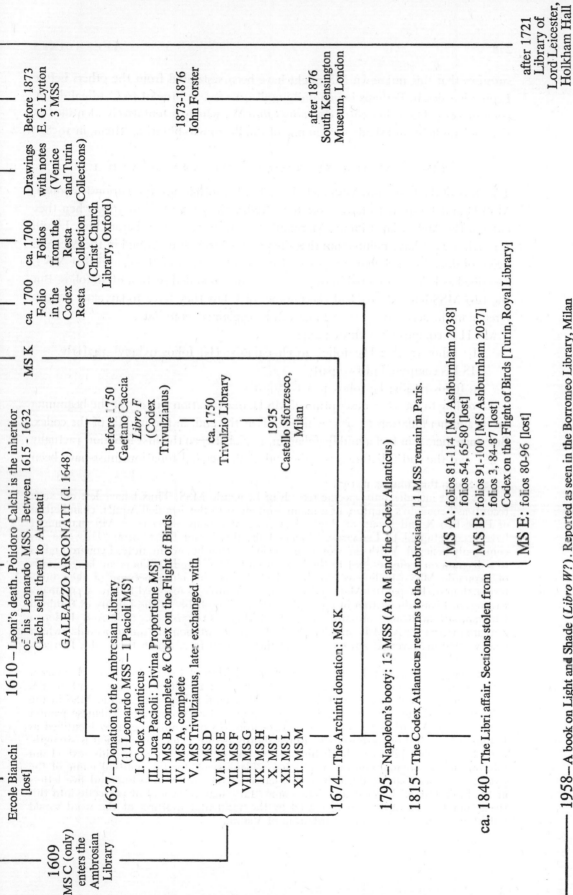

surmises that this unknown MS might have been separated from the others before Leonardo's death. Perhaps Leonardo himself gave it as a present to Cardinal d'Aragona in 1517. The other entry concerns *Libro W*, which is tentatively identified as the book on light and shade seen in one of the Borromeo libraries, Milan, in 1958.[13]

THE "ADDED SECTIONS" OF MSS H AND I

The story of the Leonardo MSS includes not only mutilations, for, curiously enough, MSS H and I appear to have more folios today than they had in 1637 when they entered the Ambrosian Library. Marinoni ([1954], p. 266) and, before him, Uzielli ([1884], p. 242) have pointed out that the present MS H is described in the Arconati deeds of donation as being composed of two parts instead of three, and that MS I, described as being composed of 91 folios, has now an added section of 48 folios. But the two MSS have always had the number of folios they have today, and the difference in the accounts of their folios can be explained as follows.

MS H is composed of three parts:

H_1: folios 1r–48v; H_2: folios 49[1]r–94[46]v; H_3: folios 95[47v]–142[1r]v.

MS I is composed of two parts:

I_1: folios 1r–48v; I_2: folios 49[1]r–139[91]v.

According to the 1637 description of MS H, one foliation (1–46) at the beginning meets another foliation (1–47), which starts at the end, in the middle of the codex. But since there is in fact a middle foliation, 1–46, between the first foliation (actually 1–48) and the end foliation 47–1, the end of the second foliation must have been

---

13. See in this volume, p. 147.

This chart includes only specific records of Leonardo MSS. Thus I have left out such records as Leonardo's mention of a manuscript given to Battista dell'Aquila, chamberlain of Pope Leo X and friend of Raphael (Codex Atlanticus 287 r-a), a MS that might have been returned to Leonardo. (Incidentally, this is not the treatise "De vocie" as commonly believed. With the words "de vocie" written below the note, Leonardo refers to a diagram on acoustics, not to the book given to Dell'Aquila.) There are later records of Leonardo MSS which have not been included in this chart because of their indeterminateness. The painter Matteo Zaccolini, for example, is reported to have seen "many writings of Leonardo written in reversed characters," probably in the Library of Cardinal Chiaramonti in Rome, around 1620. See Pedretti (1957b), p. 258. And Federico Zuccaro (1607) speaks of Leonardo rules on the representation of "moto azionale" which were written in "reversed script"—perhaps the originals from which the Codex Huygens was compiled.

According to Mazenta, Lomazzo himself owned MSS of Leonardo: "This [Lomazzo] gathered many of Leonardo's paintings, drawings, and writings, which went to the gallery and museum of Rudolf II, Emperor." No record is left of Leonardo MSS in the collection of Maximillian Rudolf II. In my opinion, the Anonymous Milanese painter mentioned by Vasari as the owner of a Leonardo MS on painting can be identified as Lomazzo himself. Lomazzo went to Rome shortly before 1568. My opinion is strengthened by a curious bibliographical hint in the text of Vasari's report. This text (I am referring to the original edition, 1568) has a blank space for the omitted name of the painter—a space that would include two letters at the end of one line and five letters at the beginning of the next line. The name "Lo / mazzo" would fit perfectly into this space, but the scurrilous pun produced by the accidental splitting of the word would not have escaped the watchful puritanism of Vasari!

mistaken for the end of the first. Baldassarre Oltrocchi, librarian of the Ambrosiana in the second half of the eighteenth century, refers to MS H as being composed of two parts, but in his quotations he refers also to passages in a third part between the two (cf. Ritter [1925], pp. 21–22). Moreover, around 1779 Count Anton Giuseppe della Torre Rezzonico describes MS H as being composed of two parts, but refers to notes and drawings that are found in a third part (cf. Monti [1914], p. 77).

In the 1637 description of MS I the total number of the folios was given as 91, overlooking the fact that the MS has two foliations for a total of 139 folios. Again Oltrocchi makes the same mistake. He quotes passages in folios 32r and 39v of MS I without specifying that folio 32 is in the first part and folio 39 in the second; in fact the passage quoted as being on folio 39v is on the present folio 87.

MS K, which was not among the MSS of the Arconati donation, is also composed of three parts (1–48, 1–32, 1–48), but Oltrocchi does not specify this either, probably because he quotes only passages in the first part.

Post Scriptum

SHORTLY BEFORE the present book went to press, in the summer of 1963, I had the opportunity to visit several institutions and libraries in Europe, searching for support to some of my hypotheses. I was fortunate enough to find positive evidence that the handwriting of the Codex Urbinas 1270 is indeed that of Francesco Melzi.

All we could say about the identity of Manus 1 in the Codex Urbinas, that is, the compiler's hand, can be summarized as follows. The handwriting of Manus 1 resembles that of a number of notes written by an unknown person on manuscripts and drawings of Leonardo's. According to Gerolamo Calvi, this person could be identified as Melzi by comparing the handwriting of those notes with that of the notes on the Ambrosiana drawing signed by Melzi and dated 1510 (plate 13). Some of those notes were also written on Leonardo's folios dating after 1517; thus it was reasonable to conclude that their author was Melzi, who in fact followed Leonardo to France. But no example of Melzi's handwriting dating after Leonardo's death was known to us. Therefore, although some of the notes written during his activity as a pupil and assistant of Leonardo show a type of handwriting resembling the calligraphy of the text of the Codex Urbinas, the identification of Manus 1 as Melzi's could be suggested on circumstantial evidence only.

We have now an example of Melzi's handwriting dated 1546 (fig. 1). This is an ownership entry written in Latin on the first folio of a manuscript of Spanish poetry [1] preserved in the Trivulziana Library in Milan:

Joannes Franciscus [2] Meltius hic scripsit die xiij mensis Junij 1546

---

1. Codex Trivulzianus M. 39. Cf. A. M. Finoli, "Lingua e cultura spagnola nell'Italia superiore alla fine del '400 e ai primi del '500," *Istituto Lombardo. Rendiconti. Classe di Lettere e Scienze Morali e Storiche*, 92 (1958), 635–647. I am indebted to Dr. Otto Kurz of the Warburg Institute in London for directing my attention to this publication.

2. Melzi's full name was Giovan Francesco, but Vasari and Lomazzo always refer to him as "Francesco Melzi" or "Francesco de Melzo." The document concerning the stipends paid to Leonardo, Melzi, and Salai in France, 1517–1518, gives Melzi's name as "Mes. Francisque de Melce," and Leonardo's will cites him as "Messer Francisco de Melzo" (see Beltrami [1919], nos. 241, 244, and 247). Melzi himself signed "Franciscus Mentius" (*sic*) in the letter to Leonardo's brothers, June 1, 1519 (Beltrami [1919], no. 245). Leonardo gives his pupil's full name in the well-known annotation on the first folio of MS E (*Libro B*): "partii da mjlano per roma addj 24 / dj sectēbre 1513 cō giovāfrāciesscho / de melsi salai lorēço e il fāfoia." But since no other source gives Melzi's full

This entry is written three times, each time with letters smaller in size.[3] The script of the third line is so small that it looks like the signature of a miniaturist. (It is well known that Lomazzo speaks of Melzi as a "great miniaturist.") These lines are identical in *ductus* to Manus 1, and furthermore they can be compared to the notes on the Windsor drawings nos. 12,416 (plate 12) and 12,684 (plate 20). To facilitate comparisons we reproduce here the 1510 signature of Melzi (fig. 2), his copy of Leonardo's note dated 1511 (fig. 3), and a passage from *Libro* A in Codex Urbinas 116v (fig. 4). The handwriting of figures 1 and 3 is identical both in *ductus* and in characteristics of individual letters. This type of handwriting, which is not so free as that of the earlier note in figure 2, is just slightly less formal than the calligraphic type in figure 4. The last word in figure 4, *Fortezza*, has the *z* as in the

name, it has always been assumed, beginning with Amoretti in his *Memorie storiche* (1804), p. 104, that Leonardo mentioned two persons: a Giovanni (identified either as Boltraffio or Petrino—cf. Richter [1883], no. 1465, and his second edition of 1939) and Francesco Melzi. G. Favaro, resuming the old question in his "Scampoli Vinciani" (1939), pp. 3–4, is inclined to accept the traditional interpretation of "Giovanni" as a reference to Boltraffio. In the Ambrosiana drawing signed by Melzi (plate 13, and fig. 2 of this *post scriptum*) there is apparently no "Giovanni," but Calvi (1925), p. 258, n. 3, reads the name "Joh[an]" at the end of the first line after the word "releuo."

Besides the new evidence of the 1546 entry we have that of the genealogy of the Melzi family given by F. Calvi, *Famiglie Nobili Milanesi* (Milan, 1881), vol. 3:

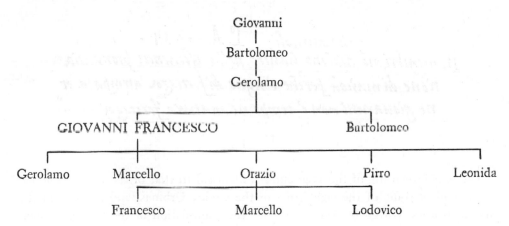

Moreover, in a document in the Archivio Storico Civico, Milan (Famiglia Melzi, no. 981), I have found the name of our Melzi given as Giovan Francesco.

Francesco Melzi must have received a good education in his youth, and from his notes in Leonardo's manuscripts we know that he was acquainted with Greek and Latin literature. This might explain the Classical names he gave to all his sons, with the exception of his first-born, who received the name of his grandfather. It is a time-honored opinion that Francesco Melzi could not have compiled Leonardo's *Trattato della Pittura* because of his lack of culture. G. Dozio (1871), p. 17, states that Melzi could not have made this compilation because of his laziness due to his wealth, and that "a letter of his, which has come down to us [i.e., the letter to Leonardo's brothers], shows him to be a rough and uncultured writer"!

3. In the second and third line Melzi writes "Julij" instead of "Junij" as in the first line, perhaps merely by mistake.

word *Suizeri* in figure 3 and the capital *F* as in the name *Franciscus* in figure 1 and
Francescho in figure 2. The *M* in the heading *De Muscoli* in figure 4 is that of the
name *Meltius* in figure 1 and *Milano* in figure 3.

Joannes Franciscus Meltius hic scripsit die xiij mensis Junij 1546
Joannes Franciscus Meltius hic scripsit die xvij mensis Julij 1546
Joannes Franciscus Meltius hic scripsit die xvij mensis Julij 1546

Fig. 1

1520   adi 14 Augusto   s' canam de releue /S
Francescho da melzo de anni 171

Fig. 2

adi 13 di decembre 1511 a hore 15 fu fatto questo
secondo incendio da suizeri piso a Milano
et luogo dicto Dexe

Fig. 3

·De muscoli,   l°. A. cor. 14.
Li, membri nõ debbono hauere nella Giouentu pronuntia=
tione di muscoli perche e' segno di fortezza attempata er
ne giouanetti non e' tempo ne matura fortezza ———

Fig. 4

The gray-brown ink of the 1546 entry is identical to that of the chapters added
at the end of some of the eight parts of the Codex Urbinas, and of most of the
marginal notes written by Manus 3. Thus the compilation of the Codex Urbinas
must be dated before 1546, because the ink Melzi used in that year is that of the
chapters added on the folios left blank at the end of each part of the Codex Urbinas.
The yellowish ink used by Manus 1 is in fact earlier than the gray-brown ink, and
is also found in certain notes written by Melzi on the Leonardo manuscripts during
his work of compilation, as well as in his slashed circles (ø) next to each passage in
the original manuscripts. I have checked the originals of all these passages in the
Leonardo manuscripts at Windsor, in the British Museum,[4] and in the Institut de

---

4. I am referring, of course, to Melzi's marks "N. d. P." and "N.la di Pita" (Nulla di
Pittura) in Codex Arundel 44, 59v, 93v, and 235v.

France. The yellowish ink used by Melzi in the preparatory phase of his work is definitely the same as that used for the greater part of the text of the Codex Urbinas. The date of the first phase of work in the compilation of the *Trattato della Pittura* can be maintained around 1530 as suggested before, the added chapters having been written at a time closer to the 1546 entry. The ink of this entry appears again in the collation notes written on the covers of the Leonardo manuscripts in the Institut de France (plate 16, *a–b*), as well as in the original code marks on the covers of those manuscripts.

The minuteness of the script in the 1546 entry somewhat resembles that of the marginal notes written by Manus 3 in the Codex Urbinas. I must admit that for a time I believed Manus 3 could also be Melzi's, and seeing again the Codex Urbinas in the original I am not able to convince myself entirely that this hand cannot be Melzi's. There are several points of resemblance between Manus 1 and Manus 3, and sometimes a marginal note by Manus 3 is written with the yellowish ink used by Manus 1. Ludwig has already indicated one of these marginal notes as being written by Manus 1, perhaps because of the color of the ink, but, as we have seen, such a note was definitely written by Manus 3.[5]

Manus 3 is usually considered as that of a consultant scholar called in by Melzi to do the work of editing. This person, who had to be quite familiar with the Leonardo manuscripts in Melzi's possession, uses the same ink as Melzi does and writes in very small script as in the Melzi entry of 1546. But against the assumption that Manus 3 is also Melzi's are the three following reasons:

1. The references to the original notebooks, *Libro A* and *Libro B*, were not written simultaneously with the chapters copied from those notebooks, but were added by Manus 3. It would be unlikely, although not impossible, that the idea of giving the source of each chapter copied from those notebooks occurred to Melzi only as an afterthought, when the whole work of compilation was accomplished.

2. The Windsor anatomical folio no. 19,102v (plate 19) contains a note written by a hand resembling Manus 3 and also a note by Melzi. It would be difficult to ascribe both notes to the same person. Both notes were written before Leonardo had filled in the page with his own notes and drawings. It is unlikely, therefore, that a long period elapsed between the two notes, so that it is not a case of the same person writing in two different ways at two different periods of his life. (And yet, since there is no real evidence that the Windsor note is written by Manus 3, Manus 3 could still be Melzi's.)

3. The handwriting of the Codex Huygens (plate 18) is also very close to that of Manus 3. The anonymous author of the Codex Huygens was indeed very familiar with the Leonardo manuscripts, and we know for certain that the Codex Huygens originated almost simultaneously with the Codex Urbinas. In fact it was based on the same method as that adopted by Melzi in compiling the Codex

---

5. See above, p. 104 and plate 9.

Urbinas: in both compilations the original Leonardo passages were first counter-signed with small circles, and then these circles were slashed after the passages were transcribed.[6]

To conclude, instead of being able to answer the question "Who was Manus 3?" we are led to another question: Was Melzi responsible also for the compilation of the Codex Huygens?

* * *

A book such as the present, which is almost entirely based on deductions, in-ferences, and hypotheses, may legitimately end with a question. And the reader may share the author's feeling that the end of a work of this kind is only the begin-ning of another: *Finiunt pariter renovantque labores.*

---

6. The Windsor drawing 12,293r, proportion of the horse's forelegs, is another indication of Melzi's work related to the contents of the Codex Huygens. In fact, the drawings on the left half of the folio are Melzi's tracings of the Leonardo drawings on the right side (note the vertical fold in between). The Melzi tracings complement the annotation of Leonardo (top center), in that they are accompanied by the actual equations (left margin, in Melzi's handwriting) according to the "minuti" system (see Panofsky [1940], pp. 51–54, for the explanation of this system). The author of the Codex Huygens copied *only* the Melzi equations, including the one near the right margin, and not the notes by Leonardo which deal with the increase and de-crease of the thickness and the length of certain parts of the leg as the leg bends or stretches (a problem that is related to the subject of *Libro A 108*). Is it a coinci-dence that the author of the Codex Huygens copied only the Melzi notes? The folio 74 of the Codex Huygens containing the copy of the upper half of Windsor 12,293 is described (but not reproduced) by Panofsky ([1940], p. 55).

BIBLIOGRAPHY

Bibliography

Accolti, Pietro, *Lo Inganno de gl'occhi*. Florence: Giunti, 1625.

Alberti, Leon Battista, *Della Pittura*. [First ed. (Thomas Venatorium, ed.; Latin text); Basle: 1540. Second ed. (Lodovico Domenichi, ed.; Italian translation); Venice: 1547.] Edited by Luigi Mallè. Florence: Sansoni, 1950. Quotations are given in Italian with reference to the English edition by J. R. Spencer (New Haven, Conn.: Yale University Press, 1956).

———, *De Re Aedificatoria*. L'Architettvra di Leonbattista Alberti tradotta in Lingua Fiorentina da Cosimo Bartoli. Venice: Francesco Franceschi, 1565. (English edition by J. Leoni; London: 1726, 1739, and 1755. Reprinted 1955; London: Alec Tiranti.)

———, *De Statua. Leon Battista Albertis Kleinere Kunsttheoretische Schriften*. Edited by H. Janitschek. Vienna: 1877.

———, *I Ludi Matematici*, in S. Timpanaro, ed. (1926), *Leonardo Pagine di Scienza*, pp. 1–36.

Amoretti, C. (1804), *Memorie storiche su la vita, gli studj, e le opere di Lionardo da Vinci*. Milan: Giusti, Ferrario.

Armenini, Giovan Battista, *De veri precetti della pittura*. Ravenna: Francesco Tebaldini, 1586.

Argan, G. C. (1957), *Botticelli*. New York: Skira.

Bacon, Roger, *Opus Majus* [First ed. (Samuel Jebb, ed.), 1733. Critical ed. by J.H. Bridges (Oxford: Clarendon Press), 1897–1900]. Quotations are from Robert Belle Burke's 2-vol. translation (Philadelphia, Penn.: University of Pennsylvania Press, 1928).

Baldinucci, F. (1681), *Vocabolario Toscano dell'Arte del Disegno*. Florence: Per Santi Franceschi al segno della Passione.

Baltrušaitis, J. (1955), *Anamorphoses ou Perspective Curieuse*. Paris: O. Perrin.

Baratta, M. (1903), *Leonardo da Vinci e i problemi della Terra*. Turin: Fratelli Bocca.

Barocchi, P. (1960), *Trattati d'arte del Cinquecento*. Volume Primo: Varchi, Pino, Dolci, Sorte. Bari: Laterza & Figli.

——— (1962), *Trattati d'arte del Cinquecento*. Volume Terzo: C. Borromeo, Ammanati, Bocchi, R. Alberti, Comanini. Bari: Laterza & Figli.

Bassoli, F. S. (1954), "Un pittore svizzero pioniere degli studi vinciani: Lodovico Antonio David," *Raccolta Vinciana*, XVII, 259–314.

Battisti, E. (1960), *Rinascimento e Barocco*. Turin: Einaudi.

Belt, E. (1948), *Manuscripts of Leonardo da Vinci. Their History, with a Description of the Manuscript Editions in Facsimile*. Los Angeles: The Elmer Belt Library of Vinciana.

Beltrami, L. (1919), *Documenti e Memorie riguardanti la Vita e le Opere di Leonardo da Vinci in ordine cronologico*. Milan: Treves.

Blunt, A. (1959), *Artistic Theory in Italy. 1450–1600*. Oxford: Clarendon Press.

Bolelli, T. (1955), "Osservazioni linguistiche sul 'Trattato della pittura' di Leonardo da Vinci," *Actes due cinquième Congrès International des Langues et Littérature modernes* (Florence), pp. 99–105.

Borzelli, A. (1914), *Trattato della Pittura di Leonardo da Vinci*. Lanciano: Carabba. 2 vols.

Boschini, M. (1660), *La Carta del Navigar Pitoresco*. Venezia: Per li Baba.

Bossi, G. (1810), *Del "Cenacolo" di Leonardo da Vinci. Libri Quattro*. Milan: Stamperia Reale.

Bressy, M. (1955), "Gioffredo Caroli Cittadino Saluzzese del Cinquecento," *Bollettino per la Societa degli Studi Storici, Archeologici ed Artistici nella Provincia di Cuneo*, Vol. 35 (31 marzo 1955).

Briquet, C. M. (1923), *Les Filigrans*. Leipzig: Karl W. Hiersemann.

Brizio, A. M. (1951), "Primo libro delle acque," *Miscellanea: Scritti Vari*, II, *Facoltà di Magistero* (Turin), pp. 1–19.

———— (1952), *Leonardo da Vinci, Scritti scelti*. Turin: Unione Tipografica Editrice Torinese.

———— (1954), "Correlazioni e corrispondenze tra fogli del Codice Atlantico e Fogli dell'Anatomia B, e dei Codici A e C su l'occhio, la prospettiva, le piramide radiose e le ombre," *Raccolta Vinciana*, XVII, 81–89.

———— (1956), "Il Trattato della Pittura di Leonardo," in *Scritti di Storia dell'Arte in onore di Lionello Venturi* (Rome: De Luca), pp. 309–320.

Calvi, G. (1909), *Il Codice di Leonardo da Vinci nella Biblioteca di Lord Leicester* Milan: Cogliati.

———— (1925), *I Manoscritti di Leonardo da Vinci dal punto di vista cronologico, storico e biografico*. Bologna: Zanichelli.

Carusi, E. (1919), "Per il 'Trattato della Pittura' di Leonardo da Vinci (Contributo di ricerche sui manoscritti e sulla loro redazione)," in *Per il IV Centenario della Morte di Leonardo da Vinci* (Bergamo: Istituto Italiano d'Arti Grafiche), pp. 419–439.

———— (1930), "Note Varie: 3. Scritture d'altra mano," in *I Manoscritti e i Disegni di Leonardo da Vinci pubblicati dalla Reale Commissione Vinciana, Volume I. Il Codice Arundel 263, Parte IV*. Rome: Danesi.

———— (1941), "Quel che c'è di Leonardo nel mappamondo a lui attribuito," in *I Manoscritti e i Disegni di Leonardo da Vinci pubblicati dalla Reale Commissione Vinciana, Disegni Geografici nel Castello di Windsor, Fascicolo Unico* (Rome: La Libreria dello Stato), pp. 27–34.

Castiglione, B. (1528), *Il Libro del Cortegiano*. Venice: Aldus.

Cennini, Cennino d'Andrea, *The Craftsman's Handbook*, tr. D. V. Thompson, Jr. New York: Dover, n.d. (An unabridged reprint of the 1933 Yale University Press publication of the Thompson translation.)

Chastel, A., ed. (1961), *The Genius of Leonardo da Vinci. Leonardo da Vinci on Art and the Artist*. New York: Orion Press.

Clark, K. (1935), *A Catalogue of the Drawings of Leonardo da Vinci in the Collection of His Majesty the King at Windsor Castle*. London: Cambridge University Press. 2 vols.

———— (1944), "Leon Battista Alberti on Painting" (Annual Italian Lecture of the British Academy), *Proceedings of the British Academy*, XXX.

———— (1952), *Leonardo da Vinci. An Account of His Development as an Artist*. London: Cambridge University Press.

———— (1959), *The Nude: A Study in Ideal Form*. Bollingen Series XXV. 2. New York: Pantheon Books.

Commissione Vinciana (1938), *I Manoscritti e i Disegni di Leonardo da Vinci pubblicati dalla Reale Commissione Vinciana. Volume III. Il Codice A (2172) nell'Istituto di Francia (Complementi)*. Rome: La Libreria dello Stato.

Crescentio, Piero, *Della Agricoltura*. Florence: Alamanni, 1478.

D'Arrigo, A. (1958), "Un frammento inedito di Leonardo sulla meccanica ondulatoria," *Rivista di Ingegneria*, pp. 3–8.

De Toni, G. B. (1924), *Giambattista Venturi e la sua opera vinciana. Scritti inediti e l' "Essai"*. Rome: Maglione & Strini.

Du Fresne, R. (1651), *Trattato della Pittura di Leonardo da Vinci, Novamente dato in luce, con la vita dell'istesso autore, scritta da Rafaelle Du Fresne. . . .* Paris: Giacomo Langlois.

Dozio, G. (1871), *Degli scritti e disegni di Leonardo da Vinci e specialmente dei posseduti un tempo e dei posseduti adesso dalla Biblioteca Ambrosiana*. Milan: Giacomo Agnelli.

———— (1939), "Scampoli Vinciani," *Atti e Memorie della R. Accademia di Scienze, Lettere ed Arti di Modena*, Serie V, Vol. IV.

Duhem, P. (1903–1913), *Etudes sur Léonard de Vinci, ceux qu'il a lus et ceux qui l'ont lu*. Paris: Librarie Scientifique A. Herman. 3 vols.

Eastlake, C. L. (1840). *See* Goethe.

———— (1869), *Materials for a History of Oil Painting*. London: Longmans, Green. 2 vols. (Reprinted under the title *Methods and Materials of Painting of the Great Schools and Masters*. New York: Dover, 1960. 2 vols.)

Eissler, K. R. (1961), *Leonardo da Vinci: Psychoanalytic Notes on The Enigma*. New York: International Universities Press.

Favaro, G. (1918–1919), "Misure e proporzioni del corpo umano secondo Leonardo," *Atti del Reale Istituto Veneto di Scienze, Lettere ed Arti*, LXXXIII, 109–190.

———— (1926–1927), "L'equilibrio del corpo umano negli studi di Leonardo," *ibid.*, LXXXVI, 227–254.

———— (1939), "Scampoli Vinciani," *Atti e Memorie della R. Accademia di Scienze, Lettere ed Arti di Modena*, Serie V, Vol. IV, pp. 3–8.

Filarete, Antonio Averlino, *Tractat über die Baukunst*. Edited by W. von Oettingen. Vienna: Graeser, 1890.

Galbiati, G. (1920), *Il Cenacolo di Leonardo da Vinci del pittore Giuseppe Bossi nei giudizi d'illustri contemporanei*. Milan: Alfieri & Lacroix.

Gantner, J. (1958), *Leonardos Visionen von der Sintflut und von Untergang der Welt*. Bern: Francke Verlage.

Gauricus, Pomponius, *De sculptura*. Firenze: Giunti, 1504. Reprinted; Lipsia: H. Brockhaus, 1886.

Ghiberti, Lorenzo, *I Commentari*. Edited by Ottavio Morisani. Naples: Ricciardi, 1947.

Giacomelli, R. (1936), *Gli scritti di Leonardo da Vinci sul volo*. Rome: Dott. G. Bardi.

Gioseffi, D. (1957), *Perspectiva Artificialis. Per la storia della prospettiva spigolature e appunti*. Università degli Studi, Trieste. Facoltà di Lettere e Filosofia. Istituto di Storia dell'Arte Antica e Moderna; no. 7.

Giovio, Paolo, *Leonardi Vincii Vita* (MS, ca. 1527). Published in G. Tiraboschi, *Storia della letteratura italiana* (Venice, 1796), vol. vii, 1641–2. Reprinted by Bossi (1810), pp. 19–22, and, with an English translation, by Richter (1939), I, 2–3.

Goethe, J. W., *Theory on Colours*. Translated from the German with Notes by Charles Lock Eastlake. London: John Murray, 1840.

Goldscheider, L. (1959), *Leonardo da Vinci. Life and Work, Paintings and Drawings*. London: Phaidon Press.

Gombrich, E. H. (1954), "Leonardo's Grotesque Heads," in *Leonardo Saggi e Ricerche* (Rome: La Libreria dello Stato), pp. 197–219.

Gombrich, E. H. (1960), *Art and Illusion. A Study in the Psychology of Pictorial Rep-resentations* Bollingen Series XXXV. 5. New York: Pantheon Books.

Gould, C. (1947), "Leonardo da Vinci's Notes on the Colour of Rivers and Moun-tains," *Burlington Magazine*, LXXXIX, 239–242.

——— (1954), "Leonardo's Great Battle-piece: A Conjectural Reconstruction," *Art Bulletin*, XXXVI, 117–129.

Gramatica, L. (1919), *Le Memorie su Leonardo da Vinci di Don Ambrogio Mazenta*. Milan: Alfieri & Lacroix.

Heydenreich, L. H. (1949), *I Disegni di Leonardo da Vinci e della sua Scuola con-servati nella Galleria dell'Accademia di Venezia*. Florence: Lange, Domsch.

——— (1954), *Leonardo da Vinci*. New York: MacMillan; Basel: Holbein.

——— (1956), "The Codex Urbinas Latinus 1270 and Its Copies," [Introduction] in A. P. McMahon, *Treatise on Painting by Leonardo da Vinci* (Princeton, N.J.: University Press, 1956), I, xi–xliii.

Hooykaas, R. (1952), "La théorie corpusculaire de Léonard de Vinci," in *Colloques Internationaux du Centre National de la Recherche Scientifique, Paris, 4–7 juillet, 1952* (Paris: Presses Universitaries de France), pp. 163–169.

Hours, M. (1954), "Etudes analytique des tableaux de Léonard de Vinci au Laboratoire du Musée du Louvre," *Leonardo Saggi e Ricerche* (Rome: La Libreria dello Stato), pp. 13–26.

Ivins, W. M., Jr. (1938), "On the Rationalization of Sight," *Metropolitan Museum of Art Papers*, no. 8.

Jordan, M. (1873), *Das Malerbuch des Lionardo da Vinci*. Leipzig: Seemann.

Klein, R. (1961), "Pomponius Gauricus On Perspective," *Art Bulletin*, XLIII, 211–229.

Lomazzo, G. P. (1584), *Trattato dell'Arte de la Pittura*. Milan: Gottardo da Ponto. (English translation by R. Haydocke [Oxford, 1598].)

Ludwig, H. (1882), *Leonardo da Vinci. Das Buch von der Malerei*. Vienna: Brau-müller. 2 vols.

MacCurdy, E. (1939), *The Notebooks of Leonardo da Vinci.* . . . London: Jonathan Cape; New York: Reynal & Hitchcock. 2 vols.

McMahon, A. P. (1956), *Treatise on Painting by Leonardo da Vinci. Translated and Annotated by A. P. McMahon, with an Introduction by Ludwig H. Heydenreich* Princeton, N.J.: University Press. Vol. I, Text; Vol. II, Facsimile.

Major, R. M. (1866), "Memoir on a Mappemond by Leonardo da Vinci," *Archaeologia* (London), XL, 1–40.

Manzi, G. (1817), *Trattato della Pittura di Leonardo da Vinci*. Rome: de Romanis.

Marinoni, A. (1952), *Gli Appunti Grammaticali e Lessicali di Leonardo da Vinci*. Milan: Treccani. 2 vols.

——— (1954), "I Manoscritti di Leonardo da Vinci e le loro Edizioni," *Leonardo Saggi e Ricerche* (Rome: La Libreria dello Stato), pp. 229–274.

——— (1957), "Il Regno e il Sito di Venere," in *Poliziano e il suo tempo. Atti del IV Congresso Internazionale di Studi sul Rinascimento* (Florence: Sansoni), pp. 273–287.

Marcolongo, R. (1937), *Studi Vinciana. Memorie sulla geometria e la meccanica di Leonardo da Vinci*. Naples: S.I.E.M.

Mazenta, Ambrogio. *See* Gramatica, L. (1919).

Michel, P. H. (1952), "Léonard de Vinci et le problème de la pluralité des mondes," *Colloques Internationaux du Centre National de la Recherche Scientifique, Paris, 4–7 juillet, 1952* (Paris: Presses Universitaires de France), pp. 31–42.

Minnaert, M. (1954), *The Nature of Light and Colour in the Open Air*. New York: Dover.

Monti, S. (1914), "Curiosità—Vinciana: 2. I diversi codici di Leonardo da Vinci nella Biblioteca Ambrosiana descritti da Anton Giuseppe della Torre di Rezzonico circa l'anno 1779," *Periodico della società storica della Provincia e antica Diocesi di Como*, XXI, 69–79.

O'Malley, C. D., & Saunders, J. B. de C. M. (1952), *Leonardo da Vinci on the Human Body*. New York: Schumann.

Pacioli, L. (1509*a*), *Divina Proportione*. Venice: Paganinus.

———— (1509*b*), *Euclidis . . . Opera a Campano interprete translata. . . .* Venice: Paganinus.

Panofsky, E. (1940), *The Codex Huygens and Leonardo da Vinci's Art Theory*. London: Warburg Institute.

———— (1952), *Idea. Contributo alla Storia dell'Estetica*. Florence: La Nuova Italia. (An Italian translation of the 1st ed., 1924, published in *Studien der Bibliothek Warburg*, ed. F. Saxl. Leipzig, Berlin: Teubner.)

———— (1954), *Galileo as a Critic of the Arts*. The Hague: M. Nijhof.

———— (1955), *Meaning in the Visual Arts*. Garden City, N.Y.: Doubleday.

———— (1960), *Renaissance and Renascences in Western Art*. Stockholm: Almqvist & Winksell.

———— (1961), *La Prospettiva come 'Forma Simbolica' e altri Scritti*. Milano: Feltrinelli. (An Italian translation of the 1st ed., 1927, published in *Vorträge der Bibliothek Warburg*, ed. F. Saxl. Leipzig, Berlin: Teubner.)

Pastor, L. (1905), *Die Reise des Cardinals Luigi d'Aragona . . . beschrieben von Antonio de Beatis*. Freiburg: Herder.

Pedretti, C. (1957*a*), *Leonardo da Vinci Fragments at Windsor Castle from the Codex Atlanticus*. London: Phaidon Press.

———— (1957*b*), *Studi Vinciani. Documenti, Analisi e Inediti Leonardeschi. In Appendice: Saggio di una cronologia dei fogli del "Codice Atlantico."* Geneva: E. Droz.

———— (1959*a*), "Un nuovo apografo del 'Trattato della Pittura' di Leonardo," *Bibliothèque d'Humanisme et Renaissance*, XXI, 446–450.

———— (1959*b*), "Leonardo's Last Drawings," *Italian Quarterly* (Los Angeles, Calif.), vol. 3, no. 11, pp. 42–57.

———— (1960*a*), "Il 'Neron da Sancto Andrea'," *Raccolta Vinciana*, XVIII, 65–96.

———— (1960*b*), "Un Inedito di Leonardo a Bayonne," *ibid.*, XVIII, 53–63.

———— (1960*c*), "Saggio di una cronologia dei fogli del Codice Arundel di Leonardo da Vinci," *Bibliothèque d'Humanisme et Renaissance*, XXII, 172–177.

———— (1960*d*), "Spigolature nel Codice Atlantico," *ibid.*, XXII, 526–548.

———— (1962*a*), "Copies of Leonardo's Lost Writings in the Ms. H 227 inf. of the Ambrosian Library, Milan," *Raccolta Vinciana*, XIX, 61–94.

———— (1962*b*), "Pietro Accolti e il 'Trattato della Pittura' di Leonardo," *ibid.*, XIX, 292–294.

———— (1962*c*), *A Chronology of Leonardo da Vinci's Architectural Studies after 1500*. Geneva: E. Droz.

———— (1963), "Leonardo On Curvilinear Perspective," *Bibliothèque d'Humanisme et Renaissance*, XXV, 69–87.

Petrarch (1545), *Il Petrarcha*. Con l'espositione d'Alessandro Vellutello. Vinegia: Gabriel Giolito de Ferrari, 1945.

Pierantoni, A. C. (1921), *Studi sul Libro della Pittura di Leonardo da Vinci*. Rome: G. Scotti.

Popham, A. E. (1946), *The Drawings of Leonardo da Vinci*. London: Jonathan Cape.

———— (1958), "On a Book of Drawings by Ambrogio Figino," *Bibliothèque d'Humanisme et Renaissance*, XX, 266–276.

Prospectivo Melanese Depintore, *Antiquarie Prospettiche Romane*. No indication of year and printer, but probably Rome, *ca.* 1500. Reprinted by G. Govi, "Intorno a un opuscolo rarissimo della fine del secolo XV . . . ," *Atti della R. Accademia dei Lincei*, CCLXXIII, 1875–1876, Serie 2ª, Vol. III, P. III, pp. 39 ff. See also A. Favaro, *Gilberto Govi ed i suoi scritti intorno a Leonardo da Vinci* (Rome, 1923), pp. 133–175.

Ravaisson-Mollien, C. (1881), *Les Manuscrits de Léonard de Vinci. Le Manuscrit A de la Bibliothèque de l'Institut*. Paris: Quantin.

———— (1888), "Pages autographes et apocryphes de Léonard de Vinci," *Memories de la Societé Nationale des Antiquaries de France*, XLVIII, pp. 132–145.

Reti, L. (1956–1957), "Leonardo da Vinci nella storia della macchina a vapore," *Rivista di Ingegneria*, pp. 3–31.

———— (1959), " 'Non si volta chi a stella è fisso' Le 'Imprese' di Leonardo da Vinci," *Bibliothèque d'Humanisme et Renaissance*, XXI, 9–54.

Richter, J. P. (1883), *The Literary Works of Leonardo da Vinci*. London: Low, Marston, Seale, and Rivington. 2 vols. (Second ed., enlarged and revised by J. P. Richter and I. A. Richter; London: Oxford University Press, 1939. 2 vols. Third edition, forthcoming, with Introduction and Additional Notes by C. Pedretti; London: Phaidon Press. 3 vols.)

Richter, Irma A. (1949), *Paragone. A Comparison of the Arts by Leonardo da Vinci*. London, New York, Toronto: Oxford University Press.

Rigaud, J. F. (1877), *A Treatise on Painting by Leonardo da Vinci. . . .* London: George Bell. (A revised, enlarged version of the 1835 edition.)

Ritter, S. (1925), *Baldassarre Oltrocchi e le sue memorie storiche su la vita di Leonardo da Vinci*. Rome: Maglione & Strini.

Rzepinska, M., ed. (1961), *Leonardo da Vinci, Traktat o Malarstwie*. Warsaw: Zarklad Narodowy Im. Ossolinskich Wydawnictwo Polskiej Akademii Nauk.

———— (1962*a*), "Light and Shadow in the Late Writings of Leonardo da Vinci," *Raccolta Vinciana*, XIX, 259–266.

———— (1962*b*), "Dwa Studia o Teorii Malarskiej Leonarda da Vinci" (with abstract in French), *Rocznik Historii Sztuki* (Komitet Nauk o Sztuce Polskiej Akademii Nauk), III, 8–43.

Salmi, M. (1955), *Luca Signorelli*. Novara: Istituto d'Arti Grafiche.

Sampaolesi, P. (1954), "I dipinti di Leonardo agli Uffizi," *Leonardo Saggi e Richerche* (Rome: La Libreria dello Stato), pp. 27–46.

———— (1960), "Studi di Prospettiva," *Raccolta Vinciana*, XVIII, 188–202.

Solmi, E. (1905), *Nuovi Studi sulla Filosofia Naturale di Leonardo da Vinci. Il Metodo Sperimentale. L'Astronomia. La Teoria della Visione*. Mantua: Mondovi.

———— (1908), "Le Fonti dei Manoscritti di Leonardo da Vinci," *Giornale Storico della Letteratura Italiana* (Turin: Loescher), Suppl. no. 10–11, pp. 1–344.

Spencer, J. R. (1956), *Leon Battista Alberti, On Painting*. New Haven, Conn.: Yale University Press.

Steinitz, K. T. (1958), *Leonardo da Vinci's "Trattato della Pittura." A Bibliography*. Copenhagen: Munksgaard.

———— (1963), "Trattato Studies. II," *Raccolta Vinciana*, XIX, 223–254.

Timpanaro, S. (ed.) (1926), *Leonardo Pagine di Scienza*. Milan: Mondadori.

Uccelli, A. (1940), *I Libri di Meccanica di Leonardo da Vinci*. Milan: Hoepli.

Uzielli, G. (1884), *Ricerche intorno a Leonardo da Vinci*. Serie II. Rome: Salviucci.

Valentiner, W. R. (1950), *Studies of Italian Rennaissance Sculpture*. London: Phaidon Press.

Vasari, G. (1568; 2d ed.), *Le Vite de più eccellenti pittori* . . . , Parte III. Florence: Giunti. 3 vols. The Life of Leonardo is reprinted in Beltrami (1919), which includes passages of the first edition (1550; 2 vols.) omitted in the second. English translation in Goldscheider (1959).

——, *On Technique*. . . . *Introduction to the Lives*. . . . Edited, with Introduction and Notes, by G. Baldwin Brown. New York: Dover, 1960. (An abridged reprint of the 1907 (J. M. Dent) publication of the Brown translation.)

Venturi, L. (1919), *La Critica e l'Arte di Leonardo da Vinci*. Bologna: Zanichelli.

Vitruvius (1521), *De Architectura*. . . . Edited by Cesare Cesariano. Como: Gottardo da Pontio. (English edition: *Vitruvius, The Ten Books on Architecture*, tr. Morris H. Morgan. New York: Dover [an unabridged reprint of the 1914 Harvard University Press publication of the Morgan translation].)

—— (1536), *De Architectura*. . . . Edited by G. B. Caporali. Perugia: Stamperia del Conte Iano Bigazzini.

White, J. (1957), *The Birth and Rebirth of Pictorial Space*. London: Faber & Faber.

Zoubov, V. P. (1960), "Leon Battiste Alberti et Léonard de Vinci," *Raccolta Vinciana*, XVIII, 1–14.

Zuccaro, F. (1607), *L'Idea de' pittori, scultori et architetti*. . . . Turin: Agostino Disserolio.

INDEXES

Index-Concordance to Libro A

The contents of *Libro* A are given here according to the carta sequence, but the chapters from the Codex Urbinas are separated from the notes from the Codex Leicester. Each heading bears the chapter number (in italic) of the present reconstruction. After each heading, when necessary, the subject of the chapter is specified between parentheses. The folio references to the Codex Urbinas include the indication of the part (I to VI). The abbreviations are those adopted in the edition of *Libro* A (see above, "Editorial Notes," p. 30). A heading is set in italic when it is not found in the Codex Urbinas. The opening sentence (also in italic) of each of the notes from the Codex Leicester is taken as a heading. The references to *Libro* A written by Leonardo himself in the Codex Leicester are given in the original spelling. The contents of *Libro* A are also indexed alphabetically in the "General Index."

Carta	*Headings*	*CU*	*Lu*	*McM*	*Rig*
1	1. On Painting (Blue of the sky)	III,154v	490	519	303
12	2. On the Quality of Lights and Shadows	V,192v–193	652	763	—
13	3. On Imitating Other Painters	II, 39v	81	77	354
	4. Quality of Expressions of Faces	III,108	287	414	—
	5. On Poses of Infants	III,127–127v	386	390	108
	6. On Poses of Women and Girls	III,127v	387	392	107
14	7. On Bending (Flexion of members)	III,113	314	304	58
	8. On Equilibrium	III,113–113v	315	340	81
	9. On Muscles	III,116v	333 & a	321	45
	10. On Creases in the Flesh	III,121v–122	353	316	53
15	11. How Figures Often Resemble Their Masters	III,157	499	437	—
	12. On Portraying the Parts of the World	III,157	500	549	335
	13. On Depicting the Four Seasons of the Year or Things Connected with Them	III,157–157v	501	548	331
16	14. On Outlines (Aerial perspective)	III,153v–154	486	506	264
	15. On Diminution of Colors and Bodies (Aerial perspective)	III,164	527	527	286
	16. On Interposing Transparent Bodies between the Eye and the Object	III,164	528	517	208
	17. *On the Object between the Eye and the Light*	III,164	528a	449	208
17	18. The Difference between Painting and Sculpture	I, 27–27v	45	54	—
18	19. On Colors (Fire and Sunset)	II, 74–74v	248	196	245
	20. On Objects (which part of them is most illuminated)	III,164	526	447	310

Carta	Headings	Codex Leicester	Leonardo's Reference
95	131. The water, which spurts out through the little opening of the vessel in which it is boiling . . .	28v	in A ha. 95

General Index

The front-matter of the present book is not indexed. Part One and Part Two are fully indexed. As the material of the *Trattato della Pittura* is fully indexed in McMahon's edition of the Codex Urbinas, the complete run of the headings of the chapters of the *Trattato* in our Part Three is not indexed here. However, names of persons in my comments to this section are included (with the exception of the names of Leonardo, Melzi, Ludwig, and McMahon). The appendixes and *Post Scriptum* are also indexed.

L'opera essendo Italiana, si perdoneranno gli errori a gli stampatori Francesi, e poi sono stampatori *

---

* The printer's concluding remark in the first edition of Leonardo da Vinci's "Treatise on Painting," Paris, 1651